Amos Oz

SUNY SERIES IN CONTEMPORARY JEWISH LITERATURE AND CULTURE

EZRA CAPPELL, EDITOR

Dan Shiffman, *College Bound:*
The Pursuit of Education in Jewish American Literature, 1896–1944

Eric J. Sundquist, editor, *Writing in Witness:*
A Holocaust Reader

Noam Pines, *The Infrahuman: Animality in Modern Jewish Literature*

Oded Nir, *Signatures of Struggle:*
The Figuration of Collectivity in Israeli Fiction

Zohar Weiman-Kelman, *Queer Expectations:*
A Genealogy of Jewish Women's Poetry

Richard J. Fein, translator, *The Full Pomegranate:*
Poems of Avrom Sutzkever

Victoria Aarons and Holli Levitsky, editors,
New Directions in Jewish American and
Holocaust Literatures: Reading and Teaching

Jennifer Cazenave, *An Archive of the Catastrophe:*
The Unused Footage of Claude Lanzmann's Shoah

Ruthie Abeliovich, *Possessed Voices:*
Aural Remains from Modernist Hebrew Theater

Victoria Nesfield and Philip Smith, editors,
The Struggle for Understanding: Elie Wiesel's Literary Works

Ezra Cappell and Jessica Lang, editors,
Off the Derech: Leaving Orthodox Judaism

Nancy E. Berg and Naomi B. Sokoloff, editors,
Since 1948: Israeli Literature in the Making

Patrick Chura, *Michael Gold: The People's Writer*

Nahma Sandrow, *Yiddish Plays for Reading and Performance*

Alisha Kaplan and Tobi Aaron Kahn, *Qorbanot*

Sara R. Horowitz, Amira Bojadzija-Dan, and Julia Creet, editors
Shadows in the City of Light: Paris in Postwar French Jewish Writing

Ilana Szobel, *Flesh of My Flesh: Sexual Violence in Modern Hebrew Literature*

Amos Oz

The Legacy of a Writer in Israel and Beyond

Edited by

Ranen Omer-Sherman

Cover image: Amos Oz, courtesy of Dani Machlis and the Amos Oz Archive, and the Heksherim Institute and Literary Archives at Ben-Gurion University of the Negev.

Published by State University of New York Press, Albany

© 2023 State University of New York

All rights reserved

Printed in the United States of America

For information, contact State University of New York Press, Albany, NY
www.sunypress.edu

Library of Congress Cataloging-in-Publication Data

Name: Omer-Sherman, Ranen, editor.
Title: Amos Oz : the legacy of a writer in Israel and beyond / edited by
    Ranen Omer-Sherman.
Description: Albany : State University of New York Press, [2023] | Includes
    bibliographical references.
Identifiers: LCCN 2022032829 | ISBN 9781438492490 (hardcover : alk. paper) |
    ISBN 9781438492506 (ebook) | ISBN 9781438492483 (pbk. : alk. paper)
Subjects: LCSH: Oz, Amos, 1939–2018—Influence. | Oz, Amos, 1939–2018—
    Criticism and interpretation. | Israeli literature—History and criticism. | Israeli
    literature—Political aspects.
Classification: LCC PJ5054.O9 Z56 2023 | DDC 892.43/6—dc23/eng/20221230
LC record available at https://lccn.loc.gov/2022032829

10 9 8 7 6 5 4 3 2 1

For my children Kesem and Julian
for all their laughter, love and mischief.
And for all the dreaming and
despairing readers of Amos Oz,
and dissidents everywhere.

Contents

Part 2.
NOMADS, VIPERS, AND WOMEN

Part 3.
COMING OF AGE:
CONSTRUCTING THE HEBREW HOME(LAND)

Introduction

Amos Oz's Arduous Truths and Ambivalences

RANEN OMER-SHERMAN

The armchair in the corner is ringed with light. No one is sitting in it. Do not fill it with men and women who belong elsewhere. You must listen to the rain scratching at the windowpanes. You must look only at the people who are here, inside the warm room. You must see clearly. Remove every impediment. Absorb the different voices of the large family. Summon your strength. Perhaps close your eyes. And try to give this the name of love.

—Amos Oz[1]

Long after his death, the seismic sense of loss left by the departure of the preeminent novelist of Israel's post-statehood generation, the public intellectual and humanitarian, remains staggering, to such an extent that the task of a proper assessment of his achievement can still feel elusive. Where to begin amidst all his myriad qualities? There is the obstinate teller of difficult political truths, the radical empathy, lyrical melancholy, the dedicated witness of kibbutz life's moral triumphs and decay; portraits of the fervor of religious ultranationalists in the West Bank, the madness and quotidian life of Jerusalem, the untamed desert expanses; all the multifarious qualities enumerated by breathless obituarists. How best to sum up the magnitude and sheer complexity of all that? Soon after

Amos Oz's death from cancer, President Reuven Rivlin eulogized him as "the Dostoevsky of the Jewish people," and given that a new book by Oz would often exceed sales of ten thousand copies a day, many of his fellow Israeli citizens certainly seemed to concur with Rivlin.[2] They knew he well understood their fears, dreams, desires, and hopes.

Years earlier David Grossman might have come closest in simply describing his friend as "the offspring of all the contradictory urges and pains within the Israeli psyche."[3] Grossman's succinct allusion to those seething oppositional forces well captures the vital creative catalyst that formed both Oz's moral and aesthetic imagination, the very wellspring of his art. Hence, it seemed especially apt that for the first chapter in this volume, to head the short reminiscences presented in the "In a Retrospective Mode" section, we selected Grossman's eloquent reflections (appearing in English for the first time in Jessica Cohen's luminous translation) on one of Oz's most important works of political writing, which, like the best of his literary art, was alternatively compassionate and scathing. For Grossman, *In the Land of Israel* was an especially acute critical intervention, a kind of moral barometer measuring the acute ailments Oz felt must be urgently addressed to ensure the ultimate health and durability of his society. And in that spirit, the contributors to this volume sought to capture the significant ways that Oz's greatness as a writer resides in the way those ailments (especially concerning the nature of fanaticism and betrayal), which he very often had the integrity to recognize in his own being, are ultimately shared by members of Oz's global audience and their own societies.

Perhaps it was inevitable that contradictory impulses resided at the heart of one who was very much the child of European Jewry yet raised in a society inculcated with the lofty ideal of "the new Jew." In a classic study that influenced later generations of Oz readers, Avraham Balaban examines the creative role of those fecund oppositions and fault lines:

> Oz's protagonists have torn personalities. The tensions between the different psychic forces as well as between the flat, secured, and lifeless existence within societal borders and the intensive, vital, alluring experiences beyond those borders, find expression in the protagonists' struggles between light and darkness, God and Satan, spirit and body, man and woman, Jews and Arabs, culture and nature. Like a wound that cannot be healed, this tension underlies Oz's works, dictating their direction. His

> works attempt to find a cure to this problem by bringing the
> warring contraries together to live in peace. (180)[4]

In pursuit of that elusive redemption to which Balaban here alludes, in capturing the variety of religious and political messianisms that saturated his society, Oz bequeathed us with the gift of achingly beautiful prose poems that are at the heart of so much of the best of the fiction, penetrating metaphors and similes, and above all else, tender, joyful, and melancholy portraits of the human condition.[5] He was a writer of towering versatility. And paradoxes. For if he was often too easily construed as a paragon of Sabra identity, he was always the consummate insider-outsider, someone whose youthful longing to conform to labor Zionist culture only underscored his own insecurities in ways that would enable the adult writer to achieve a profoundly empathic attunement to the struggles of others. Hence, as I frequently reread the short fiction, novels, and essays alongside my students, many of them immigrants, I'm often struck by what they most appreciated about Oz's language, how seemingly beset by the painful historical fissures of a very different society, he somehow seemed to speak to the problems of their own, or to the places they had left behind. Often, Oz's clarity helped to reinforce their own.

Even before the Trump years, many of those students (again, immigrants or the children of immigrants) had been wounded by the dehumanizing forms of xenophobia, intolerance, and anti-immigrant sentiment creeping into the American language. They appreciated Oz's humanity, above all his guiding ethos that insisted on precision in language as a higher ethical value.[6] In a benighted era in which we have seen the frequent devaluation and utter disregard of truth itself, he can seem positively quixotic—and yet absolutely essential. Condemning those who referred to human beings anywhere as "aliens, burdens, or parasites," Oz famously declared in one of the passages that stirred them with its resonating immediacy: "Precision is a value. . . . The moment we are precise with our nouns, adjectives, verbs and adverbs, we are closer to doing justice, in a small way. Not universal justice. Not international justice. But the way I describe a person, a mode of behavior or even an inanimate object, the closer I am to the essence, the more I evade either exaggeration or incitement. Words are important because they are one of the main means by which humans do things to each other. Saying is doing."[7] Even in more experimental postmodern works, such as *The Same Sea* [*Oto Ha-Yam*, 1999] or *Rhyming Life and Death* [*Charuzei Ha-Chayim*

Ve-Ha-Mavet, 2007], his voice remains steadfast in imaginatively grappling with the critical problem of the various distortions of identities, nationalism, and language obstructing the path to human redemption. To an unprecedented degree, Oz contributed to the (perhaps unfair) expectations held by readers around the world; that by its very definition Israeli literature must be exceptionally self-critical, that its writers dare not look away from the injustices of their state.[8]

To succeed even partially, a volume of this nature necessarily demands a genuinely multifaceted vision encompassing a range of methodologies and traditions that grapple with both the literary and polemical dimensions of Oz's legacy. To that end I am exceedingly grateful for the eager participation of some of our most accomplished veteran scholars as well as exciting younger voices whose work embraces a wide range of cross-disciplinary concerns, raising important new questions. Though I have enjoyed the considerable privilege of editing two previously well-read essay collections (*The Jewish Graphic Novel*; *Narratives of Dissent: War in Contemporary Israeli Arts and Culture*), I was intimidated by the responsibility to assemble a volume that might do even modest justice to Oz's extraordinary oeuvre. My goal was always to bring lasting critical pleasure to those who have read him over decades, while also stimulating the thinking of future generations of students and others only lately discovering him. While on this journey, I became reconciled to the fact that while an edited collection of this limited scope cannot possibly encompass every facet of such a remarkable career, there is nevertheless an extraordinary range of disciplinary perspectives on display in these chapters. Naturally, major themes and loci addressed include the kibbutz, the city of Jerusalem, the idea of a Jewish homeland, and his own life story. While some contributors examine Oz's most famous concerns, such as the scourge of fanaticism, others address unusual, critically overlooked but highly consequential dimensions of his legacy and include the ruminations of an acclaimed young novelist whose voice is provoked by Oz's progressive politics and humanism as well as its shortcomings. Others, who knew Oz in life, append piquant recollections to their critical discussions. Perhaps what most lends coherence to these essays is that all the contributors are keenly attentive to the intricate ways that the inner lives of Oz's characters are often at odds with or otherwise shaped by Israel's rural and urban environments.

If for some, Oz was famously preoccupied by the frail social fabric and complex realities of the kibbutz (in ways that bookend his entire career), it remains equally true that up to the very end of his life, Jerusalem compelled his attention again and again. In his fiction, Jerusalem is the fraught arena in which, from antiquity to the present moment, both spiritual inspiration and the corrosive force of fanaticism perpetually seem to incubate. Has any writer ever captured the literal as well as figurative light and shadows of Jerusalem of the last years of the British Mandate to such brilliant effect?[9] Few prose writers have equaled his achingly beautiful and lingering descriptions of its famous light, alleys, stony houses of worship, and pervasive melancholy.[10] Accordingly, this volume's explorations are bookended by thoughtful reappraisals of *My Michael*, Oz's second and in some ways still most controversial novel (critic Gal Beckerman memorably describes it as "a sort of *Madame Bovary* set against the backdrop of white Jerusalem stone").[11] These include the personal reflections of two extraordinarily accomplished scholars whose self-understandings were profoundly transformed by reading the novel back in the heady decade of the 1960s, one recalling his first encounter with the book as a soldier in the aftermath of the 1967 War (in which Oz had also fought), and the other reflecting on the resonances Oz's portrayal of dysfunctional domesticity had for her as a young immigrant woman learning to cope with her bewildering new environment.[12] Other contributors address Oz's important autobiographical works. Widely considered the greatest autobiographical work in modern Hebrew literature and Oz's most acclaimed achievement, *A Tale of Love and Darkness* [*Sipur Al Ahava Ve-Choshech*, 2002] is the subject of two incisive discussions by scholars whose voices have long inspired others exploring the intersections of Israeli literature, gender studies, and ethnography.

No hagiography is intended in this volume (even if there remains more admiration than disdain) and some discussants pay heed to the fact that even as Oz vigorously fought for his vision of Israel's future, both the Ashkenazi left with which he was most identified faded in his lifetime and his own voice became less relevant as those of the country's Mizrahi, Russian Jews, and right-wing Orthodox grew in influence. Whether painful for us to acknowledge or not, Oz's long insistence on the two-state solution and ending the occupation of the West Bank has come to seem utterly anachronistic in the current reality in which even Arab states seem willing to turn their backs on the plight of Palestinians. Yet even as his position was increasingly marginalized at home in later years, Oz's literary and cultural reputation continued to swell internationally. As so much of his vast international audience came to anticipate, Oz's lucid interpretations of the socio-political turmoil roiling his society was always accompanied by intensely lyrical language, deep penetrations into the vulnerabilities of the human psyche, and the consolations of transcendent hope.

Almost immediately, Oz's voice captivated European and American readers and critics, replicating his early success with his Hebrew audience. Laudatory reviews followed the translations of his early books, each of which (whether satirically or melodramatically) sharply interrogated the capacity of ideology to serve human beings in all their full complexity. In one salient example, not long after the Yom Kippur War (in which Oz had fought in a tank crew on the Golan Heights), the *New York Times* senior book critic Christopher Lehmann-Haupt hailed the startling ironies of *Elsewhere, Perhaps* [*Makom Acher, Sifriat Hapoalim*, 1966], proclaiming it a "charmingly unpious tapestry of Israeli life," praising the self-critical portrayals of the fictional kibbutz of its young kibbutz author:

> [T]he men and women of Kibbutz Metsudat Ram try to march in lockstep toward a new socialist utopia, but snapping at their ankles and tripping them into disarray are the traditions of their disparate pasts. Russian Jews are at odds with German Jews: the talkers are in conflict with the doers; the young don't see eye to eye with the old. Is kibbutz life the paradigm of cooperative living? The women gossip and kvetch over trivia, the men stop speaking to each other over nothing. And the greatest irony of all: Just as Kibbutz Metsudat Ram is preparing a heroic military sortie to establish its right to cultivate besieged borderland, the fabric of its social life is rent by a sexual scandal straight out of a French farce.[13]

The sheer audacity that Lehmann-Haupt and other early critics found so remarkable, the unstinting capacity to mock the very tropes and conventions others deemed sacred, his sophisticated understanding of the deep and perhaps fatal conflicts within the Zionist enterprise, would continue to distinguish Oz's literary imagination throughout his career.[14] Yet even his most unsparing interrogations of his society's dreams and myths were never completely devoid of affection.

One of the prevalent conventions adapted by his critics concerned the role of politics, perhaps best exemplified by Joseph Cohen who insisted that "Oz does not use his fiction directly to accommodate his political beliefs . . . rejecting an ulterior sociopolitical motive."[15] Yet over time, this claim has perhaps been somewhat overstated. To be fair, Oz himself encouraged the rise of the myth, telling numerous interviewers abroad that "I have two pens on my desk. One black and one blue. One I use to tell stories and the other to tell the government to go to hell—and I never mix them."[16] Yet while if it is not entirely inaccurate to say that there are few if any instances of raw polemic in the fiction, there is a more complex truth worth considering. Because, to put it simply, to deny the presence of an unwavering political consciousness in the fiction would require willfully looking away from the tenacious presence of Palestinian ruins (let alone the living bedouin of "Nomad and Viper") that Oz resolutely sets before us again and again. His own eyes were trained upon those remnants of indigeneity, and other inconvenient vestiges of historical truth. Memorializations of the Palestinian past haunt his most resonant novels from *A Perfect Peace* to *Judas*, where the remains of the villages of Sheikh Badr and Deir Yassin stubbornly cling to the transformed landscape in mute accusation. Indeed, persistent reminders of the Naqba and Arab indigeneity constitute some of the most haunting and abiding resonances in all of the work.[17] However, it should be stressed that if in early works such as "Nomad and Viper" it is impossible to ignore the searing indictments of the original Hebrew prose, it is also true that the confusion about the putative demarcation between politics and fiction may owe in part to the overly subtle if not altogether censorious impulses of foreign publishers and translators.

In his brilliant discussion of the Oz that readers encountered in English editions, Omri Asscher documents numerous instances in which some of the most irrational hatred and savagery of certain Jewish protagonists is tempered, obscured, or even erased in the translations. In other cases, crucial allusions to Palestinian history or the destructive nature of the 1948 War vanish. For instance, in *A Perfect Peace* (one of his most widely read novels of the 1980s), numerous disquieting references to the Palestinian village Sheikh Dahr are entirely omitted in the English version.[18] If I dwell on these matters it is because it seems vital in the reality of today's Israel to stress that, while never descending to raw polemic, Oz's art is never entirely separable from his political consciousness—and any gap between these realms narrows considerably in his final novel.

Looking back at the entire oeuvre in the wake of his passing we find an unyielding engagement with the problem of fanaticism and the fascistic personality, a theme that sadly shows little sign of becoming obsolete. Indeed, that common denominator prevails beginning in his earliest works, stories such as "Before His Time" and "Nomad and Viper," or the complementary novellas in *Unto Death* [*Ad Mavet*, 1971] that provocatively mirror Crusader butchery and 20th-century Zionist fantasies of vengeance, through the magisterial memoir *A Tale of Love and Darkness* [*Sipur Al Ahava Ve-Choshech*, 2002] to the late essays of *Dear Zealots* [*Shalom La-Kana'im: Shalosh Machshavot*, 2017]. As for the political writing itself (revered by some and abhorred by others), Oz unabashedly claimed for both himself and the secular left a direct lineage to the Hebrew Bible's prophetic mode.[19]

Judaism's greatest legacy for the modern world, as far as Oz was concerned, resided in the wisdom of its ancient prophets rather than the capricious governance of its kings. That understanding often led to some of his most incisive (and wittiest) observations, as in a memorable passage that rather elegantly exposes the hypocrisy and blinkered historical understanding of Israel's Haredim (translated here as Halakhic Judaism):

> Halakhic Judaism . . . practices Jewish heritage as a museum piece. Beyond all the fierce and petty controversies among themselves, they are all utterly convinced that they are closer to the "source" than secular Jews. Some remind us, for example, that sounding the air-raid siren on Memorial Day is a non-Jewish custom, as are the National flag and anthem. They are of course, absolutely right—right to a flaw. They are right as they wear the costumes of Polish noblemen of past centuries, right as they sing charming Ukrainian melodies, right as they piously dance Slavic folk dances. They are also right as they argue with us, using the principles of Aristotelian logic—courtesy of Maimonides, and right as they go forth to conquer the land, on the basis of Hegelian historiography—courtesy of Rabbi Kook. There is no reason to condemn halakhic Judaism for all it has taken from the Persians, the Greeks, the Arabs, the Poles and the Russians. We may raise an eyebrow, however, at the claims of *Shulhan Arukh* Judaism regarding its proximity to "the source," while accusing its opponents of "Hellenizing" and adopting "foreign customs." ("A Full Cart" 26)

As apparent in this memorable exemplar, if there was dogged constancy in Oz's embrace of secular Jewish culture and the scathing criticism he almost gleefully unleashed on religious fundamentalists, that inclination was staunchly erudite, deeply informed by the Hebrew Bible and Talmud, evident from the earliest fiction to late nonfiction works such as *Jews and Words* (coauthored work with daughter Fania Oz-Salzberger), and *Dear Zealots*. When considering the cumulative impact of the reflections in *Dear Zealots*, rather than demarcating a late phase in Oz's thought, this work should be recognized as merely one particularly eloquent riff upon a theme that had long reverberated throughout his polemics and art alike.

Oz never lost an opportunity to wield the arts of creative empathy against the insularity, tribalism, and uncritical conformity of fanatics in his fiction and was equally consistent in his polemics such as "How to Cure a Fanatic" where he identifies the greatest crisis besetting both the Middle East and the entire world as that of "the ancient struggle between fanaticism and pragmatism."[20] Building on this theme in his acceptance speech for the 2007 Asturias Prize he proclaimed that: "I believe in literature as a bridge between peoples. I believe curiosity can be a moral quality. I believe imagining the other can be an antidote to fanaticism."[21] Oz was of course too sophisticated and rigorously unsentimental a thinker to pretend that the mere act of reading literature was "redemptive" (readily acknowledging that global literary history was filled with examples of poetry and fiction used to stoke the hatreds of tribal or nationalistic fervor). Nevertheless, he tirelessly insisted that the works of the greatest writers immerse readers in the kinds of rich ambivalences and complexities that might just wean them from the seductions of doctrinal absolutes and reductive thinking.

Gogol, Kafka, Faulkner, and Amichai were favorites in that regard, and Shakespeare perhaps his preeminent exemplar: "Every extremism, every uncompromising crusade, every form of fanaticism in Shakespeare ends up either in a tragedy or in a comedy. The fanatic is never happier or more satisfied in the end; either he is dead or he becomes a joke. This is a good inoculation" ("How to Cure" 63). As one who famously insisted on precision in language, Oz took pains to stress that it was critical to avoid diluting the term's potency by applying it to anyone who was merely passionate about their convictions: "I'm certainly not suggesting that anyone who has a strong opinion is a fanatic. I'm saying that the seed of fanaticism always lies in uncompromising self-righteousness, the plague of many centuries" ("How to Cure" 51). Other ruinous attributes Oz ascribes to fanatics include an appetite for sentimental kitsch, attraction to cults of personality, and a morbid obsession with their own death.[22]

Conceding that extremists might occasionally wield a shrill sarcasm, Oz regarded them as essentially humorless. And humor was perhaps his essential deterrent for any such tendencies, whether in himself or others: "I have never once in my life seen a fanatic, nor have I ever seen a person with a sense of humor become a fanatic. . . . Humor contains the ability to laugh at ourselves, humor is relativism, humor is the ability to see yourself as others may see you, humor is the capacity to realize that no matter how righteous you are and how terribly wronged you have been, there is a certain side to life that is always a bit funny" ("How to Cure" 65).[23] Toward the end of his life, Oz revisited and refined his framing of the problem, declaring to British journalist Jonathan Freedland that "A fanatic wants to change other people for their own good. He's a great altruist, more interested in you than in himself. He wants to save your soul, change you, redeem you—and if you prove to be irredeemable, he will be at your throat and kill you. For your own good."[24] As alluded to above, the genesis of that agonistic relation with fanaticism is present in the earliest works, thematically anchoring the entirety of his 1965 debut *Artsot ha-tan* [*Where the Jackals Howl*], the seminal collection of his first stories penned at Kibbutz Hulda, which he joined in 1957 (and where his royalties went to the collective's budget). In perhaps its most representative story "Nomad and Viper" ["Navadim va-tsefa"], the malignant tensions and misunderstandings between kibbutzniks and the desperate, famine-stricken Bedouins in the desert beyond builds into a brilliant deconstruction of the "savage" and the "civilized" hierarchical binary that devastatingly overturned the self-righteous illusions of the Labor Zionist imagination in that era.[25]

In spite of its canonical status, it is perhaps too easy to forget that the story was an extraordinarily audacious cultural and literary salvo against the established cultural pieties of its time (aside from its unflinching cultural message, the story's sly recasting of Bereshit 34 warrants appreciation as a powerful contemporary midrash alongside later works such as Anita Diamant's *The Red Tent*). The grim episode of Dinah and the Shechemites, with its avowed rape and violent retribution, clearly struck the young writer with a sense of tragic timeliness, ironically foregrounding contemporary developments. By the time of the story's composition, the semi-arid northern Negev region had become a tense arena for frequent conflicts between Bedouin herders and Jewish farmers, largely due to a severe drought. That dire environmental circumstance (a phenomenon lately viewed by Israeli scientists as an early sign of global climate change) meant that while new kibbutzim expanded Israeli agriculture into traditional nomadic grazing areas, the herds of Bedouins inevitably grazed on the settlers' crops, greatly amplifying tensions and open conflict between groups that might have otherwise coexisted.

In capturing this deteriorating reality, "Nomad and Viper" sets forth numerous exemplars of both "othering" language to suggest the ways that the "enlightened" kibbutzniks might rationalize their very most violent instincts and actions.[26] As haunting as any of the earliest works, this story memorably brings Oz's powerful lyricism front and center to unforgettable effect, a singular stylistic mode that Robert Alter characterizes as "substituting for conventional narration a prose-poem method of exposition through imagistic motifs, and reiterated verbal formulas, an incantatory language used to evoke a mood, to intimate a subject beyond the grasp of words."[27] Four decades later, Alter's penetrating observation still encapsulates the very essence of what would distinguish Oz's writerly technique to the very end.

Over the years, some on the right found it convenient to dismiss Oz as just another variant of the domestic Israel-basher, too dovish or hypocritical to turn his famous critical gaze upon extremists on the left. Yet as the late essays of *Dear Zealots* remind us, Oz readily found fault with both extremes. In one revealing example ("Dreams Israel Should Let Go of Soon") he argues forcefully against "the dual brainwashing" of both the non-Zionist far left and right for insisting on "the irreversibility" of *ha-Matsav* (the occupation), condemning their efforts "to break the spirit of the Zionist left."[28] Whereas "post-Zionists" and "anti-Zionists" insist that the only way forward is "giving up the Zionist dream and accepting our fate as a minority under Arab rule," the Zionist left vehemently "opposes the occupation and refuses to rule over another nation" while refusing to repudiate the Jewish "natural, historical, legal right to a sovereign existence" in a democratic state that Oz would clearly prefer to be much smaller. But for Oz, embattled Zionist liberals were haplessly caught between a rock and a hard place: "despised by the hilltop settlers on the one hand, and by the post-Zionist and anti-Zionist front on the other. They have both been denouncing the left for years and are eager to trounce it . . . these two extremes have conspired to make us despair and force us to choose between giving up on Zionism and giving up on democracy" (*Dear Zealots* 132).[29] Notwithstanding those altogether sincere instances of evenhandedness, in an Israel that was rapidly becoming unrecognizable to him Oz undeniably reserved his greatest umbrage for the "supposed authenticity" of the religious fundamentalists' worldview, a hierarchy that relegates secular humanists to the despised lowest tier of Israeli society.

That abiding concern was most passionately expressed a year after Rabin's assassination by a Bar-Ilan University law student. As part of its institutional soul-searching, Oz was invited to deliver an address before a large audience to commemorate the university's newly established Chair for Democracy and Tolerance. That famous lecture (widely circulated in Hebrew and English), "A Full Cart or an Empty One?," ranges across time from biblical prophecy to utopian-socialist thinkers such as Berl Katznelson and A. D. Gordon to argue vehemently against those (including some among Bar-Ilan's faculty), who would condemn democracy as a foreign body rather than the quintessential expression of Jewish culture.[30]

In this address, Oz castigates the religious-fundamentalist illusions of the Greater Israel movement: "based upon the premise that some of the land's inhabitants are less important than we are: we have our Torah, nationalism, aspirations, rights, and the Messiah. The Arab has a belly and a pair of hands and can therefore be trained to be a grateful 'hewer of wood' and a contented 'drawer of water.' This twisted approach has also come to color religious-secular relations: there are people who are fully human, who have the Torah and its precepts, and the things that they hold dear and sacred are truly dear and sacred; and there are people who are not quite as human—the secular, who don't seem to hold anything dear and to whom nothing is sacred. The latter are therefore, like an 'empty cart,' that can be moved aside to make way for those who possess a 'full cart'" (27).[31] In related instances scattered throughout an essay written in the same spirit, "Many Lights, Not One Light," he pointedly cites passages from Deuteronomy, Leviticus, and Psalms, to indict the spirit of fanatic intolerance to ironic effect: "At the very bottom are the worst of the worst, the most un-Jewish, the most Israel-hating, the most goyish: the lefties, who insist on pursuing peace and protecting human rights, who won't let anyone quietly commit a minor injustice or a little nationalist usurpation, and who won't stop droning on about 'Justice, justice shalt thou pursue,' 'Ye shall have one manner of law, as well for the stranger as for the homeborn,' 'Thou shalt not kill,' and 'Seek peace and pursue it.' If you so much as . . . deliver a collective punishment to a whole Arab village, those lefties start badgering us with foreign notions like 'Every man shall be put to death for his own sin.' Where on earth did these goyim come up with all those bleeding-heart concepts?" (*Dear Zealots* 102, 103).

For those who perceived Oz as aloof or even supercilious in public appearances, it was perhaps too easy to forget what he kept well-hidden for many years, that the origins of much he had to say in both his fiction and polemics actually had its origins in the acute vulnerability, humiliations, and outsider status inflicted on him in his youth at Hulda and perhaps earlier.[32] If we manage to keep the image of that lonely youth before us, it is perhaps easier to grasp the emotional history which spurred the creation of tormented characters such as Azariah in *A Perfect Peace*, Moshe Yashar and other lonely souls in *Between Friends*, Shmuel Ash in *Judas* (perhaps traces are even visible in Hannah Gonen of *My Michael*). Though direct connections between Oz's life and fiction were often oblique, they were not entirely absent especially if one considers the poignant resemblance between Oz and his character Proffy, young narrator of his enthralling young-adult novel *Panther in the Basement* [*Panter Ba-Martef*, Keter, 1995].

As those familiar with Oz's biography will recall, when Oz was merely eight, he too befriended a biblical Hebrew speaking British Mandate policeman who had even memorized much of the Hebrew Bible: "When the other children discovered my friendship with this man, they called me a traitor" (*Dear Zealots* 9). This rueful memory of his earliest brush with infamy seems the genesis of Oz's subsequent agonistic relation with the accusatory label of "traitor": "Much later, I learned to take comfort in the thought that, for fanatics, a traitor is anyone who dares to change. Fanatics of all kinds, in all places at all times, loathe and fear change, suspecting that it is nothing less than a betrayal resulting from dark, base motives" (9).[33] Clearly the memory of those ostracisms and rejections took deep root in his moral imagination.[34] Given his utter estrangement from Yehuda Klausner after his mother Fania's suicide, his subsequent radical self-making, it doesn't seem a stretch to conclude of Oz's life that, in an almost Wordsworthian sense, the child is very much "father of the man."[35] And it should be stressed that if the unhealed wounds of those unhappy days are visible in critical aspects of his portrayals of young men and boys, it is no less evident in his portrayal of the feminine, for better and for some, decidedly worse.[36] For Nurith Gertz, Oz harbored deep reservoirs of pain never fully expressed (not even in the raw intimacy of *A Tale of Love and Darkness*), and she sees him as perpetually resurrecting his lost mother throughout his fiction: "In all his books, there's a woman like that, a mother who comes back to life, dies metaphorically, is reborn in the next book, and again and again. All his life he's resurrecting that mother. All his life he goes to that locked gate, hitting it again and again. Initially, in his first, violent books, he hits it in anger, then gradually in a different way. Underlying everything, I think, is that mother and the desire to shake her. Gradually, with the years, he got to some sort of Ithaca. To home, to places where he can forgive her."[37]

In his final years, an unexpected development would form another crucial bridge to the grim travails of Oz's early life. Contra the euphoria overwhelming most Israelis (and Jews around the world) after the six days of fighting that culminated in Israel's triumphal control of all of Jerusalem, Sinai, the West Bank, and Gaza, Oz knew that he and his fellow soldiers had witnessed or participated in horrific events. Traveling with a reel-to-reel tape recorder to kibbutzim across the country, he and other participants asked their fellow veterans to share their traumatic accounts of the war and some of their grim accounts were published a mere three months later in Hebrew by the kibbutz movement, *Siach Lochamim* (translated several years later into English as *The Seventh Day* [1971]).[38] Though an international sensation at the time, this book was largely forgotten in Israeli society in ensuing decades as a quaint relic of its time.[39] Until by chance documentary film director Mor Loushy discovered the original audio transcripts. So unsettled was she by the kibbutz reservists' grim stories about atrocities and their prescient intimations about the corruption of occupation—muted in the original publication—that Loushy immediately recognized they deserved public attention. The result was the disquieting documentary *Censored Voices*, arguably Israel's most urgent film about the horrors of war, individual conscience, and occupation.[40]

As the camera focuses on Oz and others (now fifty years older) listening for the first time to the anguished, often shocking confessions of their younger selves, their raw responses are haunting. Several make critical connections between Israel in the present moment and the past, none more memorably than a moment when Oz himself contrasts contemporary Israel with the candor and soul-searching of his generation:

> I see more apathy in today's society, more lack of sensitivity. What happens in the territories sometimes crosses a red line, constituting a war crime, but is [viewed as happening] there and not here. There is some mechanism of repression and disengagement at play. Many people don't read news items relating to the occupation when they come across them. Thus, the media doesn't adequately cover what happens there. Every day, every hour, Palestinians suffer humiliation, harassment

at checkpoints, in their villages—the settlers' sewage flows downhill into Arab villages. Already during the fighting in Sinai, I felt that this victory was sowing seeds of deep hatred toward Israel. . . . I knew we were at the beginning of a long and difficult road of a bloody war with the entire Arab and Muslim world. I knew that peace could not come from the defeat and humiliation of the Arabs.[41]

At the beginning of his statement, Oz suggests that he sees no counterpart among the soldiers serving in the checkpoints of the West Bank for what he and others had dared condemn in their own generation.[42] Yet of course the very point of Loushy's film is that the critical testimonies of Oz and his fellow reservists (including comparisons to the Holocaust) not only transgressed what their society was apparently willing to hear, but that its messengers would be deemed suspect. Perhaps the most immediate corollary to Oz's sympathy for those deemed "traitors" (those whose bold thinking might offer potential solutions for the toughest quandaries and conflicts of their society) is what Jonathan Freedland rightly hails as Oz's "defining creed," an unwavering "belief in compromise . . . because he understood that one's enemy is also, and always, a human being."[43]

In the titular essay of *How to Cure a Fanatic*, Oz revisits his earliest encounters with the strains of intolerance against which he would later rebel:

My . . . childhood in Jerusalem rendered me an expert in comparative fanaticism. Jerusalem of my childhood, back in the 1940s, was full of self-proclaimed prophets, redeemers, and messiahs. Even today, every other Jerusalemite has his or her personal formula for instant salvation. . . . I'm quoting a famous line from an old song, "they came to Jerusalem to build it and to be built by it." In fact, some of them—Jews, Christians and Muslims, socialists, anarchists, world reformers—actually came to Jerusalem not so much to build it, not so much to be built by it, but rather to get crucified, or to crucify others, or both. (*How to Cure* 42)

Even as Oz prided himself first and foremost as a "listener" in a society of self-righteous individuals (in which "no one ever listens") he readily confesses here that "as a child . . . I was myself a brainwashed little fanatic all the way. Self-righteous, chauvinistic, deaf and blind to any view that differed from the powerful Jewish, Zionist narrative of the time. I was a stone-throwing kid, a Jewish Intifada kid" (*How to Cure* 43). And in describing the development of *Panther*'s precocious Proffy, Oz remarks that the child's triumph and true coming-of-age epiphany occurs when he learns to embrace "a sense of ambivalence, a capacity for abandoning his black-and-white-views" (*How to Cure* 45). It is clear that whenever Oz later spoke of this child protagonist it was invariably in a self-referential mode. For in this bildungsroman's denouement, Proffy suffers a falling out of childhood for "[m]uch of the joy and fascination and zeal and simpleness of life has gone away" and he is scorned by his oldest friends, labeled "traitor" (*How to Cure* 45).

For those who may have overlooked this stirring young-adult novel, it bears heeding that Oz identifies an extended passage covering the story's first page and a half (beginning: "I have been called a traitor many times in my life. The first time was when I was twelve and a quarter and I lived in a neighborhood at the edge of Jerusalem" [*Panther* 1]) as his most essential statement on the scourge of fanaticism. After suffering painful rejection by his friends and left estranged and isolated at the end of the novel, Proffy comes to learn what its author knew: "Only he who loves might become a traitor. Treason is not the opposite of love; it is one of its many options. Traitor, I think, is the one who changes in the eyes of those who cannot change and would not change and hate change and cannot conceive of change, except that they always want to change you . . . to be a fanatic means to be, to some extent and in some way, a traitor in the eyes of the fanatic" (*How to Cure* 48–49). Up to the very end of his life, Oz would happily implicate himself as a "recovered fanatic," and the bittersweet essence of that hard-won ethos is encoded in many of his finest works, absolutely permeating *Judas*, his much-anticipated final novel.

In many respects his most startling and ultimately rewarding novel, *Judas* warrants some attention here especially for those unfamiliar with it. In the aftermath of his passing, it is manifestly clear that it constitutes Oz's most eloquent and fully realized response to a lifetime of being vilified as a "traitor" by some of his countrymen (from his early involvement in Peace Now to his late comparison of violent West Bank settlers to neo-Nazis, which earned him death threats). This astonishing late work represents the intellectual culmination and brilliant literary flowering of Oz's deep preoccupation with the vilification of iconoclastic thinking and heretics. For if the exceedingly malleable nature of just what "treason" and "loyalty" genuinely portend enlivened his earlier works, in his jolting final work,

Oz delivered an especially multilayered and timeless statement. Placing the "virus of treachery" front and center, *Judas* offers his most thoughtful and urgent statement concerning the uneasy relationship between nationalism and critical citizenship.[44] It is a consummate portrait of the friendlessness of the prophet. And in myriad ways it slyly illuminates Oz's own condition as one labeled a "raving radical" by his enemies on the right but who considered himself simply as "an evolutionist" or "country doctor" patiently ministering to his country's affliction ("The Order of the Teaspoon" 93).[45]

As for *Judas*'s reception, after roughly a decade devoted to essays (*How to Cure a Fanatic*, and *Jews and Words* with daughter Fania Oz-Salzberger), lean short-story collections (*Scenes from Village Life* and *Between Friends*) and a fable for children (*Suddenly in the Depths of the Forest*), Oz's late return to the novel had stirred the interest of many. Moreover, it was ultimately deemed a masterpiece in the eyes of many readers and critics (during a visit to Louisville in the spring of 2017, David Grossman told me that he considered it a magnificent return to form after less ambitious efforts). Yet if to so many, *Judas* seemed one of Oz's most accomplished, philosophically resonant works, an old-fashioned novel of ideas in the best, provocative sense, such acclaim may owe in part to the fact that it was a book that had been slowly simmering for most of his life. Oz first began reading the New Testament as a lonely teenager in the library at Hulda.[46] Today we know that over the decades he remained absorbed by the gospels as well as imaginative works on early Christianity's Jewish origins such as Sholem Asch's 1939 controversial novel *The Nazarene* (perhaps the first modern literary work to champion the "Jewish Jesus," the bestseller's wide condemnation by Yiddishists must have further piqued Oz's interest). Brimming with intricate storylines and characters who are brilliantly alive and get under one's skin, the novel is woven around a structural triptych consisting of the story's "present" set in the harsh Jerusalem winter of 1959–1960, the chief protagonist is a young biblical scholar whose investigation of the portrayal of Judas in the early Christian imagination leads to a startling conclusion, and lastly a beguiling alternate history of Roman Palestine narrated by none other than Judas himself. Initially, its antihero Shmuel Ash seems to be one of Oz's more familiar types, a luftmensch sharing many of the dysfunctional and antiheroic qualities of his predecessors (as early as the tragic paratrooper in his classic story "The Way of the Wind," which was partially based on a disaster that occurred at Hulda during a parachuting exhibition on Independence Day).[47]

We meet the protagonist at a moment of acute crisis: university studies abandoned, romantic life in ruins, and beleaguered by asthma, he faces a bleak financial horizon. In the era in which Zionist codes of identity were perhaps most prevalent, Shmuel has long anguished that (given as he is to sentiment and uncontrollable tears), he falls woefully short of the idealized norms of Sabra masculinity. Indeed, in many ways he seems to hearken back to the kinds of wistful, not-entirely-at-home European immigrants that people Oz's trenchant reminiscences of Jerusalem in *A Tale of Love and Darkness*.

At one point, he ruefully contemplates a colorful poster for the Jewish National Fund displaying his converse image: "a tough, muscular pioneer, his sleeves rolled up . . . top button of his shirt undone, revealing a suntanned, hairy chest" (28). Nebbish or not, the character is drawn with such fierce tenderness and a rich interiority that he may prove one of Oz's most lovable and enduring characters. When his prospects look particularly dire, Shmuel finds employment as caregiver for a cynical old man named Gershom Wald. Gershom's bookish household includes the provocative presence of Atalia, daughter of the late Shealtiel Abravanel, who spent his last days scorned by society for his dovish views on coexistence ("They said he was the bastard son of an Arab. Hebrew newspapers mockingly called him the Muezzin, or Sheikh Abravanel, or the sword of Islam"). Embittered by those who drove her compassionate father into a kind of exile, Atalia is also scarred by the particularly horrific death of her husband (Gershom's son), in the 1948 War. As lovelorn Shmuel becomes obsessed with Atalia, secrets are revealed and given the clamorous afterlife of the two dead men, who seem to take up at least as much room as the living, the little apartment can seem claustrophobic. Other ghosts and hauntings persist in the novel, as a quiet but insistent backdrop to the political and ideological debates teeming in these pages the presence of the ruins of a pre-1948 Palestinian village (with its "half-built festival hall") underscores what else has been lost.

Ultimately it is Atalia who most bears the burden of these losses, and as such she serves as Oz's most morally impassioned and intellectually eloquent witness to the debacle of war and the inhumanity too often rationalized in nationalist causes. In that regard, it seems worth recalling that Oz was sometimes criticized for female characters who merely function as passive catalysts for male desire. Yet if at first Atalia seems perhaps cast in that same vein, frustratingly elusive and withholding (at least through Shmuel's gaze), she ultimately emerges as one of Oz's most perceptive and starkly rational characters. Here the woman (whose husband's body was desecrated by the enemy), vehemently confronts the helplessly infatuated Shmuel with her disgust over the destructive forces of extremist male ambition and desire: "I can't love men. You've held the whole world in your hands for thousands of years and you've turned it into a horror show. A slaughterhouse" (*Judas* 187).[48] As the novel's living embodiment of the spirit of dissidence Oz long championed, Atalia emerges as one of the most fully realized and consequential characters of his career.

In thought-provoking interviews appearing around the time of *Judas*'s publication, Oz was clearly invigorated by the questions he had raised, especially concerning the marginalization of figures like Atalia and her idealist father; losing no opportunity to stress that many of the most significant political leaders in history were called a traitor by many of their own people, most poignantly his late friend Shimon Peres (who reportedly loved arguing with the novelist) a dedicated reader of all his books (on various occasions Oz tirelessly cited Abraham Lincoln, de Gaulle, Gorbachev, Begin, Sadat, Rabin, even the prophet Jeremiah among his pantheon of "traitors"). In widely varying degrees and contexts, these and other figures Oz acknowledged exhibited a propensity for both critical introspection and the conviction that change was possible, just as he tirelessly advocates in *Dear Zealots*: "Contending with fanaticism does not mean destroying all fanatics but rather cautiously handling the little fanatic who hides, more or less, inside each of our souls. It also means ridiculing, just a little, our own convictions; being curious; and trying to take a peek, from time to time, not only through our neighbor's window but, more important, at the reality viewed from that window, which will necessarily be different from the one seen through our own" (35). In this light, the Shmuel of *Judas* seems almost transparently cast as the author's ideological proxy, especially in his belated recognition that: "Anyone willing to change will always be considered a traitor by those who cannot change and are scared to death of change and don't understand it and loathe change" (249). That role becomes even more explicit in Shmuel's speech declaiming that the designation "traitor" "ought really to be seen as a badge of honor," more brazen still when he invokes many of the very same figures his creator often extolled in his late interviews and essays:

> Not long ago in France, de Gaulle was elected president by the votes of the supporters of French rule in Algeria, and now it transpires that his intention was to abandon French

rule and grant full independence to the Arab majority. Those
who previously enthusiastically supported him now call him
a traitor. . . . The prophet Jeremiah was considered a traitor
both by the Jerusalem rabble and by the royal court. The
Talmudic rabbis ostracized Elisha ben Abuya and called him
Aher, "the Other." . . . Lincoln, the liberator of the slaves, was
called a traitor by his opponents. The German officers who
tried to assassinate Hitler were executed as traitors. Every so
often in history, courageous people have appeared who were
ahead of their time and were called traitors . . . Herzl was
called a traitor just because he dared to entertain the thought
of a Jewish state outside the Land of Israel . . . Even David
Ben-Gurion . . . when he agreed . . . to the partition of the
land into two states one Jewish and the other Arab, was called
a traitor by many Jews here. (248–49)

Defending the audacious utopianism of Atalia's late father, Shmuel remarks
that "Abravanel had a beautiful dream, and because of his dream some
people called him a traitor." In such instances, of which there are not a
few, *Judas* reads as the powerful zenith of Oz's imaginative and persistent
interrogation of the toxic mingling of messianism and politics in the Jewish
state. Nor is the novel's enduring resonance limited to that consequential
legacy, for Oz had still other irons in the fire of what probably warrants
merit as his most socially and politically complex novel.

Given *Judas*'s deep engagement with the ugly distortions at the
foundation of Christian anti-Semitism, it shouldn't surprise that even
before its publication, Oz often remarked that the figures of both Jesus
and Judas had obsessed him ever since his teenage years as a voracious
reader at Hulda. (Intriguingly, this turns out to owe something to his
familial past for his great-uncle, the renowned historian Joseph Klausner,
aroused heated controversy with his 1921 book *Jesus of Nazareth*, which
reclaimed Jesus as a Jewish reformer.) Alternating chapters explore the fruits
of Shmuel's scholarship, the insidious ways that Judas came to be seen as
"the incarnation of treachery, the incarnation of Judaism, the incarnation
of the connection between Judaism and betrayal" and the "hated archetype
of all Jews, in every country and century" in the Christian imagination.
But when Shmuel's research leads him to boldly conclude that Judas was
the most *faithful* of Jesus's disciples it becomes apparent that Oz has not
only crafted a subtle allegory linking events in ancient Palestine and the

tempests and unfortunate excesses of certain strains in modern Zionism and the state of Israel but with the violent distortions of complex realities and myths to which the entire West has too often proved susceptible.

Beneath its layers of achingly beautiful and lingering descriptions of Jerusalem's famous light, alleys, stony houses of worship, and pervasive melancholy *Judas* reads like an especially urgent and profoundly universal work about dreamers and their dangerous fantasies, its characters' heartfelt struggles with their own human frailties as well as those of the state resonating far beyond Israel itself. In its melancholic (if quietly hopeful) conclusion, the reader of *Judas* recognizes that there are many forms of betrayal, not least the hyper-nationalist states, messianic fundamentalists, and fanatic revolutions whose callous disregard for the sanctity of all life destroys innocent people. Astonishingly, at the advanced age of seventy-seven, Oz delivered the gift of one of the most intricately layered novels of his entire career, and certainly his most searching exploration of increasingly urgent questions concerning the excesses of absolutism and the ever-imperiled status of critical citizenship.[49]

My own journey with Oz began in the 1970s, as a young American immigrant living in a kibbutz in the Arava desert, alienated from my own father, and rather naively enraptured by the Zionist dream of socialist communalism. And I knew how the famous story went, that Oz had left his father's house at an even younger age (the year I was born). He was only fourteen when he permanently changed his family name from the German Klausner to Oz (which denotes courage or strength).[50] Today with a parent's deeper understanding of the implications of that almost violent self-transformation, the alienation that birthed the writer and cast off the father, the story can still move me to tears. But at the time, in the Israeli desert of the 1970s and impossibly far from my southern California origins, I took comfort in both the boldness of his teenage rebellion and the adult writer's gripping portraits of other dreamers struggling with inner flaws and all the conflicts and contradictions of kibbutz life (*Where the Jackals Howl*; *Elsewhere, Perhaps*; *A Perfect Peace*).[51]

In essence, the socialist communal dream that preoccupied Oz from 1965 to 2013 resulted in some of his most critically acclaimed, morally complex novels and short fiction. Like many others, I have eagerly revisited Oz's portrayals of the kibbutz dream over the years, savoring those narratives for their moral seriousness and psychological depths, weighing the dystopian and utopian impulses, the gains and losses, of the most genuinely revolutionary endeavor in modern Jewish history. Transformed by his encounter with Sherwood Anderson's *Winesburg, Ohio* in a kibbutz library, with its revelatory portrayals of "small" lives in small-town America, Oz began to craft indelible, sometimes miniaturized portraits of the lonely, eccentric, and ideal-smitten characters he observed in daily life on Kibbutz Hulda.

Anderson, Oz once remarked, "showed me that the real world is everywhere, even in a small kibbutz. I discovered that all the secrets are the same—love, hatred, fear, loneliness—all the great and simple things of life and literature."[52] In the aftermath of his passing it seems especially meaningful that so late in life, Oz felt compelled to return once again to the very genesis of his earliest inspiration in the intricately interwoven skein of eight new stories that compose *Between Friends* where, while ostensibly revisiting the foibles of collective life on display in the fictional Kibbutz Yekhat, he actually seems to bind together the conflicted thoughts and feelings of a lifetime.[53] As Karen Grumberg observes of Oz's three short story collections, *Where the Jackals Howl*, *Scenes from Village Life*, and *Between Friends*, while each examines the vicissitudes of "aloneness in a collective setting" only the latter "nurtures a note of quiet, moderate hope."[54] While resolutely refusing to idealize kibbutz society as immune to the surrounding society's xenophobic or misogynist strains (nor its own self-mythologizing tendencies), nor ever quite forgetting the petty cruelties he and his daughters suffered at Hulda, in their respective formative years, this late collection nevertheless bears poignant witness to the moral grandeur of the kibbutz dream as I discuss in my later chapter.[55]

Many of Amos Oz's fellow writers still mourn his passing, perhaps none so eloquently as David Grossman who wrote after his death in *The Guardian* that Oz "had a greatness about him, a nobility. Even towards those who attacked him. It was a nobility that was a bit anachronistic, as if from the 19th century. It wasn't easy for him, being Amos Oz. It wasn't easy for him to be the person who so many people project so much on to: their deepest desires, their hopes and disappointments, everything that is tangled and unresolved within them."[56] Hence, it seemed fitting to include Grossman's expanded reflections in this collection.

In considering this volume's notable critical and personal reflections on *My Michael*, it is worth recalling the judgments of earlier critics like Joseph Cohen who hailed Oz's achievement in creating Hannah Gonen on a scale with that of Flaubert and Joyce.[57] Hannah's struggle to achieve "the beauty, the power, the grandeur and the freedom to be totally her own self . . . wins the reader's total sympathy and support" over that of the titular character (*Voices* 143).[58] In what still reads as one of modern Hebrew literature's most startlingly imaginative novels, as Nehama Aschkenasy (a contributor to this volume) has pointed out, Hannah's psychic disintegration is a struggle against time itself, "in its existential and historical aspects."[59] In her perilous struggle to exist "simultaneously in the world of the here and now, on the one hand, and in a romanticized sphere of total freedom and unbridled desires that knows no laws and constrictions, on the other" (Aschkenasy 122), Hannah clearly served Oz as the prototype for many other memorable urban and kibbutz dreamers tormented by internal and external fragmentation.[60] So many of them yearning for something ineffable, not quite fulfilled by their own environment. As it happens, that yearning deeply spoke to Sidra DeKoven Ezrahi a young woman who would eventually enthrall many in her deep critical explorations of the irresistible poetics of Exile and Return, and whose critically imaginative works reveal the indelible correspondences between modern Hebrew literature and the ancient continuum of Jewish literary culture.

Over the years, Oz's reputation as Israel's preeminent author and public intellectual inspired numerous critical essays and several early volumes that deserve mention. A decade earlier, the prominent critic Gershon Shaked published *A New Wave in Hebrew Fiction* [*Gal Hadash Ba-Siporet Ha-Ivrit*, Sifriat Poalim] that drew attention to Oz and other leading voices of the New Wave of Israeli authors whose narratives questioned the Zionist metanarrative or were otherwise distinguished by an anti-establishment ethos.[61] A decade later, Nurith Gertz published the first Hebrew monograph solely devoted to his oeuvre (Amos Oz, Sifriat Poalim) followed by other comparative critical works that further enhanced his reputation. Two other monographs of exceptional merit by Avraham Balaban (*Between God and Beast: An Examination of Amos Oz's Prose*) and Yair Mazor (*Somber Lust: The Art of Amos Oz*) that appeared in Hebrew in the 1980s and 1990s were subsequently translated into English.[62]

Yet despite that prodigious industry of scholarship, apart from a special issue of the *Journal of Israeli History*, it has been over a decade since the publication of a major work of Oz criticism last appeared.[63] In the aftermath of his passing I was eager to help make room for what might have shifted and offer readers an opportunity to grapple with the profound ramifications of his extraordinary legacy. In pursuing that goal, it has been a joy and a privilege to work with the eighteen other contributors to this volume. The following chapters adhere to a thematic structuring of five sections, which also happen to follow a roughly chronological arrangement with just a few exceptions. Some of the earliest critics whose voices directly contributed to Oz's canonization in Hebrew literature are present in this volume ("In a Retrospective Mode"). While many of the contributors happen to be Israelis and native-born Hebrew speakers, the diverse range of our essayists in the four remaining sections ("Nomads, Vipers, and Women"; "Coming of Age: Constructing the Hebrew Home(land)"; "Oz and the Other: Mizrahis and Palestinians"; and "Dreamers, Iconoclasts, and Traitors") reflects the indisputable fact that Oz was a lasting and formidable presence in the lives of a truly global audience and that his critical and popular reception elsewhere often seemed to have an impact on his own thinking and public voice.

The first of these sections features memoiristic writing and a conversation addressing the impact of Oz's earliest publications, especially the complex and surprisingly intertwined role of gender and politics in works such as My Michael and "Nomad and Viper." We open with "Hannah and Me," Sidra DeKoven Ezrahi's pensive recollection of her self-recognition ("Like Hannah, I also wended my way with inverted umbrellas through the brown-gray streets of Jerusalem under the incessant assault of winter rainstorms; like me, she tried to submerge her own memories, insights and ambitions under the cloak of her husband's grander, more recognized scholarly achievements"), experiencing social claustrophobia, the material and metaphorical entanglements of both Jerusalem and domesticity for herself as a young married woman in Jerusalem. Aside from that intimate connection, Ezrahi's reflections ultimately encompass a political edge, ruefully measuring what has changed and not changed vis-à-vis the Palestinians in the years since that time.

Nurith Gertz's "The History of a Long Conversation" steers the conversation still closer toward lived experience, examining many of the profound and sometimes disquieting revelations that emerged throughout a 45-year friendship with Oz, candid exchanges that encompassed war and peace, family, love, loyalty, betrayals, and perhaps most poignantly, the intricate relation between art and death. Throughout their lively and sometimes testy dialogue, we see Gertz gently but firmly prodding the author for the psychological, spiritual, and political motivations that inspired some of his greatest works (and we find Oz's own intriguing interpretation of his conclusion to Judas). Above all, we witness Oz's journey from a dreamer who once sought human redemption in its most global sense to one quietly reconciled to finding it in its most local and domestic forms, on the level of the most modest yet perhaps sustaining human connections.[64] As the author of *Between God and Beast: An Examination of Amos Oz's Prose* and other essential works, Avraham Balaban has long been established as one of Oz's most important critical interlocutors and in "Homeless between Two Homes" he describes their early friendship at Hulda (for one of them the kibbutz was "hell" while for the other it was a "redemption" of sorts) as well as the revelatory role that Jung played in his appreciation of Oz's earliest works. And rounding out this section, Nissim Calderon's "*My Michael*, May 1967" offers a bittersweet glance back at Calderon's time as a young soldier, grappling with the premonitions of Oz's foreboding and staunchly antiheroic novel amidst the post-Six Day War euphoria.

In the next section, "Nomads, Vipers, and Women," Nitza Ben-Dov delves with keen insight into the tragic origins and unhealed wound that lie behind Oz's complex relation with the feminine, inspiring some of his most haunting works. In Ben-Dov's revealing analysis ("Maternal Illness and the Israeli Body Politic at War"), understanding the role of Oz's "hidden heroine" in her many guises and variations, proves essential to understanding the psychological complexity, painful resonances, and haunting artistic effects, of much of his oeuvre, as well as the author's gift for transforming personal trauma into a disturbing collective allegory. In "The Little Plot and the Big Plot in Oz's Early Fiction," Oded Nir situates two novels and two shorter works against earlier generations of modern Hebrew literature to propose a new way to understand the significance of Oz's vital role in the 1960s "New Wave," illuminating the critical shift between a national-social register to the psycho-ethical (individual) one in these narratives.

Over the years, a few scholars have found it a fascinating exercise to observe the traces of when Oz's conscious effort to forge a literary attachment to Europe began to emerge. We find veiled allusions to the rootedness of the Klausner family in the Polish district of Grodno in narratives such as *Touch the Water, Touch the Wind*, and Oz once told the interviewer Nitza Rosovsky that his European inheritance was carried in his genes: "I am neither proud nor ashamed of it. This is my birth before birth. My parents used to speak with a mixture of longing and fear about the beautiful countries in which they grew up. They hoped that someday Jewish Jerusalem too would become a real city. It took me years to understand that by 'real city' they meant a place with a cathedral, a river, and thick forests."[65] Improvising on Bloom's renowned revisionist critical theory of the "anxiety of influence," Sheila E. Jelen's "Oz's Literary Genealogies: Salvage Poetics in *A Tale of Love and Darkness*" presents a captivating new paradigm of hermeneutic genealogy, a sophisticated argument paving the way for new understandings of Oz, presenting cogent evidence of the author's resolute reconciliation with the feminine and the maternal in his sprawling yet intimate künstlerroman.

The essays of the volume's third section, "Coming of Age: Constructing the Hebrew Home(land)," map out both the crucible of childhood and the emergence of the young Jewish state. Though Oz's fiction contains a staggering degree of characters and personas, for some readers his most enduring portraits are those of his child protagonists. In the first essay of this section, Adam Rovner thoughtfully considers the relationship of the author's enduring preoccupation with literary beginnings of works by other writers (and of course his own wounded origins), to the child narrators of his most poignant works. Rovner's "Cat People: Coming of Age in *Mr. Levi* and *Panther in the Basement*" ultimately directs our attention to ways in which the "uneasy synthesis between boy and man" in those narratives also seem to comment obliquely on the growing disjunction of the writer and his society that became apparent over time as the latter wearied of his leonine status as Israel's official "voice of conscience."

Drawing on Lukács and others in what is perhaps this volume's richest theoretical discussion, Eric Zakim situates Oz's early works such as "Derekh ha-ruah" within an ecocritical framework, yet one that ultimately departs from the Anglo-American literary tradition, bound instead to "a modernism of interiority." In "Tilling the Soil of National Ideology" Zakim regards that ethos as defined less by the romantic certitudes of A. D. Gordon or Labor Zionism than an aesthetics of unresolved anxieties and contradiction and the unraveling of his characters' subjectivities. By way of further contrast, in examining Oz's 1970s rewriting of those ideologically disruptive works, Zakim ultimately identifies a turn to nostalgia and the defense of a historical ethos that flattens the dissonance of the original language. For Oz, few questions were more consequential than the Jew's fateful identity crisis, the perpetual divide between diaspora and homeland and in Liam Hoare's far-ranging consideration of novels, short fiction, essays and interviews ("On Eternity: Homelessness and the Meaning of Homeland"), he underscores just how conflicted the author himself could be, in ways that inspired some of his most richly ambivalent literary creations. If over the years, a number of critics have touched on the biblical resonances scattered throughout Oz's fiction, few have done so with such penetrating insight as the formidable feminist biblical scholar Nehama Aschkenasy and here she does more than justice to the ingenious and often ironic reinventions of the plots and themes of sacrifice, sexual violence, and the bitter entanglements of fathers and sons that weigh so heavily in the narratives of Genesis, and in Oz's fiction to such startling effect. In "The Dialogic Encounter between New and Old: The Biblical Intertext in Oz's Fiction" Aschkenasy suggests that in vital respects, the Hebrew Bible serves Oz as "a form of a Zionist manifesto, and he wrestles with it, just as he does with Israeli politics and society, with combativeness and reproach, but also as a source of solace and comfort. . . . Oz's engagement with the Bible reflects his relationship with his homeland and its people, disillusionment and harsh criticism together with fierce loyalty and awe."

"Oz and the Other: Mizrahis and Palestinians" brings together several essays addressing the highs and lows of Oz's portrayals of those who challenged Ashkenazi hegemony in its various cultural and political manifestations. In "Oz's Contentious Journey: *In the Land of Israel*" Adia Mendelson-Maoz incisively addresses controversial aspects of Oz's reflections on his immersive encounters with outspoken members of Israel's diverse and often antagonistic communities in the early 1980s, a work that would inspire later bold forays into hostile environments by literary writers including David Grossman and Nir Baram. When it comes to mirroring the country's charged political climate in the 1980s, *Black Box* stands out as one of Oz's most ambitious if misunderstood novels, its tense choreography of moral, sexual, gender, and political themes perhaps also a manifestation of the human condition at large. Both politically and romantically, *Black Box*, Oz's sole epistolary novel, is thus a work of paradoxes and extremes and Joshua Leifer's "Oz against Himself: Between Political Romanticism and Social Realism" examines the fractious ethnic conflict at its heart, emphasizing that this is Oz's only novel to grapple directly with the fraught relationship between Ashkenazim and Mizrahim as well as perhaps gesturing toward the fatal stagnation of Oz's approach to the Israeli-Palestinian conflict. In a related examination of Oz's political legacy (" 'Like Belfast, Rhodesia, or South Africa': Oz and the Ideologies of Oslo"), Moriel Rothman-Zecher weighs the fate of Amos Oz's early radical vision against the demise of the two-state solution and the violent deaths of Palestinian civilians and the need to acknowledge that the grim future Oz once prophesied has become reality. Concluding this section

("And They Lived Separately Ever After: The Two State Solution as Literary Ending"), Vered Karti Shemtov's richly comparative essay considers the wider cultural implications and development of the intricate relationship between Oz's politics and the metaphoric denouements of his literary works, alongside those of his old friend A. B. Yehoshua as well as other popular artists and writers including contemporary works such as the Palestinian screenwriter and director Sameh Zoabi's provocative 2018 film comedy *Tel Aviv on Fire*.

The volume's fifth and final section, "Dreamers, Iconoclasts, and Traitors" presents the plight of Oz's often lonely or isolated protagonists grappling with both the consequences of ardent ideology and the stigma of heresy in Zionist culture. Yaron Peleg's "Of Howling Jackals and Village Scenes: A Lament" examines the variable cultural legacy of Oz's mantle as "prophet," contrasting the radical disruptions of the early fiction with the late nostalgia of his final short works. For Peleg, Oz's lofty status as "seer depended on a number of conditions and on the existence of a distinct cultural and political community that shared the kind of values that created the role of prophet to begin with." Intriguingly, Peleg argues that if that role of consummate moral authority lost its relevance in a society that had undergone dramatic social and political change, it was Oz himself who played an active part in its cultural decline, reconciled to addressing his global audience from a new (and diminished) position that Peleg calls "confessional nostalgia" in his cleareyed assessment. My own contribution to this section explores the legacy of Oz's memorable critical literary portrayals of the Zionist institution perhaps closest to his heart and mind, in "Exultation, Disillusionment and Late Inspiration: Oz's Once and Future Kibbutz."

No collection of this nature could satisfy without addressing the powerfully resonant final novel *Judas* (shortlisted for the Man Booker Prize), surely one of Oz's most urgent and profoundly universal works about political and romantic dreamers and the tragic dimensions of their fantasies; its characters' heartfelt struggles with both their own human frailties and those of the state resonating far beyond Israel itself. In the penultimate contribution to this volume, Sam Sussman addresses one of the most fascinating creative contradictions in the late novel that many have come to regard as one of Oz's finest works. "From Tragedy to Betrayal: *Judas* and the Subversive Politics of Oz's Last Act" examines the thought-provoking enigma of just why Oz, the quintessential Sabra writer, "child and champion of the Jewish state, prophet of the two-state solution, spokesman of the Ashkenazi labor Zionist elite," might have chosen to create such a hauntingly eloquent spokesman for an alternative to Zionist hegemony and the Middle East's lost multinational legacy, a startlingly different story of the Israeli-Palestinian conflict ("a radical critique of Israel's very founding") than what he had long championed, as what he likely knew would be his final literary act. For Sussman, the novel's legacy offers a "richly historic alternative to the one state/two state paradigm, one that promises to shape future debate about justice in Israel-Palestine."

Like many others, I experienced shock and dismay at the revelations concerning Galia Oz and her allegations of emotional and even physical abuse in her autobiography, *Something Disguised as Love*.[66] I cannot exaggerate the pain that the contributors and I felt at the time and few of us would deny that Oz's reputation has been profoundly tarnished even though his other children, Fania Oz-Salzberger and Daniel Oz have passionately insisted that their sibling's accusations were grievously exaggerated distortions of the past they knew. I struggled for a long time before writing a collective email to the other contributors. It seemed that Oz, eloquent witness to the tormented lives of his parents and fictional chronicler of so many other wounded families, managed to remain tragically oblivious to dangerous truths about himself.

As the son of an abusive father, I did not take any of this lightly. In the end I wrote an anguished statement to the effect that writers die, and then at some point uglier realities than we knew of in their lifetimes force their way to the surface for one reason or another. We should not look away. And as lovers of literature, it behooves all of us to accept that the noblest among us all too often have feet of clay. Some of us may have thought we were writing only about a wholly exemplary human being rather than a complex and tormented artist who had received pain early in life and was fully capable of bringing pain to others close to him. In the passing of almost every revered individual, it is almost inevitable that painful truths later surface and they must be aired. Certainly, such has been the case with other writers whose literary legacy otherwise remains at a high stature (Saul Bellow, J. D. Salinger, Philip Roth, and Henry Roth, and on and on through the ages). Having expressed that, I can only add that those wishing for a fair accounting of Oz's life and legacy will surely find Fania Oz-Salzberger's revelatory Afterword to this volume essential reading. Suffice it to say that one could not hope for a more judicious and eloquently thoughtful consideration of what it meant to experience Oz, not only as a father but as an intellectual partner. Those seeking a better understanding of the sources that inspired Oz's early iconoclasm will also find much to ponder here.

To underscore what I stated earlier, this volume was never intended as a hagiography. To my mind, the extraordinary work and often courageous life still warrants the benefit of our deep critical engagement and moral consideration. I am profoundly grateful to all the contributors for their efforts and understand that it is going to take time, perhaps many more years, to fully absorb this pain. At the same time, I would gently like to suggest that it worth heeding the imperative that Galia Oz herself rushed to emphasize: "Personally I don't boycott art. Tolstoy was a terrible family man, so was Dickens. I think that you can see a person in a complex way. There's no need to go on a crusade. You can tell the truth without boycotting."[67] Nevertheless, at least two contributors reluctantly determined that they no longer felt comfortable about their association with the volume and so we parted ways, to my great regret.

Ultimately, each of us must grapple with the significance of the uncertainty of what we can ever truly know. Ours was not the only major Oz project profoundly affected by the explosive news. Acclaimed film documentarian Yair Qedar labored for two and a half years (often in close collaboration with Nurith Gertz and others close to Oz and the family) on his Oz documentary *The Fourth Window*, the penultimate installment of his acclaimed "The Hebrews" literary series. He had just completed editing when the Kinneret Zmora publishers announced Galia Oz's new book. To Qedar's credit, he realized that he had to reimagine the contours of his film and the result is a sensitive, richly psychological, and emotionally layered project that does full justice to Oz's intricacies and contradictions, his virtues as well as terrible failings.[68] I would strongly urge anyone interested in Oz's life and works to seek out this extraordinary film. In a similar vein, this book aspires to offer its readers numerous pathways into the rich moral and political complexities.

My deep conviction is that this collection richly demonstrates that Oz's work constitutes an aesthetically wrought corpus that will always lend itself to being approached from a variety of different perspectives and methodologies to yield fascinating literary, cultural, political, and psychological insights and complexities, including but not limited to inter-textuality, Marxist criticism, ecocriticism, and feminist criticism. Some of the contributors focus on the challenges of different narrative modes or narrative closure in Oz's works. Others offer exciting insights into Oz's literary and psychological development and his emergence and various stages of his life as a public intellectual. Each of these approaches provides crucial building blocks for subsequent research. Moreover, it is surely worth noting that to date, there has been only limited critical attention to the remarkably innovative aspects of Oz's late works, *Between Friends* (2012) and *Judas* (2014), and no scholarly work has yet been written that addresses Oz's literary career from its beginning to its conclusion, the author's full and often combative life as a public intellectual, or the interrelationship between these two areas of his writing. As editor it is my great hope that this volume will successfully illuminate these issues and help others to make their own independent assessments of Oz's literary career and legacy—arguments that will surely unfold for decades to come and undoubtedly attract scholars to his archive. While it would be sophomoric to suggest that any single book could accomplish all these goals so soon after Oz's death, the time is surely ripe to begin the work of reassessing both the literary work and that of the public intellectual and it is my modest hope that the present volume will contribute mightily toward those efforts and hopefully steer future readers to his remarkable achievements, with all their joys as well as aching melancholy.[69]

Finally, I am profoundly grateful to all the essayists for their perseverance and dedication to this project. It has been a long journey for us. At this point in my life, I cannot refrain from mentioning my oldest Israeli friends, whose extraordinary accomplishments and deep affection has inspired and sustained me over the years ever since the days of our youth at Kibbutz Yahel: Rafael Bar, Avi Camchi, Dr. Shmulik Friedman, Dr. Yonaton Gold, Dr. Robert Hoffman, "Gingi" Shlomo Mordechai, Chip Nobil, Ellis Shuman, and Dr. Mark Weiser. My appreciation also goes to my wonderful colleagues and friends in Jewish Studies and the Department of Comparative Humanities at the University of Louisville and to the Jewish Heritage Fund for Excellence for their support. I deeply appreciate the gracious participation of Fania Oz-Salzberger and thank Éditions Gallimard for their permission to include the translation, which appears as the Afterword to this volume. When it comes to an incisive reading of the entire manuscript, I couldn't have wished for a better critic than Karen Grumberg. Her terrifically thoughtful comments and suggestions led to significant improvements in many of the individual essays, and indeed strengthened the entire organization and structure of the entire book, and I am very grateful. It was a genuine pleasure to work with James Peltz and his conscientious staff at SUNY Press. And I warmly thank Ilan Bar-David, Jessica Cohen, translator extraordinaire, and Deborah Harris, of the Jerusalem-based Deborah Harris agency, for their helpfulness at critical moments. As always, my wife and life partner Michali Kofman lifted my spirits during difficult times, put up with all my angst and uncertainty, and inspires me every day through her own grace under pressure in a challenging academic environment and beyond.

Notes

1. *Elsewhere, Perhaps*. Translated by Nicholas de Lange. Harcourt Brace Jovanovich, 1973. The title of this essay is inspired in part by Johann Hari's complex portrait of the author in "A Life in Focus: Amos Oz, Israeli Literary Colossus and Lifelong Advocate of a Two-State Solution." *Independent*, 31 Dec. 2018, https://www.independent.co.uk/news/obituaries/amoz-oz-dead-israeli-writer-novelist-palestine-israel-tale-love-and-darkness-a8705681.html.

2. To be precise, Rivlin was quoting a remark made to him years earlier by Yossi Sarid when they were both members of the Knesset. In his eulogy, Rivlin recalled his effusive response: "I am not reading Dostoevsky, I am reading myself. That's me there in those small letters, I am in that book. When Amos wrote of love and darkness, he was writing about me." Rivlin, Reuven. "Eulogy for Amos Oz." *J-Wire*, 1 Jan. 2019, https://www.jwire.com.au/eulogy-for-amos-oz/.

3. Edemariam, Aida. "A Life in Writing: Amos Oz." *The Guardian*, 13 Feb. 2009, https://www.theguardian.com/culture/2009/feb/14/amos-oz-interview.

4. Balaban, Avraham. *Between God & Beast: An Examination of Amos Oz's Prose*. Pennsylvania State UP, 1993. With Oz's passing, Balaban's assessment concludes with a declaration that poignantly endures with even greater resonance: "Because of the contradicting features of the forces that the protagonists try to unite, that unity can only be temporary, a springboard for a renewed struggle and a new book" (239). Cf. Yair Mazor's similar explication: "On the one hand, Oz's world is founded on logic, discipline, pure reason and solid, cogent rationality; on the other hand, it is a dark, demonic world of unbridled desire, echoing with the hoarse shrill shrieks of passion and lust. The turbulent, murky world of gushing, untamed emotions threatens to invade the sober, well-lighted world of rationality and spread its deadly venom there. It seeks to undermine and destroy its order, balance, and serenity; to instill a sinister and evil spirit of malignancy and nightmare that will rob the other domain of its happiness and tranquility." In *Somber Lust: The Art of Amos Oz*. Translated by Marganit Weinberger-Rotman, State U of New York P, 2002, p. 2. Or Avner Holtzman's

argument that the recurring conflict in Oz's works are variations on a messianic attraction to zealous militancy, and a pull toward rationality. Holtzman considers this as a 'religious' yearning for the peaceful synthesis of these warring cultural binaries. "Fima mekhake l'nes." ["Fima Waits For a Miracle"]. Hebrew. *Haaretz*, 15 Feb. 1991.

5. Or perhaps not altogether "elusive" after all. One thinks of the conciliatory formation of unlikely extended families and the kibbutz's pacifying containment of potentially explosive enmities in novels like *Elsewhere, Perhaps* or *A Perfect Peace*. In a 1986 interview, Oz succeeded in crystalizing the concerns that drove his post-1960s generation of writers in terms that seem to stand the test of time in illuminating his own preoccupation with the transcendent to the very end of his life, a concern "with soul-searching and a secret fascination with theology . . . a theological quest underneath" and "a quest for something that goes beyond the boundaries of politics and ideology." Addressing his enthusiasm for the Latin American novelist Garcia Marquez, Oz described *The Autumn of the Patriarch*: "On the surface . . . a novel about a ruler, about a tyrant. But this tyrant is a metaphor for God Almighty. . . . The political reality provides the springboard to writing a metaphysical . . . novel about God." Cohen, Joseph. *Voices of Israel: Essays on and Interviews with Yehuda Amichai, A. B. Yehoshua, T. Carmi, Aharon Appelfeld, and Amos Oz*. State U of New York P, 1990, pp. 181, 189. Perhaps the fullest ripening of Oz's provocative insistence that secular writers like himself were the most legitimate inheritors of religious concerns (and not the ultra-Orthodox) can be found in his essay, "A Full Cart or an Empty One?" The text was translated by Shmuel Sermoneta-Gertel and published by Meitar: The College of Judaism as Culture in where it appeared under the title "A Full Cart or an Empty One?" It was reprinted in the U.S. in Malkin, Yaakov, editor. *Secular Jewish Culture*. The Library for Secular Judaism, 2017, pp. 16–31.

6. In his authoritative study, Yair Mazor illuminates the unwavering honesty, discipline, and control in Oz's language, through "highly methodical observations of reality . . . his writing shows a crystalline logic, sharply honed, polished and precise . . . [he] approaches the reality under examination like a careful scientist in a laboratory, one eye closed and the other screwed to a sterile microscope, a sharp scalpel in hand. With great concentration and lucidity, he . . . formulates decisive, well-founded observations and draws clear, accurate, and perfectly logical conclusions." By way of aesthetic contrast, as Mazor underscores, Oz's meticulous observations of reality clash with memorable effect against the passions of his protagonists: "currents of libido and eroticism [that] are always somber, sinister, untamed, and defiant of the dictates of reason and restraint." Thus "the most pervasive and permanent element . . . in his writing is a state of rivalry and animosity, struggle and strife between two extremes that are irreconcilably hostile and antagonistic to each other." *Somber Lust: The Art of Amos Oz*. Translated by Marganit Weinberger-Rotman. State U of New York P, 2002, pp. 1–2.

7. Quoted in Oz's interview at Princeton with Lisa Meyer, "Employing Language in the Service of Peace." *Los Angeles Times*, 28 Jan. 1998, https://www.latimes.com/archives/la-xpm-1998-jan-28-ls-12760-story.html.

8. As argued most recently by Omri Asscher, Oz "seems to have been instrumental in creating Hebrew literature's moral, oppositional image [his] works were often perceived as representing Hebrew literature and he himself as a metonym for Hebrew literature." *Reading Israel, Reading America: The Politics of Translation between Jews*. Stanford UP, 2020, p. 65.

9. One immediately thinks of the three novellas of *The Hill of Evil Counsel*, as well as *Panther in the Basement*, and *A Tale of Light and Darkness*, among others.

10. The late Joseph Cohen speculated that Oz, contra centuries of expressions of Jewish secular and messianic hopes and yearning, was "the first Jewish writer . . . to recognize and exploit the negative literary potential of Jerusalem." For Cohen, the stolid and determined geologist Michael merely wants to get on with existence while Hannah "represents the powder keg waiting to explode that Israel was, and in some respects, still is" and embodies the novel's "indirect sociopolitical message . . . there can be no peace and contentment until Israel gets beyond its hysteria over its enforced embrace with the Arabs and finds a means of 'furious wrestling' with them that is less lethal than playful" (*Voices* 148, 149).

11. The first of his books to be translated into English, *Michael Sheli* (*My Michael*) was a departure from his first two books, the short story collection *Artzot Ha-Tan* (*Where the Jackals Howl*) and *Makom Acher* (*Elsewhere, Perhaps*) both focused on the drama of kibbutz life. Readers outside of Israel are sometimes confused by this bibliography; the Hebrew original of *Elsewhere, Perhaps* was written two years prior to *My Michael*. Oz's first Hebrew book, *Where the Jackals Howl*, appeared in English only after the novels *Elsewhere, Perhaps*, *My Michael*, and *Touch the Water, Touch the Wind*.

12. As Nehama Aschkenasy eloquently observes, "Time and history are weighted with a special significance in the context of modern Jerusalem, a city charged with past memories and looking towards renewal and change. The city Jerusalem is a place where, perhaps more than anywhere else, an impressionable person like Hannah might experience the oppression of history, the sense that the individual is called upon to harness his energies and commit his whole life to an idea rooted in history and transcending the individual's need for personal happiness." See "Women and the Double in Modern Hebrew Literature: Berdichewsky/Agnon, Oz/Yehoshua." *Prooftexts*, vol. 8, no. 1, Jan. 1988, pp. 113–28. Quotation appears on p. 121.

13. Lehmann-Haupt, Christopher. *Books of the Times: Elsewhere, Perhaps*, 14 Nov. 1973, https://archive.nytimes.com/www.nytimes.com/books/97/10/26/home/oz-elsewhere.html. Though I generally refer to Oz's critical reception and popularity in the U.S., it seems worth noting that his books often fared even better in French, German, and Italian editions.

14. What Lehmann-Haupt and other readers of the early kibbutz fiction sometimes overlooked was that the utopian enclosure of kibbutz life stood for nothing less than humanity, in their poignantly overweening aspirations, as a *whole*. As Robert Alter observes, "The kibbutz enterprise is seen as a dream of overweening rationality, an attempt to impose a net geometric order on the seething chaos of the natural world . . . a reflex of turning away from the unsettling darkness of reality to an illusory light." Alter, Robert. *Modern Hebrew Literature*. Behrman House, 1975, p. 331. However, lest any of us underestimate Oz's genuine (and lifelong) regard for kibbutz socialism, on many occasions, as in the essay "The Kibbutz at the Present Time," he stresses that the kibbutz embodies "a social system that, for all its disadvantages, is the least bad, the least unkind." Later, he rhapsodically delineates its adaptive nature in organic terms as a society "striking deeper roots, producing leaves, flowers, and fruit in due season and occasionally shedding its leaves [living] in its own inner legitimacy, far from the domination of . . . legislators." In *Under this Blazing Light*. Cambridge UP, 1996, pp. 125–32. Quotations appear on pp. 128, 131.

15. Cohen, Joseph. *Voices of Israel*, p. 142. And Oz himself often grew impatient with the many readers who demanded an unreserved political message from his work: "Every day, my mailbox drowns in invitations to lecture before all sorts of conferences and symposia about 'The Image of the Israeli-Arab Conflict in Literature' or 'The Reflection of the Nation in the Novel' or 'Literature as a Mirror of Society.' But if all you want is to look in a mirror, why read books?" *The Story Begins: Essays on Literature* [*Matchilim Sipur*, Keter: 1996]. Translated by Maggie Bar-Tura. Harcourt Brace & Company, 1999, p. 115.

16. See for example, Bronner, Ethan. "Amos Oz, Approaching 70, Sees Israel With a Bird's-Eye View." *The New York Times*, 12 Apr. 2009, https://www.nytimes.com/2009/04/13/books/13oz.html.

17. Gil Hochberg incisively addresses the role of the "emptied Arab village" in Israeli fiction, which "unfold a semantics of ambiguity located between presence and absence, the visible and invisible" thus forming the very antithesis of "sealed fragments of the past." Hochberg, Gil. "A Poetics of Haunting: From Yizhar's Hirbeh to Yehoshua's Ruins to Koren's Crypts." *Jewish Social Studies*, vol. 18, no. 3, 2012, pp. 55–69. Quotation appears on p. 66. See also Karen Grumberg's authoritative discussion of the role of the "Hebrew gothic" in *My Michael* and other works in chapter 4 (Dark Jerusalem: Amos Oz's Anxious Literary Cartography between 1948 and 1967) of her *Hebrew Gothic: History and the Poetics of Persecution*. Indiana UP, 2019.

18. Elsewhere, I have argued that much of the internal crisis of the kibbutz protagonist Yonatan Lifshitz owes to the haunting proximity of the village ruins in his formative years, however that catalyst is simply far more visible to the Hebrew reader than in Hillel Halkin's translation. See Omer-Sherman, Ranen. *Israel in Exile: Jewish Writing and the Desert*. University of Illinois, 2006, pp. 66–95. Such

editorial censorship, if that is what it is not only diminishes our appreciation of both Oz's conscience and that of his protagonist but by extension, constitutes a second, symbolic assault on Palestinian memory. In English, the reader encounters faithful renderings of the festering animosities between Russian and German Jews, between generations, between militarist hawks and doves. But here is one of the salient instances of the troubling omissions Omri Asscher identifies: "A grindstone fragment that Yonatan came across had to be left for drier weather when a tractor and a wagon could be used to haul it back. . . . Suddenly, Azariah started and grabbed unto Udi's shirt." Asscher's essay includes a striking number of other instances in which "ideologically charged aspects of the text" are significantly subdued. In each, Oz's distressing allusions to the destruction or dispersal of the original inhabitants is nearly invisible to the reader of Halkin's translation. Asscher astutely speculates that "as Sheikh Dahr is representative of the history and fate of other Palestinian villages, the connotations of this sentence within the political-ideological discourse about 'the right to the land' are clear, and may be the reason behind its omission." Asscher also addresses the striking extent to which Nicholas de Lange's 1973 translation of *Elsewhere, Perhaps* (which appeared in a revised and truncated version) softens the wild irrationalism and aggressive impulses of Reuven Harish, kibbutz educator and poet, by omitting a crucial passage. Little of his hatred toward the Arab enemy is retained from a "ferociously violent stream of consciousness, full of murderous connotations as well as several biblical allusions." The result is a significant loss of the novel's unsettling ambiguities as the reader encounters "a less pathologically haunted" protagonist. See Asscher, Omri. "The Ideological Manipulation of Hebrew Literature in English Translation in the 1970s and 1980s." *Journal of Modern Jewish Studies*, vol. 15, no. 3, 2016, pp. 384–401. Quotations appear on pp. 394, 389. In the case of *Elsewhere, Perhaps*, it seems that Oz himself was complicit as he collaborated on the translation.

19. Never in his career was that quality more of a force to be reckoned with than his early warning soon after the 1967 War: "Even unavoidable occupation is a corrupting occupation," he declared in an editorial published in the now-defunct Labor Zionist newspaper *Davar*.

20. Oz, Amos. "How to Cure a Fanatic." *How to Cure a Fanatic*. Princeton UP, 2006, pp. 37–71. Quotation appears on p. 40.

21. Oz, Amos. "2007 Asturias Prize Acceptance Speech," http://www.fpa. es/en/princess-of-asturias-awards/laureates/2007-amos-oz.html?texto=discurso.

22. Oz argued that "there is something in the nature of the fanatic that essentially is very sentimental and at the same time lacks imagination" ("How to Cure" 53).

23. Oz aligns the gift of humor with the ability to both "enjoy diversity" and "live in open-ended situations" (66) traits that many might ascribe to a diasporic consciousness, an ethos that Israel's ultranationalists find antithetical.

24. Freedland, Jonathan. "Interview with Amos Oz: 'I Love Israel, but I Don't Like It Very Much.'" *The Guardian*, 23 Sept. 2016, https://www.theguardian.com/books/2016/sep/23/amos-oz-i-love-israel-bit-i-dont-like-it-very-much-interview.

25. Yigal Schwartz offers an excellent overview of this binary and its two overlapping narrative "maps" in chapter 5 of his *The Zionist Paradox: Hebrew Literature and Israeli Identity*. Translated by Michael Sapir. Brandeis UP, 2014.

26. For a cogent example of Oz's conscientious activism on behalf of the Bedouin in his later years see Khoury, Jack, and Maya Sela. "Amos Oz: Situation of Bedouin in Negev Is 'Ticking Time Bomb.'" *Haaretz*, 18 Aug. 2010, https://www.haaretz.com/1.5101538.

27. Alter, Robert. *Modern Hebrew Literature*, p. 330.

28. *Dear Zealots*. Houghton Mifflin Harcourt, 2018, p. 131.

29. Though well aware that the Israeli left has never been culpable in the kind of violence that the rightwing settler movement, Oz would often complain of certain colleagues in the Israeli peace movement who passionately despised him "just because I advocate a slightly different strategy on how to make peace with the Palestinians" ("How to Cure" 50).

30. The text was translated by Shmuel Sermoneta-Gertel and published by Meitar: The College of Judaism as Culture where it appeared under the title "A Full Cart or an Empty One?" It was reprinted in the U.S. in Malkin, Yaakov, editor. *Secular Jewish Culture*. The Library for Secular Judaism, 2017, pp. 16–31.

31. If asked to identify the single work of Oz's nonfiction that most resolutely speaks to the future of Israeli citizenship one could do worse than turn to the prickly and intellectual forceful argument of "A Full Cart or an Empty One?" With much sorrow, I suspect this essay will one day be read as the embodiment of the legacy (and perhaps final protest) of the secular, Israeli left. With erudition and wit, Oz demolishes ultra-Orthodox Judaism's insidious role as "pretender to the throne" of Judaism's richly complex legacy, arguing that those who most authentically bear it on their shoulders are secular writers:

On the whole, Halakhic Judaism was unable to present a religious approach to the Nazi phenomenon. . . . It was in fact modern Hebrew literature that developed profoundly religious approaches to the genocide of the Jews and to the founding of the Jewish state. A number of writers and poets took upon themselves the task that the halakhists had avoided. One might almost speak of a separation of religion—not from the state, but from the religious. The shocking fact is that theology has not disappeared; it has simply shifted from the religiously observant to the most creative force Jewish culture has witnessed in recent generations: modern Hebrew literature, prose, poetry and scholarship. These have refused to let God off the hook, tugging at his sleeve, showing a modicum of understanding, or taking him to court. Authors who have, for the most part, considered themselves secular, have dealt incessantly with theological perplexities. A broad range of authors—from Bialik, Berdyczewski and Agnon, through Uri Zvi Greenberg, to Yizhar, Dan Pagis, Amichai and others—have written, in some way or another, of "God's withdrawal from the affairs of the world" (hester panim). It would appear to be the case that most of the dynamic and creative discoveries of the past century have taken place beyond the realm of Halakhah, albeit in dialectic or iconoclastic relation to it. Iconoclasm is also a kind of relationship however, often more intimate than the relationship of the museum curator who polishes a locked display case. Heresy too is a part of Jewish culture, as are disbelief and blasphemy. All of these approaches are eminently religious. (22–23)

32. Oz was seven years old in the tumultuous years of 1946–47, which marked the end of the British Mandate and the violent prelude to the War of Independence and his childhood impressions inform the impressions of the vulnerable young protagonists in *Panther in the Basement* [*Panter Ba-Martef*, 1995] and even earlier, in each of the three novellas that compose *The Hill of Evil Counsel* [*Har Ha-Etza Ha-Ra'ah*, 1976]. Of the latter novellas, Joseph Cohen notes that "central to each . . . is a boy Oz's age, perceptive, sensitive, highly imaginative, awkward, pudgy, tormented by the neighborhood children" (*Voices of Israel* 165). And while Oz may have sought to remake himself at Hulda, his inability to dance or excel in kibbutz sports were obstacles to his full acceptance. Hence, in a psychological sense, these narratives are almost nakedly autobiographical.

33. There was a later, less famous but equally compelling repetition of the charge during Oz's early Hulda years after he changed his name to avoid association with the famous Klausner clan: "I asked [the school principal] not to tell the other boys, and they didn't know my real name. But somehow, I have no idea how, they found out that I was from a right-wing Revisionist family, and Revisionism was the ideological enemy of the labor Zionists who founded the kibbutz movement. So some of them suspected I was a kind of fifth column, maybe I'd come to spy. It really wasn't fair, because I was the most left-wing person in Kibbutz Hulda. I can tell you another secret: in Hulda, at elections, the entire kibbutz always voted for the center-left Mapai Party, and they were very proud that Mapai received one hundred percent of the votes. In the evening, right after the votes had been counted, they would post a note on the bulletin board: 'This time too, Mapai received one hundred percent of our votes.' That's how it was until the 1960 elections, when there was a huge scandal. . . . As the votes were being counted, they suddenly found one vote for the left-wing party, Mapam. The entire kibbutz moved heaven and Earth to find out who the traitor was. But they never did. They suspected Elyosha, suspected Honzo, but it was me. That was the first time I had the right to vote, and I simply betrayed them and voted for Mapam, and I didn't tell anyone. I was that kind of fifth column. Today they're gone, that older generation. . . . If they had known about it, they would have killed me." "A Room of One's Own: Amos Oz in Conversation with Shira Hadad." Translated by Sondra Silverston. *Granta*, vol. 145, 15 Nov. 2018, https://granta.com/a-room-of-ones-own/. In any case, the charge of "traitor" frequently followed Oz through

his adult life, to the extent that, at the memorial held December 31 at the Tzavta Theater in Tel Aviv, President Reuven Rivlin, a childhood friend, concluded his eulogy by remarking of Oz's outspoken opposition to Netanyahu and the rightwing establishment: "Not only were you not afraid to be in the minority and hold a minority opinion, but you weren't even afraid to be called a traitor. On the contrary, you saw the word as a title with honor.": https://www.timesofisrael.com/liveblog_entry/rivlin-eulogizes-amos-oz-you-werent-afraid-to-be-called-a-traitor/.

34. I am profoundly grateful to the observations of an anonymous reader of this volume: "While sympathetic to the desire to fit in, Oz used his work to point to the dangers of wanting to fit in too much and advocated in favor of 'treachery'—the willingness to go against mainstream views and behaviors when he recognized that these . . . proved harmful to people. This manifested itself as rebellion in his early fiction and was not characterized as treachery. Yet it took on a different character in his later fiction and came to be understood as 'treachery' when Oz promoted the value of difference and the importance of resisting conformist pressures."

35. The phrase occurs in the final three lines of Wordsworth's 1802 poem, "My Heart Leaps Up": "The Child is father of the Man/; And I could wish my days to be/Bound each to each by natural piety." The utterance reappears as the epigraph to "Ode: Intimations of Immortality," composed in 1804.

36. it is true that Oz can sometimes seem perplexed by the mystery of the feminine, as readers will note in his candid admissions to Nurith Gertz in "The History of a Long Conversation" included in this volume. For exemplary critiques of Oz and the feminine see also: Wheatley, Natasha G. "'It Is the Hunter and You Are the Harpooned Dolphin': Memory, Writing, and Medusa—Amos Oz and His Women." *Jewish Quarterly Review*, vol. 100, no. 4, 2010, pp. 631–48; and Fuchs, Esther. "Amos Oz's Treacherous Helpmate: Toward a Feminist Critique of His Fiction." *Literature East and West*, vol. 26, 1990, pp. 149–60.

37. In perhaps his most important confession over their years of friendship, Oz reportedly told Gertz, "'I always felt guilty, and I feel guilty now, too, that if I had been a good boy it wouldn't have happened, if I had been worthy of love, it wouldn't have happened, it couldn't have happened. A mother doesn't do that to a boy unless she doesn't love him.'" Gertz is quoted in Izikovich, Gili. "'Amos Oz Spent His Whole Life with a Black Hole Inside and Nothing Could Fill It.'" *Haaretz*, 7 Nov. 2020, https://www.haaretz.com/israel-news/.premium.HIGHLIGHT.MAGAZINE-amos-oz-spent-his-whole-life-with-a-black-hole-inside-1.9294066.

38. In addition to Oz, the strikingly intimate and revealing interviews with hundreds of kibbutz reservists were conducted by Abba Kovner, David Alon, and Yariv Ben-Aharon, among others. Two hundred hours were recorded but the published result was a striking softening and elision of the original as the government prevented seventy percent of the material from being included and sent those recordings to Yad Tabenkin, the Kibbutz Movement's archives. The resulting

book was edited by Oz's collaborator, historian Avraham Shapira (a student of Martin Buber), who in later years refused to release the excluded audio tapes until approached by Mor Loushy who prevailed only after months of dogged efforts. Ironically, just before the release of *Censored Voices*, Deputy Defense Minister Eli Ben-Dahan initially threatened to censor it (though he hadn't yet seen it) because of the film's perceived threat to Israel's official heroic narrative of the war. Of Oz's "very crucial" participation in the film as one of the primary interviewees, Loushy later declared that "His testimonies are so emotional and so smart and so moving and he initiated this idea [with Shapira]. It's so much to understand that beneath all, the dancing you had to be sensitive to know that we had to deal with all this. It was a brave act to initiate these conversations." Steinberg, Jessica. "Six Day War's *Censored Voices*." *Times of Israel*, 19 Nov. 2015, https://www.timesofisrael.com/six-day-war-revelations-of-censored-voices-come-to-ny-la/.

39. Gili Izikovich perceptively captures the book's divisive reception when it first appeared: "Its supporters viewed its antiwar character and universal sensitivities to the horrors of war as decisive proof of moral superiority. Discussion about the burden of fighting, recoiling from violence and the oppression of victory—all were perceived as yet another justification for being victorious. However, most people saw it as something completely different. Among all the victory albums, the adoration of the military, of holy places and of liberated swaths of land, this book was perceived as a defiant downer. Some people considered the censored and lean testimonies to be sanctimonious, or miserable wailing. The book even got the derogatory moniker 'Shooting and Crying,' while some people described it as an apology for winning the war. The subversive, competing narrative of the book was ridiculed, and the winners were also victorious in the underlying battle over national memory and the country's history books." Izikovich, Gili. "The 'Seventh Day': Censored Voices from the 1967 War." *Haaretz*, 6 July 2005, https://www.haaretz.com/the-seventh-day-censored-voices-from-1967-war-1.5369889.

40. In one especially memorable description, one film critic hailed Loushy's oral history as a "debriefing of the soul." Abele, Robert. "*Censored Voices* Revisits 1967's Six Day War." *Los Angeles Times*, 26 Nov. 2015, https://www.latimes.com/entertainment/movies/la-et-mn-censored-voices-review-20151127-story.html.

41. *Censored Voices*. Directed by Mor Loushy. Music Box Films, 2015.

42. Though of course such an assumption would overlook the important work of Breaking the Silence, an organization of veteran soldiers who strive to expose the Israeli public to the daily abuse of Palestinians in the occupied territories through video testimonies, publications, and lectures.

43. Freedland, Jonathan. "The Radical Empathy of Amos Oz." *The New York Review of Books*, 14 Jan. 2019, https://www.nybooks.com/daily/2019/01/14/the-radical-empathy-of-amos-oz/.

44. In *Judas*, Gershom Wald, the oldest character in the novel, asserts that "the name Judas has become . . . a synonym for Jew. Millions of simple Christians think that every single Jew is infected with the virus of treachery" (250).

45. van Rheinberg, Brigitta. "The Order of the Teaspoon: An Interview with Amos Oz." *How to Cure a Fanatic*. Princeton UP, 2006, pp. 73–95.

46. At 3:30 p.m. the kibbutz children went to visit their parents' homes, and of that time Oz told his lifelong confidant Nurith Gertz that "those who didn't have families went to their adoptive families, or they went to the basketball court, or they went to hang out with girls. I went to the library and read the New Testament." Izikovich, Gili. " 'Amos Oz Spent His Whole Life with a Black Hole Inside and Nothing Could Fill It." *Haaretz*, 7 Nov. 2020, https://www.haaretz.com/israel-news/.premium.HIGHLIGHT.MAGAZINE-amos-oz-spent-his-whole-life-with-a-black-hole-inside-1.9294066.

47. It is hard to exaggerate the remarkable degree of Oz's success as a debut author. After experiencing the rejection of just a single short story, he sent "The Way of the Wind" to Aharon Amir, editor of the prestigious literary magazine *Keshet*. Not only was the story immediately accepted but within less than five years it was included on the Ministry of Education's mandatory reading list for the literature matriculation exam. Notwithstanding that early success and his prolific output in the decades following, Oz and his wife Nili faced years of economic struggle after leaving Hulda (following the diagnosis of son Daniel's asthma) for the high desert town of Arad where they raised their three children. Now approaching the age of fifty, to make ends meet Oz was forced to work at several jobs including stints at Ben-Gurion University and Sapir College, and writing a weekly column for the newspaper *Davar* as well as lecture trips abroad.

48. And elsewhere: "You wanted a state. You wanted independence. Flags and uniforms and banknotes and drums and trumpets. You shed rivers of innocent blood. You sacrificed an entire generation. You drove hundreds of thousands of Arabs out of their homes. You sent shiploads of Holocaust survivors straight from the quayside to the battlefield. All so there would be a Jewish state here. And look what you've got" (*Judas* 183).

49. Readers enthralled by this late flowering of Oz's artistry are encouraged to seek out *What Makes an Apple: Six Conversations about Writing, Love, Guilt, and Other Pleasures* (Princeton UP, 2022), posthumously published dialogues with Shira Haddad, Oz's editor on *Judas*.

50. Toward the end of his life, prompted by his editor Shira Hadad to revisit this storied act of spontaneous self-invention, Oz offered these rueful reflections: "I don't remember exactly, but maybe when I felt I was going to leave home to go to a kibbutz, courage and strength were what I lacked the most. It was like jumping off a diving board at night without knowing whether there's water in the pool. So that name, Oz, was a bit of wishful thinking. Besides, maybe—and I'm not quite sure about what I'm about to tell you, because really, it's been more than sixty years—maybe because there was a slight similarity between the middle letters of Klausner and the word oz. Maybe, but I'm not sure. It's the name a fourteen-year-old boy chose, like whistling in the dark. Today, I would never choose such a resounding name for myself." See "A Room of One's Own: Amos

Oz in Conversation with Shira Hadad." *Granta*, vol. 145, 15 Nov. 2018, https://granta.com/a-room-of-ones-own/.

51. In yet another novel (less discussed today), the richly philosophic and experimental *Touch the Water, Touch the Wind* [Laga'at Bamayim Laga'at Baruach, 1973], in which Oz, drawing on principles of metaphysics, music and mathematics, departed altogether from the norms of realism major characters survive their victimization in the Holocaust and join a kibbutz. Though the novel bewildered many readers and critics at the time, Joseph Cohen favorably compares its sophisticated fusion of relativity and Jewish mysticism to works by Borges, Durrell, Pynchon, and Ozick (*Voices of Israel* 160). Today, this neglected novel's triumphant affirmation of Jewish philosophy and sly repudiation of the philosopher and Nazi-collaborator Martin Heidegger is worth revisiting, especially in the wake of the publication of the latter's antisemitic *The Black Notebooks*.

52. Mitgang, Herbert. "Amos Oz: A Kibbutznik in the Colorado Rockies." *The New York Times*, 6 July 1985, section 1, p. 9. The following year he exulted to Joseph Cohen about his excitement in discovering in Anderson his own potential for revealing "the whole world in a microcosm, in a drop of water, a whole world of ordinary people lying there on the surface with their lives described colloquially" (*Voices of Israel* 183). That epiphany led directly to the use of interrelated stories with recurring characters in *Where the Jackals Howl*.

53. In the interviews that followed the publication of these late stories, he would often tell journalists variations of the following: "Although I left the kibbutz 27 years ago, I still go back there in my dreams at least once a week. This signaled to me that it's time to go back and have a distant look at the kibbutz over the 1950s as I found it when I came there first at the age of 15 to start my life anew. And in *Between Friends* I tried to watch the kibbutz not with nostalgia, not with anger, but with precision and compassion." Estrin, Daniel. "Amos Oz Is Still Writing After All These Years." *The World*, 14 Oct. 2013, https://www.pri.org/stories/2013-10-14/amos-oz-still-writing-after-all-these-years-and-waiting-his-nobel-prize.

54. Grumberg, Karen. "The Greatness of Smallness: Amos Oz, Sherwood Anderson, and the American Presence in Hebrew Literature." *Journal of Israeli History*, vol. 39, 2020, https://www.tandfonline.com/doi/full/10.1080/13531042.2020.1834913. Quotation appears on p. 19.

55. Beginning in the mid-1980s (and with greater frequency over the ensuing years), Oz reaffirmed that little had changed in his sympathetic outlook on the kibbutz: "I have the feeling and belief that . . . the kibbutz is the 'least bad' place to live, the 'least bad' of all the places I know." Oz, Amos. "The Quality of Equality." Center for Kibbutz Studies, Overseas Department of the United Kibbutz Movement. Among other venues, this widely circulated article was reprinted in the *Greater Phoenix Jewish Times*, 17 Sept. 1986, p. 15. And in the month before his death, Oz told Shira Hadad that the enduring qualities he most prized about his often very disappointing society had their origins in the kibbutz experiment:

"Several kibbutz genes have remained in the DNA of Israeliness, genes I consider good. Do you remember Stanley Fischer, who was once the governor of the Bank of Israel? On one occasion he told a story about flying to Cyprus with his wife Rhoda. At two thirty in the morning, a very tired Stanley and Rhoda Fischer were standing at the conveyor belt in Limassol waiting for their luggage. An Israeli passenger came over to them and asked politely, 'Excuse me, sir, are you the governor of the Bank of Israel?' He said yes. 'Where's the best place to change money? Here in the airport or in the bank tomorrow?' Shira, I love that so much. They ask me what I love about Israel. That. He didn't insult Stanley Fischer, he wasn't rude, but he knew that Stanley Fischer worked for him. That would never have happened in, let's say, France, or to the president of the bank of Germany. That's the gene the kibbutzim left for Israeli society, and I love it. The anarchism, the directness, the chutzpah, the argumentativeness, the absence of hierarchy. 'No one's going to tell me what to do.' That's the gift from the kibbutz of that period, the time of the first waves of immigration to Israel. I know, of course, that this is a time for slaughtering sacred cows. When I wrote *Where the Jackals Howl* and came out against Ben-Gurion in the Lavon Affair, I was filled with the joy that comes with slaughtering sacred cows: the kibbutz ethos, the myth of the 'Father of the Nation' and all that. Today, when I see a swarm of slaughterers eagerly attacking one old sacred cow, the kibbutz, I suddenly feel that I've moved slightly to the side of the cow. Not because I worship it; I remember very well how it kicked and how it stank. But at least it gave milk that wasn't half bad." "A Room of One's Own." https://granta.com/a-room-of-ones-own/.

56. Describing their last meeting, together with their wives, Michal and Nili, a month before his death, Grossman recalls that "Amos was at his peak—entertaining, witty, ironic, brilliant. He mostly did not speak about his illness, which at that point was already critical. He just said: 'The architect of the body was a genius, but the contractor skimped on the materials.' Michal and I laughed, but Amos apparently saw my expression and said: 'Don't pity me. I have had a very good life. Much better than I ever could have imagined. I have loving children, I have Nili, my beloved wife. My books are read around the world. I received so much more than one can ask from life.'" Grossman, David. "Amos Oz Expressed the Painful Turbulence of Israeli Life." Translated by Danielle Harris. *The Guardian*, 5 Jan. 2020, https://www.theguardian.com/commentisfree/2020/jan/05/amos-oz-painful-turbulence-israeli-life-books. However, it should be noted, as is discussed later in this introductory essay, that while Oz enjoyed close relations with both his older daughter, Fania, and his son Daniel, his daughter, Galia, was estranged from him and her 2021 autobiography *Something Disguised as Love* (Tel Aviv: Kinneret Zmora) describes a physically and emotionally abusive parent, claims that both the other siblings and Nili have vehemently denied or insisted were exaggerated.

57. In an origin story too good to exclude here, Oz recounts living at Hulda at the time, back in the days he was allotted only one day a week for writing,

and as he tells it, *My Michael* was written entirely at night in the bathroom, "the size of a toilet seat. . . . I would write in the bathroom and smoke until midnight or . . . for as long as I could hold out. I would sit on the toilet seat cover, a Van Gogh album we'd received as a wedding gift on my lap, a pad of paper on the album, a ballpoint pen in one hand, a lit cigarette in the other. That's how I wrote *My Michael.*" Little wonder the novel so successfully conveyed an atmosphere of stifled claustrophobia! In Hadad, Shira. "A Room of One's Own: Amos Oz in Conversation with Shira Hadad." Translated by Sondra Silverston. *Granta*, vol. 145, 15 Nov. 2018, https://granta.com/a-room-of-ones-own/.

58. In later years, Oz would occasionally remark on the somewhat unusual choice (at the time) for such a young male writer to attempt to fully immerse himself in a woman's consciousness. In his 1979 essay "Like A Gangster on the Night of the Long Knives, But Somewhat in a Dream," he describes Hannah's almost mystical persistence in spite of his dismissive reluctance: "she nagged me for a long time, she wouldn't give up, she said, look I'm here, I shan't leave you alone, either you write what I tell you or you won't have any peace. I argued, I apologized. I said, look, I can't do it, go to someone else, go to some woman writer, I'm not a woman. I can't write you in the first person, let me be. No. She didn't give up. And then, when I did write, so as to get rid of her and get back somehow to my own life, still every day and every night, she was arguing about each line." See *Be'or hatkhelet ha'aza*. Sifriat Poalim, 1979, p. 213. *Under this Blazing Light*. Translated by Nicholas de Lange. Cambridge UP, 1979, pp. 185–86. It seems worth recounting that at this time in his life, Oz had been granted just a single day out of the week by the kibbutz general meeting to work on his fiction. Hannah had such a hold on his imagination that he spent many sleepless nights in trying circumstances to tell her story: "I used to go into the bathroom to write *My Michael*. At the time, we lived in a one-and-a-half-room apartment and the bathroom was the size of an airplane toilet. And I didn't sleep half the night. I would write in the bathroom and smoke until midnight, or one o'clock, for as long as I could hold out. I would sit on the toilet seat cover, a Van Gogh album we'd received as a wedding gift on my lap, a pad of letter paper on the album, a ballpoint pen in one hand, a lit cigarette in the other. That's how I wrote *My Michael*. . . . Often, when people tell me they're traveling somewhere to find inspiration for a book, a place of mountains or lakes or forests or the ocean shore, I recall that tiny bathroom of ours in Hulda." See "A Room of One's Own." https://granta.com/a-room-of-ones-own/.

59. Aschkenasy, Nehama. "Women and the Double in Modern Hebrew Literature: Berdichewsky/Agnon, Oz/Yehoshua." p. 121.

60. Though not always acknowledged as a "feminist" narrative, I see *My Michael*'s pervasive influence in the works of Israeli women writers in later generations including Orly Castel-Bloom's (b. 1960) dystopian *Dolly City* where the dangerous obsessions of the psychically damaged titular character led to grotesque

consequences for her son and many others. It is worth noting that the figure of Hannah aroused great ire among some Hebrew critics when the novel first appeared (and some have compared the novel's early notoriety to the frenzied reception of Philip Roth's *Portnoy's Complaint* in the same decade). Significantly, Omri Asscher notes "Baruch Kurzweil's memorable statement . . . that the character of Hannah Gonen was more dangerous to Israel than all of the Arab armies put together—attests to the emotions that often erupted out of the tension between the defiant 'autonomy' of literary writing and the collective significance attributed to it in Israeli discourse." In *Reading Israel, Reading America: The Politics of Translation Between Jews.* p. 11.

61. Other prominent figures of the literary era of disillusionment that took root after the establishment of the state include Amos Kenan, A. B. Yehoshua, Yoram Kaniuk, and Ruth Almog.

62. Later Oz-centered Hebrew scholarship worthy of note include Yigal Schwartz's *Zemer nuge shel Amos Oz: Pulhan ha-sofer ve-dat ha-mdina* (*A Melancholy Song by Amos Oz: Cult of the Author and the State Religion*). Kinneret Zmora-Bitan Dvir, 2011. In addition, Schwartz's *The Zionist Paradox: Hebrew Literature and Israeli Identity* (Translated by Michael Sapir, Brandeis UP, 2014), which contains roughly 100 pages devoted to Oz, is available in English. Nitza Ben-Dov's (a contributor to this volume) Hebrew study of Agnon's influence on Oz and A. B. Yehoshua is also recommended; *Ve-Hi Tehilatekha* (*And It Is Your Praise*): *Studies in the Writings of S. Y. Agnon, A. B. Yehoshua and Amos Oz* (Schocken, 2006 [Hebrew]).

63. Arie Dubnov edited the special issue titled "Amos Oz's Two Pens: Between Literature and Politics." *Journal of Israeli History*, vol. 38, no. 2, 2020.

64. For a fuller exploration of that dialogue, see Gertz's new book in Hebrew, *What Was Lost in Time: Biography of a Friendship* (Ma She-Avad Ba-Zman). Kinneret Zmora-Bitan Dvir, 2020.

65. Rosovsky, Nitza. "The Novelists: Amos Oz." *The New Republic*, vol. 179, no. 16, 14 Oct. 1978, pp. 25–27. Quotation appears on p. 26. Oz boasted to Rosovsky that European critics had written to express their astonishment at the verisimilitude of his landscape imagery, whether northern Italy or the Rhône regions, in spite of his never having visited.

66. While at the time of this writing, Galia Oz's Hebrew autobiography, published early in 2021, has not been translated to English, *Haaretz* printed the first chapter in its entirety. See Oz, Galia. "My Father, Amos Oz, Sadistically Abused Me. The Punishment Was Endless." *Haaretz*, 25 Feb. 2021, https://www. haaretz.com/israel-news/.premium.HIGHLIGHT.MAGAZINE-my-father-amos-oz-sadistically-abused-me-the-punishment-was-endless-chapter-1-1.9568562.

67. See Izkiovich, Gili. "Amos Oz's Daughter Calls Not to Boycott His Work, After Accusing Him of Abuse." *Haaretz*, 24 Feb. 2021, https://www.haaretz.com/israel-news/. premium-amos-oz-s-daughter-calls-not-to-boycott-her-father-s-work-1.9565073.

68. Asked by a journalist how his reading of Galia's memoir affected him, Qedar admitted that "I have an image from 'A Clockwork Orange.' Like Malcolm McDowell with his eyelids held open by force, I was looking at something I didn't want to see. I think a lot of other people didn't want to see it, it had a destructive power and was unpleasant, but I couldn't turn away." So it has been for many of us. As Izikovich remarks, the portrait that emerges in the film is of "a man full of pain and contradictions, one carrying past traumas beneath a sophisticated layer of concealment, remorse and endless iterations, still questioning and confused, asking for forgiveness." See Izikovich, Gili. "'Amos Oz's Image Is Struggling to Recover. It's Been Defiled.'" *Haaretz*, 29 Sept. 2021, https://www.haaretz.com/israel-news/.premium.HIGHLIGHT.MAGAZINE-amos-oz-s-image-is-struggling-to-recover-it-s-been-defiled-1.10252225.

69. Here I would like to express my deepest appreciation to the anonymous readers for SUNY UP whose profoundly constructive criticism led to great improvements in many of the chapters and certainly my own contributions. In addition to the worthy essays gathered in this volume, Hebrew readers are strongly urged to consult the entry on Oz and related critical online resources in the Lexicon of Modern Hebrew Literature: https://library.osu.edu/projects/hebrew-lexicon/00397.php.

PART 1

IN A RETROSPECTIVE MODE

Chapter 1

Reflections on *In the Land of Israel*

David Grossman

Reading this book, which is no less stirring now than when it came out, is like reading the medical charts of a patient with innumerable complications. Almost all of Israel's immunity failures, as a state and as a society, are here, as are the powerful forces of life and renewal that might help it heal. Ultimately, however, this "illness chart" has been written over the course of many years, and anyone who reads it already knows that the patient has yet to recover—in fact, his condition has deteriorated, and at times he seems to be turning his disease into a peculiar sort of ideology: he flaunts it, clings to it at any cost, even willing to pay with his life.

I do not know if this is how Amos Oz sees it, but in the echo chamber of the decades since his journey, the words on these pages now strike me as a lamentation. A lamentation for the country and the grand dreams pinned on it, for what the national anthem terms "all the hopes," which will probably not come true. Perhaps it is precisely because the hopes and dreams were so great, so messianic and utopian, that they ultimately derailed even the possibility of fulfilling a modest, normal, safe "day of small things." Almost thirty years after Oz's travels, Israel has not turned into "Ashdod," as he hoped at the end of his journey. It is not a country that exists for its people, the country "of human proportions" that he wished for, but rather a land that continues to "eateth its inhabitants"—and at times devour them.

∿

I remember reading the book for the first time when it came out, in 1983. After almost every chapter, I had to put the book down and take a deep breath. Over and over again, I thought to myself: That's it, this isn't going to work. There's no chance of us ever living a normal life here. With these kinds of fears and this kind of hatred, we shall never be free.

I wish I could say that now, twenty-six years later, I feel differently. But it's quite the opposite. Today, we readers know that some of the most outrageous, radical aspirations expressed on the pages of this book have since become the norm. A worldview that espouses power, paranoia, and racism, as formulated by Z., in his chilling monologue, now characterizes the attitude and actions of large sectors of Israel's public and political spheres.[1] The settlements are flourishing exponentially compared to the early eighties, and, as their founders hoped, they have become a hindrance to ending the occupation and achieving a stable peace treaty. Moreover, two bloody intifadas have occurred since then. The fragile peace process that began between Israel and the Palestinians has turned into a farce and a tragedy. Prime Minister Rabin was murdered by a right-wing Jewish assassin. There has been a Second Lebanon War, and a war in Gaza. Social disparity in Israel grows deeper and deeper. Every page in this book is horribly relevant, creating the impression that the State of Israel, rather than moving forward, is trapped in an infinite loop, doomed to repeat the same mistakes and experience the same catastrophes.

In his monologue, Z. quotes Moses: "And among these nations shalt thou have no repose, and there shall be no rest for the sole of thy foot; but the Lord shall give thee there a trembling heart, and failing of eyes, and languishing of soul. And thy life shall hang in doubt before thee; and thou shalt fear night and day, and shalt have no assurance of thy life." Z. goes on to explain, with his characteristically cheerful serenity: "That is an accurate description of the *zhid*, and that is what Zionism set out to demolish. But you can't demolish it until the *zhids* understand where they're living and what awaits them if they aren't home before dark." Z. mocks the "*zhids*," by which he means the diasporic Jews—both those who live in the Diaspora and those in Israel—but reading the book as a whole offers a different explanation for why there really is "no rest for the sole of our foot" even here, in Israel, even after sixty-one years of independent sovereignty, even with a massive army that was supposed to provide us with security. From these pages it transpires that our enemies are not the sole reason for our inability to attain "rest." Israel's adversaries certainly were, and still are, active partners in creating the disheartening conditions that serve to deepen the conflict, but surely they do not bear the sole responsibility. Reading the conversations in this book, we understand something profound and frightening about our own inability, the inability of Israel's Jewish citizens, to be a "normal" state or, simply, a nation like all nations. A nation that lives a full and normal life, to the greatest extent possible, within its reality and given its history. A nation that does not insist—as do those who have been outcast and hurt, an insistence that is both heartrending and disastrous—on remaining stuck in the myth, in the larger-than-life, grandiose story that it has been telling itself for generations.

Through the fascinating, expressive, sharp-minded, passionate people Oz met in his non-accidental wanderings in the fall of 1982, we touch upon a slippery secret that sits at the foundations of Israeli existence. It is hard to define in words, but it is a sort of constant tremble in our souls and minds. The tremble of age-old memories and unbearable traumas, which have still not been truly digested and comprehended. A tremble of deep, existential insecurity, frequently accompanied by excessive self-regard and rash confidence. A tremble of inconsolable affront built up over millennia, and the permanent, almost violent defiance resulting from that affront. Fervent outbursts—of intellect, emotion, creativity—and winds of unenlightened zealotry and absolute idealism. And all these are bolstered by a spiteful, megalomaniacal faith, convinced of its own ability to subjugate reality and force it to change. How exciting to find all this in a book. How difficult to live with.

There is no doubt that different writers who made the same journey would have discovered and revealed different facets of Israel and Israelis. Each writer, each person, would have underscored those aspects of reality for which they set out to search and were therefore destined to find. In this respect, it is all the more fascinating to read Amos Oz's report today, after having read his great memoir, *A Tale of Love and Darkness*. The country we see in *In the Land of Israel* is, to a great extent, a reflection of the author's familial history, its diverse political and ideological factions, its desires and contradictions, its intense absorption of the past, and its embodiment of story and myth.

It is these forces that make this book and its characters—as well as its writer, as he is written along with them—so interesting and so relevant. Only complete fanatics, after all, on both sides of the political map, hold the absolute truth in their pockets and are able to contemptuously dismiss any parts of reality that do not accord with their worldview. Amos Oz, in his biography and perhaps in his soul, contains the extremes, the contradictions, the oxymorons, and the entire continuum between them. To me, that is his forte as a documentarian of this multifaceted Israeli reality. Even if at times he seems to have foreseen his conclusions before he began the journey, he reestablishes them only after confronting—not easily, not without inner resistance—arguments that provoke in him fear, shock, shame, and guilt. And they arouse all these responses not only because they are indeed sometimes shocking and disgraceful, but because they exist in him, too. They animate something within him, they seduce him, and he cannot completely deny nor dismiss them.

Even if at the end of each encounter Oz presents a clear moral, political, and human standpoint, we readers have gone through the process with him. We have felt a broad array of feelings and thoughts spread out inside us, including some we find loathsome, some we know are distortions and deformities that have been "in the family" for generations. We have now spent many long moments inside them, seduced by them, burned by them, and we have sensed the doubts of the man who documented them. At times we have distanced ourselves from him, when he seemed like a character from one of his own books: the bleeding heart, the "watchman unto the house of Israel," who frustrates and occasionally infuriates us with his inability—which we sometimes share—to change our belligerent, nightmarish existence through his exceeding goodwill and his eminently reasonable wishes.

Today's readers understand how greatly this book influenced public discourse in Israel. How it brought to the surface the uncontrollable, authentic currents at the depths of Israeli being (*Jewish* Israeli being, that is; regrettably, there is only one brief encounter with an Israeli Palestinian in the book). As readers, we cannot help but feel surprised that Israel is able to withstand these contradictory forces at work in it, and that it manages to survive and to prevent the bands that hold it together from breaking. That is one of the great riddles of Israeli existence, yet perhaps it is this great survival effort that has led to the perpetually tied score in a country trapped in a repetitive, paralyzing loop.

One could argue, of course, that in the years since Oz's travels, a large left-wing bloc has emerged and is slowly, unenthusiastically, coming to terms with the constraints of our reality and the limits of force. It is comprised of people who seek a peaceful, comfortable, "Ashdod-like" life, one that is not constantly burning ideological flames that occasionally erupt into "strange fire." The problem is that these people's desire for quiet normalcy is not merely a wish, but also their mode of action. And so, despite its size, the bloc remains ineffectual against the unbridled determination of its opposing forces, those which enslave its future and may decide its fate.

༄

When I read the book for the first time, I was twenty-nine, the father of a child. I had recently returned from reserve duty in Lebanon and my first novel, *The Smile of the Lamb*, which dealt with Israelis and Palestinians in a state of occupation, had already been published. Four years later, in March 1987, I took my own journey and subsequently wrote *The Yellow Wind* (which, at the time, I privately referred to as "In the Land of Ishmael"). For roughly two months, I traveled around the occupied territories and talked with Palestinians and settlers. I went to Ofra, among other places, where I found the people who had talked to Oz. Partly because of that encounter, they were suspicious of me, and their arguments were directed at him—and at what he had seen in them—no less than at me. I do not think I fully understood how much I had been influenced by *In the Land of Israel* when I wrote my book. These words are, in part, my way of expressing gratitude to Amos for his work, and for many hours of closeness as a writer, a teacher, and a friend.[2]

Editor's Note: David Grossman's reflections were previously published only in Hebrew, as the Afterword to *In the Land of Israel*. Less than two weeks after Oz's death, David Grossman wrote these words about both their friendship and Oz's stature in Israeli society: "I didn't gain his trust easily. In our first meetings he would sit in an armchair across from me, but his body and face were turned away. In those meetings he would listen very little and speak a lot. He basically lectured. But with each subsequent meeting he turned himself in his chair a few centimeters in my direction. With each meeting he lectured less and instead spoke—and listened—more and more. And when he finally sat with his face fully towards me, I knew he had begun to trust me. He had a greatness about him, a nobility. Even towards those who attacked him. It was a nobility that was a bit anachronistic, as if from the 19th century. It wasn't easy for him, being Amos Oz. It wasn't easy for him to be the person who so many people project so much on to: their deepest desires, their hopes and disappointments, everything that is tangled and unresolved within them."[3]

Notes

1. Editor's Note: "Z" alludes to the spokesman from the settlement of Ofra whose monologue is essentially all of Chapter 5 ("The Tender Among You, and Very Delicate") in Oz's *In the Land of Israel*.

2. Translated by Jessica Cohen.

3. See *In the Land of Israel* ([*Po Ve-Sham Be-Eretz-Israel*: Bi-Stav] revised edition, Keter Publishing, 2009). David Grossman's later comments appeared in "Amos Oz Expressed the Painful Turbulence of Israeli Life." Translated by Danielle Harris. *The Guardian*, 5 Jan. 2020, https://www.theguardian.com/commentisfree/2020/jan/05/amos-oz-painful-turbulence-israeli-life-books.

Chapter 2

Hannah Gonen . . . and Me

A Personal Essay

Sidra DeKoven Ezrahi

Our apartment was rather gloomy, and the plumbing was antiquated, but the rooms were very tall, which I liked. We discussed plans for painting the walls in bright colors and growing plants in pots. We did not know then that in Jerusalem potted plants never flourish, perhaps because of the large amounts of rust and chemical purifiers in the tap water.

—Amos Oz, *My Michael*

A young married woman sits in her small apartment in West Jerusalem. She stirs her tea in solitary despair, watching the potted plants struggling for life, listening to the patter of the falling rain or, on rainless days, to the hammer of the stonemasons building a city over the Syrian-African rift of geological, religious, and political volatility.

That woman, of course, is Hannah Gonen, the protagonist of Amos Oz's *My Michael*. But it is also a portrait of myself, living in West Jerusalem when, like Hannah, and the Jewish part of the city, I was young and slim. Like Hannah, moreover, I was a student of literature, recently married, lonely, and frightened. She lived in Mekor Baruch with her new husband in the 1950s; I lived in the newer section, Rehavia, with mine in the early 1960s. Oh, and one more difference: as a character in fiction, she will always be trapped between the covers of a novel, in that tiny apartment with its quiet desperation; I moved on. But more than any fictional character, I identified with her when I first read the novel—and I still do, as I contemplate my younger self.

Loneliness in the city is not a new subject for fiction. It almost defines the urban novel, from Dickens's *David Copperfield*, to Dreiser's *An American Tragedy*, to Joyce's *Ulysses*, to Henry Roth's *Call it Sleep*, to Paul Auster's *New York Trilogy*. And the loneliness of a woman in the city also has its pride of place on the bookshelf dedicated to the sorrows of Anna Karenina, Sister Carrie, Clarissa Dalloway, Plath's Esther.

And yet: anyone who has spent more than a few hours in Jerusalem knows that it never really was a "city," at least not in modern times. Biblical Jerusalem is indeed delineated as urban space: "Jeremiah" laments the City that sat alone, like a widow [ישבה בדד העיר רבתי עם היתה כאלמנה איכה Lam. 1:1]. Nearly always figured as a woman, she appears frequently as God's beloved faithful—or faithless—wife, widow (!!), or daughter.[1] But in modern times, Tel Aviv was already an urban space when it was only a few sand dunes and three "white" buildings; whereas Jerusalem, capital of Israel, with all the requisite edifices of a modern metropolis—a government center, a major university, a few museums, municipal taxes, and almost-passable roads—has always felt like a small village, with the attendant claustrophobia (or claustro-philia[2]). As Hannah herself notes: "this isn't a city . . . it's an illusion. We're crowded in on all sides by hills. . . . [It is] a landscape pregnant with suppressed violence. Jerusalem can sometimes be an abstract city: stones, pine trees, and rusting iron."[3]

In an essay written shortly after the novel was published, Robert Alter described not so much the representations of the city as the mythic impulses it fosters: "Jerusalem the city surrounded by ancient mountains and enemy forces, as it is mediated through the consciousness of [the first-person narrator], becomes the flimsy structure of human civilization perched on the lid of a volcano of chthonic powers."[4] Alter's use of geological imagery to describe Oz's Jerusalem is not coincidental to this novel, whose male protagonist is a budding geologist; Hannah actually relishes the implications of a paper her husband Michael is writing on "geomorphology."[5]

The ground is unstable, in Hannah's eyes, because of the unresolved political enmities that mimic the constantly shifting geological formations.

"We can say that the earth is being continuously recreated," is the way Michael describes the instability of the tectonic plates below them. But when he explains to his wife that the sea had once covered the hills that surround Jerusalem, Hannah retorts with her own apocalyptic prophecy: "at the end of time, the sea will cover Jerusalem again."[6]

These terms, reflecting the material and metaphorical status of Jerusalem, would have been especially acute between 1948 and 1967, when the absence of a horizon, of a coastline like the one that hugs Tel Aviv and Haifa, was exacerbated by the inimical presences just beyond the armistice line. Only the old-timers in our midst remember the famous Red Rock, the "sela ha-adom" of Petra, which enticed daring youths to risk their lives to cross over.[7] The Arabs, as we then called the Palestinians, were the Other who beckoned and threatened from beyond: "Villages and suburbs surround Jerusalem in a close circle, like curious bystanders surrounding a wounded woman lying in the road: Nebi Samwil, Shaafat, Sheikh Jarrah, Isawiyeh, Augusta Victoria, Wadi Joz, Silwan, Sur Baher, Beit Safafa. If they clenched their fists the city would be crushed."[8] Those of us with some historical perspective know that it was Jewish Jerusalem that would eventually crush those Palestinian villages. But in the twenty years between the declaration of the State of Israel and the Six Day War, our sense of claustrophobia was acute. And it haunts the fantasy life of Hannah Gonen: Halil and Aziz, the twins with whom she had played as a child in pre-1948 Jerusalem, become phantoms in the sexually infused dreams and daydreams of her unhappy young adulthood. Like the Arab stonemasons with their incessant pounding, irregular metronomes of the daylight hours penetrating through thick walls, Halil and Aziz are nightly apparitions, sneaking across the border into Hannah's semi-consciousness. And, at the end, it is her imagination that sends them to blow up a water tower and ignite the apocalypse.[9]

There are two dates that frame the Hebrew original of this novel: "Jerusalem, January 1962" and "May 1967"—signaling the five years in which *My Michael* was composed. Strikingly, the novel, which narrates events unfolding in the 1950s, was completed just weeks before the outbreak of the Six Day War; indeed, we could go so far as to say that, as Hannah's imagination ignited the war, so her creator foretold it.[10] Even descriptions of the 1956 war in which Michael is called up for service, carry premonitions of the 1967 War. In autumn, 1956, Michael and Hannah's friend, Avraham Kadishman, predicts that "there is going to be a great war, and the Holy Places will once again be ours."[11]

My own story as a young married woman in Jerusalem began several years after Hannah's, in the November of 1963. Living for several weeks above a coffee shop on Azza Street—enough time to develop a lifelong aversion to the smell of Arabic coffee laced with "*hell*" (cardamom), and to experience from afar the shockwaves of J. F. K's assassination—we then moved to a fourth-floor walkup on Metudela Street. In addition to the incessant metronome of the stonemasons, the "light footfall" of the milkman making his morning rounds and the repetitive click of the spoon stirring the glass of afternoon tea complete the soundscape of my own young adulthood.[12]

In those years, you didn't have to be a geologist to know about Jerusalem's many fault lines. One of them was the Valley of the Cross—now a thoroughfare where drivers hardly take any notice of the church they are passing that purports to be built on the site where the tree grew on which Christ would be crucified. But for all of us who lived on Metudela (the misnomer signifying the 12th century explorer, Benjamin OF TUDELA), on the valley's rim, there was magic and menace in that valley. As Hannah reflects, connecting the topography and the scholarly intensity of West Jerusalem in the post-1948 decades: "At a lighted window sits a gray-haired sage at his work, his fingers tapping at the keys of his typewriter. . . . Who could imagine that beneath his western balcony spreads the Valley of the Cross, an ancient grove creeping up the slope, clutching at the outermost houses of Rehavia as if about to enfold and smother them in its luxuriant vegetation? Small fires flicker in the valley, and long-drawn-out, muffled songs rise out of the woods and reach out towards the windowpanes."[13] The gray-haired sage at his work might have been Hannah's professor of literature at Terra Sancta College, the converted convent that housed the Hebrew University in the decade after the founding of the State of Israel. My own studies were conducted in the new buildings on Givat Ram after the University moved there in 1958. She would have scribbled her classroom notes on Hebrew literature in the same standard gray-green notebook that I used ten years later at Hebrew University. Her teacher was a semi-fictionalized version of Professor Yosef Klausner (Oz's great-uncle); mine was the poet Leah Goldberg, founder of the Department of Comparative Literature. Like Hannah, I also wended my way with inverted umbrellas through the brown-gray streets of Jerusalem under the incessant assault of winter rainstorms; like me, she tried to submerge her own memories, insights, and ambitions under the cloak of her husband's grander, more recognized scholarly achievements. "You know, Michael, still, to this day, I sometimes think that I shall marry a young scholar who is destined to become world-famous," Hannah confides to her new beau, channeling her father's admiring attitude, but also that of the entire generation. "I shall creep in on tiptoe to put a cup of tea down on the desk, empty the ashtray, and quietly close the shutters, then leave without his noticing me."[14]

We of course don't know what would have become of Hannah had her story continued, had the aftermath of the Six Day War let air into her own rooms and her own mind in claustrophobic Jerusalem. Would she have met those Arab twins in the sequel, relinquished her delusions of their seditious actions wearing "commando uniforms"[15] and recovered their childhood friendship out of mutual respect? Or would she have adopted her creator's eventual position that a "divorce" was necessary between Israelis and Palestinians in order to ensure a more stable coexistence? The Palestinians, as we finally learned to call them, never became truly visible; even today, as I look out of my study window on the top floor of my home in the Greek Colony at the building that has arisen across the street over the COVID months, the sound of Muslims at prayer and the sight of Arab construction workers wielding cranes with great slabs of concrete are still muted by the cloak of their invisibility.

But of course, trapped between the pages of a novel, Hannah will never be able to escape her miserable claustrophobic existence, any more than Anna Karenina will be able to pull herself away from the railroad tracks.

I, however, have changed and evolved; and yet, since I first encountered this book, soon after it was published, and long after I outgrew those first unhappy years in Jerusalem, I have not been able to dissociate the sounds of Arab stonemasons, the gray-brown of Jerusalem's broken sidewalks wet with rain and overflowing sewers, the scribbles in the gray-green notebooks, from the loneliness of a lost soul. But today I would look Hannah directly in the eyes and assure her that she can break out of her isolation and silence. I would try to convince her that she does not have to remain a creature trapped inside a fervid literary imagination but can, indeed, rewrite her story of boredom, terror, rage, and the simplistic equivalences between internal states and "reality." And as professor of literature, I might acknowledge her talents and perhaps even offer to mentor her—maybe even help her see that not all the works of the Hebrew renaissance are saturated with what her esteemed professor called the "crisis of disappointment and disillusionment" and what she called a "quality of desolation."[16] If we view her not as an extension of that desperation, as the doomed prototype of the "mad woman in the attic," prefiguring the suicidal mother in *A Tale of Love and Darkness*—but as a temporarily lost woman who can still liberate herself from the silences and the dybbuks, who can yet find her poetic muscle and companions for the journey—well, then, we would write the sequel to our own lives if not to Oz's novel.

Notes

1. See for example, Hosea 2, Ezek.16. Elaine Follis argues that biblical Jerusalem, and ancient Athens, more or less concurrently (sixth and fifth centuries, BCE) were not just personified in the conventional way, but were "divinely favored, the centers of their respective civilizations, close to the heart of the God of Heaven. . . . And both were regarded in figurative language as the daughter of that high god." "The Holy City as Daughter." *Directions in Biblical Poetry*. Edited by Follis. JSOT, 1987, p. 182.

2. This is a term attributed to Arthur Koestler. *Promise and Fulfillment: Palestine, 1917–1949. https://archive.org/stream/promiseandfulfil006754mbp/promiseandfulfil006754mbp_djvu.txt.*

3. *My Michael*. Translated by Nicholas de Lange in collaboration with the author. Harcourt, Inc., 1972, p. 37. All English quotes in this essay are from this edition, pp. 22, 14.

4. Alter, Robert. "New Israeli Fiction." *Commentary Magazine*, June 1969, https://www.commentarymagazine.com/articles/robert-alter-2/new-israeli-fiction/. Alter presents a very insightful contemporary review of *My Michael* and other fiction of the period, especially by A. B. Yehoshua, and an overview of the atmospherics and cultural responses of the time.

5. *My Michael*, p. 39.

6. *My Michael,* pp. 119, 152.

7. The plaintive and popular song, "Ha-sela ha-adom," describing the yearning and acts of trespass, was banned from the airwaves in 1958. https://segulamag.com/en/articles/red-rose-petra/. See also: https://www.nytimes.com/1971/01/17/archives/the-ballad-of-red-rock.html.

8. *My Michael*, p. 98.

9. *My Michael,* pp. 93, 253.

10. The novel was first published in Hebrew by Am Oved in 1968.

11. *My Michael*, p. 167.

12. *My Michael,* pp. 5, 7. The sounds of the stonemason and the click of the teaspoon are especially emphasized in the soundtrack of the 1974 film version,

"Michael Sheli." Directed by Dan Wolman. See https://jer-cin.org.il/he/movie/27560 and https://www.youtube.com/watch?v=23KO1_Be8Ck

13. *My Michael*, pp. 95–96.

14. *My Michael,* p. 10.

15. *My Michael,* p. 93.

16. *My Michael,* pp. 201, 259.

Chapter 3

The History of a Long Conversation

Nurith Gertz

Introduction

Forty-five years ago, I met Amos Oz to discuss my master's thesis, "Literature and Ideology in the Works of Amos Oz." Our conversations, which started in Café Peter in Jerusalem, continued until his death; the more recent ones were recorded and transcribed, providing the basis for the book *What Was Lost to Time: Biography of a Friendship*. Out of the recordings I extracted a few questions and answers on recurring themes in our talks, which occasionally led to vociferous arguments. We didn't agree on everything. I have organised that choice here by the chronology of ideas which flowed between the books, changing form from one book to the next. I begin with the collection of stories *Where the Jackals Howl*, and with the socialist dream and the decay of the kibbutz, which Amos described in his books. From our discussions of the dream that failed, I move to the books seeking what could take its place, some whole harmony, a kind of salvation that might be found in endless spaces, in the heavenly Jerusalem, in places that do not exist (*My Michael* and *Unto Death*).

The conversations that follow explore those books' protagonists—who seek but never find, who don't abandon the quest, and who persistently try to reach certain places, even though the road to them is barred and can only be accessed through wild delusions and acts of violent lunacy.

Grouped together towards the end are our talks centering on what can replace those visions of redemption and offer a substitute for the egalitarian, socialist culture of the kibbutz. Throughout our talks, his mother was ever-present. She committed suicide when he was a boy of twelve, and all his protagonists are trying to reach her, initially with anger and violence, and ultimately in order to understand and forgive her. The conversations presented here are verbatim, organized by theme, under relevant headings: transitions between them are marked with three dots (. . .).

Twilight

NURITH: Okay Amos, let's discuss something more fun. I'm reading in parallel *Under this Blazing Light, Where the Jackals Howl*, and some other things. And now I've reached an article where you talk about twilight, about *Under this Blazing Light*. You dedicated that article to me, which is nice.

AMOS: Yes, you deserve it.

NURITH: You say there that we are in a period of twilight, you know that, can you summarize it for me? And then I'll take it onwards?

AMOS: Nope, I don't remember.

NURITH: So, I'll tell you.

AMOS: You're talking to me as if I won the International Bible Contest—someone who knows the entire Bible by heart. It's been years since I read those books.

NURITH: Okay but I don't have those beautiful words, so my summaries sound lame. That's the problem—take it into account. Great Jewish literature flourished in a twilight era—when an entire culture imploded. Now we live in a blazing blue light, in a period of growth and construction, so that sort of literature can't take root here. So, while you were writing it, you didn't notice what you were actually doing, because you did exactly what you argue the great Jewish authors did. In *Where the Jackals Howl*, you portray the kibbutz culture we were raised on—socialism and fraternity of peoples—the magnificent dream. You describe it with love and hate, criticize and undermine it, and for years you've been searching for something to replace it.

AMOS: Yes.

NURITH: It was something metaphysical, then. We no longer dreamed of the kibbutz, but let's say rather different places: galaxies, spaces, the heavenly Jerusalem—everything we move towards but never reach.

AMOS: Yes.

NURITH: But you don't describe that in the article, that means—did you see it? I know when you're inside it, you can't tell it's a process. Retrospectively, though, you can see that in fact the chasm you identify find within Jewish culture as a whole, is the very same chasm that you rent while trying to bridge, it's the socialism of the Kibbutz, the very thing we clung to. What do you say about that?

AMOS: I say you're wrong.

NURITH: I'm wrong.

AMOS: Yes. Because I didn't write those stories as if I was seated in the control room of the kibbutz idea.

NURITH: Obviously not. Why do you think Berdichevsky and Brenner were sitting in the control room?

AMOS: They were. And at twenty I didn't feel I was in the control room. Rather that I was feeling my way along some path, outside the fence.

NURITH: It's unimportant what you felt, not interesting at all, it's what you did.

AMOS: You can judge what I did, not me. How can I judge, Nurith? Really, how can I judge?

NURITH: Read, you can judge, you read well too, you don't just write well. *Where the Jackals Howl* with Sashka and Damkov, what are you describing there? You're capturing that safe culture, people in a room, writing, they have vital things to share, and outside are the jackals, evil, wickedness, and violence, everything which can assail the protected room. So, what is it exactly?

AMOS: There, the dogs were inside, the jackals outside.

NURITH: And the jackals within the dogs too.

AMOS: Nurith, you've just described it from a sweeping sociocultural historical perspective, which I didn't have at the time. Not when I was writing the stories.

NURITH: No, but you didn't really need it.

AMOS: In the articles, yes, definitely, I said that, but didn't connect it. I didn't connect the two.

NURITH: But if you had connected them, it would have been awful; the result would have been an article, not a story.

AMOS: Right. I don't know, I wrote *Where the Jackals Howl* when I'd just turned twenty. I wrote *Under this Blazing Light* and all those generalisa-tions some fifteen years later. I wasn't the same man, it's not that I wrote simultaneously—at night I wrote *Where the Jackals Howl* with Damkov and the jackals, in the daytime I wrote *Under this Blazing Light* about the twilight of culture. It wasn't the case, there were fifteen years between them, and I wasn't the same person.

NURITH: Yes. So, I'll phrase it differently, not while you were writing, let's delete that, but it's actually what you did, and what you did with the kibbutz. It's what Berdyczewski and Brenner—and who else? Even Y. L. Gordon before both of them—did with the great Jewish culture.[1]

AMOS: That's exactly what you'd write because it's the perspective of a cultural researcher who's familiar with the whole map, from Y. L. Gordon to Etgar Keret, someone who knows the entire map, the right place to position me, to pronounce "you're among the first" or "the first who," but without actually completely understanding what you're doing, that's what you did. You broke out of the box, which you built yourself in *Under this Blazing Light*, but you can say that, you don't need my confirmation to say it, Nurith, I can't confirm it.

NURITH: No, I don't want your confirmation, I want to discuss it with you, I don't need confirmation.

AMOS: See, my difficulty in talking about it is that if I say you're right, then you apparently are right, it would be a huge lie because I simply didn't think about it. The status of Brenner, the position of Berdichevsky, and the significance of Bialik—I knew nothing about them.

NURITH: It's not important, though, it's not that important.

AMOS: I don't know if it's important or not, maybe it's crucial. What I swear to you under oath is that while I was sitting and writing about nomads and vipers, or the paratrooper who landed on power cables, I wasn't thinking about Brenner and Berdichevsky, not even about "Whither the Kibbutz?".

NURITH: Well, that's obviously not the case; it's really clear it's not so.

AMOS: That's your work, Nurith, I can't teach you anything about that. Because when I look at it now retrospectively it's difficult, I can't read it the way I read the early stories of Buli (A. B. Yehoshua) or Yitzhak Ben-Ner, or Kenaz, and I can't compare or position them, I can't. I look at those stories and I say: Could you do a thing like that? Why did you have to do it? Or, look how well that description turned out, or I remember how it took shape. But now I can't describe it or position it within a complete picture, I'm incapable of that. Even when you told me "read *Unto Death*" and I read *Unto Death* because you told me to, I read Buli's "Facing the Forests," because you told me to, but I can't read it with the same gaze as yours, Nurith, it's flesh of my flesh, I can't.[2]

NURITH: So, from now on I'll tell you, I won't ask you.

AMOS: Please—that, yes. I'm willing for you to tell me, I'll listen, I'll even nod my head when I think you're talking common sense.

NURITH: Do talk to me, though, a conversation needs two voices.

AMOS: I'll try, it's hard for me to say something significant about *Unto Death*, which I read the day before yesterday, or whenever, I can't say anything meaningful about it. I know it contains some chilling sentences, but I really don't recall them. But as a story—where is that story's place, where to position it on the map—today I can't say. Because over the years, with those old things, a tension built up between yearning on one hand, and disappointment on the other. It shouldn't have been like that, *Unto Death* should have been written in a lower key with fewer exclamation marks, and even fewer poetic bells and whistles. That's how I feel now but I could be wrong. Maybe if I'd try to do *Unto Death* in Yehoshua Kenaz's language, nothing would have come of it.

NURITH: If you had written *Between Friends* in 1963, it wouldn't have worked.

AMOS: Right, it wouldn't have worked, you're right there.

NURITH: That's the answer, in fact.

AMOS: What you're asking of me, now that the statute of limitations has ended and a few decades have elapsed, something objective about the books, something not subjective. I can't, Nurith, even when your children turn fifty, they're still your babies, you can't be objective. I'm incapable of it, I can't place that on some continuum, or I allocate some pattern, I'm not good at that. I'm excellent at doing this with everyone else—with Buli, Kenaz, Amalia Kahana-Carmon, Grossman. Just ask, I'll immediately take a sheet of squared paper and draw you a map for each one, in the right slot, but not me, I can't. I've taught literature all my life, and I draw maps, say that Bialik is like this, and Rachel like that, Lea Goldberg's like that, but I don't know, I have a kind of resistance to being involved in marking my place on the map, I don't know, it's something irrational, but there's something disturbing in it. So, I just listen to you and nod.[3]

NURITH: Fine, so I'll tell you something else. It's all on the maps, it can't be helped.

AMOS: Yes.

NURITH: Because I want to see the picture you prefer not to see.

AMOS: You deserve it, and you need it. And I think that's what you need to do in the book, exactly that—present the map.

NURITH: Good.

[. . .]

AMOS: Nurith, maybe I'm not lenient enough with you here, but it's because you're asking me to confirm things that you don't need my confirmation for.

NURITH: No, it's not a request for confirmation, it's about talking, I sit alone, and ponder things, draw up lists, and I want to talk to someone, so who can I talk to about this?

AMOS: I'm here, I'm here, I'm here. Not going anywhere, and I do want to talk to you, only what I want is to contribute more to our talks, I don't contribute much.

NURITH: Okay, we can talk about other things too. Kisses, and have a good day.

Under this Blazing Light

NURITH: You always give the feeling there's something whole, look I'm showing you, it's there because I write so powerfully about it. Even if I write that it's not there, you see that it is.

AMOS: Yes.

NURITH: When Hannah talks of the infinite spaces, and Shraga talks about the galaxies, and Guillaume de Touron speaks of Jerusalem, we see them, all of them, as nonexistent. With a minus sign, as you like to say, although a non-nullifying minus sign.

[. . .]

Amos: I didn't think I was marking out a road, I thought I wanted to tell a story.

Nurith: Not to mark out a road, that sounds a little clichéd, like Berl Katznelson. But rather to look up, to raise your head, not where you were searching, not there, but somewhere else. There's nothing there but look all the same. From Pascal. There is a search, and that's where you started searching.

Amos: Yes.

Nurith: What's interesting that in the books and in our meetings too, I can state that the captivating thing with the something whole, different, not from here, is located just a few centimeters above us. And we can look up and see it, somehow, the way you propose. Tell me how you see it.

Amos: Yes, it seems that's what it was. One needs great caution when using the word religious because the word's been corrupted.

Nurith: So, one can use religiosity, Aharon Appelfeld used religiosity instead of religious, I don't know what he solved with that.[4]

Amos: But there is, yes. I think that in almost everything I wrote, certainly in my early books, there was some sort of religiosity, not a proposition for religiosity, but a search.

Nurith: Yes.

[. . .]

Amos: Yes, I'm far from those books now, I haven't even read them for years.

Nurith: But you're not far from yourself.

Amos: No, not far from myself, I can tell you something like this: that all the time there was a feeling of telling the readers: we're not alone. That means it's not only us, it's also *tikkun olam*, us and the formulas, us and the slogans, us and social change, us and Zionism—there are more things in heaven and earth.

And in a Conversation We Had towards the End of His Life

I scattered promises freely, but at tough times I wonder whether they were false promises—made by someone walking in the dark and whistling. Impressed by that whistling, others say: great, there's something in that darkness. Someone's whistling, he surely knows why he's whistling, he can see something.

WHY SO VIOLENTLY?

NURITH: I'm constantly saying—I understand the need to merge with the world, to be a part of it, to flow rather than freeze up, to find the real people, the ones who are on fire, yet restrained. But why do so violently? Why with urges? Why must it be so destructive? Once I explained this by the fact that it's our history, while today I believe it's a malignant merging with the mother, just as that merge culminated in death, so must every relationship.

AMOS: There was a sense of siege and claustrophobia, specific to 1950s Jerusalem. We already discussed it once.

NURITH: Yes, and it passed through romanticism, life unfolding at a different intensity, that was life until the year before, in the War of Independence, during and after the war. We were the captives of the bleak reality which remained. Our deep connection with the whole was taken away and shattered in the war, and we're still trying to recreate that war.

AMOS: Something stirring that existed but was taken from us and no longer exists—the morning after.

NURITH: Today though I take a different direction, the forbidden one, so I find it doesn't stem only from that, but also derives from the deep relationship with the mother. The relationship which ended in death. Here they join together. I know, one mustn't connect them, but I'm allowed to.

AMOS: You're allowed everything.

NURITH: I don't write about it either, it's just for myself.

[. . .]

NURITH: The personal story, with the attraction to death and violence in the national narrative, the return to the national trauma of death and violence. Going back, recreating the great moment, but also the loss it entailed.

AMOS: Apparently, I didn't do it deliberately, I didn't intend it. I made some kind of connection between the way in which I sustained my private blow, and the way in which the Zionist dream gave itself a series of blows, or the kibbutz dream, yes that's right, it fits. Why does it fit? Because the same guy absorbed the blow and inflicted it, and he's the connection between them. If in the course of a day a man stumbles and falls on the pavement, and also spills boiling water on himself, then he's connecting the two.

[. . .]

AMOS: Why with violence? Because apart from this, human nature also has a violent element, perhaps not to the same degree in each human being, but there's an element in human nature, which almost longs for a surge of violence.

NURITH: Maybe, but not everyone.

AMOS: Not everyone.

NURITH: It could be the mother who killed herself and it can also refer to childhood, school—a place of violence and blows.

AMOS: True.

NURITH: Both guilt and revenge.

AMOS: True.

And in One of Our Last Conversations

AMOS: Look, I was terribly angry, there was immense anger during those years, yet it's completely vanished, nothing remains of it. For a long time, there's been no trace of it. But in those years, there was huge anger, which started with anger at my mother, then spread into anger with the entire female race—all the girls who were off-limits to me, who were not for me but for someone else. There was anger, it was jealousy mixed with frustration, but frustration about sex, and violence too. Those girls on Kibbutz Hulda, when I arrived there, they were all beautiful. It seemed to me that everything was possible, anything goes, certainly by the criterion of their peers. Today they'd seem puritanical, but then it looked like another planet to me, a planet where everything that happens is possible, the girls walk hand-in-hand with the boys through the fields, and who knew what they did there, what they didn't do, and even with older boys, even with soldiers on leave from the army. It astounded me, alarmed me, and captivated me; you name it.

NURITH: But there were things you told me later, about your need to humiliate, and your fear of it, and that you pull away the moment you feel you are about to hurt someone. It should fall into place but doesn't really.

AMOS: That, I told you that, first of all it's completely gone. For many years I haven't had any urge to humiliate or hurt anyone. It vanished years ago. It disappeared because my life is good, and because life altogether has been good to me. I say that despite everything happening to me now, it has even blessed me, and I'm grateful. When I was very young, I was seething with insults from the kibbutz, and then I had some kind of urge to act on it. But the truth is that I never acted on that urge, not once.

NURITH: It seems to me too that you never acted on it, but I do recall you telling me that nonetheless there was a very real urge, but I've never seen it in you.

AMOS: No, no, I think I never acted on it. I had fantasies, I had urges of that kind, but my foot on the brakes was always very heavy. And for years I haven't had the desire to humiliate anyone.

LOVE COMES AND GOES

NURITH: Don't tell me love is connected to hate, and ultimately, it's hate with an added minus.

AMOS: That's exactly what I'm going to say.

NURITH: If you can, don't say it.

AMOS: I say this: everyone who read the book [*Judas*] and found links between the traitor Abravanel and the traitor Judas Iscariot, are wrong about my opinion. They don't resemble each other, perhaps the rabble of internet commenters who slander them and call them traitors are similar, but they're not the same. Judas Iscariot in this book resembles Shmuel Ash exactly because ultimately they both lose their belief. Who does Abravanel resemble? He resembles Jesus. In what way? In his belief that the principal universal love of the whole of humanity for the whole of humanity, and also in his belief that love is also fraternity—and generosity, gentleness, altruism, the desire to give and bestow, and nonviolence, everything they taught us in the 1960s in fact, make love not war, and the flower children. And before that too, everything we were taught in childhood, that love is a boy and girl holding hands and walking through a field of flowers towards the sunset. Gershom Wald doesn't believe it's true and neither do I, because that's what Gershom Wald says—love isn't a sweet sentiment, not an emotion that's close to generosity, or altruism and pacifism. In love there's a powerful element of desire to control the loved one or the wish to guide the loved one's path. Or both things together, they don't contradict each other. There's also something highly possessive, covetous, and egotistic in love, because when we love someone, we constantly keep them on our screen—where is he now, where's he going now, perhaps he's cold, maybe he hasn't eaten, who's he meeting now? And in fact, when we hate someone it's the same, they're always on our screen—what's she up to now, where's she going, who's she meeting now, perhaps God forbid she's happy now. Gershom Wald quotes Thomas Mann who wrote somewhere, I'm not sure where, that hate is simply love to which a mathematical minus sign has been added. Do you remember that?

NURITH: You more or less told me that, I can't say how many times.

AMOS: Wait, can I go on a little more?

NURITH: Yes, yes, I'm listening.

AMOS: Love doesn't spring from the family of friendship, generosity, forgiveness, concession, and altruism, it's a scion of the family of jealousy.

And who knew that perfectly, better than anyone? It's the woman poet who wrote the Song of Songs, and you know why I say the woman poet.

NURITH: Yes, we spoke about it.

AMOS: She knew it because this is what she wrote: "Love is strong as death; jealousy is cruel as hell (the grave): the coals thereof are coals of fire, which hath a most vehement flame." Very harrowing words, anti-romantic, potentially contradicting everything the sixties taught us, and what Jesus taught us. She analogizes love with death, not fields in the sunset, and jealousy with hell, which is the same, it is hell (שזה אותו דבר, מוות הוא דבר שאול). Parenthetically, jealousy is exactly the site where love and hate meet. So, she knew something that neither Jesus nor Abravanel knew. I add something else to this. All my life I've said that we were created-me, you, and everyone I know—to love five people, sometimes ten, very infrequently we can love fifteen. Loving more than fifteen is no longer love, it's become something else, it's already identity politics. If someone tells you "I love Latin America," that's not love. If someone declares, "I love the Third World," that's something else, not love. Or if someone says, "I really love womankind," you can be sure he doesn't love a single woman. So, love is first of all an intimate emotion, a feeling given to us, if we are lucky, not everyone is granted it, but when it's given, it comes in small, minuscule doses. And it's packed with egotism, full of covetousness, jealousy, and it's inherently control-seeking, with perhaps a dash of masochism too, or both together. That's not what people think. Don't get me wrong, I'm not against love. If there were no loves in my life, I would be long dead. I love my mother, I love my father, I love Nili, I love you, and Fania, Galia, and Daniel, and my grandchildren—I love fifteen people. Fifteen people, I once counted, and I wouldn't be alive without those loves. But I also know that love is something volcanic and joyous that we learned about in the sixties—forget about it, it's childish, part of the world of kindergarten teachers, or Jesus and Abravanel. Forget it. It doesn't exist. Even the most powerful of all loves in the world, a mother's love for a child, a parent's love for a child, is tangled up with immense desire for control, such a strong urge to be in control, so much desire to guide, to know and be involved in everything the child does, as well as egotism: our love for our children also contains egotism.[5]

NURITH: I don't think so, I don't think that's it. I believe love is something different. Love is the place, the situation in which you really care about someone, what happens to him affects you.

AMOS: Yes.

NURITH: And all the rest, as you say—there's jealousy, friendship, hate. Don't you think so?

AMOS: Look someone once told me somewhere, I don't recall who, that I've written too many books, I think it's in *A Tale of Love and Darkness*, I think it's my mother who says that friendship between a man and a woman is something more rare and more precious than love, because love comes and goes. And also because love, and I don't remember exactly how she put it, love has many sharp angles and all sorts of things mixed up in it that are not friendship, and that friendship is something rare. Perhaps it's in *The Same Sea*, I don't recall exactly where.

NURITH: Friendship is compromise, okay, compromise is good. It's compromise between what's perhaps impossible, or at least for a long period isn't possible, and something that doesn't exist—that's compromise.

AMOS: You know that compromise has been my theory of life for countless years.

NURITH: Yes.

AMOS: So many years. I think that even in the turbulent years of the Lavon Affair, something in me sought compromise. And my love for Levi Eshkol was grounded on compromise. In fact throughout my life, I wanted compromise between my parents, for there to be a compromise. That's what I wanted above all.[6]

NURITH: There was some kind of compromise but it wasn't enough for them, at least for her.

AMOS: She didn't make it, no she didn't make it.

LATE LOVE

NURITH: I once told you that you'd be a good friend of Levinas, but it's not only Levinas—today there's something rather depressing in things I read. A kind of argument and attempt to find where multiculturalism and identity politics have taken us. They have brought us to a place where every group defines itself by a single thing—hate for another group. Mizrahim are Mizrahim because they hate Ashkenazim, and vice versa. Then comes Levinas and offers a solution—love at a distance. Today though, people are suggesting new, gloomier solutions. There's Jean-Luc Nancy, for example. I'm reading him at the moment and trying to grasp if he has some sort of revelation, because what are we looking for? A revelation. That is, we know there isn't one, but nevertheless we want to search. And he says we must simultaneously live together and live apart. He calls it Singular Plural—living alone but within society too. Now let's see how it's to take place, I don't know, I don't see how.[7]

AMOS: In fact, it's a glorious message, not depressing at all.

NURITH: And not implementable.

[. . .]

AMOS: I want to tell you another thing, what's the name of the latest prophet, the one you're reading now?

NURITH: Jean-Luc Nancy.

AMOS: So—something from me, I have a message for him. Tell him I said—I think I said it before he did, some 20 years ago—that when John Donne wrote "no man is an island," he wrote sublime words.

NURITH: Yes, the peninsula, you told me.

AMOS: Peninsula—part of us is connected and must be connected, to family, to society, to language, to culture, to status, to the father—everything, to the community we live in, to the extended family—and some of us turn silently to the elements, and that's the way it must be. I always, always feared ideologies that demand you become a molecule of the continent. And equally I feared ideologies claiming we're all solitary islands, each island in a state of war with the rest of the archipelago, even if it's a question of a single island, or part of a group.

NURITH: Yes.

AMOS: Peninsula. You might say that the gospel according to Amos Oz—not the gospel according to Judas—the gospel according to Amos Oz is not only that we are born as peninsulas, that's the way to live. Even in marriage, even in a couple relationship, the best relationship I can envisage consists of two peninsulas. You know what, even in parenting—the best kind is peninsula parenting, not single islands, but not symbioses either.

NURITH: Amos . . .

AMOS: It's the gospel according to Amos Oz in his old age, there'll be no more. Alterman has a poem: an old philosopher went up to his attic, closed the door, and this he said—he speaks beautiful words, I'll read it to you at some point, I don't have it here.[8]

NURITH: "And this he said." It could be wonderful to end it there, perhaps more wonderful than quoting what the philosopher said.

AMOS: It could be great. It's the place where I'm standing now, or more precisely where I'm lying now. I need to turn over every minute from side to side, so the liquid will work its magic, and now I need, excuse me a moment, I've turned over. Nurith, I'm with you. So, tell your prophet, I've forgotten his name again—identity politics—please, peninsulas—please, but not solitary islands each one at war with the rest of the archipelago.

NURITH: Yes, but you know that the past century was an attempt to combat solitary islands. So initially they said okay, nations, then they said races, and then multiculturalism, statuses, ethnicities, groups, and the latest idea is to be inside and outside simultaneously. That's the peninsula, okay.

LOVE BETWEEN FRIENDS

NURITH: The protagonists of your early books are looking for total love—merging, becoming one, some sort of redemption. Now they want to step out of that, to something else.

AMOS: To step out, yes, step out.

NURITH: To step out. Then on one hand for me it's Levinas: let's not go to the great themes, the absolute ones, but to the minor ones. And that minor isn't enough for me and you too, it's what the generation of Rona, and Shlomi, Fania, and Galia, will do, and all those who come after them.[9]

AMOS: Those who come after them.

NURITH: The ones who will come after are not looking but would like to find a different sort of connection, not to take control, not to connect, not to distress—and that's *Between Friends.*

AMOS: Yes, I call it the minor miracle, a mini miracle.

NURITH: Well, that's where I don't agree, but why do you call it a miracle?

AMOS: Why do I call it a miracle? Because it almost counters human nature, these comings together of one individual with another, it's almost miraculous in my eyes. It happens, I know, it happens to people but it's a miracle.

NURITH: But *Between Friends* isn't a miracle, it's finding uncomplicated relationships without miracles, without salvation, some sort of connection that's deserving, nothing more, it's very little. To me it's too little. For you too, Amos.

AMOS: I'm not sure that now it's too little for me, not sure. Once it was, not today.

NURITH: Yes? Truly?

AMOS: Today it's all I need, yes.

NURITH: At night as well? When you dream?

AMOS: I don't need more. Compassion, gentleness, attentiveness, sometimes a signal of solidarity—what does a person need?

NURITH: But look, people who found it, for example the characters in *Judas*, what do they do once they find it? They split up.

AMOS: Yes.

NURITH: And that's what you forget to say in all your conversations about the book. They find each other, they love, they separate. It's a miracle, but what sort of miracle is it when they split up?

AMOS: Look, they separate in order to save that young man, otherwise he would turn to stone, covered with lichen.

NURITH: Yes, there are reasons, but the fact is they go their separate ways.

AMOS: Yes. But it's not just a separation, I remind you that at the end of the book he is actually born. It's a description of birth, the expulsion from the womb is a description of birth. It's also a departure from the winter, from the basement, leaving that claustrophobic house as well as leaving Jerusalem for the desert, the open spaces, and it's also birth. In fact the old man, Wald, and Atalia give birth to him into the outside world.

NURITH: Yes, right, I do see that. Yet at the same time, the simple decisive fact is that they discovered the possibility of loving each other and compassion, and then they separate.

AMOS: Yes, but they gave him this opportunity, put it in his hands, so he doesn't leave them empty-handed, it's not just the stick. He does take the stick, but also takes the option to love, which he didn't know before.

NURITH: Which isn't in that book, and not in the other later books. Even in that story, what's it called?

AMOS: In "The King of Norway" (*Between Friends*).

NURITH: Yes.

AMOS: In the first story in the book, yes.

NURITH: And there too he can love her, and they build a relationship when she's absent, when she's far away, those are the facts, you can't deny them.

AMOS: No, I'm not denying it, I'm just saying that an option presents itself. I wouldn't say there's a happy end. I can't write a story they lived happily ever after and had six delightful children. I can't write something like that, it's not for me. But at least an option emerges.

NURITH: Yes.

AMOS: A light flickers on in the darkness. It's not enough, I would gladly bring salvation to the world, for everybody to be happy, no one suffers or is alone, no one is abandoned or hurt, everyone lives joyfully but I can't do it, Nurith.

NURITH: I know, yes.

AMOS: No writer can do that.

NURITH: Of course, but Hannah didn't give up, Guillaume de Touron didn't surrender, and the people here do give up—that's the difference. It was clearly necessary, but I regret it a little.

AMOS: I regret it too, but on the other hand if someone suggested I could be seventeen again I'd say, "Thank you, no."

NURITH: I'd like to. Or maybe not.

AMOS: I wouldn't enjoy it.

[. . .]

NURITH: It's interesting, that revolution you launched then, and Buli and others as well.

AMOS: Yes.

NURITH: You can see it in *Between Friends*. That is, let's climb down from the heavens, let's stop seeking it there, let's look for it in the distances dividing us, no more.

AMOS: Yes, but it started well before that, not even in *A Tale of Love and Darkness*, it was already there in *To Know a Woman*. *Black Box* not yet, but in *To Know a Woman*—everything was minimized into a closed intimate setting, everything happened within the home, almost everything.

NURITH: *To Know a Woman*—there are things I've forgotten . . .

AMOS: There's *To Know a Woman*, *Fima*, and *Don't Call it Night*—they all have intimate chamber-music settings, exploring what you can and can't find in parenting and relationships.

NURITH: *Fima*, less so I think, but *To Know a Woman* yes. I'm reading it at the moment.

AMOS: *Fima* is a more historicist, political book, but it's unusual—the major turn was in *The Same Sea*, where there's no Jerusalem, no Jewish history, no Holocaust, no Mossad, no *hityashvut ovedet*, no left and right.

NURITH: Still, it's not a question of the *hityashvut ovedet*,[10] or left and right, which is also in *Between Friends*, in some ways, it's a question of something else, between people, that's new.

AMOS: It started in *The Same Sea*. Perhaps even before, where there's something else between people, and it's as if I suggest—instead of changing the whole world, changing the home. First of all, changing society, changing the couple relationship.

NURITH: For me it's not changing each other, rather to stop looking up to the heavens. Making the transition to here, on the beach, with a tiny spade, collecting water drop by drop to extinguish the flames.

AMOS: *Between Friends*, yes *Between Friends* is my position still now.

NURITH: Yes, but look, after *Between Friends* something else will appear, perhaps not you, but someone else.

AMOS: Someone will undoubtedly emerge.

NURITH: The ones who say, "it's not enough . . . we want more."

AMOS: Of course, the ones who say, "what's this? It's nothing, just crumbs, what's he selling us—broken shards?" Of course, it will emerge because it's a dialectic, when there's no redemption, people say "bring us redemption," when redemption emerges people say "enough with that redemption."

NURITH: Amos, tell me how are you?

AMOS: Apart from fatigue I'm perfectly fine, I don't have any pain.

NURITH: All those other symptoms now.

AMOS: No, no pain, no wounds or nausea, nothing. Only extremely tired and it's hard to concentrate.

NURITH: And your fever is gone?

AMOS: Yes, completely. I had a fever on Friday, and I think it's gone, yes completely.

NURITH: And what do you do the whole day? Are you with the kids?

AMOS: I sit in the armchair, read a little, chat with Nili, talk a little on the phone with people, and take naps, I don't do much, but I go out in the morning for a walk and take some steps on the staircase during the day, walk a little. That's all I do, not much. Look, Daniel is here and Neta's here, Nir and Nadav were here yesterday, Fania and Eli were here today and yesterday. What do I need to do?

NURITH: I'll tell you what, I've got an idea, Amos.

AMOS: Yes, let's dream.

NURITH: Okay, that's good too.

Epilogue

The first collection of "kibbutz stories" that Amos Oz wrote, *Where the Jackals Howl*, described the stifling atmosphere, resentment, and narrow-mindedness that dominate the very setting where the socialist dream of total equality where "each give according to their ability, and receive according to their needs" came true. People there wove dreams about

living life intensely and to the full, dreams that would end in decline
and disintegration. The protagonists of *Where the Jackals Howl* failed to
conform with the socialist dream, and their other dreams encountered violence and horror, jackals, Arabs, a burning and consuming light. In a later
book by Oz, *Between Friends*, sparks of those dreams still flicker—leaving
the kibbutz, traveling to far-away countries—while the world outside, the
spaces, the jackals, and the Arabs are still threatening, and the world inside
is still controlled by violence, wickedness, small-mindedness, and gossip.
These however are not the principal themes of *Between Friends;* rather
Oz returned to the kibbutz of the past, in search of the old dreams out of
which he now aspires to create a new prophecy. A modest prophecy with
neither "light unto the Gentiles" nor "light unto the Jewish people." He
has no aspirations to bring people together under some sort of religious,
national, or ethnic banner, nor to change the world, and instead seeks
compassion, concern, and responsibility between individuals. There, where
the old hopes collapsed, the book sets out to find small promises, human
connections—no more. In our last conversations, that was what we spoke
about. We held those last conversations when he was already sick, but it
was still clear that the treatment would help, his sickness would halt, and
in the years ahead of him there would be more books, he would continue
his quest for other dreams, new prophecies. But he wasn't granted those
years, and the sequence of our conversations ended with that message of
compassion and responsibility, no more.[11]

Notes

1. **Micha Josef Berdyczewski** (1865–1921) was a Ukrainian-born Hebrew
writer born to a family of Hasidic rabbis who, though a collector of Jewish legends
and folklore, was influenced by Hegel and Nietzsche and passionately urged Jews
to abandon the religious dogmas of the past. **Yosef Haim Brenner** (1881–1921)
was a Russian-born writer widely considered a major pioneer of modern Hebrew
literature, who immigrated to Palestine, eventually teaching literature at the Gym-
nasia Herzliya in Tel Aviv until murdered during the 1921 Jaffa riots. **Judah Leib
(Y. L.) Gordon** (1830–1892) was born in Lithuania, studied European culture and
languages (Russian, German, Polish, French, and English), and eventually taught
and wrote poetry, satirical stories, fables, and polemics essays calling for the
revival of the Hebrew language, denouncing both antisemitism and the intractable
religious dogmatism of Jewish leaders as well as fiercely advocating for the rights
of Jewish women, the poor, and the oppressed.

2. **A. B. Yehoshua** ("Buli"), born in 1936 to a fifth-generation Jerusalem family, has written numerous Israel and international award-winning novels, short stories, plays, and essays and, alongside Amos Oz and David Grossman, is one of Israel's most widely translated and internationally known authors. **Yitzhak Ben-Ner** (b. 1937), writer, screenwriter, playwright, and journalist who has been awarded the prestigious Agnon-Jerusalem Prize (1981), the Bernstein Prize (1981), the Ramat Gan Prize for Literature (1983), the Prime Minister's Prize (2006), and the ACUM Prize for Lifetime Achievement (2008). **Yehoshua Kenaz** (1937–2020) was long considered one of Israel's most important writers, best known for his 1986 novel *Infiltration* (nominated one of the ten most important books since the creation of the State of Israel), and was a strong advocate of the two-state solution to the Israeli–Palestinian conflict.

3. **Amalia Kahana-Carmon** (b. 1926) is the author of novels, novellas, short stories, and essays whose distinctive feminist narrative style influenced subsequent generations of Israeli writers; her 1966 collection of stories, *Under One Roof*, was named one of the ten most important books since the creation of the State of Israel. **David Grossman** (b.1954) is one of Israel's most nationally and internationally acclaimed, widely translated, and award-winning authors of novels, short stories, novellas, drama, essays, and books for children. **Hayim Nachman Bialik** (1873–1934) was born in Ukraine where he received a traditional Jewish education but later embraced the Enlightenment movement. In Odessa, he became active in Jewish literary circles. After moving to Berlin, he founded the Dvir Publishing House before permanently settling in Tel Aviv, establishing himself as a cultural beacon of the Hebrew renaissance. He is still regarded as "the national poet of Israel." The Russian-born poet **Rachel** (Bluwstein) (1890–1931) published her poetry exclusively under her first name Rachel. After immigrating to Palestine in 1909, she lived in an agricultural school for girls on the shores of the Sea of Galilee until leaving for France to study agronomy and drawing in 1913. After the outbreak of World War I she returned to Russia to work with refugee children. After contracting the tuberculosis that would eventually kill her, she returned to live on Kibbutz Degania in 1919. Prevented from working with children because of her illness, she left the kibbutz and lived in a one-room apartment in Tel Aviv during the final five years of her life. She was buried near the Sea of Galilee to which much of her poetry was devoted, weighted with themes of longing, loneliness, and heartbreak. Over time, Rachel's tragic life has taken on the aura of legend and her beloved collected verse is still one of Israel's greatest bestsellers. One of Israel's most influential poets, **Lea Goldberg** (1911–1970) was born in East Prussia (now Kaliningrad, Russia), and began writing Hebrew verse in childhood. In addition to her esteemed poetry, she was a highly successful children's author, theater critic, and translator. She established the Hebrew University of Jerusalem's Department of Comparative Literature and served as its chairperson until her death. Goldberg published

nine books of poetry during her lifetime and was awarded the Israel Prize for Literature (1970) the year of her death.

4. Aharon Appelfeld (1932–2018) a survivor of the Holocaust and an Israeli writer whose prolific oeuvre was devoted almost entirely to richly metaphoric and spiritual portrayals of the suffering, disorientation, and displacement of Europe's Jews, prior to, and immediately after World War II.

5. Oz's wife, **Nili** Oz, and their three children: **Fania Oz-Salzberger, Galia Oz,** and **Daniel Oz.**

6. The **Lavon Affair** was a highly controversial unsuccessful Israeli covert operation in Egypt (codenamed Operation Susannah), carried out in the summer of 1954. A nucleus of Egyptian Jews was recruited by Israeli military intelligence to plant bombs inside civilian institutions and cultural centers, attacks intended to be blamed on the Muslim Brotherhood and others, to instill a climate of violence and instability to influence the British government to retain its occupying troops in Egypt's Suez Canal. Though there were no civilian casualties, two operatives committed suicide after their capture and two others were executed by the Egyptian authorities. The botched operation later became known as the Lavon Affair after Defense Minister Pinhas Lavon, who was forced to resign as a consequence. **Levi Eshkol** served as Israel's third prime minister from 1963 until his death in office in 1969 from a heart attack.

7. **Emmanuel Levinas** (1905–1995), French philosopher and Talmudic commentator whose thought encompasses Jewish philosophy, existentialism, ethics, phenomenology, and ontology and focuses primarily on the radical primacy of humanity's "face-to-face" relation with the Other. **Jean-Luc Nancy** (b.1940) is a major French philosopher whose work has influenced many artists, filmmakers, and writers whose writing addresses questions concerning the nature of community and coexistence, politics, German Romanticism, psychoanalysis, and literary hermeneutics.

8. **Natan Alterman** (1910–1970), one of Israel's most culturally influential poets, whose works were often adapted to song and whose strong political affinities shifted from socialist Zionism to the Greater Israel Movement.

9. **Rona Kenan** (b.1979), Israeli singer and songwriter, youngest daughter of Nurith Gertz and novelist Amos Kenan. **Shlomzion (Shlomi) Kenan** (b.1969) is an Israeli journalist, critic and artist, oldest daughter of Nurith Gertz and Amos Kenan.

10. The Labor-affiliated settlement movement.

11. Translated by Diana Rubanenko.

Chapter 4

Homeless between Two Homes

AVRAHAM BALABAN

I

My mother was not an educated woman, but decades of providing childcare on Kibbutz Hulda sharpened her powers of discernment when it came to both children and adults. She once told me, years after I left the kibbutz, "When I see Amos Oz walking toward me in the morning, I can tell that he's saying to himself: ten steps from now I'll have to say good morning to that woman." Like most kibbutz members, she admired Oz, and she was aware that he had arrived from Jerusalem, at the age of fourteen, as a wounded child, his mother having committed suicide two years prior. With her caregiver's instincts, she saw a man who had erected a wall around himself and who, to a great extent, had lost his capacity for unmediated contact with the people around him.

Oz flourished on Hulda. After reading the memoir I wrote about my childhood on the kibbutz (*Shiva*, published in English translation as *Mourning a Father Lost: A Kibbutz Childhood Remembered*, in 2004), he told me: "For you, Hulda was hell. For me, it was redemption." There were several reasons for his saying this, but a primary one was undoubtedly the school and its unique curriculum. Ozer Huldai, our school principal, aspired to educate his students in the socialist-Zionist spirit of the Gordonia youth movement (based on the doctrines of A. D. Gordon). All the children studied from 7:00 a.m. to 1:00 p.m. and starting in the fifth grade we worked after school in various kibbutz industries for two hours a day. The goal was to raise children who would perpetuate their parents' traditions. But Huldai wanted us to be educated farmers, not bumpkins. Since the school was a small kibbutz institution, he had a lot of discretion when it came to the curriculum. And so in high school, alongside the standard subjects, we also studied sociology, philosophy, and psychology. Encountering Freud, Jung, Schopenhauer, and Nietzsche as a sixteen-year-old boy changed my life, and to a great extent made me who I am today. I have no doubt that Oz had a similar experience, having been exposed to these thinkers at a young age along with all our classmates. In Jung, he found a savior and a guide whom he followed for the rest of his life.

II

My path to discovering Amos Oz was largely paved by the story "Where the Jackals Howl," the first in the collection of the same name (published in 1965). During my first year in high school, I began publishing poems in the local children's magazine. Oz, who was a soldier at the time, called me over one day and said that if I was going to write poems, I ought to know something about modern poetry. He let me borrow three of his poetry books: collections by Uri Zvi Greenberg, Walt Whitman, and Yehuda Amichai. The first two did not speak to me at all, but Amichai's first book, *Now and in Other Days*, was an astonishing discovery for me.

After that, I often visited Amos in his kibbutz apartment and showed him drafts of my poems. In one of those meetings, when I was in the eleventh grade, he gave me a stack of densely typed pages bearing the title "Where the Jackals Howl," and asked for my opinion. I was taken by the vivid language and the precise descriptions of jackals and the way light and darkness change on the kibbutz fields. But the nature of the encounter between Matityahu Damkov, the stranger who arrives on the kibbutz after World War II, and Galila, the young kibbutz native, rattled me. It was hard for me to make sense of Matityahu revealing to Galila that he is her biological father and then trying to seduce her. I praised Oz for his rich, picturesque language and left it at that, explaining that I needed to reread the story in order to better understand it.

In fact, I did not like the story, nor the book that was published three years later. The luxuriant language reminded me of the Amos Oz who used to turn up at holiday parties and weddings dressed in khaki, long after his classmates had abandoned that fashion. He would try to dance and sweat like the rest of us, but not a single bead of sweat appeared on his forehead. When the kibbutz recruited workers for extra shifts on Saturdays, so that we could pick all the cotton before the rains came, he would again appear in his ironed khaki outfit. I sensed that he was working hard to accomplish something that came naturally to the other kibbutz kids. As a student at Tel Aviv University, I read his stories more closely. The dichotomies they hinted at, between light and dark, between nurture and nature, struck me as artificial and, above all, too familiar from literature and psychology. This artificiality seemed to accord with the pressed-khaki style of the stories.

The originality and richness of "Where the Jackals Howl" become fully evident to me some two decades after first reading the manuscript. In 1981, I taught a writing workshop for beginners at Tel Aviv University. I assigned Oz's story to my students, intending to discuss the character of the narrator, the function of the landscape descriptions, and so forth. Reading the familiar text in preparation for my class, the story of Matityahu Damkov enticing Galila to his room so that he can tell her he is her biological father and, in the course of the evening, try to get her to go to bed with him, was revealed to me in a completely new light. The story as I had previously read it was a fairly simplistic one, comprising traditional conflicts between light and dark, between man and beast. Damkov represents the primary, unchanging world of "nature." He is described as a jackal who walks to the dining room from his "lair," and the story hints at a parallel between the stud horse he talks about and Damkov himself, who assaults Galila. Of course, the protagonist's name also attests that he is nothing more than a forest animal (in Hebrew, *dam* means "blood," *kof* is "monkey"). Conversely, the character of Sashka, the kibbutz ideologue and Galila's ostensible father, represents the reasoned, illuminated, cultural world.

My close reading of the story illuminated something else: most of Damkov's identifying features resemble those of Hephaestus, the Greek god of metalworking. He, like Hephaestus, is remarkably ugly and works half-naked. Furthermore, like Hephaestus who was cast off Olympus by his mother, Damkov "fell to us" after World War II.[1] This suggested analogy turns the story upside down: the representative of nature contains elements that characterize the Olympic gods. In other words, the binary conflict between light and dark is purely external, for in fact there are clear indicators of darkness in the light and vice versa. What emerges from the story is that there is enormous vitality in darkness, whereas light is a weak, atrophied element. Sashka's enlightened world turns out to be a sterile, barren realm disconnected from nature. Not uncoincidentally, Sashka is completely unaware of the affair his wife had with Damkov and is not Galila's biological father. As if not fully content with this stark outcome, the narrator concludes his story with clear advice on how to live one's life: "The path of the seasons is well trodden. Autumn, winter, spring, summer, autumn. [. . .] Whoever seeks a fixed point in the current of time and the seasons would do well to listen to the sounds of the night that never change. They come to us from out there."[2] In other words, we should not leave the jackals outside the fence, we should not shun them, but rather we must learn to live with them and make peace with them. Needless to say, this is a very pessimistic worldview, because it maintains that the only constant in our world is the sounds of the night, which reach us from the land of the jackals. All notions of enlightenment, of historical and cultural evolution from darkness to light, are summarily rejected here.

And so, twenty years late, I discovered a profound and fascinating story. Twenty years late, I understood that the key to Oz is Schopenhauer and, more pointedly, Carl Jung. That week, at the archives of the Writers Association, I found the first story Oz had ever published, "A Crack Open to the Wind" (Davar, 1961), which buttressed my opinion. In this story, Oz follows Jung step by step. Jung published twenty volumes of research, all of which essentially deal with individualization, a process in which a person seeks, or finds, his "self"—the profound internal point at which all of the personality's opposing facets live in harmony. The structure of "A Crack Open to the Wind" in many ways concretizes this process: the kibbutznik protagonist notices large cracks appearing in his apartment wall. He asks the kibbutz secretary for help but is refused. When he falls ill because of the draughts entering his room through the cracks, he goes to Tel Aviv to seek help from a wealthy relative. The relative also turns him down, and the young man heads home. Since it is late at night and there is no direct bus to the kibbutz, he has to make the last part of his journey on foot. Walking along the side of the road in the dark, he encounters a jackal pup. He tries to shoo the creature away by throwing stones at it, but the pup will not leave. Eventually he picks it up and warms it under his coat. When he arrives home, he puts the sleeping jackal on a pile of sacks under his house. Although it's late at night and he has no construction experience, he goes to the kibbutz warehouse, mixes some mortar, and repairs the hole in the wall with his own two hands. He is certain that from now on he will be able to keep the room free of cracks and other defects.

It is not difficult to infer that the crack in the wall represents a fissure in the protagonist's soul. Throughout the story there are allusions to the onslaught of nature against culture and civilization. An airplane's contrail, for example, is described as a "white scar" on the flesh of the sky, and the road the protagonist takes to the kibbutz is an "abrasion" on the damp fields. By taking in the jackal, he is accepting the jackal-like forces of nature inside him. Having reconciled with the suppressed urges in his soul, his room (and he himself) are no longer in danger. This is precisely the individualization process discussed by Jung.[3] Both of these early stories revealed to me that Oz's seemingly flowery prose conceals an utter lack of faith in the ability of human language to express primary, contradictory emotions, and that Oz's poetics are a poetics of insinuation, pointing from afar at mental states that have no name. Having devoted a separate book to this topic (*Toward Language and Beyond: Language and Reality in Amos Oz*, Am Oved, 1988), I shall not expound upon it here.

III

A year later, I was invited to Harvard University as a guest scholar, and I decided to spend the year researching Oz's works. The result was *Between God and Beast: An Examination of Amos Oz's Prose*. The book was preceded by a long article in *Achshav*, the journal edited by Gabriel Moked, entitled "Amos Oz, An Introductory Essay,"[4] in which I argued that one cannot fully understand Oz's writing without recognizing its clear affinity with Jung's theories, manifested in three main realms. Firstly, the structure of the human mind: the ego as a weak, unsteady tip of a pyramid that is largely composed of the collective unconscious. Secondly, individualization as a central theme in Oz's stories and novels. Jung argued that the only way to achieve harmony in the second part of life is by connecting with the mental forces that were repressed in the first part. The "self" is reached by exposing the darkest layers of one's soul to light and making peace with them. Jung tried to show that the various myths depicting a treasure hunt are in fact describing a journey in search of oneself. The Golden Fleece and the Holy Grail are concrete representations of this yearned-for self. What I came to see is that the depth structure in all of Oz's works is, essentially, a treasure hunt. *A Perfect Peace*, which came out while I was researching my book, is a fine example: Yonatan, the main character, leaves the kibbutz without knowing where he is going. Only when he hitches a ride, heading south, does he realize that "this essential journey that calls to him from the depths of his soul" leads to Petra in Jordan. After facing his deepest fears and desires, Yonatan is able to return to the kibbutz and find "a perfect peace." The character of Azariah, a stranger who arrives on the kibbutz in the dark of night, is initially portrayed as Yonatan's adversary, but after Yonatan's return the two men are depicted as one and the same, and we do not know which of them impregnates Yonatan's wife Rimona. The third realm is the descriptions of the emotional processes at the center of Oz's writing, which repeatedly employ Jung's system of symbols. For example, in *A Perfect Peace*, Azariah finds a tortoise in the field and brings it to Yonatan as a gift. According to Jung, the tortoise symbolizes selfhood, because it represents a union between sky and land, thanks to the shape of its body (a half-sphere on a flat surface). While this may appear to be an insignificant detail, I offer it as an example of the way even marginal details bear the meanings assigned to them by Jung and allude to the novel's primary process.

I was teaching at the University of Michigan, Ann Arbor, when my article appeared in *Achshav*, and I awaited Oz's response with curiosity. To my delight, he wrote to thank me for revealing the Jungian elements in his writing. However, he added, "I was a Jungian before I read a single line of Jung." I had no trouble believing this. Jung, after all, did not invent the central processes characterizing the human soul—he merely interpreted them. When I visited Oz at his home in Arad that summer, he showed me the complete works of Jung displayed on his bookshelf. He opened a volume and explained that the land surveyor in *A Perfect Peace* (Yonatan meets this character in the desert before traveling to Petra, and lives with him for a few months before going home) began to emerge in his mind after he saw one of the pictures of demons at the end of Jung's book.

IV

In his famous essay, "The Hedgehog and the Fox," Isaiah Berlin draws a distinction between writers who see the world through one window and those who view it through a large and evolving array of windows. Amos Oz undoubtedly belongs to the former. In fact, anyone who fully comprehends his first story, "A Crack Open to the Wind," will understand the rich oeuvre of fiction that followed. The same elements that connect "Where the Jackals Howl" with "Strange Fire" (the first and last stories in the original edition of *Where the Jackals Howl*) are repeated over and over again in his later works. In all of them, we encounter a protagonist with dual parents (a recurrent feature of mythological heroes), a treasure hunt, and the discovery of the treasure. Each novel essentially ends with a compromise or reconciliation between rival emotional forces, only to be followed by another novel that begins with passionate loathing between adversaries who will, once again, reconcile at the end of the story.

That pervasive depth structure also explains the profound pessimism that hangs over all of Oz's fiction, which stems from the impossibility of the synthesis that concludes each novel. Harmony between man and jackal is possible in fiction, but in life it can last for a moment or two, at most. It is not by chance that *Where the Jackals Howl* ends with "Strange Fire," the story of a man torn between two homes—the sterile, lifeless Jerusalem apartment, and the vibrant Jerusalem Zoo—neither of which offer him a satisfactory or enduring spiritual existence. All of Oz's main characters, from the stories in *Where the Jackals Howl*, to his first novel, *Elsewhere, Perhaps* (1966), and through his final novel, *Judas* (2014), swing back and forth between two such homes that invalidate each other. Sadly, the political and cultural developments of the last few years (including the enormous influence of social networks on the power of populist leaders and movements, both in Israel and in the United States) demonstrate that this pessimism was fully justified.

V

I began with an anecdote about my mother, and I shall end with one. When Amos Oz came to the *shiva* for my mother, he told me a story about the first time he'd met her. He had come to Kibbutz Hulda, as we know, at the age of fourteen, as an "outside boy." Shortly after arriving, he was sitting alone on a bench near the dining hall. He did not know a single person on the kibbutz, and he could tell that the class he was joining was a very cohesive group of children who had grown up together, and that it would be extremely difficult for him to fit in and find a sense of belonging. He sat on the bench with his eyes closed, allowing the evening breeze to cool his face. To his surprise, he suddenly felt a hand smoothing down his hair: a caress, and then another. He opened his eyes and saw my mother standing there. She smiled and said, "It'll be all right. You'll see, it'll be all right." Half a century later, he still recalled that caress with great emotion. My mother would have been astonished to see tears in the eyes of this grown man who, years ago, used to prepare himself for saying "good morning" to her when they passed each other on the kibbutz paths.[5]

Notes

1. This is from the first edition. In the second edition, published roughly a decade later, Oz rewrote the story and the phrasing is slightly different. The second edition is the one translated into English.

2. "Where the Jackals Howl." Translated by Philip Simpson. *Where the Jackals Howl*. Houghton Mifflin Harcourt, 2012, pp. 3–20. Quotation appears on p. 19.

3. Oz allowed me to publish the story as an appendix to my book, *Between God and Beast: An Examination of Amos Oz's Prose*. Penn State UP, 1993.

4. *Achshav* 49, Spring 1984.

5. Translated by Jessica Cohen.

Chapter 5

My Michael, May 1967

Nissim Calderon

I first read Amos Oz's *My Michael* after the Six Day War. The book was published in April 1968, and the writing was completed in May 1967. Oz felt the need to let his readers know that he had not written the book as a response to the war. And yet it was a post-war reading. It was also my first year as a student in the Hebrew literature department at Tel Aviv University, where Dan Miron said, "You like the book, I don't. Let's argue." He arranged for an auditorium on campus, and we debated the novel. There was a healthy tension in the air.

I no longer know, at this point, what I said at the time and what built up in me years later, when I reread *My Michael*. As a soldier, I had read Oz's *Where the Jackals Howl* and the novel *Elsewhere, Perhaps*. His first collection of short stories interested me but did not stir my senses. His first novel seemed to me a respectable failure. *My Michael* did stir my senses. At the time, I knew I was approaching the book with a sense of gratitude due to the fact that "Homeland," a series of articles that Oz had published in the newspaper *Davar* after the war, had expressed the most scathing objection to the "Greater Israel" notion. (Yeshayahu Leibowitz, who likewise opposed that ideology, spoke as an apocalyptic prophet who was above politics. He spoke, in fact, from a religious perspective, which was, and remains, foreign to me. By way of contrast, Oz emerged from Israel's two most forceful political traditions: Revisionism, into which he

was born, and the Labor movement, which he adopted. Hence his criticism
of the occupation seemed more rooted in the land, having gone through
the channels that most Israelis experienced.) But precisely because I was
so grateful to Oz, the enemy of the occupation, I suspected that I was
flooding my own literary world with an unwelcome political deluge. I did
not wish to read *My Michael* as political allegory. *1984* and its ilk had
always bored me. And by specifying when he had written his book, it
seemed to me that Oz himself was warning against such a reading. But
how could one expunge politics from one's orientation as a reader after
the war? Furthermore, I was still reeling, not just from the war but from
the impact of my entire military service. Somehow, the influence of the
army's discipline lingered oppressively years after I'd emerged from it (at
one point, the chaos of army life had also landed me in hospital with
jaundice). Little wonder that I grasped at literature as though it were
a lifebelt. I devoured literature, reading almost every Hebrew book as
soon as it came out, as well as classics like the works of Berdyczewski,
Asher Barash, and Ibn Gabirol. And I knew that the hand clinging to
that lifebelt was confused: beyond those classics it also wanted Brecht
and what felt to me Mother Courage's scream against the Israeli cult of
power, and it also wanted the playwright Nissim Aloni, with his far-flung
modern princes who were beyond all screaming, beyond all Israeliness.
W. H. Auden once suggested that critics should state what sort of climate
they like best before pronouncing their opinion of a book. This was the
climate in which I was living, whether I liked it or not, when I first read
My Michael. I was immediately struck by its heartfelt writing, beginning
on a note of authenticity that persisted through the final page.

My Michael is shadowed by death. Its opening line is unforgettable:
"I am writing this because people I loved have died." Even as early as
1968, there were those who recognized that Oz had written something
of his late mother into the book. But Hannah Gonen does not die in *My
Michael*. The only characters who die are elderly people whose time has
come. Nathan Zach once listed all the numerous young characters who
die in Hebrew fiction, most of whom commit suicide. Zach saw them as
articulating a romantic failure on the authors' part: they send their heroes
to die because they, the living, do not have the courage to live the ordi-
nariness of life, whether banal or not. Because they prefer a death that is
romantic, literary-unto-death, over the unromantic grappling with what
life has to offer, and what it does not.

Oz was wary of that kind of romanticism. This was manifestly evident in the degree to which he distanced Hannah Gonen from his own mother's psychology. Moreover, it would be a mistake to read any woman's psychology in this novel. Oz was not trying to understand Hannah. He was not at all trying to understand the reasons for her suffering. Consider how many times Hannah repeats the doubts she harbors regarding the word *reason*. She does not believe that there are, in a profound sense, *reasons*. By way of contrast, I would argue that Oz the person, and certainly the political person, seeks and finds very necessary reasons for the things we do, or the things done by the fascists that sprout from the same ground as we do. But Oz as storyteller is a loyal son of the literary-philosophical-emotional tradition that maintains that we must describe our path to death because life without the shadow of death is a great lie that begets a thousand little lies. Reasons are the surface layer of that path. "Gone is the cause of things and their effect," wrote Natan Alterman, "the world occurs in the middle." The most important things have no reasons. They "just happen." Death, too, "just happens." It is not a reason, nor a result, nor a coming full circle, according to the literary tradition embraced by Oz, which resists psychology.

Oz is a quintessential writer of literary traditions. Agnon's Tirza from *In the Prime of Her Life*, is present in Hannah Gonen no less than is Oz's mother. This is the Tirzah whom Agnon portrayed so that the death of the soul lived in her, without the death of the body serenading her in any literary-romantic way. This is the Tirzah who tried to repair—through her body, her love, and her marriage—that which was corrupted by her mother's death. But her attempts fail, and she lives and does not die in the twilight zone between reality and fantasy.

It should be noted here that *My Michael* paved the way for many dozens of translations, though it is a book so deeply rooted in Hebrew literature, and a certain dimension of it is lost to readers in other languages. It is no coincidence that Hannah Gonen's life is invaded, at critical junctures, by Hebrew writers whose names are scattered throughout the novel, and by their literary qualities: Abraham Mapu, Peretz Smolenskin, Y. H. Brenner, Tchernichovsky, Jacob Fichman and others, such as Agnon, who is not mentioned by name precisely because his affinity here is the greatest. Oz embeds the full weight of Hebrew literature's past into this book, while he also conducts a substantial quarrel with that past (the book includes many small arguments with each of those writers, a topic

that should be written about some day). Above all, however, he incorpo-
rates new Hebrew literature's most valuable facet, which is that it did not
uncritically celebrate the figure of the New Jew but, rather, attacked him,
exposing his weaknesses and contradictions, settling the score with his
various lies and deceits. Hannah Gonen is a living-dead woman because,
like Agnon's Herschel (in *A Simple Story*), S. Yizhar's Koby (in *Days of
Ziklag*), and Shabtai's Caesar (in *Past Continuous*), she is not a walking
reason, she is a walking dearth. She is everything we lack, everything we
gave up, everything we compromised on, everything that's screwed up in
us (and yes, that includes Arab twins as a fantasy and not a reality—that,
too, is something screwed up in us). This is why it was such a revelation
for me to receive *My Michael* from Amos Oz the day after the Six Day
War. My reading eye needed the book's dearth, its unyielding refusal to
accept the euphoria, its presence of the wound, its unromantic catastrophe.

I did not like everything about the book. It has too many "murmurs,"
too much "nail-biting tension" and "thrusts of the dagger." The language
tries too hard, to the point of artificiality. It certainly tries when Jerusalem,
and Holon, and Hannah's dreamscapes, all become one endless, tightly
woven symbol. By means of excessively eloquent and accentuated words,
and an array of loud metaphors, Oz digests and conceals the book's most
precious quality: *observation*. If "the cold wind spoke to the cypresses in
a soft and hostile language," and if that soft and hostile language is also
spoken by the many cats in the book, and by the Arab twins in Hannah's
dreams, and by the religious boy who falls in love with her, and by the
Jerusalem hills, and by the streets of Holon—there is not much left in
the world for Oz to observe, or a way to listen to the many different
languages it speaks.

This was no minor flaw in 1968. I was not alone in my need to
rediscover Avot Yeshurun, to submit to the energies of Yona Wallach, to
await the translations of Nili Mirsky. What these very different authors
had in common was literature that opens doors to the world, and a language free of excessive literariness. This may seem to some like stylistic
squabbles among a literary cult (the cult later associated with the literary
journal *Siman Kria*). But there are times when literary cults argue with
a fervor that is necessary not only for their own insular sake but for the
benefit of broader cultural arenas. The literary republic of 1968 observed a
tight-lipped, tight-brained Israeliness. It wanted to read without Alterman
weighing down its words, without the Israeli weighing down the Jew, or

the Arab (by the time we got to Emil Habibi, we were prepared), and without a stifling literariness.

There are a number of points in My Michael at which Amos Oz's power of observation is thwarted by his need to somehow describe the anarchic while using tamed language that is antithetical to anarchy. Perhaps it is a desire for control. Perhaps he is so threatened by anarchy that he dispatches words to contain it too tightly. This is not evident in the heart of the book: in the character of Hannah and in her relationship with Michael. Almost all the other characters, however—Hannah's son, her religious and Revisionist neighbors, her adolescent student, her *yekke* doctor, her socialist father-in-law from Holon—verge on caricature. Oz keeps them on a tight leash, bending them into their roles vis-à-vis Hannah. Only Michael evades caricature by the skin of his teeth, perhaps because Oz saw in him the shadow of his own father, and that concreteness refused to let him become a caricature.

What was perhaps most interesting, and surprising—for those of us who arrived at the book from Oz's two previous ones—was to encounter not only Hannah breaking free from the grip of language, but also her plotline breaking free from literary patterns. Nothing dramatic happens to Hannah. What happens to her is the ordinary progression of a young Israeli woman in the 1950s: going to university, meeting a man, getting married, giving birth, working as a kindergarten teacher, another pregnancy. No literary reversals. No literary inventions. Moreover, what little does happen to her—goes right over her head. From page one to the very last page, she does not appear to change, carrying on with the same inexhaustible hunger for excitement, the same endless frustration with her unexciting life. Thus it seems surprising that so many readers, whether in Hebrew or other languages, were fascinated with My Michael despite its failure to provide the minimal element that most readers expect of a novel: a change undergone by the protagonist. (This is usually not required of the short story.) Hannah does not change. The seasons change, Michael comes into her life, she gives birth to Yair—but this all remains outside her skin. She intrigues us even though the author has given her no plotline dramas. She has enough internal drama.

The nine years of Hannah and Michael's marriage, from 1950 or '51 to 1959, are wisely bisected by the Sinai Campaign of 1956. Without constructing an explicit political allegory, yet with astute political intimation, Oz puts a slight crack in Hannah's dramatic borders by introducing the IDF spokesman who celebrates "the Sinai Desert, the Israeli nation's historic cradle." The foolishness of Israel's alliance with England and France at the pathetic end of their colonial theft was short-lived. So were, in 1956–1957, the voices that reach Hannah from "the nation's historic cradle." But a month after Oz finished writing *My Michael*, Israel's project of occupation and enslavement began in Hannah and Michael Gonen's Jerusalem, following its war of true salvation. And this time it was long-lasting and left none of the Israelis' imperviousness intact. Oz's novel was one of the books that prepared me for this.[1]

Note

1. Translated by Jessica Cohen.

PART 2

NOMADS, VIPERS, AND WOMEN

Chapter 6

Maternal Illness and the Israeli Body Politic at War

NITZA BEN-DOV

My Michael, the only Israeli novel that the Bertelsmann Publishing House placed on its illustrious list of the "Twentieth Century's One Hundred Greatest Novels," tells the story of Hannah Gonen, a young, frustrated housewife living in the divided Jerusalem of the 1950s.[1] Although the narrative is positioned squarely in an Israeli literary and social milieu, its descriptions of the stifling routine and disintegrating marriage of Hannah and her husband Michael are in dialogue with the traditional nineteenth-century realistic novels such as *Anna Karenina* by Leo Tolstoy, *Madame Bovary* by Gustav Flaubert, and *Effi Briest* by Theodor Fontane. Also common to all of the aforementioned novels are the themes of depression, psychological despair, and death. In the earlier novels, omniscient narrators tell the protagonists' stories, and are therefore able to narrate the accounts of the character's death. In *My Michael,* Oz chose to tell the story from Hannah's perspective, in her own "voice." She hints early on that her suicide may become a possibility in the future; but the text sets up as an equally possible scenario the idea that the very act of constructing her own "confessional narrative" is therapeutic, that the reader is witnessing the process whereby suicide might be exchanged for a life of writing. Those familiar with Amos Oz's biography know that in his novels the authorial voice and the speech of various female characters, often mothers, sometimes merge.

Written partly in response to Oz's recent death, this essay considers the autobiographical sources of Oz's oeuvre and in particular, the sources of his persistent portrayals of ailing mothers. The suicide of the writer's mother when he was aged twelve may be an interpretative key to many of his novels and stories. By first examining Oz's most direct treatment of this event in the autobiographical *A Tale of Love and Darkness*, I proceed to argue that we may trace in many other of his novels an attempt to rewrite the story of the mother's life and death in multiple variations and from different vantage points. What these repetitions of the narrative of the mother's death share are the interwoven themes of illness, fantasy, and death. Finally, I show how Oz links these themes to the collective story of the illness of the Israeli body politic at war. The ability to narrate the story of war and illness as threshold states, verging on madness and confounding any simple sense of individual or collective sovereignty, implicitly enables Oz's text to escape the repression which characterizes the ailing mother's text and thereby enables a life of creative endeavor.

The titles of many of Oz's most memorable texts—"Before His Time," *A Perfect Peace* (in Hebrew: "A Perfect Rest," "rest" as euphemistic expression indicating "death"), *Black Box*, *Unto Death*, *Rhyming Life and Death*, *A Tale of Love and Darkness*—are strikingly suggestive of morbidity and impending doom. The texts themselves also tend to invoke death, which remains a pervasive presence throughout: "Hot and strong was the bull on the night of slaughter"—starts his early short-story entitled "Before His Time"; "I am writing this—says protagonist Hannah Gonen—because people I loved have died. I am writing this because when I was young I was full of the power of loving, and now that power of loving is dying. I do not want to die"—thus she opens the story of her ten-year marriage to "Her Michael." The novel *Fima* opens: "Five days before the disaster, Fima had a dream that he wrote down at five-thirty in the morning in his dream journal."

When I first learned of Amos Oz's death and was subsequently requested to write a piece on his work for the literary supplement of *Haaretz*, I sat for a long time, full of hurt, facing the white screen. I did not know where to begin. In his handbook entitled *The Story Begins*, Oz writes about the author struggling as he sits facing the blank page, not knowing how to start. He wrote: "sometimes there is in the opening paragraph, a hidden, secret, contract between writer and reader formed over and above the heads of the characters." I decided therefore to open this chapter with the titles of his books that had always enchanted me and with the opening words of his stories that always constituted—they still do—a veiled contractual link between the stories and myself.

Why was the bull slaughtered before its time? Why is the inner strength of *My Michael*'s Hannah Gonen's love dying and why, in its stead, is the fear of death lurking within her? What is the disaster hiding within the opening allusion of *Fima*? What unspoken contractual commitment is to be found, from the outset, hovering over the head of Shimshon, the bull ready for slaughter, over Hannah Gonen, (in her story Eros and Thanatos mingle chaotically from the outset), even over Fima-Ephraim's dream? I believe that many of the titles, the "opening acts," as well as the endings of Oz's stories, hint one way or another at a childhood wound that never healed. The same wound annihilated his trust in love yet sprang wings of inspiration that led him to the world of dreams, imagination, and creativity. From the wound of his mother's premature death, he drew the strength to contend with attacks by physical blows, harassment by childhood play-mates, and, later, with the words of critics. "Do not be afraid Ephraim," says the woman-child in Fima's first dream in the opening of *Fima*, and so Fima puts his trust in her, and follows, elated with happiness, and does not wonder how this woman-child has changed into his mother (40). In my own and other readers' contractual relation to the works of Oz, we suspended the sense that all the women, and sometimes the men too, and even Shimshon the bull, change into the mother that committed suicide when he was twelve and then became the ostensible heroine of his life, and the hidden heroine in all his writings. But after the publication of his autobiographical novel, it became almost impossible to continue to ignore the significance of this event for his writing.

From his debut as a writer until his death, Amos Oz wrote more and more alternative narratives, variations, of the story of his mother's premature death—the story of his becoming an orphan. Hannah Gonen, who studied literature at the Hebrew University of Jerusalem, was cre-ated in the image of his mother Fania, in his own image, and that of the mother of Agnon's heroine, Tirza.[2] *My Michael* is structured in the form of diary entries by Hannah—one can glean an especially meaningful insight from a particular segment of Hannah's text: "At the root of the poetry of the Hebrew Enlightenment Period we find (solid as a foundation) the condition of being orphaned; what might be its source and nature is not for me to say."[3] Israeli readers have generally conjectured the source and nature of Oz's vast oeuvre lay in the condition of being an orphan, but after the publication of *A Tale of Love and Darkness,* we know for certain. Like a man scratching a wound, knowing he should stop, but cannot, Oz burrowed, with novels, with literary analysis, with personal, cultural, and political essays, into the childhood wound that had never healed. In *A Tale of Love and Darkness* he gave this wound its most clear and explicit expression: "My mother ended her life in her sister's apartment on Ben Yehuda Street in Tel Aviv on the night between Saturday and Sunday, January 6,1952, the 8th day of the month of Tevet, in the year 5712." So starts the last chapter of the novel.

Documenting with such exactitude the time and place of his mother's tragic death, redoubling the day and month and year by adding the Hebrew date to the Gregorian, the two versions cross each other, anchoring the tragedy as a singular event and imbuing it with a sense of awe that is chillingly festive, imparting a feeling that this day would be forever remembered. The seemingly dry chronicle of the details of the private tragedy spreads to encompass nature as well as nation: "all over the country that winter it rained heavily almost without a break all over Israel through that winter of 1951–52. The river Ayyalon, the dry riverbed of Musrara, burst its banks and flooded the Montefiori district of Tel Aviv, and threatened to flood other districts as well. Heavy flooding did extensive damage to the transit camps with their tents and their corrugated iron or canvas huts, crowded with hundreds and thousands of Jewish refugees who had fled from Arab lands, leaving everything behind and refugees from Hitler, from Eastern Europe, and the Balkans. Some transit camps were cut off by the floods, and there was a risk of starvation and epidemic" (62). The private and the public blend together in Oz's work, turning *A Tale of Love and Darkness* into what many other readers conceived as their own story.

Amos Oz himself also passed away while torrential rains were falling non-stop in the winter of 2018–19, thus weaving an imaginary thread between the time of his mother's death and his own. Even the Hebrew dates turn out to be close together. His mother took her life between Saturday and Sunday on the 8th of the month of Tevet and his came to an end on a Saturday evening on the 20th of Tevet. The twelve-and-a-half-year-old Amos Klausner stayed in Jerusalem at the beginning of January 1952 while his mother traveled alone to Tel Aviv, where she put an end to her life in her sister's apartment. Nevertheless, with the precise details of an eyewitness, he depicts her aimless wanderings, first on a rain-drenched and windblown Saturday morning in a Tel Aviv teaming with cats, debris, and trash, and later on in the evening, a few hours before her death. In the last chapter of *A Tale of Love and Darkness*, the son—now an adult, a parent himself, and a well-known writer—is trying to enter the waterlogged boots of his mother and, with empathy and identification, to accompany her last steps. He who was not with her on her path that cold and rainy day in Tel Aviv on the eve of her death is creating it anew for her. It is as if the "authenticity" of documentation forces him to push his imagination further, to better accompany her melancholy walk through deserted streets: "there cannot have been many people in the streets of North Tel Aviv on that wet and windy Saturday morning"; "She may have crossed Ben Yehuda Street and turned left, or perhaps northward, toward Nordau Boulevard"; "My mother was very tired that morning, and her head must have been heavy from lack of sleep, hunger and all that black coffee, all those sleeping pills"; "She may have left Ben Yehuda street before she reached Nordau Boulevard and turned right into Belvedere Alley, which despite its name offers no beautiful panorama" (535–36). Four additional "maybes" and one "it seems" make it clear to the reader that the vivid representation the son offers of his mother's final hours springs from his own imagination.

Apart from her morning walk, the mother goes on an additional walk at sunset, perhaps a more successful one because the weather had calmed, the city lights had come on, the passersby were now more numerous. Yet all this did not mirror her feelings: "to her it all looked tawdry and second-hand, like an imitation of an imitation of something she found pathetic and miserable" (537). Fania Klausner's imagined resignation is strikingly similar to the way Hannah Gonen, in *My Michael* expresses her own sense of ("what was is what will be") eternally recurring banality: "The days are the same, the same, just as I myself am the same." Both of them feel that nothing in this world is going to surprise them, everything is known and cliché and ground-down and, ad nauseam, recognizable. Significantly, despair at the sterility of life is associated with creative sterility and despair: "We are all discarded drafts" says Hannah to "her" Michael, "we copy onto a clean page and then copy on yet another clean page and then discard it, and crumple it and toss it into the trashcan and then copy it out again onto yet another clean page, making a minuscule change. What foolishness, Michael, what dreariness, what an insipid joke."[4] The inability to tell a meaningful story or produce a worthwhile draft of the mother's story is what is at stake. The potential meaninglessness, sterility, and compulsivity of the act of retelling reverberates beyond the level of diegesis to cast doubt on Oz's own retelling.

At the very end of *A Tale of Love and Darkness*, two paramedics carry the unconscious mother on a stretcher to the ambulance that had arrived at the sister's house, before sunrise, on Sunday the 6th of January 1952. From there the paramedics transport her to the hospital. Yet father and son had already, like the two paramedics carrying her stretcher, cared with devotion for the sick mother for a whole year before her death. But from the day of her death and until the day of his own, her son carried her alone, as he copied onto a clean page and then copied onto yet another clean page and then discarded it and crumpled it and tossed it into the trashcan and then copied it out again onto yet another clean page, making a large or minor change; but always creative and surprising, innovative and humane, connecting the story of her life and death. His many loyal readers, in Israel and elsewhere, did not see foolishness or drudgery in all this but were excited by the originality of each reiteration, and in this way, they perhaps lightened the load of trauma.

Fima's dream of disaster at the beginning of *Fima*, in which he is not surprised when the woman-child dream-figure transforms into his mother, ends with the words: "And I will not see her anymore and I woke up with sadness and even as I am finishing this sketch the sorrow has not ended."[5] The sentence that seals the last chapter of *A Tale of Love and Darkness* describes the bird "Elise" that calls out from the branches of the Ficus tree in the garden of the hospital to the mother who sunk in relentless sleep. It "called to her, baffled, and called to her again and again in vain, and yet again it went on trying over and over again and still, sometimes, it tries sometimes" (538). Just like the bird Elise, the son called and called to his mother and even when she did not respond he tried again and again and forced his readers to read about her.

My Michael is perhaps Oz's most direct and extended treatment of the story of the ailing mother, torn between a rich inner world of fantasy and a mundane family life in which she finds little meaning or room for authentic expression. Hannah Gonen's narrative follows a precise timeline of events. A date and location is provided at the beginning of the novel: "Jerusalem, January 1960." It soon becomes clear that the narrative will encompass ten years of Hannah's marriage to her husband Michael. Intriguingly for a first-person narrative, Hannah does not name her story after herself. Rather it is named after her husband, whom she considers the central figure in her sad life. In the title "My Michael" one hears the resonance of her possessive voice; Michael belongs to her, and he is also that part of the "self" that inspires her distress, a motif that is sustained throughout the text. Hannah "writes" the story of her accidental meeting with the geology student Michael Gonen and her marriage to him in 1950, a decision she regards in retrospect as hasty and which she will ponder again and again while writing her memoirs. "I am thirty years of age and a married woman. My husband is Dr. Michael Gonen, a geologist, a good-natured man. I loved him. We met in Terra Sancta College ten years ago. I was a first-year student at the Hebrew University, in the days when lectures were still given in Terra Sancta College" (1). Following the initial description of the most consequential transformation in her life through marriage and pregnancy, Hannah reveals each event in her life with careful attention to detail, using specific dates to endow the passing time with mimetic authenticity. Most of the dates are connected with her private or family experiences: "Our son Yair was born [. . .] in March 1951" (56); "There was a day, for instance, late in July 1953, a bright blue day full of sounds and sights" (87); "I bought Michael the first volume of the *Encyclopedia Hebraica* as a present on our fourth wedding anniversary" (97); "One evening in the autumn of 1954 Michael came home carrying a grayish-white kitten in his arms" (105); "In the summer of 1955 we took our son for a week's holiday in Holon, to relax and swim in the sea" (122). Periodically, some outside news items filter into the closed family chronicle, recounted by Hannah accurately but always channeled through her narrow domestic consciousness. For example, in July of 1953 Michael bought an evening newspaper "which mentioned South Korea and gangs of infiltrators in the Negev" (87).[6] These events occurred three years before the 1956 Sinai War, which is the "climax of the novel's thematic structure," but the reader is given a hint that Hannah has no real interest in geopolitical events.[7] Similarly, in the autumn of 1956, when the signs of war are multiplying, the readers become aware of the imminent military conflict through various characters who express their opinions of the unfolding events. One of them is Mr. Kadishman, a frequent visitor to Hannah and Michael's home, who says:

> There is going to be a war. This time we shall conquer Jerusalem, Hebron, Bethlehem, and Nablus. The Almighty has wrought justly, in that, while He has denied our so-called leaders' common sense, He has confounded the wits of our enemies. What

He takes away with one hand, as it were, He restores with the
other. The folly of the Arabs will bring about what the wisdom
of the Jews has failed to achieve. There is going to be a great
war, and the Holy Places will once again be ours. (163)

To this premature "prophecy,"[8] Michael retorts: "Since the day the Temple
was destroyed, the power of prophecy has been granted to men like you
and me. If you want to know my opinion, the war we are about to fight
will not be over Hebron or Nablus but over Gaza and Rafah" (163–64).[9]
Both men's opinions about the "Sinai War" illuminate their personalities.
Analytical, straight-thinking Michael forecasts the events rationally and
correctly, thus serving as an antithesis to those who dream grandiose
nationalistic dreams, like Kadishman, or those who dream lurid private
dreams, like his wife Hannah. Yet the cause of Hannah's dissatisfaction
with her married life is precisely this admirable quality, her husband's
mild and balanced character, as a man who does his utmost to protect
their tranquil life from her over-excitement, her fantasies, and her mental
illness. His name, Gonen (which in Hebrew means "protector") and his
correct prediction are suggestive: although he is able to assess the nature
of the coming war, and to protect Hannah from feeling anxious, he cannot
appreciate or protect her from her own more turbulent inner world, her
"dreams," which eventually result in her grave illness, which coincides with
that war. Michael's true "prophecies" do not gain him any favor with her:

> At lunchtime Michael commented on the radio news: There is
> a well-known rule, established—if his memory did not deceive
> him—by the German Iron Chancellor, Bismarck, according to
> which when one is faced by an alliance of enemy forces, one
> would turn and crush the strongest. So it would be this time,
> my husband declared with conviction. First of all, we would
> scare Jordan and Iraq to death, then we would suddenly turn
> around and smash Egypt.
>   I stared at my husband as if he had suddenly started
> talking Sanskrit (165).

Unlike war plans and strategies, which are nothing but "Sanskrit" to her,
the sight of soldiers clad in uniform is striking to Hannah's romantic
consciousness: "In Café Allenby in King George Street I saw four handsome French officers. They were wearing peaked caps, and purple stripes

gleamed on their epaulets. Only in films had I seen such sight before"
(166). She finds Israeli soldiers attractive as well: "In David Yellin Street
[. . .] I passed three paratroopers in mottled battle dress. Submachine
guns hung from their shoulders [. . .] One of them, dark and lean, called
after me 'Sweetheart.' His comrades joined in his laughter. I reveled in
their laughter" (166–167). Hannah would like "to live in films"; she
detests what for her is a dull real life, and she does not join the home
front's preparations for war. She merely buys *matzah* (normally bought in
springtime for Passover, not in autumn), while others are grabbing canned
foods, candles, and paraffin lamps from the grocery store shelves (166).[10]
Moreover, while the frantic food hoarding and the tense atmosphere make
most people alert and over-active, she becomes ill and ceases to function.
In reality, the soldiers had merely called her "sweetheart," but that had
left her half-satisfied. In her fantasies: "The soldiers thronged and closed
around me in their mottled battle dress. A furious masculine smell exuded
from them in waves. I was all theirs. I was Yvonne Azulai. Yvonne Azulai, the opposite of Hannah Gonen" (170). The soldiers who proceed to
gang rape her are the extreme opposite of her husband, who receives his
call-up papers with the utmost restraint while Hannah inwardly shouts:
"When will this man lose his self-control? Oh, to see him just once in
panic. Shouting for joy. Running wild" (177–78).

The noble calm with which Michael receives his call-up papers is
characteristic of his accustomed position in their relationship, as a voice
of reason, which drives Hannah, literally, out of her mind. Describing
a typical scene, she narrates Michael's words rather than quotes them
directly. The indirect telling, or "free indirect speech," is meant to ridicule
his assessments and his character, although what he says is very sensible:

> Michael explains tersely that no war was likely to last longer
> than three weeks. The talk is of a limited, local war, of course.
> Times have changed. There wouldn't be another 1948. The
> balance between the Great Powers is very unsteady. Now that
> America is in the throes of elections and the Russians are busy
> in Hungary, there's a fleeting opportunity. No, this war won't
> drag on, for certain. Incidentally, he is in Signals. He is neither
> a pilot nor a paratrooper. (178)[11]

Hannah's repeated emphasis of the fact that Michael serves in the army
signal corps adds a sarcastic dimension to his pronouncement, which he

repeats with a chivalrous apology, that he is not a "real" fighter, since he is neither a pilot nor a paratrooper. Her piercing irony is directed at Michael not only through requisitioning his words and reporting them in indirect speech, but also by ways of analogy and projection. Of all the radio broadcasts on the eve of the war, Hannah is struck most by the fact that: "an excited newscaster spoke of an ultimatum issued by the President of the United States. The President called on all parties to exercise restraint" (175). This ultimatum, coming at a moment when the conflict between the parties had already reached the boiling point, serves as a striking analogy to Michael's absurd ability to accept his call-up papers with restraint and to speak, even at that moment, with cold logic. Even the "excited" news-caster cannot maintain composure when reading the president's demand. It seems that Michael is the only one able to maintain a sense of calm. Michael repeats for the third time his measured and reassuring estimate concerning the war, and once again his words and actions are recounted from Hannah's ironic point of view: "He is leaving me a hundred pounds. And here on a piece of paper under the vase are written his army number and unit number [. . .] The war won't last long at all. He means to say, that is what political reason dictates. After all the Americans [. . .] never mind now" (178).[12] For his part, Michael is only marginally aware that his estimates of the length of the war or the deployment of forces are not a major concern for Hannah. Her lack of interest in the war on the national and political levels can be seen through the way she reports the frequent radio bulletins, once again through indirect speech. She begins by quoting authentic news, but changes them into clipped reports, pick-ing from the news trite combinations, "white-washed expressions," and unrelated clichés, which portray the war's aims and triumphs ironically:

At nine o'clock the radio announced: Last night the Israel Defense Forces penetrated the Sinai Desert, captured Kuntilla and Ras en-Naqeb, and have occupied positions near Nahel, sixty kilometers east of the Suez Canal. A military commenta-tor explains: While from the political point of view. Repeated provocations. Flagrant violation of freedom of navigation. The moral justification. Terrorism and sabotage. Defenseless women and children. Mounting tension. Innocent civilians. Enlightened public opinion at home and abroad. Essentially a defensive operation. Keep calm. Must not wander outside. Must enforce blackout. Must not hoard. Must obey instructions. Must not

panic. Must be on the alert. The whole country is the front.
The whole nation is an army. On hearing the warning signal.
So far events have proceeded according to plan. (180–81)

Except for the first sentence, Hannah's report of the radio's nine o'clock
bulletin is devoid of real information. Hannah creates a parodic internal
monologue of the news, especially in the parts of alternative "musts and
must nots," giving the civilian public military-like instructions. Hannah
carries on with her subjective and ironic reporting of what is heard on
the radio every fifteen or thirty minutes: "At a quarter past nine: The
armistice agreement is dead and buried and will never be revived. Our
forces are overrunning. Enemy opposition is giving ground [. . .] Till half
past ten the radio played marching songs from my youth: 'From Dan
to Beersheba we'll never forget,' 'Believe me, the day will come'" (181).
Hannah's detached ironic perspective violates the familiar patriotic songs.
In her responses to the lyrics, it is clear she has no intention of taking
any part in the national celebration. All the messages, all the slogans, are
worthless to her: "Why should I believe you? And if you don't forget,
what of it?" (181). The dramatic and ceremonial report at half past ten:
"the Sinai Desert, historic cradle of the Israelite nation," is also met with
Hannah's sarcastic response: "As opposed to Jerusalem," she adds, neither
agreeing with nor rejecting the assertion regarding the importance of the
Sinai Desert. Then she says either earnestly or ironically: "I try my hardest
to be proud and interested" (181), hinting that her make-believe effort is
fruitless. As far as she is concerned, the war is a golden opportunity to fall
ill, to abandon all her obligations, to indulge in fantasies, to get even with
her maddeningly "square" husband. Hannah, like the war itself, represents
the destabilization of order, the breaking of routine. Like a nation at war,
she does not have the ability to see things outside of herself.

The analogy between Hannah's illness and wartime existence in a
divided Jerusalem, in which Hannah and Michael live "on the threshold,"
in the shadow of a hostile border splitting the city in two, is the source of
the novel's drama. Oz turns Hannah's ailing body into a kind of metaphor
for the young Israeli body politic in 1956. Hannah's mental and physical
condition is of existence on the brink of disaster, courting madness, perhaps even death. She is described as sick, delirious, indulging with equal
measures of terror and delight in fantasies of forbidden sexual boundary
crossing. As such, her condition becomes representative of a kind of national
subconscious at the time of the Sinai War. If Michael's speech stands for

the Israeli text, Hannah's diary entries are what is repressed by this text: in her rich fantasy life she both celebrates and dreads the porousness and flexibility of borders even as a war is ongoing to enforce their fixity. Thus, during a visit by the German-born physician, Dr. Urbach, the latter speaks alternatively of her state of health and the state of the nation as an analogy between two states of sickness that are simultaneously states of exhilaration:

> "These are important days," says Dr. Urbach, "fateful days. At times such as these it is difficult to refrain from scriptural thoughts. Is our throat still inflamed? Let us look inside and find out. It was bad, very bad, dear lady, what you did when you poured on yourself cold water in the middle of winter, as if it was possible to bring peace to the mind by bringing afflictions to the body [. . .] Well, today the news from the war is optimistic. The English and the French also will fight together with us against the Moslems. The radio this morning spoke even of 'the allies.' Almost like in Europe." (186)

Both Hannah's mental illness and the ecstatic state in which the Israeli nation finds itself in the autumn of 1956 are brought together in her physician's words: "There is a serious defect of the intellect in some Jews; we are unable to hate those who hate us. Some mental disorder. Well, yesterday the Israeli army climbed up Mount Sinai with tanks. Almost apocalyptic, I would say, but only almost" (186–87). In his medical diagnosis of both Hannah and the Jews—"defect of the intellect," "inflamed throat," "to bring peace to the mind by bringing afflictions to the body," "mental disorder," "almost apocalyptic"—Dr. Urbach uses expressions that work on both levels. Hannah's psychosomatic and psychotic state serves as a metaphor for the state of the Jews, while the state of the Jews serves as a metaphor for Hannah's fantastical despair. In one of her most startling fantasies, she dreams about her relationship with two Arab boys, with whom she played with as a child and "bossed around,"—they now become fantasy figures who attack and rape her. This rape-fantasy is similar to the one she has about the soldiers who called her "sweetheart," in terms of its position relative to her relationship with Michael, but this time the fantasy involves Arabs raping her and "raping" the State, following the argument about Hannah's "mental condition" as an analogy to the "war." Oz's association between the Israeli state and the ailing, mentally frail figure of Hannah is striking when considered against the backdrop of contemporary portrayals of the typical Israeli Sabre, usually a robust male devoted to agriculture and ready to defend the nation in battle.

It is worth noting here that Oz was not seduced by the "scriptural thoughts" and the feeling of elation shared by Israelis during the swift and relatively self-contained first war following the War of Independence. He also remained firmly detached from the messianic wave that subsequently flooded the country and the people during the Six Day War. Through Hannah, who remains unmoved by the decisive victory and turns through her dreams and illness into a mirror for the distorted, abnormal state of a nation during war, Oz reveals his reservation concerning the political dreams of grandeur, which cause illness and war. Perhaps there is a literary-ideological message here: If Hannah Gonen becomes an analogy for the nation, it is precisely her position as a "Gonen"—a woman who is both protected and imprisoned, guarded to the point of driving her to madness—that causes her illness, culminating at a time when Israel's protective and threatening borders are again in question. Oz's ability to tell this other story, not the story of Michael's detached sanity but of Hannah's madness and delirium, is, in this context, the saving grace separating a life of creative work from one of repression, despair, and death. In this way *My Michael* turns personal trauma into a collective allegory—an aesthetic strategy that is arguably the central characteristic of Oz's work. In his writing, the intimate story of the stricken family, which disintegrated so tragically, is interwoven with the story of the nation, transvalued as a kind of myth of origins. The orphaned child, helpless before his mother's decision to end her life, becomes the masterful writer who tells the story of his people, as though trauma might be subsumed through an identification with the public. And yet, as the numerous stories of Oz's vulnerable heroines show us, trauma continued to press its claims, insistent and irreducible, much like the madness of Hannah Gonen, demanding to be read on its own terms.

Notes

1. Unless otherwise specified, all quotations from the novel are from the English translation by Nicholas de Lange in collaboration with the author, first published in London by Chatto and Windus in 1972, and in paperback in New York by Bantam Books in 1976. *My Michael* was originally published in

Hebrew in 1968, but it was completed in May 1967, about one month before the Six Day War.

2. *In the Prime of Her Life*, (Schocken, 1991 [Bi-Dmi Yameha]). Agnon's narrative is related by the protagonist, Tirza, a young woman whose mother died "in the prime of her life." Tirza becomes entranced by Akaviah Mazal, a lecturer at the college where she is studying, who is discovered to be the dead mother's former lover. The mother's illness and death are central themes in this influential novella.

3. The translation is my own. While Nicholas de Lange chose "desolation" for Hebrew יתמות, Oz's Hebrew specifically refers to the condition of being an orphan, יתום. De Lange's version reads:

> "I recorded in my exercise book that the quality of desolation pervades the works of the poets of the Hebrew renaissance" (*My Michael*, Vintage, pp. 50–51).

4. My translation. Nicholas de Lange's version reads: "One fresh draft is made after another, and each in turn is rejected and crumpled up and thrown in the wastepaper basket, to be replaced by a new, slightly improved version. How futile it all seems. How dull. What a pointless joke" (*My Michael*, p. 198).

5. My translation. The English translation by de Lange: "And that I would not see her again. I woke with sadness and even now as I conclude these notes the sadness has not left me" (*Fima*, Chatto & Windus, p.3).

6. The civil war between North and South Korea broke out in June 1950, with China and the Soviet Union supporting the North and the United States and United Nations allies supporting the South. Approximately 1.2 million people were killed in the war, which ended in a stalemate and armistice in July 1953. Following the Israeli-Arab armistice in 1949, Arab terrorists from Egypt and the Gaza Strip attacked Israeli settlements in the Negev.

7. Gertz, Nurith. *Israeli Prose Fiction in the 1960s*. Units 4–5, The Open University, 1982, p. 20 (Hebrew).

8. Hannah is narrating an event that occurred on the eve of the Sinai War in 1956, rather than the Six Day War that occurred eleven years later. Oz's readers would know that Kadishman's predictions will indeed happen.

9. For Oz's readers, the great loss of life in the Korean War, its ending in a stalemate and cease-fire in 1953, later in a partition of the Korean peninsula in 1954, which is still a source of conflict, are familiar aspects of Israel's War of Independence, its armistice line, and continuing conflict with the Arabs.

10. In the English translation *matzah* is replaced by "cookies."

11. Yehoshua Kenaz, in his novel *Infiltration* set in 1955, stresses how crucial it was for men of that generation to serve in the paratroops. The Sinai War began on October 29, 1956, in response to repeated terrorist incursions into

Israel and Egypt's seizure of the Suez Canal and blockade of Eilat, and with the acquiescence of the British and the French. The Americans were caught up in the presidential election, and the Soviet Union had just invaded Hungary to suppress their rebellion, October 23–November 10, 1956.

12. In the aftermath of the Sinai War, the re-elected president, Dwight D. Eisenhower, and his secretary of state, John Foster Dulles, humiliated Britain and France, and demanded that Israeli forces leave the conquered territory in the Sinai.

Chapter 7

The Little Plot and the
Big Plot in Oz's Early Fiction

ODED NIR

Until recently, the 1960s have always been considered as the most momentous period of transformation in Israeli fiction, one in which the hegemony
of the "Zionist metanarrative," as Gershon Shaked put it (*Hasiporet Ha'ivrit
1880–1980* 16), gave way to other forms of writing. Amos Oz's work is
widely acknowledged as one of the central representatives of the 1960s
"New Wave," as Shaked called it (*Gal khadash basiporet ha'ivrit*), if not
the most important representative of it. Oz's challenge to previous Hebrew
literary hegemony is many times framed as taking place at both a larger
scale than national concerns, and simultaneously at a smaller scale than
them. Larger than the narrowly national is his focus on universal human
questions, smaller than national collectivity is the individual, which in Oz's
work takes center stage and becomes more dominant than outside events.
Thus Oz's challenge is many times articulated, for example, by moving
away from the celebration of collective settlements, or by questioning the
heroism of the sabra, or focusing works on protagonists very different than
the pioneers that dominate Zionist realist fiction (Omer-Sherman 69–70).

In this chapter, I suggest a new way to conceptualize formally Oz's
challenge to previous literary hegemony. I will be looking very briefly at
two of Oz's early novels: *Elsewhere, Perhaps* and *My Michael* and two of
his well-known early short stories: "Where the Jackals Howl" and "Nomad

and Viper." As I hope to demonstrate, Oz's early fiction is characterized by juxtaposing a big plot—the main narrative line—with a little plot (or more than one), which is many times not related in any strong narrative sense to the big plot. The relationship between these two textual parts, as I hope to show, is where the work of dissolving collective interpretation, and establishing an individual one, takes place. I will conclude the discussion by suggesting that the dominant theme of this turn to the individual, as it emerges in these works, itself posits a different collective interpretation, one not consciously evoked by the works themselves.

To demonstrate most clearly the existence of what I am calling the two plots in Oz's early fiction, I want to turn to the short story "Nomad and Viper," published in 1965, only a year before Oz's first novel, *Elsewhere, Perhaps*. In the story, a group of Bedouin nomads are pushed by a drought to make camp next to a kibbutz. Quickly enough, tensions arise between kibbutz members and Bedouins. As the short narrative progresses, that these tensions will end in violence seems inevitable, strangely despite the best of intentions of the members of the kibbutz, or so it seems. I will return below to this irrational emergence of violence. For now, I only want to emphasize that the story's particular presentation of common Zionist themes, has many times been taken as a critique of kibbutz life and the Israeli state, which it clearly allegorized (Grumberg 37–38). In what follows, I will demonstrate how the story's division into big and small plots is vital for this critique.

In the beginning of the story, the narrator uses "we" to refer to the kibbutz members, signaling to the reader that the story is narrated by a member of the kibbutz. He later uses the first person, which strengthens this impression. However, when Geula—a former love interest of the initial narrator—walks out of the kibbutz to meet one of the Bedouins, the narration follows her, referring to her in the third person and narrating the events of the encounter as they are happening from her perspective. This contradicts the initial assumption about the narrator, or at least makes the reader assume that there are multiple narrators. This contradiction joins many other narrative contradictions or incoherencies. For example, the narrator holds fast to his belief that the Bedouins are stealing from the kibbutz, even as he mentions that there is no evidence for such theft ("Nomad and Viper" 122–23). The kibbutz meeting provides another example: the narrator mentions having spoken, yet he immediately follows that with a long complaint about the younger kibbutz generation—of which he is part—not being given the right to speak (133). But perhaps the sharpest level of contradiction has to do with the characterization of the Bedouins: they are described as both masculine and feminine; both strong and weak; both cunning and cognitively deficient—and the list of binaries goes on. I will return to this contradictoriness a bit later in the analysis.

To this contradiction-laden main narrative several side stories—or small plots—are juxtaposed. Their causal relation to the main narrative is tenuous at best, and for at least one it is completely absent. This is the tiny plot of Geula's attempt to break a glass that she finds lying on the ground. This plot is given in two separate vignettes:

> Near the Persian Lilac Geula saw a bottle dirty with the remains of a greasy liquid. She kicked it repeatedly, but instead of shattering, the bottle rolled heavily among the rosebushes. She picked up a big stone. She tried to hit the bottle. She longed to smash it. The stone missed. The girl began to whistle a vague tune. (124)

> Viciously Geula picked up another stone to hurl at the bottle. This time she did not miss, but she still failed to hear the shattering sound she craved. The stone grazed the bottle, which tinkled faintly, and disappeared under one of the bushes. A third stone, bigger and heavier than the other two, was launched from ridiculously close range: the girl trampled on the loose soil of the flower bed and stood right over the bottle. This time there was a harsh, dry explosion, which brought no relief. Must get out. (125)

That this small plot is intertwined with Geula's general characterization helps dissociate it from the time of the main narrative, setting it apart and encouraging the reader to view it as having universal validity, or as constituting significance that transcends the unimportant event in itself. I will return in what follows to the last line in the quote, "Must get out," and to the associative relation of Geula to a "vague tune," which are left ominously unexplained. My argument is that the story encourages the reader to see this small plot as an interpretive key for understanding the larger narrative in which it is embedded, but to which it does not causally belong. Two factors are important here: first, that the contradictions in the main narrative block or neutralize any explicit social interpretation that the reader might entertain. Initially the reader might conclude that the Bedouins are stealing from the kibbutz. But that premise is quickly put in doubt, as no evidence is produced, and as it quickly becomes apparent that the narrator's characterization of the Bedouins cannot be trusted; secondly, the reader might think that internal tensions to the kibbutz—the generational conflict, for instance—simply find displaced expression in the violent response to the Bedouins. But this interpretation cannot really be maintained, since, as I mentioned earlier, the younger people do in fact get to speak and take action. Thus, any explicit social interpretations are neutralized. Needless to say, this neutralization already enacts a critique of national ideology, since all the allegorical elements neutralized—primarily, the nation and its other—fail to produce a stable understanding of the events.

But then the little plot comes into play, offering us an interpretation that is stripped from social or historical specificity, providing a stable substitute. Geula's irrational attempt to break the bottle can be said to model something like the Freudian death-drive—a destructive impulse, as Yigal Schwartz has it (12), one that entails action that is no longer motivated by an coherent hope of transcendence or change, often expressed in irrational-seeming repetition such as Geula's.[1] It is this irrational death-drive through which one slowly begins to understand the main narrative, too: aggression toward the Bedouins, sexual exploitation, generational conflict—all of these gradually become symptoms of the same death-drive (interesting in this regard is the status of sanity itself in Oz's work. See Bar Yosef).

Other formal characteristics strengthen this reading. The small lyrical asides that emphasize a feeling of entrapment are perhaps the most visible of these. The "must get out" with which the previous quote ended is joined here by other openings and endings of small sections of the story, expressing the same sense of being trapped, like "no relief . . . must go now" ("Nomad and Viper" 126), or the sentence fragment "the night fell, damp and hot and close" (124) that closes a section of the story, only to reappear in the beginning of the following section in very slight variation: "Damp and close and hot the night fell on the kibbutz [. . .]." These repetitions invoke lyrical verse, typically associated with subjective consciousness rather than realistic narration. To these, one can add the observation, made by others, that the landscape descriptions in the story constitute an obviously self-conscious "pathetic fallacy"—directly reflecting the state of mind or inner nature of this or that character (Barzel 635–44). And so, all that gives rise to the suspicion that we are not really dealing with events in the world but rather with the nightmarish daydreams of someone's mind, a hypothesis that matches the contradiction in narrative voice mentioned earlier, and one which Oz's *My Michael*, which I discuss below, takes up explicitly.

It is in this way that interpretive focus is shifted from the national-social register to the psycho-ethical (individual) one. While the former is neutralized in the main narrative, the latter is established by the small plots juxtaposed to the main narrative. I would like to first note that there is a problem with certain traditional critiques of the representation of Arabs in 1960s fiction, when we consider Oz's story. It is sometimes claimed that the figure of the Arab in this period is merely an element of an essentially Jewish-Israel drama (Oppenheimer 212). But Oz's short story, as I tried to argue, does not present the Arab in this way, but rather *reflects on* such use of the Arab as a figure. It is clear that for the kibbutz members, the Bedouins serve as the medium, code, or language through which some psychic dynamic is acted out. Thus, if anything, Oz's short story brings up this tendency for critical reflection, rather than merely expressing it. I raise this issue not in order to take a position on this moralizing register of literary critique, but to pursue a different point altogether: namely that, *for the story itself,* a certain gap exists between explicit literary material and its interpretation. In other words, the story contains—quite consciously—commentary about itself.

Here it is worth pausing to consider just what to make of this formal juxtaposition of big narrative and small narrative, which seem to lead us from realism to psychological symptom? I will try to suggest an answer in what follows. First let us consider some of Oz's other works from the period that reveal the presence of similar formal arrangements. Take, for example, another short story, "Where the Jackals Howl," published around the same time as "Nomad and Viper." Here, again, a strong spatial imagery distinguishes the civilized kibbutz from its natural outside (or, the *symbolic* from the *real*). Here, the division between big and small plots is even more explicit: the main narrative takes place within the kibbutz, telling the story of young Galila's irrational attraction to Damkov, a kibbutz member who represents precisely what is forbidden or frowned upon in the kibbutz (a clear internal-outsider to the kibbutz). Galila's attraction to Damkov is at the center of the main narrative of the story, narrated as some unwanted inevitability, in a similar fashion to the violence between kibbutz members and Bedouins in "Nomad and Viper."

Meanwhile, the small plot takes place outside the kibbutz, and it is not causally related to the chain of events of the main narrative. Jackals rather than people populate it, and the narrator's essayistic tone in these passages, abstracted from the time of the main narrative, again helps set this little plot apart, and suggests that we read it as interpretive reflection. In that small plot, a baited trap attracts a young jackal, despite its vague intimation that there is something dangerous about it. All too late it finds out that it cannot escape the trap ("Where the Jackals Howl" 9–10). This clearly echoes what I have called the articulation of a death-drive above. But here, there is one further elaboration:

> Finally, the others appeared.
> Jackals, huge, emaciated, filthy and swollen-bellied. Some with running sores, others stinking of putrid carrion. One by one they came together from all their distant hiding places, summoned to the gruesome ritual. They formed themselves into a circle and fixed pitying eyes upon the captive innocent. Malicious joy striving hard to disguise itself as compassion, triumphant evil breaking through the mask of mourning. The unseen signal was given, the marauders of the night began slowly moving in a circle as in a dance, with mincing, gliding steps. When the excitement exploded into mirth the rhythm was shattered, the ritual broken, and the jackals cavorted madly like rabid dogs. Then the despairing voices rose into the night, sorrow and rage and envy and triumph, bestial laughter, and a chocking wail of supplication, angry, threatening, rising to a scream of terror and fading again into submission, lament, and silence.
> After midnight they ceased. Perhaps the jackals despaired of their helpless child. (16)

The obvious allegorical function of this small plot is clear: the inter-generational drama in the kibbutz is to be understood along some code of psychic (human) nature, at the core of which lies some attraction to non-symbolic destructiveness, which I earlier called the death-drive. But here, the little plot turns the allegorical screw even tighter: the actions of adults not only do not prevent the child from falling in the trap; rather, they enjoy its desperate suffering, in what is a clear example of the Lacanian jouissance, or excess enjoyment (which, as Žižek argues in "From Desire to Drive: Why Lacan Is Not Lacanian," is strongly related to the death-drive). One immediately includes the human adults in the kibbutz in the same judgment, even if for the kibbutz members, the suffering-jouissance is not expressed explicitly. The pagan ritual is here added as an interpretive valence. Yet it is not a new social perspective, one that stands in opposition to nature, but rather clearly an extension of the latter, a kind of natural religion. I will enlarge on this pivotal interpretive element below, when I discuss Oz's relation to Berdyczewski.

For now, I just want to note that the interpretation offered by this little plot again stands in opposition to the accepted social or national one invoked by the main narrative itself. For Galila's father is something like the kibbutz's ideologue, an ardent Zionist, "forged in fury, in longing and in dedication" ("Where the Jackals Howl" 15). Education and care for the youth is one of his primary roles. And it is the powerlessness of his own Zionist worldview that is dramatized in Galila's attraction to the artist Damkov, who is presented as an anti-Zionist: people "like him, [. . .] know nothing of the longing that burns and the dedication that draws blood from the lips" (15). Thus, just like in "Nomad and Viper," the accepted "social" interpretation—the Zionist one—is neutralized, and a psychological one, invoking a certain sense of human nature, is established in its place.

This is perhaps an apt juncture to briefly address Oz's first novel, *Elsewhere, Perhaps*, published a few years after the short stories. This novel is essentially an expanded version of "Where the Jackals Howl," almost replicating the narrative setup of the short story. The kibbutz's leader is here Reuven Harish, a Zionist worker-intellectual. His daughter, Noga, is attracted to the ominous figure of Ezra Berger. In "Nomad and Viper," the Bedouins, but also Geula, to a lesser extent, provided the occasion for Freudian condensation of what is threatening for the kibbutz members (but not exactly for the narrator). In *Elsewhere, Perhaps*, the two figures are condensed into that of Ezra Berger: a kibbutz insider-outsider—a truck driver, whose figure connotes Arabness (189–94), physical prowess and the animalistic (18–19). But also, by way of his brother, with diasporic Jewishness, queer sexuality, and dominant artistic proclivities (177–78). In the novel, this association of Ezra with what is outside the kibbutz is important. Indeed, it is precisely this externality, of what lies outside the kibbutz, which is the subject matter of the reflections in what I call the little plot in *Elsewhere, Perhaps*. Opening many of the sections of the novel are disembodied reflections on the kibbutz which sometimes seem like a parody of Zionist narration in their strong affirmation of kibbutz as a success, and its celebration of Zionism (Schwartz 235–37). One suspects these are written by Harish himself, but the speaking "we" speaks of Harish in the third person, and thus remains stubbornly behind a protective layer of disembodiment and abstraction from narrative time—just as was the case for the little plots of the short stories.

Right from the start, the little plot establishes the leading opposition for the kibbutz itself: "there is a kind of enmity between the valley with its neat, geometrical patchwork of fields and the savage bleakness of the mountains. Even the symmetrical architecture of Kibbutz Metsudat Ram is no more than a negation of the grim natural chaos that looks down on it from above" (4). And so, what is outside the kibbutz is identified with that which threatens it, for the ideological script that distinguishes the kibbutz (clearly standing for the nation) from its outside (the nation's Other). But as the novel progresses, these musings of the little plot start wandering, almost unconsciously moving beyond the stable interpretive framework it has established between the kibbutz and what is not-it. This wandering ends up neutralizing the stable "social" register of interpretation:

> Our village is encircled. Outside the fence something stirs. If only you could interpret the signs. A snarling menace surrounds the fence trying to penetrate and disrupt our tidy order. Base treason whispers already on the outskirts of the camp. Mute objects mutiny first. In the panting darkness they slowly change their shape. Take on other forms. You look at them, and they seem alien; their angles soften and curve. You look at the trusty bench half hidden, as always, among the flowering shrubs, and you find all its lines altered. You sharpen your gaze and try to put down the treachery, and it intensifies with a snicker. There are no lines to be seen. Only shapes, unconnected shapes, black within black wrapped in black. You fix your eyes on a pleasant arbor, but they seem to detect a cautious movement. Look up at the mighty sky. There, at least, things are as they were. But no. Even above you something is happening. From the top of the water tower a bluish light hits you with a terrifying wink. A spasm has seized dumb objects. They are rebelling against good order. Even the searchlight beam quivers apprehensively. Unruly shadows respond with a riotous dance." (154–55)

And so, what begins as a neat distinction between what is inside the kibbutz from its threatening outside, slowly disintegrates in the mind of the narrator of these small plot sections. The threat that belongs outside creeps into the kibbutz itself in this passage—as internal elements start moving suspiciously for the narrator. Again, the formal similarity to "Nomad and Viper" should be clear: what begins as a description of the external world starts to seem like evidence of some obsession of the narrator, a neurotic symptom of some deeper psychic cause. Again, one finds the double operation that I have been describing: the strategic neutralization of overt "social" interpretive codes—those of the national narrative forms—and their replacement with a psychological-individual one through the allegorical key provided by the little plot. Here, too, a stubborn self-destructiveness, one that does not signify any reason outside itself, seems to be the defining feature of this psychology, or what I have called a death-drive.

I would like to offer one last example, from Oz's novel *My Michael*, published in 1968, which demonstrates the pervasive existence of the plots and the intricate relationship between them. *My Michael* is a significant departure from my previous example not only in that it no longer uses the kibbutz as its main allegorical terrain (the couple at the center of the novel lives in Jerusalem) but that it is narrated through the consciousness of a married woman. As one might expect, here the "social" or national narrative that will be neutralized has less to do with Zionist pioneering ideology. Instead, the urban and (imagined) feminine perspective allows for tackling other collective narrative forms, ones that have to do with the narrative figurative relation between successful heteronormative marriage, motherhood, and the implicit success of nation-building. That the protagonist Hannah Gonen becomes increasingly alienated from her husband and their life together is therefore clearly a challenge to national ideology.

It is easy to distinguish at least several small plots from the main narrative of the novel. Perhaps the most conspicuous of those is the one to which Hannah's thoughts often turn: her relationship to a pair of Arab twins, whom she remembers from her childhood:

> When I was nine I still used to wish I could grow up as a man instead of a woman. As a child I always played with boys and I always read boys' books. I used to wrestle, kick, and climb. We lived in Kiryat Shmuel, on the edge of the suburb called Katamon. There was a derelict plot of land on a slope, covered with rocks and thistles and pieces of scrap iron, and at the foot of the slope stood the house of the twins. The twins were Arabs, Halil and Aziz, the sons of Rashid Shahada. I was a princess and they were my bodyguards, I was a conqueror

and they my officers, I was an explorer and they my native
bearers, a captain and they my crew, a master spy and they
my henchmen. (5)

But what starts as relatively benign memories (because they are safely
contained in the past) of playful gender queering and ethnic mixing,
quickly turns threatening. Right before their wedding, Hannah dreams
that the twins kidnap her, and Michael is unable to help her. The twins'
virility, and a hint of sexual desire strongly dominate the memory: "They
were dark and lithe. A pair of strong gray wolves. 'Michael, Michael,' I
screamed, but my voice was taken from me. I was dumb. A darkness
washed over me. The darkness wanted Michael to come and rescue me
only at the end of the pain and the pleasure" (42). This nightmarish fantasy
keeps developing as the novel progresses, alongside the main narrative:
the twins become inseparable intertwined with fantasies of Jerusalem's
conquest by evil powers, and the sexual significance attached to them is
further developed.

What quickly becomes clear in this example is that national-ideolog-
ical narrative elements are neutralized as literal signifiers, clearly becoming
so many symptoms, indicators of some other problem of which these
narrative elements are mere indirect suggestions. And so, again, we can
discern the double movement generated by the co-presence of the big
plot and little plot: the "social"-national interpretation is neutralized, and
is replaced by a "deeper," hidden one, in which the previous narrative's
elements are its language or code. That this new interpretation seems to
express some destructive primal impulse, or the death-drive is not that
difficult to see. Passages such as the following one, which can be treated
as small plots in their own right, help drive the point home:

> I lie in bed, holding a novel by John Steinbeck which my best
> friend Hadassah brought me when she came to visit me last
> night. [. . .] A fly dashes itself against the windowpane. A fly,
> not a sign and not an omen. Just a fly. I am not thirsty. [. . .]
> At nine o'clock the radio announced: Last night the Israeli
> Defense Forces penetrated the Sinai Desert, captured Kuntilla
> and Ras en-Naqeb. [. . .] A military commentator explained.
> While from the political point of view. Repeated provocations.
> Flagrant violations of the freedom of navigation. The moral
> justification. Terrorism and sabotage. Defenseless women and

children. Mounting tension. Innocent civilians. [. . .] Keep calm.
Stay indoors. Blackout. No hoarding. Obey instructions. The
public is requested. No panic. The whole country is a front.
The whole nation is an army. (209–10)

The feeling we have encountered before of entrapment—and the need
to break through the trap—is here highlighted through the apparently
random mention of the fly dashing itself against the window, and denying
its significance without being asked for either—an answer given without
being asked a question being one way to define a symptom, as Althusser
puts it. But the same feeling is also expressed formally: the broken-up
sentence fragments taken from the radio broadcast are drained of their
literal "social" significance, becoming something like formal imitations of
the fly's repetitive dashing itself against the window—and just like Geula's
repeated attempt to break the bottle in "Nomad and Viper," at the end of
each short sentence one can feel the hope of breaking through.

Until this juncture I have sought to demonstrate how the little
plot provides an interpretive key to the events of the big plot (or main
narrative) in Oz's early fiction. The operation is twofold, I argued: first,
the "social" or national interpretation is neutralized or made ineffective.
Then, a different interpretive register is suggested in the little plots: one
that is strongly psychological, dominated by what the text sees as a kind
of natural or irrationally stubborn drive towards destruction. Were I to
stop at this point, my argument might serve as a minor variant of the
standard understanding of Oz's work: presenting a critique of national
ideology, and a rewriting of Israeli experience in universal human terms.
To that, one could add that the coexistence of dominant and subordinate
plots is something Oz borrows from predecessors such as Agnon, Mendele,
and others (see for example Perry, Shaked, *Omanut Ha-Sipur Shel Agnon*)
who share with Oz commitments seen as antagonistic to national ones.
And so, the formal borrowing from these authors only strengthens the
anti-national interpretation.

This interpretation, however, is a-historical and insensitive to the
periodization of literary forms. One critique that is easy to articulate is
the non-historical view of form: that the same formal structure can mean
different things at different moments, and so Oz's use of a structure could
mean something else from his predecessors'. A related claim only when
modernism stops being a challenge to artistic hegemony, and is adopted
by it instead, becoming a set of sensibilities or artistic tastes in its own

right (Jameson, *Postmodernism, or, The Cultural Logic of Late Capitalism* 4; Jameson, *A Singular Modernity: Essay on the Ontology of the Present* 179; Wegner 20), that one can say that Oz's fragmented, barely narrative, subjects are emblematic of some essential or natural human experience. Therefore, it is necessary to move beyond this reading of Oz, interrogating further its relation to history itself (rather than just in relation to the discursive apprehension of history in Oz's time).

Such a reading of Oz's early work means not only situating it vis-à-vis its discursive context—its rejection of the "social" or national dominant ideology of its moment—which we have already done. Rather, it means to understand this explicit discursive relationship as a way of grasping historical movement, which remains necessarily unrepresentable in global capitalism, as the Marxist interpretive tradition has it. As I have argued above, Oz's fiction posits a necessary distance or gap between overt represented content and what its representation in the work means. And so, I would be respecting the literary works' own logic, rather than violating it, by positing a deeper meaning to be uncovered.

Thus, in the next section of my argument, I will suggest a different social interpretation for Oz's early fiction, which will allow us to understand the small plot's rewriting of literary meaning in terms of psychological death-drive as the result of some loss rather than a liberation from ideological constraints. Two other literary coordinates will help me elucidate the social significance of the pairing of big and small plot, and the interpretive operation this pairing performs. The first of these is Oz's relation to Berdyczewski's work, which other scholars have discussed extensively, and has crucially been acknowledged by the writer himself.[2] The second literary coordinate that is important for my argument is that of 1920s–1940s Zionist realist fiction, the narrative modes of which can be considered Oz's direct object of critique. I will discuss both briefly.

One of the nodes of the considerable commentary on the relation of Oz to Berdyczewski has to do with mythical intertext and its inseparability from some supposed natural or primal human psychic traits (Holtzman and Seymour 151), which are of course closely related to the interpretive code of the little plots I have been describing. To exemplify the relationship here, we can consider Berdyczewski's "The Red Heifer," which includes both of these elements. In the story, hard times have fallen on a small Jewish town. Its residents are divided into two groups: ritual slaughterers and butchers: the ritual slaughterers are described as more pious and well off; while the butchers are poorer, brutish, and less devout, especially when their livelihood is on the line (21–23). Belonging to neither camp is Reuben, an "average fellow," righteous and content, owner of a red cow whose milk production quickly becomes legendary (26). Hard times befall the town, and some of the butchers and slaughterers become jealous of Reuben's luck and piety. They steal his cow and kill it:

> One of the butchers, himself a ritual slaughterer, stood up calmly and sharpened the old blade; he took it out and rubbed its point with his fingernails. Once again, the butchers leaned on the back of the heifer. Some took hold of her thick legs below and above, and two especially strong men twisted her head with incredible might. It was as if doom filled the air, an awful decree of the end of days, and suddenly the butcher who was a slaughterer took up his blade and ran it back and forth across his delicate neck. The heifer let out an earth-shattering groan and blood poured out like a fountain. (27)

The mythical-ritualistic valences should be clear here, and the similarity to the jackals' ritualized revelry is Oz's "Where the Jackals Howl" evident. That those killing the cow are described a few lines later as "priests of Ba'al" (27) only goes to strengthen the mythical-ritualistic meaning. It should also be emphasized that Berdyczewski's story has what I called a little plot of its own: the framing story—which appears in the beginning and end of the story—is where the narrator introduces the townspeople and also discusses Jewish customs and laws. The end of the story, in which the killers' punishment is presented as divine in origin, revisits the same frame of reference (28).

To see how the frame story, and narrative form itself, interprets the events of the story for us (just like in the case of Oz's works discussed earlier), one must turn to the marginalized Marxist understanding of the revival period (*Techia*) in Hebrew literature. The social antagonism in the story is, clearly, class antagonism: the ritual slaughterers are the figure for the dominant class, and the butchers for the subordinate one. Thus, what we see in the story is precisely an encounter between class antagonism, brought about by capitalism's creeping into the Jewish town, and the older Jewish life world. This is precisely what was argued by the Marxist interpreters of the revival literature: in it, we see the shtetl's beliefs and social world encountering capitalist reality (Orbach, "Horata Vehuladeta Shel Habikoret Hare'alistit Ha'ivrit, Part One"; Orbach, "Horata Vehuladeta

Shel Habikoret Hare'alistit Ha'ivrit, Part Two"; Ben Nahum; Banbaji).
Revival Hebrew literature, and not the derivative 1980s pastiches by Meir
Shalev, is essentially the Jewish version of magical realism: that coexistence of older and newer forms of life, which produces the odd pairing of
realism (the literary mode of properly capitalist social form), and Jewish
structure of feeling or belief-world (in which capitalism and commodity
production do not dominate social life), as Jameson argues for the case
of Latin American magic realism ("On Magic Realism in Film" 311).
The presence of ritual, myth, and nature is here the proof of belonging
to that Jewish structure of feeling, invoking not so much its formalized
and codified knowledge, but its informal web of beliefs, prejudices, and
oral knowledge. That the narrator hurriedly mentions rumors, gossip, and
incidents that have no direct bearing on the story strengthens this sense
of belonging to this older (non-capitalist) Jewish life-world. This kind of
narration is common in revival texts—Mendele's narrator's ruminations is
a good example—and continue appearing as late as in Agnon's "Agunot,"
and later in Hazaz's work.

The ultimate referent of antagonism or threat in "The Red Heifer," is
therefore unrepresentable capitalism itself, and its creative-destruction of
social form. The overt antagonisms of the plot—such as the one between
the ritual slaughterers and butchers—are so many forms of grasping the
advent of capitalism and its effects on the shtetl. These explicit antagonisms
are not thereby minimized or reduced away in this reading: rather, these
invented symbolic figurations are essential for perceiving the unrepresentable, which would remain forever beyond reach without these imagined
antagonisms. And they are crucial for the operation of ideology—that
imagined (represented) relations to real (unrepresentable) conditions
of existence, as Althusser puts it (*On the Reproduction of Capitalism*
171–208). The containment of the contradiction or rift in reality is the
divine punishment of the killers of the cow. Thus, the contradictions of
capitalism find their imaginary rest in divine power in Berdyczewski's work.
This solution is of course no longer available for Oz, since precapitalist
Jewish-European life is long gone by the 1960s. I would simply like to
note at this point the dynamic revealed when we look at Berdyczewski's
fiction: the source of social antagonism is clearly the advent of capitalism
and class conflict that it entails.

Here my brief historical survey can turn to Oz's immediate predecessors, those whose writing is supposedly under the spell of the same
ideology that is the target of Oz's writing: the Zionists literary realists that

dominated Hebrew fiction from the 1920s to the mid-1950s.[3] Take, for example, the work of Meir Vilkanski, derided by Shaked and others of Oz's generation as a good exemplar of the reproduction of the so-called Zionist metanarrative against which they were writing. Vilkanski's "Bakhr" follows a group of Zionist immigrant-pioneers, readying a plot of land for cultivation. The story's title is a Hebrew transliteration of the Arabic word for "sea," metaphorically used to designate the undulating landscape of a field ready for cultivation. The adoption of Arabic terms, as Lital Levy argues, was a result of the romanticized admiration of the pioneers for Palestinians (*Poetic Trespass* 30–33). The narrator describes in detail the difficulty of the work, and the group's commitment to it; almost didactically the different skills and practices one must adopt, and competition with Palestinian workers. Ideological debates are common: "And there stood several people heatedly arguing with one of the workers, a disciple of Marx, who is speaking negatively about the valley. Everyone attacks this 'defiler of the bakhr.' Is this a bourgeois business? Are we working for money or in the name of ideals? But this is *bakhr*! Of course, it is *our land*, the land of the people, that we are working! And then talk turns about the additional workers needed for the land" (Vilkanski 11; my translation. Emphasis in the original). All of these contradictions are somehow contained in the short story. But at the end of the story, the hired workers are ordered to leave the field. That opens up an unsurmountable gap or ideological failure: "A warrant came out: go home! We walk slowly through the field, and we are already *outside its pale*. . . . Looking once more at the field, at our bakhr. The farewell is difficult. We had land, and it was taken from under us. We had a fortress, strangers took it. And you pick up the wanderer's staff" (Vilkanski 24; my translation. Emphasis in the original). The enthusiastic "our land" of the first quote suddenly turns out to have been erroneous, the land proving to have not been the workers' after all—in the literal sense. Interestingly, it is those driving them off the land—Zionist landowners—that become "strangers," or some unnamable threat, rather than Palestinian workers or any other antagonistic group encountered in the narrative.

And so, class antagonism—between wage laborers and the bourgeoisie—remains the contradiction under whose sign the story is written. I will not be able to demonstrate here in any detail how this contradiction is reconciled in the writing of the period. I can simply suggest that the ideologeme of work and its relation to making history is what allows for this antagonism to be reconciled in this story as well as many other ones that belong to the Zionist realist camp.[4] Works such as Ever Hadani's *The Wooden Cabin* or Yisrael Zarchi's *Barefoot Days*, written in the 1930s, are good later examples; and earlier work by Moshe Smilansky also exemplifies the same imaginary solution to similar contradictions. Thus, if in Berdyczewski's case, ideological reconciliation depended on divine power, for the early realists, human direct making of history is the active ideology, that which makes it possible to unify reality into a space of action.

But more important than ideological reconciliation for my argument are the social forces that the textual oppositions are able to encompass. I have already argued, following 1950s Marxist criticism of Hebrew literature, that in Berdyczewski's case, it is the entry of capitalism into the small Jewish shtetl that is the unrepresentable process grasped by the text's antagonisms. I can now add a similar argument about early Zionist realism. Even if for a while the Zionist project was a real battleground between socialism and capitalism, what won in the end was capitalism. In hindsight, it becomes clear that the Zionist commitment to work and nation-building actually helped establish capitalism as the dominant social form in Palestine (Ben Porat; Gozansky). To be sure, this process happened behind the backs of the (mostly socialist) believers themselves, as an unintended consequence of their action. Tragically, it was partially socialist aspirations, that brought about the dominance of wage-labor (and thus capitalism) in Palestine, and later Israel.[5]

And so, in the early Zionist realists, the social process undergirding textual oppositions is the emerging dominance of capitalism in Palestine/ Israel. In the cases of both Berdyczewski and that of early Zionist realists, this is not the conscious topic addressed by the text. In both of these, what we can say about them in hindsight could not have even been articulated in their respective contexts, let alone be the explicit subject of representation. But these processes are what is unconsciously and only figuratively expressed in them, nonetheless. And this gap—between overt meaning and unrepresentable referent—is one that literature itself posits, rather than a critical imposition, as I argued above. At this juncture, the significance of my brief exploration of these earlier moments of Hebrew literature for the interpretation of Oz's early work should become evident. That the way of life of older Jewish communities and its structure of feeling is no longer available for Oz is of course clear. Thus, in borrowing from Berdyczewski, the ideological frame that generates closure must be replaced. What takes the place of the life-world of the Jewish community is the psychic frame of Oz's work, that I mentioned earlier. What should be more surprising, however, is that the Zionist realists' ideological solution, that of work's relation to the making of history, is also no longer available in a satisfying way for Oz and his contemporaries. The antagonisms that working "our land" had the power to reconcile for the realists—Jew and Arab, rural Halutz and urbanite, religious and secular, laborer and land-owner, to name just a few examples—can no longer be contained by the same ideological framework.

The important point is, of course, not to debunk these ideologies, but to consider what they make possible. In the cases of both Berdyczewski and the Zionist realists, divine law and the making of history, respectively, allow its contemporaries to grasp something about the transformation of their own social form—the becoming-dominant of capitalism—that is not available to them in any other way. Violence or antagonism in these works is always the result of the destructive forces inherent in the advent of capitalism (the destruction of previous ways of life, but also new class tensions, jealousies, and vengefulness). I have argued that Oz's psychic solution is the equivalent of the ideologemes of divine law and the making of history in the previous moments. Thus, it can be argued that the grounding psychic death-drive in Oz's fiction, that registering of antagonism that is completely stripped from significance, is precisely its way of registering this violence of capitalism. The little plots of Oz's narratives, insofar as they are the ones that rewrite antagonism in terms of this death-drive, are actually a way of preserving the possibility to register the violence of capitalism.

Here it is possible to glimpse the new social interpretation for Oz's fiction that I promised in the beginning of the article, which stands at a remove from its critique of national ideology or the so-called "Zionist metanarrative." The individual-psychic interpretive ground in Oz's early fiction preserves the possibility of registering capitalism's contradictions. In this new social interpretation, the focus on the individual in Oz's work is not some rebuke to collectivity as such; rather, the focus on interiority is precisely the way in which collectivity and its antagonisms are registered. Compared to his predecessors, Oz ideological stand-in for capitalism's con-tradiction is utterly a-historical. Berdyczewski still had Jewish temporality and eschatology, inseparable from divine law; The Zionists realists had the "teleology" of the nation-state or socialist revolution to replace the older divine time with human-made one. But Oz's death-drive has no such explicit temporal or historical content. It is no longer able to project some concrete temporality. It is precisely this absence, this lack of some different time, for which the death-drive's empty destructiveness ultimately stands in; occupying the place of a time-to-come with an empty placeholder.

Notes

1. The concept of the death-drive is introduced by Freud. Slavoj Žižek's elaboration of it is particularly important for my use of it here (Freud; Žižek, *The Most Sublime Hysteric: Hegel with Lacan* 176–82; Žižek, "From Desire to Drive: Why Lacan Is Not Lacanian"; Johnston 187–48).

2. See for example Oz, " 'Ha-Adam Hu Schum Ha-Het ve-Ha-Esh Ha-Atzura Be-Atzmotav' ('A Person Is the Sum of His Sin and the Fire Locked in His Bones')" 30; Ben Mordechai 93–94; Holtzman and Seymour 150–52.

3. See Shaked, *Modern Hebrew Fiction* 44; Gertz 31.

4. A. D. Gordon's anti-socialist "Religion of Work" doctrine is of course the most well-known example of the special place reserved for physical labor in much of the halutzic imaginary. A more contemporary take on this role of work is provided in Boaz Neumann's work. Needless to say, much of the discourse about work was inextricably tied with the substantial socialist tendencies among the halutz movement.

5. I discuss this transition to capitalism at greater length in "Towards a Renewal of Israeli Marxism, or Peace as a Vanishing Mediator." *Mediations*, vol. 32, no. 2, 2019, pp. 71–97.

Works Cited

Althusser, Louis. *On the Reproduction of Capitalism*. Verso, 2013.

Banbaji, Amir. " 'Mifne Shel Shavu'ot Me'atim Shina et Pnei Olamenu Kulo': David Kna'ani Veharealizm Hasotzialisti." *Sifrut Uma'amad: Likrat Histori-yografya Politit Shel Hasifrut Ha'ivrit Hahadasha*. Edited by Amir Banbaji and Hannan Hever. Va Leer Jerusalem Institute; Hakibutz hame'uhad, 2014, pp. 204–31.

Bar Yosef, Hamutal. "Ma'amada Ha-Musari Shel Hashfiyut Be-Yetzirato Shel Amos Oz (On the Moral Significance of Sanity in Amos Oz's Work)." *Sefer Amos Oz (Amos Oz Book)*. Edited by Yitzhak Ben Mordechai and Aharon Komem. Ben Gurion UP, 2000, pp. 41–49.

Barzel, Hillel. *Ha-Me'a Ha-Hatzuya: Mi-Modernizm Le-Post-Modernizm (the Split Century: From Modernism to Post-Modernism)*. Sifriyat Po'alim, 2013.

Ben Mordechai, Yitzhak. "Ha-Tanim ve-Ha-Ra'am: Bein Micha Yosef Berdyczewski Le-Amos Oz (Jackals and Thunder: Between Micha Yosef Berdyczewski and Amos Oz)." *Sefer Amos Oz (Amos Oz Book)*. Edited by Yitzhak Ben Mordechai and Aharon Komem. Ben Gurion UP, 2000, pp. 93–108.

Ben Nahum, Daniel. *Bema'ale Dorot: Iyunim Besifrut Hahaskala*. Sifriyat Po'alim, 1962.

Ben Porat, Amir. *The State and Capitalism in Israel*. Greenwood Press, 1993.

Berdyczewski, Micha Josef. "The Red Heifer." *Reading Hebrew Literature: Critical Discussions of Six Modern Texts*. Edited by Alan Mintz. UP of New England, 2002, pp. 21–28.

Freud, Sigmund. *Beyond the Pleasure Principle*. Dover, 2015.

Gertz, Nurit. *Sifrut ve'ideologia Be'eretz Yisreal Beshnot Hashloshim*. The Open UP, 1988.

Gozansky, Tamar. *Hitpatkhut hakapitalism bepalestina [The Formation of Capitalism in Palestine]*. U of Haifa P, 1986.

Grumberg, Keren. *Place and Ideology in Contemporary Hebrew Literature*. Syracuse UP, 2011.

Hadani, Ever. *Tzrif Ha'etz*. Mitzpe, 1930.

Holtzman, Avner, and Chaim Seymour. "Strange Fire and Secret Thunder: Between Micha Josef Berdyczewski and Amos Oz." *Prooftexts*, vol. 15, no. 2, 1995, pp. 145–62.

Jameson, Fredric. *A Singular Modernity: Essay on the Ontology of the Present*. Verso, 2002.

———. "On Magic Realism in Film." *Critical Inquiry*, vol. 12, 1986, pp. 301–25.

———. *Postmodernism, or, The Cultural Logic of Late Capitalism*. Verso, 1991.

Johnston, Adrian. *A New German Idealism*. Columbia UP, 2018.

Levy, Lital. *Poetic Trespass: Writing between Hebrew and Arabic in Israel/Palestine*. Princeton UP, 2014.

Neumann, Boaz. *Tshukat Hahalutzim*. Am Oved, 2009.

Nir, Oded. "Towards a Renewal of Israeli Marxism, or Peace as a Vanishing Mediator." *Mediations*, vol. 32, no. 2, 2019, pp. 71–97.

Omer-Sherman, Ranen. *Imagining the Kibbutz: Visions of Utopia in Literature and Film*. Pennsylvania State UP, 2015.

Oppenheimer, Yochai. "The Arab in the Mirror: The Image of the Arab in Israeli Fiction." *Prooftexts*, vol. 19, no. 3, 1999, pp. 205–34.

Orbach, Yosef. "Horata Vehuladeta Shel Habikoret Hare'alistit Ha'ivrit, Part One." *Orlogin*, vol. 9, 1953, pp. 166–88.

———. "Horata Vehuladeta Shel Habikoret Hare'alistit Ha'ivrit, Part Two." *Orlogin*, vol. 10, 1953, pp. 75–98.

Oz, Amos. *Elsewhere, Perhaps*. Harcourt Brace Jovanovich, 1973.

———. " 'Ha-Adam Hu Schum Ha-Het ve-Ha-Esh Ha-Atzura Be-Atzmotav' ('A Person Is the Sum of His Sin and the Fire Locked in His Bones')." *Be-or Ha-Tchelet Ha-'aza (Under This Blazing Light)*, Sifriyat Po'alim, 1979, pp. 30–36.

———. *My Michael*. Alfred A. Knopf, 1972.

———. "Nomad and Viper." *Sleepwalkers and Other Stories: The Arab in Hebrew Fiction*. Edited by Ehud Ben Ezer, Lynne Rienner Publishers. 1999, pp. 119–34.

———. "Where the Jackals Howl." *Where the Jackals Howl and Other Stories*, Mariner Books, 2012, pp. 1–20.

Schwartz, Yigal. *The Zionist Paradox: Hebrew Literature and Israeli Identity*. Project MUSE, 2014.

Shaked, Gershon. *Gal khadash basiporet ha'ivrit*. Sifriyat Po'alim, 1971.

———. *Hasiporet Ha'ivrit 1880–1980*. Hakibutz Hame'ukhad, 1993.

———. *Modern Hebrew Fiction*. Indiana UP, 2000.

Smilansky, Moshe. "Zmira." *Sipurim: Mekhaye Hayishuv*, vol. 1, Yavne, 1924, pp. 123–66.

Vilkanski, Me'ir. "The 'Bakhr." *Sipurim Mechaye Ha'aretz*, Kadima Press, 1917, pp. 3–24.

Wegner, Phillip. *Life between Two Deaths: US Culture in the Long Nineties*. Duke UP, 2009.

Zarchi, Yisrael. *Yamim Yekhefim*. Sefer, 1934.

Žižek, Slavoj. "From Desire to Drive: Why Lacan Is Not Lacanian." *No Subject: An Encyclopedia of Lacanian Psychoanalysis*, 1996, https://nosubject.com/Articles/Slavoj_Zizek/why-lacan-is-not-lacanian.html.

———. *The Most Sublime Hysteric: Hegel with Lacan*. Polity, 2014.

Chapter 8

Oz's Literary Genealogies

Salvage Poetics in A Tale of Love and Darkness

SHEILA E. JELEN

On winter evenings a few members of my parents' circle used to get together sometimes at our place or at the Zarchis' in the building across the road: Hayim and Hannah Toren, Shmuel Werses, the Breimans, flamboyant Mr. Sharon-Shvadron, who was a great talker, Mr. Haim Schwarzbaum the-red headed folklorist, Israel Hanani, who worked at the Jewish Agency, and his wife Esther Hananit. They arrived after supper, at seven or half-past, and left at half past nine, which was considered a late hour. In between, they drank scalding tea, nibbled honey cake or fresh fruit, discussed with well-bred anger all kinds of topics that I could not understand; but I knew that when the time came, I would understand them, I would participate in the discussion and would produce decisive arguments that they had not thought of. I might even manage to surprise them, I might end up writing books out of my own head like Mr. Zarchi, or collections of poems like Bialik and Grandpa Alexander and Levin Kipnis and Dr. Saul Tchernikhowsky, the doctor whose smell I shall never forget.

—Amos Oz, *A Tale of Love and Darkness*

Amos Oz's *A Tale of Love and Darkness* (2002), a novel-cum-memoir about growing up in Mandate Palestine and divided Jerusalem as the only son

139

of two European refugees, presents us with a fascinating chiasmus. In it, Oz presents a portrait of the founding fathers of Hebrew literature in a familial light, humanizing them and de-familiarizing them by casting them more as extended family members than as literary models. At the same time, he describes the ways in which his nuclear family, and specifically his late mother, becomes the source of his literary genius even as it fails to nurture him as a son. In this essay I will trace this crossover, from canonic literary genealogy to family and from family to literary genealogy. Through this chiasmus, Oz embraces a woman whose life was defined by her frustrated literary aspirations as his greatest literary influence while refusing to acknowledge the literary giants of Hebrew literature's influence on him as a Hebrew writer of the next generation. This movement from family to text and from text to family branches out in a variety of ways that illuminate the role of women in what seems on the surface to be a misogynist oeuvre, and the role of Eastern Europe in what, on the surface, appears to be the work of the quintessential sabra.

In the generational literary historiography of Israeli belles lettres, Amos Oz has long been identified as a poster boy for the literary gener-ation of *Dor ha-Medinah*, the Statehood Generation of Hebrew writers, who were mostly born in Palestine and whose first language was Hebrew, by and large.[1] Therefore, by genealogical default, Oz, alongside Yaakov Shabtai, A. B. Yehoshua, Yoram Kaniuk, Yehoshua Kenaz, and others,[2] were the natural inheritors of the *Dor ha-Tehiyah*, the Revival Genera-tion of Hebrew writers, who heralded from Eastern Europe. Included in that earlier generation, were Hayim Nachman Bialik, S. Y. Agnon, Saul Tchernichovsky, and Dvora Baron, all of whom immigrated to Palestine in the first half of the twentieth century. Critical lip service is given as well by Israeli literary historiographers to earlier Hebrew writers who did not make it to Palestine but who set the tone and tenor of the Hebrew Revival, most notably S. J. Abramowitz (Mendele), M. Y. Berdyczewski, U. N. Gnessin and M. Z. Feierberg.

With the creation of generations of writers, the canon-makers assign each generation to carry the torch of the generation that came before it. There is, in other words, an implicit understanding that the second generation is, in some way, responsive to the first generation, aligned with it, departing from it in subtle ways that do not negate the sense of indebtedness and influence that drives it. In his study of canonicity in modernist Hebrew poetry, Michael Gluzman discusses inclusion and exclusion at a time of Israeli nation building, paying especially close attention to the different affiliative vectors that grow out of a close analysis of canonic writers' attitudes towards their place in the canon. Instead of fathers and mothers who bequeath literary obligations to their children, he identifies, in the tradition of Russian formalist Victor Shklovsky, the selection of aunts and uncles by the younger generation from among the older generation and beyond.[3] In so doing, Gluzman elaborates on the following questions: Why should literary generations embrace their schematization wholeheartedly? How does accepting one's placement as a generation of inheritors over-determine one's literary path in debilitating ways? How does our reading of writers within canonic genealogies limit the scope of our critical understanding?

More than anything else, *A Tale of Love and Darkness* is a künstler-roman, a novel of artistic becoming. In it, Amos Oz situates himself at a nexus of literary influences that is constituted primarily by two major threads: a familial thread, and a national literary thread. The two, however, as described above, function in a chiastic structure, with the national literary thread taking on a familial genealogical role in his literary conception of himself, and his familial thread taking on the role of literary genealogy. The quote that opened this essay provides a beautiful illustration of the progressive overlap between the familial and the literary threads that Oz introduces in his novel and paves the way for the displacement of the national literary by the familial, to dramatic effect.

In his description of winter nights during his childhood, when his parents got together with neighborhood friends to discuss politics and literature, Oz equalizes well-known literary and lesser-known personalities that populated his early life. Shmuel Werses, the well-known critic of Hebrew and Yiddish literature is placed alongside Dr. Shlomo Breiman, administrator and instructor of modern Hebrew literature at the Hebrew University, and his wife.[4] Hayim Nachman Bialik the foremost Hebrew national poet is situated alongside Grandfather Alexander, who could barely write in Hebrew. And Levin Kipnis, a writer of Hebrew children's books, is aligned with Saul Tchernichovsky, another Hebrew national poet. For the child Oz, Grandfather Alexander was as important a poet as Bialik, and Levin Kipnis was as inspiring an author as Tchernichovsky. The most important indication of Oz's unorthodox equivalencies can be found, however, in the final line of this passage. Tchernichovsky is identified as memorable not by virtue of his poetry, but by virtue of his smell. And this smell keeps returning as Tchernichovsky's leitmotif in Oz's account:

Almost sixty years have gone by, yet I can still remember his smell. I summon it, and it returns to me, a slightly coarse, dusty, but strong and pleasant smell, reminiscent of touching rough sackcloth, and it borders on the memory of the feel of his skin, his flowing locks, his thick mustache that rubbed against the skin of my cheek and gave me a pleasant feeling, like being in a warm dark old kitchen on a winter day. The poet Saul Tchernichovsky died in the autumn of 1943, when I was little more than four years old, so that this sensual recollection can only have survived by passing through several stages of transmission and amplification . . .

> But in the picture in my mind, which my parents' recurrent searchlight beams may have helped me preserve but did not imprint in me, in my scenario, which is less sweet than theirs, I never sat on the poet's lap, nor did I tug at his famous mustache, but I tripped and fell over at Uncle Joseph's home, and as I fell I bit my tongue, and it bled a little, and I cried, and the poet, being also a doctor, a pediatrician, reached me before my parents, helped me up with his big hands, I even remember now that he picked me up with my back to him and my shouting face to the room, then he swung me around in his arms and said something, and then something else, certainly not about handing on the crown of Pushkin to Tolstoy, and while I was still struggling in his arms, he forced my mouth open and called for someone to fetch some ice, then inspected my injury and declared: "It's nothing, just a scratch, and as we are now weeping, so we shall soon be laughing."[5]

As a young child at his Uncle Joseph Klausner's house, Oz fell down. Saul Tchernichovsky, who was visiting Klausner, picked Oz up, held him, comforted him, and reassured the young parents. Oz's association with this great poet of the Hebrew Revival is a familial, domestic one. His memory of him is not text centered, but sense oriented. Oz even goes out of his way to deny any literariness in the encounter, saying that he certainly wasn't discussing Tolstoy or Pushkin with the great poet (the fact that Oz was about three years old probably played a significant role in that discursive choice). Tchernichovsky is embodied as hands, a mustache, a smell. He is a man to the young boy, not a poet. Acknowledging that this memory was certainly influenced by his parents' awed retelling of the day that Oz was scooped up into the great poet's arms, we return to the earlier quote and consider the position of the child protagonist as narrated by the adult. One could argue that Oz, by focusing on the poet's smell, and not his poetry, is only giving us access to the experience of the pre-verbal, or at least the pre-literary, child. But Oz goes out of his way, in further reflections on this experience, to decouple Tchernichovsky from any kind of literary consciousness: "So far as I can remember, no witty aphorism worthy of immortalization was exchanged on that occasion between the giant among the poets of the formative Generation of National Revival and the sobbing little representative of the later so-called Generation of the State of Israel."[6] In this passage, Oz acknowledges Tchernichovsky's literary identity, but he denies any kind of passing of the torch. Even as he names their canonic literary positions with respect to one another Oz repudiates that relationship. In a final statement on Tchernichovsky, Oz elaborates on his identity vis-à-vis Oz as a fatherly, comforting figure, but not necessarily as a writer:

> It was only two or three years after this incident that I managed to pronounce the name Tchernichovsky. I was not surprised when I was told that he was a poet: almost everyone in Jerusalem in those days was either a poet or a writer or a researcher or a thinker or a scholar or a world reformer . . . But he was not just any old doctor or poet. He was a pediatrician, a man with a disheveled mop of hair, with laughing eyes, big warm hands, a thicket of a mustache, a felt cheek, and a unique, strong, soft smell. To this day, whenever I see a photograph or drawing of the poet Saul or his carved head that stands in the entrance of the Tchernichovsky Writers' House, I am immediately enveloped, like the embrace of a winter blanket by his comforting smell.

Here, Oz first minimizes Tchernichovsky's stature by asserting that during his childhood everyone in Jerusalem was some kind of intellectual (a poet, a writer, a researcher, etc.). Then he downplays the importance of being a poet altogether saying that "he was not just any old doctor or poet." Although we would expect Oz to say: "He was Tchernichovsky!" instead, he says, "He was a pediatrician . . ." as if being a children's doctor is what made him special to the exclusion of all else. Also, characterizing him by his smell, his size, his body, his warmth, Oz does not represent him literarily. Even the final statement: "to this day . . ." addresses Tchernichovsky on the basis of photographs, drawings, and sculpture, not on the basis of language. And what do these images bring up for Oz? "I am immediately enveloped like the embrace of a winter blanket by his comforting smell." As before, this is clearly a fusion of Oz's parents' association with Tchernichovsky as a literary giant, and his childhood reminiscences of him as simply a man, or even a kind of parent—comforting, sentient, warm. It seems that Oz assigns to Tchernichovsky the role that he would normally assign to a mother—nurturing him after a fall.

Tchernichovsky is not the only canonic Revival writer that Oz neutralizes and de-familiarizes by bringing him into the familial fold. In describing his father's father, Alexander Klausner, Oz brings him into a circle of literati, with unexpected results:

> As he made his way around the sun washed streets of Odessa, a harbor town with a heady atmosphere colored by the presence of several different nationalities, he made friends of various kinds, courted girls, bought and sold and sometimes made a profit, sat down in a corner of a café or on a park bench, took out his notebook, wrote a poem (four stanzas, eight rhymes), then cycled around again as the unpaid errand boy of the leaders of the Lovers of Zion society in pre telephone Odessa: carrying a hasty note from Ahad ha'am to Mendele Mokher Seforim or from Mendele Mokher Seforim to Mr. Bialik, who was fond of saucy jokes, or to Mr. Menachem Ussishkin, from Mr. Ussishkin to Mr. Lilienblum, and while he waited in the drawing room or the hall for the reply, poem in Russian in the spirit of the Love of Zion Movement played in his heart.[7]

Who from the generation of the Revival doesn't Grandfather Alexander hang around with in Odessa? He seems to have been something of an intimate with Bialik, Mendele, Ussishkin, Lilienblum and even Ahad ha'am! But Grandfather Alexander whom we encountered in the opening passage cited above as a counterpoint to Tchernichovsky himself only writes in Russian! Grandfather Alexander, in other words, claims an association with these writers, but not on literary terms by any means. By associating in this intimate way with the Hebrew greats, Grandfather Alexander becomes one of them, as it were, and they become a part of Oz's family. This pattern of naturalizing, de-familiarizing and rendering familial the giants of the Hebrew Revival continues with Bialik:

Once, it may have been in the late 1950s, a brand new ten-lira note came into circulation bearing a picture of the poet Bialik. When I got hold of my first Bialik note, I hurried straight to Grandpa's to show him how the state had honored the man he had known in his youth. Grandpa was indeed excited, his cheeks flushed with pleasure, he turned the note this way and that, held it up to the lightbulb, scrutinized the picture of Bialik (who seemed to me suddenly to be winking mischievously at Grandpa as if to say "Nu!?"). A tiny tear sparkled in Grandpa's eye, but while he reveled in his pride, his fingers folded the new note and tucked it away in the inside pocket of his jacket. Ten liras was a tidy sum at that time, particularly for a kibbutznik like me. I was startled: "Grandpa, what are you doing? I only brought it to show you and to make you happy. You'll get one of your own in a day or two, for sure." "Nu," Grandpa shrugged, "Bialik owed me twenty-two rubles."[8]

The young Oz excitedly shares the new currency with his grandfather Alexander because he knows about Grandfather Alexander's association with Bialik. And how does Grandfather Alexander relate to this recognition of the icon that is Bialik? He calls in his debts. Not only does this vignette domesticate Bialik, as was the case with Tchernichovsky in Uncle Joseph's house, but it renders Bialik somewhat ridiculous.

Another instance of this familial connection with the tradition established by Oz can be found in a reference to a literary salon established by Oz's grandmother Shlomit, his father's mother and Grandfather Alexander's wife, in Odessa:

Occasionally Bialik would drop in for an evening, pale with grief or shivering with cold and anger—or quite the contrary: he could also be the life and soul of the party. "And how!" said my grandmother, "Like a kid he was! A real scalawag! No hold barred! So risqué . . ."

The poet Tchernichovsky, too, might burst into the salon, flamboyant but shy, passionate yet prickly, conquering hearts, touching in his childlike innocence, as fragile as a butterfly but also hurtful, wounding people left, right and center without even noticing . . .

Tchernichovsky stoked his spirits with a *glazele* or two of vodka, and sometimes he would start to read those poems of his that overflowed with hilarity or sorrow and made everybody in the room melt with him and for him: his liberal ways, his flowing locks, his anarchic mustache, the girls he brought with him, who were not always too bright, and not even necessarily Jewish, but were always beauties who gladdened every eye and caused not a few tongues to wag and whetted the writers' envy—"I'm telling you as a woman (grandma again), women are never wrong about such things, Bialik used to sit and stare at them like this . . . and at the goyish girls he brought along . . . Bialik would have given an entire year of his life if only he could have lived for a month as Tchernichovsky."[9]

Ventriloquizing his grandmother in her description of Tchernichovsky and Bialik, we see another form of domestication. Bialik, morose, depressed, and jealous of his fellow poet's sexual prowess and masculinity is described in keeping with Oz's father's and uncle's favoring of Tchernichovsky's "masculine" poetry as opposed to Bialik's "effeminate" poetry. This view of these famous poets as squabbling teenaged boys from Oz's grandmother Shlomit's perspective illuminates a further aspect of the kind of defamiliarization and familial domestication that Oz performs on the writers of the Revival.

Rather than just referring to him in passing over and over again, Uncle Joseph Klausner deserves some in-depth treatment here as we discuss the genealogical chiasmus between literary generation and family. Uncle Joseph was a famous member of early Zionist literati on the Yishuv and played a major role in Oz's sense of both his family and his literary development. His grandfather Alexander's brother, Joseph Klausner, was a historian of the Revival, curating and cultivating a nationalist literary and political discourse in the milieu of European-born scholars at the Hebrew University in the early decades of the twentieth century. Twice a month, or so, Oz as a young child, along with his parents would walk on Saturday afternoon across Jerusalem from Kerem Avraham to Talpiot, where Klausner lived, and there he would observe the cult of personality that surrounded his uncle. Within the context of actual familial ties, Uncle Joseph did very little to further the aspirations and ambitions of his nephew, Oz's father Aryeh Leib Klausner, who sought an academic post in literature at the Hebrew University: "While Uncle Joseph definitely encouraged my father, who was one of his star pupils, he never chose him, when the time came, as a teaching assistant, so as not to give malicious tongues anything to wag about. So important was it for Professor Klausner to avoid aspersions on his good name that he may have behaved unfairly to his brother's son, his own flesh and blood."[10] At this interesting interlude in the text, we see that family does not guarantee literary continuity; Oz indicates here, in his presentation of Joseph Klausner, that family associations with great literary figures may actually impede one's literary progress. Therefore, all the work Oz has done to establish his familial connection to Bialik, Tchernichovsky, et al. has accomplished the opposite of what one would expect. Their familial relationship with him, as he depicts it, is not in any way meant to indicate a furtherance of his career. While relating to his father throughout the memoir as a somewhat limited man, Oz does sympathize with him in this, among other arenas.

The Generation of the Revival is presented by Oz as intimately intertwined with his family. Grandpa Alexander was buddies with Bialik and knew Lilienblum intimately. Grandma Shlomit understood the animosity between Bialik and Tchernichovsky from the perspective of a woman with a husband and two sons who was deeply familiar with the ways of men. Tchernichovsky's smell remains with Oz from childhood. Joseph Klausner, on the other hand, his actual uncle, demonstrated very little warmth, very little allegiance toward his own family members. He was so enamored with himself he couldn't see a way to assist his nephew's suffering—something that was eminently within his power. All this is to say that Oz explicitly develops a literary genealogy in *A Tale of Love and Darkness* that does not take us in an expected direction; Oz does not admit any serious literary allegiance to most of the Revival Generation.[11] With the exception of Y. H. Brenner and S. Y. Agnon whom he begrudgingly acknowledges as literary influences, Oz seeks his inspiration elsewhere.

But what of Oz's actual familial genealogy and its impact on his writing life? Certainly, Klausner's impact was one of alienation. In Oz's own preference for Brenner and Agnon, he rejects his uncle's evaluation of writers who were "stuck in the diaspora," who cried and moaned and engaged in sophistry and solipsism, as he saw it. Oz's father's variation on this theme is described in the book in the following way:

> My father, who at Agnon's request translated the article "Buczacz" for him from a Polish encyclopedia when Agnon was writing *A City and the Fullness Thereof*, would twist his lips as he defined him as a "Diaspora Writer,": his stories lack

wings, he said, they have no tragic depth, there is not even
any healthy laughter but only wisecracks and sarcasm. And
if he does have some beautiful descriptions here and there,
he does not rest or put down his pen until he has drowned
them in pools of verbose buffoonery and Galician cleverness.
I have the impression my father saw Agnon's stories as an
extension of Yiddish literature and he was not fond of Yiddish
literature. In keeping with his temperament of a nationalistic
Lithuanian *Misnaged*, he loathed magic, the supernatural and
excessive emotionalism, anything clad in foggy romanticism
or mystery, anything intended to make the senses whirl or
to blinker reason—until the last years of his life when his
tastes changed.[12]

When Oz was a child, then, it seems that he was a champion of the
negation of the diaspora. Even so, it must be noted that his uncle, Joseph
Klausner, promoted Zalman Schneour (1887–1959), a Hebrew and Yiddish
poet who never lived in Palestine or Israel. Uncle Joseph also rarely, if
ever, wrote about Hebrew writers active in Palestine. Just as Oz tempers
his representation of his father's dislike for Agnon by acknowledging
that his attitude toward Yiddish and the diaspora changed at the end of
his life (in fact, he ultimately wrote his dissertation, in London, on Y. L.
Peretz), it is important to view the anti-diasporic rhetoric Oz remembers
from his family members during childhood, with a grain of salt.[13] These
champions of the "New Jew" came from Europe. They were educated
in European universities. They were raised in European languages. Oz's
familial genealogy was a European genealogy.

It is this genealogy outside of Palestine and Israel, outside of the
Revival Generation, which we will consider as we continue our discussion
of the familial/literary chiasmus we have been tracing here. Amos Oz's
family—mainly his mother, as we will discuss—created the central axis of
his literary consciousness. In a 2010 review essay on *A Tale of Love and
Darkness* and S. Yizhar's *Preliminaries*, I focused on the European background that both authors acknowledge in their late life novel-cum-memoirs.
There I argued that:

> In *A Tale of Love and Darkness* and *Preliminaries*, Oz and
> Yizhar negotiate the countervailing powers of the self and the
> nation, depicting their psychological development alongside

the political development of the State of Israel whose heavy
mantle they were forced, as the children of Zionist idealists
(to a greater or lesser degree), to bear. Implicit in each text
is a profound awareness of the burdens of growing up as a
first-generation Israeli with spiritual and intellectual leanings
toward a kind of aesthetic and consciousness that cannot
be confined to a single landscape or a single language. Each
of these writers, reflecting on his position as a native-born
"Eretz-Israeli" Jew to East European immigrants within an
imminent Israeli landscape, plays with the expectations heaped
upon him—the embodiment of the Zionist ideal—against a
backdrop of longing (as in Yizhar's case) or ambivalence (as
in Oz's case) for broader, richer, and more culturally resonant
European homelands left behind.[14]

Written as I was just beginning to conceive of my notion of "salvage poetics"
or the poetics that grow out of post-Holocaust works that attempt to wed
ethnography and art in order to "salvage" the remains of the destroyed
culture of Jewish Eastern Europe, my essay on Yizhar and Oz gingerly
approached the possibility that these poster children for the Generation
of the State were "returning" to their European origins late in their lives
just as S. Ansky, the great ethnographer of the Pale, "returned" to Judaism
after a failed attempt to join the Russian socialists, or Vladimir Medem,
baptized at birth, "returned" to Judaism when he formed the Jewish Bund.[15]
In all these cases, what we observe is a "return" to a culture and a means
of acknowledging that culture as a turning point in these men's careers.
For Ansky it was ethnographic, for Medem it was political, and for Oz it
was literary. What are the parameters of Oz's particular return to Europe
in *A Tale of Love and Darkness*?

As we continue our exploration of the different types of genealogies
developed by Oz in *A Tale of Love and Darkness* (particularly the fact
that he designates the literary generation preceding his as members of
his family), I would like to posit here that his mother, whom he lost as
a child to suicide, becomes the key figure in his literary genealogy. His
mother, in other words, takes on the role of a literary predecessor without
any of the maternal qualities you would expect to see in his description
of her, while figures like Tchernichovsky take on a maternal role, with
his pungent smell, his warm hands, and his ability, as we saw earlier, to
comfort and heal. Fania Mussman is at the center of a constellation of

forces that come together for Oz as he engages in his own sort of salvage poetic in *A Tale of Love and Darkness*.

What is Oz salvaging? Eran Kaplan argues that *A Tale of Love and Darkness* serves as a kind of found text on Zionism's formative years both in Europe and Jerusalem as told by Oz. Citing Yigal Schwartz, Kaplan says:

> Throughout most of his artistic and public career, Oz occupied a prominent place at the forefront of Israeli high art. He was one of the main pieces on exhibit on the Israeli artistic and intellectual scene. But, as Schwartz has revealed, for many readers of *A Tale of Love and Darkness* it is the real objects and real places described in the book that have registered most deeply with them. As opposed to traditional novels (including Oz's own earlier work), Oz does not draw on personal memories or the memory of personal objects in order to take them on a psychological journey with universal (middle-class) insights. Rather, Oz seems to lead his readers to specific memories and objects that serve as modern-day talismans to a specific social group.[16]

In a similar vein, Iris Milner views this book as part of the "back to our roots" movement that contemporary Israelis, many of whose grandparents Hebraized their names upon emigrating from Europe and spoke only Hebrew to their children, are now promulgating.[17] *A Tale of Love and Darkness* was thus written at a moment when it became acceptable to reclaim one's European roots, and provided a portrait of first generation Israelis for their children and grandchildren. Centered as it is in Jerusalem of the 1940s, however, it presents a very particular spin on European culture, one that is geographically situated in the Promised Land even as it provides windows into the world that preceded it. Irving Howe in his depiction of nineteenth-century East European Jewish culture in his 1976 American classic *World of Our Fathers*, situates his overview of that world primarily on the Lower East Side, or the New York in which Howe himself was introduced to that culture through his family home and his parents' generation.[18] Oz too, through his rich description of Jerusalem, and his anchoring of his background storytelling about his grandparents within that milieu, uses a similar strategy. He introduces us to European Jewry through his accounts of the early Israelis in his own family who came from that world and raised him in Jerusalem.

In addition to the culture of Zionism in Jerusalem, on the Yishuv, and in Europe between the World Wars, Oz is salvaging, it would seem, the stories told over and over again by his mother to Oz as a child. Of this, Oz remarks: "I spent my whole childhood in Kerem Avraham in Jerusalem, but where I really lived was on the edge of the forest, by the huts, the steppes, the meadows, the snow in my mother's stories, and in the illustrated books that piled up on my low bedside table: I was in the east, but my heart was in the farthermost west. Or the 'farthermost north,' as it said in those books."[19] Many critics have acknowledged the role of Oz's mother in his literary psyche, particularly in his early works, which grapple with depressed young women in soulless marriages (Hannah Gonen in *My Michael*, Mrs. Kipnis in *The Hill of Evil Counsel*), but very few have acknowledged the active place of his mother's stories, her storytelling, within his literary genealogy. There are countless descriptions throughout *A Tale of Love and Darkness* of the stories that Oz's mother told him during his childhood and the impact they had on him: "My mother liked telling me stories about wizards, elves, ghouls, enchanted cottages in the depths of the forest, but she also talked to me seriously about crimes, emotions, the lives and sufferings of brilliant artists, mental illness, and the inner lives of animals."[20] Elsewhere, Oz acknowledges the fear that his mother's stories instilled in him: "Surely my mother would never have been so crazy as to tell a horrible story like that to a four or five year old child?"[21] But he forgives her and embraces these stories immediately after this assertion:

> My mother's stories may have been strange, frightening, but they were captivating, full of caves and towers, abandoned villages and broken bridges suspended above the void. Her stories did not begin at the beginning or conclude with a happy ending but flickered in the half light, wound around themselves, emerged from the mists for a moment, amazed you, sent shivers up your spine, then disappeared back into the darkness before you had time to see what was in front of your eyes.
>
> Her stories were full of blackberries, blueberries, wild strawberries, truffles, and mushrooms. With no thought for my tender years, my mother took me to places where few children had ever trodden before, and as she did so, she opened up before me an exciting fan of words, as though she were picking me up in her arms and raising me higher and higher to reveal vertiginous heights of language.[22]

Oz's mother is said by Oz to have spent her free time reading Turgenev, Chekov, Agnon, and Gnessin. One of the ways that Oz is able to describe her descent into despair and depression is evident when she stops reading. She sits by the window with a book, upside down in her lap, and she gazes outside. But the stories she tells her young child are not drawn from the classic belle lettres of European literature. They are folktales and fairy tales, tales of the European landscape and its ghosts and sorcerers. Even the stories that she told Oz about her own life, and the stories her sister Sonia told Oz about her upbringing alongside Fania in Rovno, all resembled these ghost stories and folktales. The house they lived in was inhabited by a variety of different personages—mainly mothers and daughters—who had been abandoned by men and lived beneath the radar of society. They subsisted in quiet desperation like madwomen in the attic. It was unclear where their income came from, and they created an undercurrent in the house of dark brooding and salaciousness.

This brings to mind Art Spiegelman's meditation in *Maus*, on the loss of his mother's wartime diaries. After her suicide when Spiegelman was in his early twenties, his father, in a fit of grief and rage, destroyed her diaries. Thus, the only stories we know about Spiegelman's mother's experience during the war, because she refused to speak of it to Art, have to be mediated by his father's stories. Art turns on his father when he hears of what his father has done to his mother's diaries, and calls him "murderer," which to some extent he is, having taken Art's mother's story—all that is left of her after her death—and destroyed it.[23] Here, in Oz's recollections of the stories his mother told him as a child, we hear a kind of abstracted variation on her life. We see the resemblance between the folktales she used to tell him when he was a child and the stories about her that Aunt Sonia told Oz when he was an adult—stories of magic and the fears it invokes, of grief and the possibilities it inspires. These stories are all Oz has left of his mother and to a large extent their tonalities—the darkness, the emotionality, the lyricism—make their way into his work, particularly in his meditations on Jerusalem—a dark divided space caught up in the emotions of its inhabitants,[24] or in his depictions of despair and madness in both his Jerusalem works as well as his kibbutz works. He is not only salvaging his mother's stories in *A Tale of Love and Darkness*, but he is also salvaging the language she bequeathed to him, the tone, and tenor of psychological despair and unexplored landscapes which "reveal" to him "the vertiginous heights of language."

Robert Alter, in his reading of this book, beautifully correlates two scenes that further illuminate this understanding of the place of Oz's mother within Oz's literary genealogy. The first he identifies as the scene of inspiration where the child Oz recognizes his calling as a writer:

> You will never forget this evening: you are only six or at most six and a half, but for the first time in your little life something enormous and very terrible has opened up for you, something serious and grave, something that extends from infinity to infinity and it takes you, and like a mute giant it enters you and opens you, so that you too for a moment seem wider and deeper than yourself, and in a voice that is not your voice but may be your voice in thirty or forty years' time, in a voice that allows no laughter or levity, it commands you never to forget a single detail of this evening: remember and keep its smells, remember its body and light, remember its birds, the notes of the piano, the cries of the crows and all the strangeness of the sky running riot from one horizon to the other before your eyes, and all of this is for you, all strictly for the attention of the addressee alone.
>
> . . . slowly there descends over all a deep dim blue gray color like the color of silence with a smell like that of the repeated notes on the piano, climbing and stumbling over and over again up a broken scale, while a single bird answers with the five opening notes of Für Elise: Ti-da-di-da-di.[25]

Oz, like many other child protagonists in classic künstlerromans, has an epiphanic moment in which his vocation becomes clear. Here, for Oz, it is the environment in which he grew up, the East European smells and tastes and sounds of immigrant Jerusalem that will inspire him. But this moment of inspiration does not end here, Alter points out. In the very last lines of *A Tale of Love and Darkness*, after his mother's suicide, Oz invokes a bird, Elise:

> My mother fell asleep, and this time she slept with no nightmares, she had no insomnia, in the early hours she threw up and fell asleep again, still fully dressed, and because Tzvi and Haya were beginning to suspect something, they sent for an

ambulance a little before sunrise, and two stretcher bearers carried her carefully, so as not to disturb her sleep, and at the hospital she would not listen to them either, and although they tried various means to disturb her good sleep, she paid no attention to them, or to the specialist from whom she had heard that the psyche is the worst enemy of the body, and she did not wake up in the morning either, or even when the day grew brighter, and from the branches of the Ficus tree in the garden of the hospital the bird Elise called to her in wonderment and called to her again and again in vain, and yet it went on trying over and over again, and it still tries sometimes.[26]

Oz's re-creation, from his imagination, of his mother's last night and last morning is marked by the same song he heard during his epiphany: Für Elise. Oz ends the book in the present, with himself listening to the song he heard at those two watershed moments in his life—his vocational epiphany and his mother's death. The two are intimately connected in his life, not simply because of the trauma, but because his mother opened his eyes to language and made him the writer that he is.

This attention to the mysteries of language as rendered in the words of an important female figure in his life is duplicated in his lyrical homage to the poet Zelda, one of his earliest teachers and a crossover figure for Oz who inhabits both a familial and a literary genealogy. Of her, he says: "She would call stars the 'stars of heaven,' the abyss was 'the mighty abyss,' and she spoke of 'turbid rivers' and 'nocturnal deserts.' If you said something in class that she liked, Teacher Zelda would point to you and say softly: 'Look all of you there's a child who's flooded with light.'"[27] While Zelda may have been speaking lyrically, she may also have been speaking archaically, being as she was an orthodox Jew from Eastern Europe who made her home in Jerusalem writing poetry and teaching children. She found her spoken idiom, like those writers of the Enlightenment and the Revival, in texts and she turned it into a kind of poetic vernacular. But there is more to the charms of Zelda for Oz than that. She opens the world of the Revival writers to him in a literary way that no one else ever could, not even his grandfather Alexander and Uncle Joseph and Grandmother Shlomit who hobnobbed with those very writers. In describing the way that he and his friends stayed at school for hours upon hours beyond the end of the school day to hear Zelda tell stories, Oz uses the language of Bialik himself: "we seemed forgotten under the wings of teacher Zelda's stories."[28]

Even while providing a link to the writers of the European Revival, Zelda, in Oz's narrative, is enveloped within a domestic economy as well, like Tchernichovsky whose warmth and comforting smell Oz remarks upon throughout the book. The summer after second grade, he wanted to spend as much time with her as possible and tells us, "I had willingly volunteered to help her with her morning chores. I ran off to the shops for her, swept the yard, watered her geraniums, hung her little washing out on the line and brought in the clothes that had dried . . ."[29] In representing his participation in her domestic life, Agnon brings her into the genealogy of Bialik and Tchernichovsky, Ahad ha-Am and Mendele, humanizing her and defamiliarizing her. But he also characterizes her in keeping with the way he characterizes his mother, as someone whose language excited and inspired him, who shared orally a European corpus of literature that would have a lasting effect on his writing: "She would read to me what she might have been intending to read anyway that morning: Hasidic tales, rabbinic legends, obscure stories about holy kabbalists who succeeded in combining the letters of the alphabet and working wonders and miracles . . . day by day she raised the crossbar of my comprehension. I remember, for example, that she told me about Bialik, about his childhood, his disappointments, and his unfulfilled yearnings."[30]

Whereas the corpus his mother introduced him to were fairy and folk tales from Europe, Zelda, a cousin of the Lubavitcher Rebbe, Menachem Mendel Schneerson, introduced him to a different body of work—the work of Hassidut, of rabbinic legend, and the Zohar. Emerging from a wholly secular family, Oz's exposure to these texts in oral form "raised the crossbar of his comprehension" and impacted his choice of theme and language immeasurably. Like his mother, Zelda was able to communicate her rarefied experience of the Hebrew language to the young boy:

> Teacher Zelda also revealed a Hebrew language to me that I had never encountered before, not in Professor Klausner's house or at home or in the street or in any of the books I had read so far, a strange, anarchic Hebrew, the Hebrew of stories of saints, Hasidic tales, folk sayings, Hebrew leavened with Yiddish, breaking all the rules, confusing masculine and feminine, past and present, pronouns and adjectives, a sloppy even disjointed Hebrew. But what vitality those tales had! In a story about snow, the writing itself seemed to be formed of icy words. In a story about fires, the words themselves blazed. And what a strange, hypnotic sweetness there was in her tales

about all sorts of miraculous deeds! As though the writer had dipped his pen in wine: the words reeled and staggered in your mouth.[31]

In an interview published in *The New Yorker*, Oz discusses his lifelong fascination with the limitations of language as tools for the mimetic representation of human experience, particularly in a Hebrew idiom that is still, to this day, developing vernacular muscles.[32] Having been raised only in Hebrew when his father was proficient in seventeen languages and his mother in eight, he had always felt the pinch of the limitations of his native tongue. When asked, however, in the pages of *The Paris Review* why he chose to write in Hebrew, Oz scoffs at the absurdity of the question.[33] How could he write in any other language? Hebrew is his native tongue, he says. But that doesn't mean that he is impervious to the power of other languages, to the possibility of language taking on a kind of sentience that Hebrew in the early days of its revival may not have possessed. Zelda's Yiddish inflections and presentation of language that was gleaned from religious texts taught him about Hebrew's "echo chamber," about the possibilities inherent in this ancient language that could be put to good vernacular literary use.[34]

Like Zelda and his mother, there was one other figure who played an important role in Oz's journey beyond the state of Israel and the limitations imposed on him by the expected literary genealogies. S. Y. Agnon was central to Oz's consciousness of his writer's vocation. As a child he would visit Agnon with his parents after having spent Saturday afternoons at his uncle's literary salons (Agnon lived next door). In contrast to Tchernichovsky, Bialik, and Mendele, Agnon was not incorporated by Oz into the Klausner extended family in *A Tale of Love and Darkness*. We have already seen how Agnon was viewed by Oz's father, and by extension, his Uncle Joseph Klausner from whom Oz's father gleaned his political and literary sensibilities—he was seen as fatally "diasporic" or European in style and theme. What, however, did Oz's mother think of Agnon? Oz's description of his mother's feeling about Agnon is as follows:

"That man sees and understands a lot."

And once she said:

"He may not be such a good man, but at least he knows bad from good, and he also knows we don't have much choice."

She used to read and reread the stories in the collection *At the Handles of the Lock.* I too sometimes reread the words of Tirtzah Mazal, née Minz, at the beginning of In the Prime of her Life: "In the prime of her life my mother died. Some one and thirty years of age my mother was at her death. Few and evil were the days of the years of her life. All the day she sat at home and she never went out of the house. . . . Silent stood our house in its sorrow; its doors opened not to a stranger. Upon her bed my mother lay, and her words were few."[35]

Oz's mother, described in the book as having been an astute observer of the human character, saw in Agnon a kindred spirit. His stories were distinguishing by psychological depth even when rendered in a pseudo-folk idiom that would seem anathema to that kind of depth. In Agnon's *bi-Dmey Yamehah,* the story of a young mother's death after having found very little emotional satisfaction in life, Oz finds an appropriate literary means of expressing the angst and sadness of his mother's life. Indeed, Agnon himself, in a letter to Oz, refers to Oz's mother in the language of *bi-Dmey Yamehah:* "She stood upon the doorstep, and her words were few."[36]

Oz discusses having resisted his intense attraction to Agnon's oeuvre in the following way:

For several years I endeavored to free myself from Agnon's shadow. I struggled to distance my writing from his influence, his dense ornamented, sometimes Philistine language, his measured rhythms, a certain midrashic self-satisfaction, a beat of Yiddish tunes, juicy ripples of Hasidic tales. I had to liberate myself from the influence of his sarcasm and wit, his baroque symbolism, his enigmatic labyrinthine games, his double meanings and his complicated, erudite literary games.

Despite all my efforts to free myself from him, what I have learned from Agnon no doubt still resonates in my writing.

What is it, in fact, that I learned from him? Perhaps this. To cast more than one shadow. Not to pick the raisins from the cake. To rein in and polish pain. And one other thing, that my grandmother used to say in a sharper way than I have found it expressed by Agnon: "If you have no more tears left to weep, then don't weep. Laugh."[37]

In this description we see traces of his attraction as well to Zelda—in her Yiddish and her hassidut—and to his mother, in her casting of shadows, in her polishing of pain. Agnon is the one canonic writer, the one Revival writer that he could not push out of his literary genealogy and into the Klausner family clan. Rather, Agnon comes to be included, in *A Tale of Love and Darkness*, in the constellation of women who introduced the joys and mysteries of language into his writerly soul.[38] Indeed, when we consider Agnon's alliance in Oz's literary universe with his mother and Zelda, we can't help but consider Oz's complicated engagement with women in *A Tale of Love and Darkness*.

Both Karen Grumberg and Natasha Wheatley discuss the place of women in Oz's corpus, with Grumberg discussing Oz's attempt to exorcise his mother's ghost in *A Tale of Love and Darkness* and Wheatley discussing Oz's pained approach to memory in a memorable passage wherein memory is an old female friend who approaches him and medusa-like tries to attack him.[39] Writing is his form of resistance, the only way he can get away from her:

> It's like a some woman you have known for a long time, you no longer find her attractive or unattractive, whenever you bump into each other she always says more or less the same few worn-out words, always offers you a smile, always taps you on the chest in a familiar way, only now only this time she doesn't, she suddenly reaches out and grabs your shirt, not casually but with all her claws, lustfully, desperately, eyes tight shut, her face twisted as though in pain, determined to have her own way, determined not to let go, she doesn't care any more about you, about what you are feeling, whether or not you want to, what does she care, now she's got to, she can't help herself, she reaches out now and strikes you like a harpoon and starts pulling and tearing you but actually she's not the one who's pulling, she just digs her claws in and you're the one who's pulling and writing, pulling and writing, like a dolphin with the barb of the harpoon caught in his flesh and he pulls as hard as he can, pulls the harpoon and the line attached to it and the harpoon gun that's attached to the line and the hunter's boat that the harpoon gun is fixed to, he pulls and struggles, pulls to escape, pulls and turns over and over in the sea, pulls and dives down into the dark depths, pulls

and writes and pulls more; if he pulls one more time with all his desperate strength he may manage to free himself from the thing that is stuck in his flesh, the thing that is biting and digging into you and not letting go, you pull and pull and it just bites into your flesh, the more you pull the deeper it digs in and you can never inflict a pain in return for this loss that is digging deeper and deeper, wounding you more and more because it is the catcher and you are the prey, it is the hunter and you are the harpooned dolphin, it gives and you have taken, it is that evening in Jerusalem and you are in this evening here in Arad, it is your dead parents and you just pull and go on writing.[40]

In this passage, Oz fights off a female aggressor through writing. Why must this aggressor be female? Throughout the memoir, Oz describes his fear of women—caregivers and strangers molest him, pursue him, damage him. He succumbs to them as a child and resists them as an adult by developing literary conceits about the horrors of critics, for example, in the guise of women who can't keep their hands off him and tear him to pieces.

What he betrays here is anxiety not over his mother's early death, but over her impact on his writing life. For the first time, in *A Tale of Love and Darkness*, by bringing his mother into the circle of Zelda and Agnon, he acknowledges the fact that while his mother didn't play the role of a mother in his life, having died when he was so young and having been depressed and disengaged through so much of his upbringing, she played a significant role in his literary development. The wild woman who tries to harpoon him in the passage above is, perhaps, his mother begging him to acknowledge her. His resistance to her, through writing, betrays his anxiety over her impact on his writing.

Oz's depiction of his mother as the backbone of his literary genealogy as opposed to his familial genealogy, in conjunction with his designation of the writers of the Hebrew Revival as extended family members instead of literary antecedents, indicates an attempt to salvage many things that converge here. First, there is his mother herself who died in his youth; then there are her stories, her allegiance with European literature and landscapes; there is the kind of Hebrew that could only grow out of continuity with European Jewry—its sacred texts and vernacular language; there is European Jewry itself and the writers who continued to write in its cadences and rhythms, like Zelda and S. Y. Agnon; there is Jerusalem as a shelter for European Jews in the early years of the state and the culture that existed there.

His mother, Oz says near the end of his narrative, in a description of his father's criticism of the types of stories his wife told the young Oz "in her usual way, challenged the walls of censorship."[41] Salvage poetics are about defying censorship—the censorship imposed on the voices of a culture by the violence of historical circumstance. Oz's allegiance to his mother's literary traditions and his mother's memory, narrated near the end of his life in *A Tale of Love and Darkness*, presents a uniquely poignant variation on "the anxiety of influence." While Oz may have resisted explicitly acknowledging his mother's literary influence on him throughout his writing career, he brought her back in this late, monumental, salvage meditation.

Notes

1. There are two notable exceptions to this schema. Aharon Appelfeld and Yehudah Amichai are both considered "statehood" writers even though they were born in Europe and raised in Germany. Also, for the canonic generational schematics, see Gershon Shaked, *ha-Siporet ha-Ivrit, 1880–1980* (Yerushalayim: Keter, 1977).

2. Yehoshua, A. B. "The Literature of the Generation of the State." *The Israel Review of Arts and Letters*, 1998, pp. 107–08.

3. Gluzman, Michael. *The Politics of Canonicity: Lines of Resistance in Modernist Hebrew Poetry*. Stanford UP, 2003. Viktor Shklovsky writes: "Art history has a very important feature: in it, it's not the eldest son who inherits seniority from his father, but the nephew who receives it from his uncle." See Shklovsky, Viktor. "On Cinema." in *Viktor Shklovsky: A Reader*. Edited and translated by Alexandra Berlina. Bloomsbury Academic, 2017, pp. 352–53. In Russian, see: Shklovskij, V. B. *Gamburgskij schyot: Stat'i—vospominaniya—esse (1914–1933)*. / Sost. A. Yu. Galushkin, A. P. Chudakov, Moscow: Sovetskij pisatel', 1990, p. 121. Thank you to my colleague, Molly Blasing, for helping me to locate these texts.

4. https://library.osu.edu/projects/hebrew-lexicon/02378.php.

5. Oz, Amos. *A Tale of Love and Darkness*. Translated by Nicholas de Lange. Houghton-Mifflin Harcourt, 2015, pp. 34–36.

6. *A Tale of Love and Darkness*, p. 36.

7. *A Tale of Love and Darkness*, p. 86.

8. *A Tale of Love and Darkness*, p.89.

9. *A Tale of Love and Darkness*, pp. 95–97.

10. *A Tale of Love and Darkness*, p. 127.

11. For an archeology of Oz's actual literary debt to the writers of the Revival, not just his own admitted debt, see Govrin, Nurit. "ha-Mishpahah ha-Sifrutit shel Amos Oz." *Gag*, 24, 2011, pp. 151–66.

12. Oz, Amos. *A Tale of Love and Darkness*. Translated by Nicholas de Lange. Houghton-Mifflin Harcourt, 2015, p. 68.

13. *A Tale of Love and Darkness*, p. 471

14. Jelen, Sheila. "Israeli Children in a European Theater: Amos Oz's A Tale of Love and Darkness and S. Yizher's Preliminaries." *The Jewish Quarterly Review*, vol. 100, no. 3, 2010, pp. 504–18.

15. Jelen, Sheila. *Salvage Poetics: Post-Holocaust American Jewish Folk Ethnographies*. Wayne State UP, 2020, pp. 198–99.

16. Kaplan, Eran. "Amos Oz's A Tale of Love and Darkness and The Sabra Myth." *Jewish Social Studies*, n.s. 14, no. 1, Fall 2007, p. 130. Schwartz, Yigal. "Nikhnasta le-armon mekhushaf ve-shihrartah oto meha-kishuf: Al sipur 'al ahavah ve-hoshekh ke-sefer pulhan." *Israel*, vol. 7, Spring 2005, p.188 (cited in Kaplan).

17. Milner, Iris. "Sipur mishpahti: mitos ha-mishpahah ba-sipur 'al ahavah ve-hoshekh uve-yetsirato ha-mukdemet shel Amos Oz." *Yisrael: Hoveret myuhedet ha-mukdesher le-sifro shel Amos Oz sipur 'al ahavah ve-hoshekh*, Spring 2005, pp. 73–106.

18. Howe, Irving. *World of Our Fathers*. Harcourt Brace Javonovich, 1976.

19. Oz, Amos. *A Tale of Love and Darkness*. Translated by Nicholas de Lange. Houghton-Mifflin Harcourt, 2015, pp. 137–38.

20. *A Tale of Love and Darkness*, p. 252.

21. *A Tale of Love and Darkness*, p 270.

22. *A Tale of Love and Darkness*, p 271.

23. Spiegelman, Art. *Maus: A Survivor's Tale*. Penguin, 2003.

24. Wirth-Nesher, Hana. "The Modern Jewish Novel and the City: Franz Kafka, Henry Roth and Amos Oz." *Modern Fiction Studies*, vol. 24, no. 1, Spring 1978, pp. 91–109.

25. Oz, Amos. *A Tale of Love and Darkness*. Translated by Nicholas de Lange. Houghton-Mifflin Harcourt, 2015, p. 248.

26. *A Tale of Love and Darkness*, p. 538.

27. *A Tale of Love and Darkness*, p. 284.

28. *A Tale of Love and Darkness*, p. 286, and Bialik's poem "Alone," opens in the following way: "Wind blew, light drew them all./New songs revive their mornings./Only I, small bird, am forsaken/under the Shekhina's wing." (translated by Ruth Nevo), https://allpoetry.com/Hayyim-Nahman-Bialik.

29. *A Tale of Love and Darkness*, p. 289.

30. *A Tale of Love and Darkness*, pp. 290–91.

31. *A Tale of Love and Darkness*, p. 294.

32. Koplewitz, Gal. "Amos Oz and the Politics of the Hebrew Language." *The New Yorker*, 12 Nov. 2019, https://www.newyorker.com/books/page-turner/amos-oz-and-the-politics-of-the-hebrew-language.

33. Guppy, Shusha. "Amos Oz: The Art of Fiction." *The Paris Review*, no. 148, issue 140, Fall 1996, https://www.theparisreview.org/interviews/1366/the-art-of-fiction-no-148-amos-oz.

34. On Modern Hebrew as an echo chamber, see Alter, Robert. *The Invention of Hebrew Prose: Modern Fiction and the Language of Realism*. University of Washington, 1988.

35. Oz, Amos. *A Tale of Love and Darkness*. Translated by Nicholas de Lange. Houghton-Mifflin Harcourt, 2015, p. 69.

36. *A Tale of Love and Darkness*, p. 69.

37. *A Tale of Love and Darkness*, p. 74.

38. One of only two books of literary criticism ever written by Oz is a study of Agnon, based on lectures he gave at Ben Gurion University where he was on the literature faculty: Oz, Amos. *The Silence of Heaven: Agnon's Fear of God*. Princeton, 2012. His other work of non-fiction is The Story Begins: Essays on Literature. Harcourt, 1999.

39. See Grumberg, Karen. "Of Sons and Mothers: The Spectropoetics of Exile in Autobiographical Writing by Amos Oz and Albert Cohen." *Prooftexts*, vol. 3, no. 3, Fall 2010, pp. 373–401. Also see Wheatley, Natasha. " 'It Is the Hunter and You Are the Harpooned Dolphin': Memory, Writing and Medusa—Amos Oz and His Women." *The Jewish Quarterly Review*, vol. 100, no. 4, Fall 2010, pp. 631–48.

40. Oz, Amos. *A Tale of Love and Darkness*. Translated by Nicholas de Lange. Houghton-Mifflin Harcourt, 2015, pp. 236–37.

41. *A Tale of Love and Darkness*, p. 331.

PART 3

COMING OF AGE

Constructing the Hebrew Home(Land)

Chapter 9

Cat People

Coming of Age in Mr. Levi and Panther in the Basement

Adam Rovner

Critics often approach Amos Oz's fiction as if the author's works channel the moral voice of Israel's conscience. Oz emerged as a leonine, square-jawed sabra, a symbol of "the good Israel." Never mind that within Israel Oz's humanity has come under recent personal attack, his creative and intellectual influence on Hebrew belles lettres has waned over time, and his liberal politics have long been sidelined by a powerful right wing or eclipsed by more progressive views on the left. People surely read Oz, but they stopped listening to him. Unendurably handsome and charismatic, the elder Oz became a victim of his own charm, ubiquity, and success, perhaps as all writers who achieve prominence in their lifetimes are fated to become.

An *éminence grise*, a commodity saturating the market, Oz's media appearances were greeted with a yawn. His novels and story collections were paid due, though unenthusiastic, fealty in the few pages dedicated to literature in Israel's intellectual daily *Haaretz*. The author began to seem a relic. One no longer *had* to read his latest novel or collection. It didn't help that in his final years Oz lived north of Tel Aviv proper, in what might as well be Arad in terms of café culture, and beyond the Yarkon

River, the city's Sambatyon. Over coffee and cigarettes, the catty *bohème* of central Tel Aviv could smirk knowingly at Oz's inconsequence.

The worldwide acclaim that greeted Oz's autobiographical novel *A Tale of Love and Darkness* ([2002] סיפור על אהבה וחושך), despite its *longueurs*, further hastened professional jealousies that equate popularity with mediocrity. That memoiristic novel's adaptation into a much-hyped film (2015) directed by Natalie Portman and starring the actor as Oz's ill-fated mother only increased critical suspicions. When Hollywood calls, and when Portman is your mom, it's hard to rein in the literati's cynicism. So for some, Oz could be more easily dismissed. A persona. An unwitting parody. He even appeared in veiled caricature in one lovingly acidic novel, Agur Schiff's *Anonymity* ([7102] אנונימיות). All these facts may further tempt critics to turn Oz's slow drift towards irrelevance into a metaphor for an increasingly corrupt Israeli polity and the vulgarization of that country's cultural and intellectual life. Oz, it seems, cannot escape becoming an elegiac symbol.

Of course, this is not how the story began.

Oz himself was forever engaged by beginnings—his family mythology and his own origins. He famously re-birthed himself at the age of fourteen, moving from Jerusalem to Kibbutz Hulda, and along the way he discarded his original storied surname, Klausner, for Oz, an aspirational sobriquet that denotes "strength" or "power" in Hebrew. Oz even published a collection of ten breezy essays that examine the openings of stories and novels he taught in classes and workshops, *The Story Begins* ([6991] מתחילים סיפור). Most of the authors and fictions Oz explored in *The Story Begins* are well known in the Hebrew or global canon, including S. Y. Agnon's *In the Prime of Her Life*, Nikolai Gogol's "The Nose," Franz Kafka's "A Country Doctor," Gabriel Garcia Marquez's *The Autumn of the Patriarch*, and Raymond Carver's "Nobody Said Anything." The choices are indicative of Oz's cosmopolitan tastes and restless reading habits, as well as his devotion to craft.

Oz treats these works in terms of their initial overture to the reader, their devices, pacing, tone, voice, and structure. Late twentieth and early twenty-first century Hebrew literature may be replete with imaginative scenarios, telegraphed themes, and heady concepts ready-made for the application of political readings and theoretical frameworks. Sometimes they are even fun to read. But precious few writers of Hebrew determinedly practice craft. With its painstaking attention to world-building and character creation, craft demands precision, syntactic rigor, *le mot juste*, and a tempered style that avoids gimmickry and sentimentality as it weaves its themes and allusions. There are reasons aside from the psycho-sexual plot dynamics that Oz's much fêted *My Michael* ([86/91] מיכאל שלי) echoes Gustave Flaubert's *Madame Bovary*.

Among the pantheon of major artists and works Oz discusses in *The Story Begins* is one relatively "minor" Hebrew work, Yaakov Shabtai's "A Private and Very Awesome Leopard" "נמר חברבורות פרטי ומטיל אימה") ([2791]. Israeli readers are likely familiar with Shabtai and this comic tale, but English-language readers would be hard-pressed to even locate the translation of this story, though it is worth seeking out in the collection *Uncle Peretz Takes Off* (2004). Oz's writerly attention is drawn to the story's first-person retrospective narration in which Shabtai's ironic and perceptive narrator is an adult version of the wonder-struck child protagonist. The adult narrator reports on past events; the boy functions as the internal focalizer communicating his contemporary impressions of those events. Oz does not invoke these terms or engage with the technicalities of narrative theory in his essay in *The Story Begins*, entitled "From Tnuva to Monaco." Instead, Oz effectively summarizes the narration as offering "a subtle blend of what the child had understood and what the narrator had realized much later" (106/98).[1] For most readers, this description of Shabtai's double-voiced narrative technique is all that is required.

Oz's essay goes on to discuss the manipulations of perspective afforded by this technique. The story's innocent child focalizer fails to make sense of the deeds and misdeeds of his con-man uncle, Fink, while the adult narrator clearly does understand all that has come to pass.[2] The boy cannot shake his affection for Fink or his attraction to Fink's frivolities and fantasies, though he is simultaneously beholden to his parents' flinty Labor Zionist worldview. Against his better judgment then, the boy is mesmerized by Fink's financial schemes and exotic dreams for the creation of a "Universal Circus" in Tel Aviv (Shabtai 149/111). Uncle Fink enthuses that his circus will feature "the awesome spotted leopard, the embodiment of strength, flexibility, and nobility, the symbol of the circus" (Shabtai 149/111). When Fink's pipe dreams dissipate into thin air, he absconds and leaves in his wake debts, shame, domestic detritus, and jilted lovers.

The boy focalizer, however, lacks full awareness of Fink's grift and its destructive effects on those left behind. In "From Tnuva to Monaco," Oz comments that within Fink's family, "scandals are not discussed in front of the children, and dirty linen is not washed in view of the younger generation" (108/100). The boy focalizer is enchanted by the magic circle

Uncle Fink draws around him, and even after its ignoble end, the wised-up adult narrator evinces sorrow at the circus' immateriality. The reader senses that the adult narrator sometimes longs for his enchanted childhood self, and in so doing he adopts a less moralistic and condemnatory attitude towards Fink's manic energies. The narrator does not regret that his boyhood self fell prey to illusion; rather, he regrets the necessity of having been disillusioned. No awesome spotted leopard ever found its way to Tel Aviv. That symbol of strength, flexibility, and nobility never even existed.

I believe that Oz's discussion of Shabtai's story is significant, as the precise narrative technique he describes as structuring "A Private and Very Awesome Leopard" also frames two of Oz's own works that I often teach: *Mr. Levi* ([57/91] "אדון לוי") and *Panther in the Basement* (פנתר ([59/91] במרתף). Likewise, these two works incorporate cat motifs and hence borrow from Shabtai's story a curious play with those attributes that felines connote: tensed power, stealth, sinewy sleekness, and regal bearing, but also ambivalence, aloofness, sexuality, and even treachery.[3] The use of cat imagery to structure narratives that explore the psycho-sexuality of a masculinity threatened by devouring feline eroticism runs from Honoré de Balzac's "A Passion in the Desert" (1837), in which a soldier finds sanctuary and a kind of love with a pantheress, to Val Lewton's pulpy "The Bagheeta" (1930), in which a virginal teen must triumph over a were-leopard—a story later revised and filmed as the Hollywood classic *Cat People* (1942), to Moacyr Scliar's *Max and the Cats* (1981), in which a jaguar and a boy must survive together after a shipwreck, and Yann Martel's *Life of Pi* (2001), which reimagines portions of Scliar's novella and substitutes a tigress for the jaguar. Oz was himself a cat lover. To those exercised by biographical criticism: make of that what you will.

The novella *Mr. Levi* and the short novel *Panther in the Basement* are separated by two decades, and both exist as "beginnings" for the still later *A Tale of Love and Darkness*. The two earlier texts feature character types, interpersonal relations, locations, motifs, and events that are reworked and expanded in Oz's autobiographical novel. Cats, large and small, also surface in *A Tale of Love and Darkness*, though only in minor roles. Stray cats flee from Amos's "doomed" mother when they sense her unhappiness (536/591), and in one memorable scene the young Amos tries to impress an Arab girl by transforming himself into a "resplendent new Hebrew youth [...] a lion among lions" (327/372). I will not undertake the task of identifying how elements of *Mr. Levi* and *Panther in the Basement* are recombined and appear in *A Tale of Love and Darkness*.

Hebrew readers may refer to Nitza Ben-Dov's preliminary gloss on this issue in *Ve-hi Tehilatekha* (295–96). Instead, I want to follow Oz's own method in *The Story Begins* and examine the overtures these two earlier narratives make to the reader—how these two stories begin—and what their opening lines may signal to us about Oz's later and more expansive *A Tale of Love and Darkness*.

Mr. Levi relates the drama of the final days of the British Mandate through the character of Uriel Kolodny, a bookish adolescent. Uriel observes the adult world and skirts its periphery while navigating his Jerusalem neighborhood of Tel Arza. The male child as protagonist in Jerusalem appears in other works by Oz, including the "pudgy, awkward" (15/51) Hillel from the novella *The Hill of Evil Counsel* "הר העצה הרעה" ([6791]), the eleven-year-old Soumchi from the eponymous young adult novella ([7791] סומכי), and of course in *Panther in the Basement*. The emotionally stunted Shmuel Ash, protagonist of *Judas* הבשורה על פי יהודה) ([4102], presents as a similarly lovelorn man-child drifting from Tel Arza to other points in Jerusalem, but the most significant intertext for Oz's final novel is Sholem Asch's brilliant Yiddish epic *The Nazarene* דער מאן פון נצרת [3491]) and not a revision of previous works in Oz's own corpus. All these protagonists are decidedly not men; they are daydreamers who play at being men and possess only an imperfect understanding of the conflicts, family dynamics, and degrees of sexual expression they witness from the rooftops, windows, and dusty lots as they wander Jerusalem.

Uriel shares a great deal, including his last name, with intertextual "twin" Proffy Kolodny from *Panther in the Basement*.[4] Both protagonists exist on the cusp of sexual maturity and are torn between juvenile attractions to older girls or women, while still seeking the approval of and succor from their depressive and fragile mothers. Readers familiar with Oz's biography may safely assume that Uriel and Proffy (and Hillel and Soumchi, and perhaps Shmuel) all exist as shadows from Oz's own past, or as refractions of the author's psyche. Concluding as much may illuminate the psychological origins of these narratives in Oz's biography, but such an approach simultaneously explains too much, and too little. Too much, because fact-checking Oz's life story suggests that literary interpretation is then barely required. Too little, because Oz's focus on preteen protagonists is unusual among Israeli writers of the author's generation and the generation that preceded him, and therefore assumes some significance.

Unlike the military-age males typically featured in representative works by the so-called Statehood Generation, Oz's child focalizers are twice removed from tragic or thwarted heroism. Nor are they sacrificial Isaacs bound to the national altar by their founding fathers' convictions. Oz's child protagonists live amidst an enchanted world of adolescent power fantasies, either playacting at heroism or entirely impotent to act beyond the inner realm of their imaginations. There are, of course, a few notable exceptions to this preference among Oz's approximate generation for the military-age male. Readers familiar with literature of the 1970s–1980s might bring to mind some of the better known exceptions, though these were tellingly written by authors or featured protagonists then on the margins of the literary establishment. Classics in this vein include Aharon Appelfeld's (b. 1932) *Age of Wonders* ([87/91] תור הפלאות), which depicts the vanished European world of thirteen-year-old Bruno, and Eli Amir's (b. 1937) *Scapegoat*, which follows the painful assimilation of thirteen-year-old Baghdadi immigrant Nuri. Unlike Bruno or Nuri, Oz's Uriel and Proffy are socio-culturally marginal only with respect to their allegiances to their fathers' Revisionist political affiliation, which cuts against the grain of the then prevailing Labor Zionism. Nor are either Uriel or Proffy victims of their circumstances or potential sacrifices to their fathers' beliefs. Both boys are instead enamored of violent revenge fantasies of murder and destruction, far more so than their cultivated, mild-mannered fathers. Oz's repeated use of child protagonists thus stands out among his peers, and his deployment of the technique of double-voiced retrospective narration requires closer attention.

Mr. Levi, which forms the middle novella of the trio collected in *The Hill of Evil Counsel*, begins with an unmistakable fairy tale introduction: "Once upon a time, many years ago, there lived in Jerusalem an old poet by the name of Nehamkin" (63/55). The use of a formulaic opening cues the reader to anticipate a supernatural world harboring violent threats to children. In fairy tales, children may become innocent casualties of parental deception or greed, abandoned in dangerous circumstances, or adopted by wicked stepparents. Or children might accidentally become separated from their parents, lost, abducted, victimized by humans acting as beasts, or devoured by beasts masquerading as humans. In such enchanted settings, landscapes and characters can shape shift at an instant to become hostile and wild. These dark narrative tidings are not fully realized in *Mr. Levi*, which hews firmly to a realist sensibility. If anything, it is the child-protagonist who feels impelled towards transformation and escape from his parents, as when he repeatedly imagines fleeing beyond Tel Arza to the mountains or desert beyond.

This first sentence of *Mr. Levi* implies that the narrator persona addresses a child narratee by virtue of the fact that fairy tales are typically told to children. However, no visible narratee emerges in the text. There is no child obviously present in the text at the time of the narrator's telling. Few casual readers will recognize, let alone seek out, an invisible narratee. Most readers, or even impatient critics, will content themselves to magically (and erroneously) assume that the narrator (or even Oz the author) "speaks" to them. This cannot be the case, at least according to prevailing models of narrative theory. The novella's power derives in part from the ambiguity Oz's retrospective narrative technique encourages. This double-voiced device oscillates between adult narrator, who suggests ideological interpretations of past events, and the child focalizer, who provides a contemporary and decidedly juvenile perception of those events. The narratee likewise appears doubled: the first-person narrator addresses an invisible narratee, and in so doing this persona seems to metanarratively communicate with a reader.[5]

As the story progresses, the adult narrator's "once upon a time" overture reveals itself as ironic. What exceeds comprehension is not supernatural at all; it is only the adult world whose significance escapes the perception of the child focalizer, young Uriel. Dangers do appear in the form of the distant nimbus of war, but proximate threats are mostly in the child's mind, or are the products of wishful thinking indulged in by the boyish would-be hero. The lost world of 1940s Jerusalem thus appears not as uncanny, but as the site of staid domesticity, albeit a home inhabited by imposing giants—the nameless Mother and Father. These perplexing adults are however entirely human and wholly devoted to Uriel's protection. Indeed, the narrator provides clues that enable the reader to fill in gaps in Uriel's perceptions of his parents and the actions they conscientiously undertake for his protection and benefit.

In Hebrew, the beginning of the story makes use of the standard folkloric phrase *hayo haya* [הָיֹה הָיָה], an originally biblical locution that uses two past tense forms of the infinitive "to be." The phrase commonly serves to translate "once upon a time" into modern Hebrew. This near repetition of the verb serves as an emphatic in the Hebrew Bible and may even be used in spoken Hebrew in a jocular or mock-biblical manner. *Hayo haya* indicates a past that is distantly past, or may signify an imaginary past: the time of "once upon a time" never really existed. In Hebrew as in English this was-(not)-was formulaic introduction enjoins the reader to enter the time of legends, a kind of eternal narrative present in which the fates of the heroes retain a timeless relevance, especially to children who form the core audience for such tales. The "once upon a time" of the story's beginning thus invites the reader to access the realm of childhood, a developmental stage marked by as-if play, illusion, and enchantment. However, an adult reader cannot naively respond to this invitation and enter into the fantastic past that (never) was. The adult reader remains marooned on the far shores of maturity and can only understand or play along with the "once upon a time" invitation; he cannot slip innocently into childhood's domain.

Time in childhood is often inchoate, whereas chronology is strictly measured and apportioned to govern adult life. A child's perception of past and future dissolves into a fuzzy present that encompasses past and future, real-time and fantasy-time. To a child, events that are highly anticipated seem to take forever to arrive. Recent events often seem to a child to be enveloped in a haze of the distant past. For this reason, time as indistinct or with its chronological progress stubbornly deferred appears throughout *Mr. Levi*. The hands of the clock tower in the Schneller barracks remain fixed at 3:03 (70/61). Uriel's mother plays the same passage of an étude without progressing towards the composition's conclusion (73/63). At one point, Uriel seeks to halt his own maturation, to "stay little" forever (98/85). Uriel, the child focalizer, desires to remain static within the "once upon a time" enjoined by the narrator, a narrator whom readers come to learn is none other than the adult Uriel. The reflective "I" of the narrator and the experiencing "I" of Uriel are revealed to be one—but not the same—on the novella's second page.

The overture of the initial sentence in *Mr. Levi* does oddly depart in one way from the formula of fairy tales. Rather than introduce a premise or an agent that sets the action in motion, Oz's story instead introduces a secondary character, Mr. Nehamkin. Readers might expect the story's introduction to foreshadow the title's mysterious "Mr. Levi," or the more central figures of Uriel's parents, or even the character of Ephraim, Mr. Nehamkin's impulsive son believed to be active in the Underground's armed struggle. But Nehamkin is merely a poet. He is a bardic figure who does not initiate narrative action. Instead, he is depicted as only able to manipulate language. Mr. Nehamkin may thereby serve as a stand-in for the adult narrator who weaves his tale, or perhaps he is an avatar of the implied author. Regardless, Nehamkin serves as a conduit to the distant past and remote spaces of the "once upon a time" the text summons forth.

As the story's second sentence explains, Nehamkin "had come from Vilna and settled in a low stone house with a tiled roof in a narrow alley off Zephaniah Street" (63/55). In the post-Holocaust reality of the story, the decimated center of Yiddish culture and Jewish learning, Vilna, the Jerusalem of Lithuania with its meandering lanes, is collapsed with the neighborhood warrens of postwar Jerusalem, whose residents fear a coming conflagration. Much as time in a fairy tale abjures rational chronology, so too does space appear as boundless. The natural and supernatural worlds of folklore border one another, shift, disappear, or are concealed. So too in *Mr. Levi*. Vilna and Jerusalem are overlaid one upon the other as if Uriel could wander Zephaniah Street, step into an alley, and end up in the Great Synagogue courtyard off Žydų Street in Vilna. This heterotopic quality reinforces the timelessness (or stasis) already evoked by the story's deployment of motifs of deferred progress.

The reference to the real-world location of Zephaniah Street, which borders Tel Arza, signals an additional collapsing of time and space that relates a 1940s Jerusalem facing an uncertain future to the biblical era of the prophet Zephaniah, who warned of the destruction of Jewish sovereignty over the holy city. Nehamkin, likely a name of endearment, hints at Nahum, a prophet of consolation, or perhaps to the biblical figure of Nehemiah. All these related names contain the Hebrew root word indicating "comfort." Nehamkin's flowery utterances and gnomic pronouncements alluding to hidden redeemers of Israel living in the desert (103/89) mean that the old poet does in fact provide comfort and camaraderie to the lonely Uriel. But Nehamkin's endless and fruitless construction of a matchstick model of the Temple (77/67)—yet another frustration of progress—imply that salvation is forever deferred. In addition to whatever consolations his "secret alliance" with Uriel offers the boy (66/58), Nehamkin imagines Hitler alive and hiding amidst the *yishuv*'s Arab enemies and plotting destruction (68–69/59). Such a vision of cataclysm would be more appropriate to the latter prophet Zephaniah than to any prophet of consolation. Ancient and modern Israel, salvation and apocalypse, Diaspora and Zion, all collide in the epochs and spaces invoked by Nehamkin to fashion the realistic story's peculiarly folkloric chronotope.

If the "once upon a time" of the first sentence recalls childhood, the description of Nehamkin as an "old poet" points to senescence. Nehamkin totters between his home and the Kolodny house, supporting himself on a cane bearing the carved head of a "tiger" (נמר), which perhaps symbolizes

Nehamkin's former vigor (60/69). The Hebrew *namer* would more likely be translated as "leopard" idiomatically, but Nicholas de Lange, working with Oz, chose to render the word "tiger." Nehamkin, now in his twilight years, falls asleep in the midst of conversations. He speaks in an old-fashioned Hebrew and quotes Jewish law and lore while those around him appear almost entirely alienated from religious tradition. Due to his age, Nehamkin lacks an expansive future. He possesses only a past. Because of his youth, Uriel lacks an understanding of the mature motives of the adults around him. Uriel exists in a present marked by juvenile fantasies of heroism: X-ray submarines (73/64), death rays (74/64), and anti-gravity weapons (76/66). Neither Nehamkin nor Uriel is firmly in the present. Therefore, neither the old poet nor the young boy is capable of exerting agency in the adult world. Both lack generative potential and hence cannot materially aid the Underground's decolonization struggle against the British. Uriel's father does print up posters bearing anti-British slogans in his shop, located in their home's cellar. So while the father takes some active part in the struggle, his contributions are limited to secreting items in his basement and using mere words to fight the enemy. Of the adult men in the story, only Nehamkin's son Ephraim appears to physically abet the Underground, though the extent of his role remains ambiguous.

Ephraim's stolen glances at Uriel's mother also mean that he possesses real erotic charge, unlike Nehamkin, Uriel, or his father. The naïve Uriel believes that "love"—which the adult narrator reveals as in fact consisting mostly of sexual liaisons—fundamentally endangers Ephraim, whom he believes to be an Underground hero. Uriel dimly fears that Ephraim's exploits will lead him to fall victim to feminine wiles like those heroes he has seen in movies (65/56). Nehamkin, who presumably understands the sexual nature of his son's trysts, enlists Uriel to delay and deter the women who come to pay their nocturnal visits to Ephraim. Nehamkin's meddling may derive as much from jealousy over his son's potency as his stated desire to avoid sin (67/58). Thus, on the one hand, sexual potency and martial prowess are decoupled in the story; they may in fact be inimical. Both Uriel and Nehamkin aim to forestall Ephraim's sexual dalliances which they believe sap his purity and vigor, and even endanger his "missions." This suggests that sexual expression and the expression of armed power are not one and the same thing in the virile, masculine world of political struggle. Uriel and Nehamkin (and the passive, potentially cuckolded Father) can thus all plausibly view themselves as contributing to the Underground's struggle for independence through words, prophecies, and sloganeering.

On the other hand, potency and prowess are in fact bound in the text, at least for the adult narrator (and careful reader). Uriel and Nehamkin only *play* at contributing to the Underground, the narrator reveals. In fact, youth and old age, the infantile and senile, can only indulge in martial fantasies, much as they can only imagine or recall sexuality. Despite his leopard- or tiger-head cane, Nehamkin is no longer a threat, if indeed he ever was. And Uriel has as yet not gained the knowledge of Eros; he is no leopard either.

Uriel's near peers—their age is uncertain—are the brothers Boaz, Yoav, and Avner Grill. They appear to be older than Uriel, so perhaps are in their young teens. They exclude Uriel from their games and taunt him with childish rhymes and insults, graffiti the walls with sexualized slurs about him and his mother or him and their own older sister, torture stray cats, pound drums, and generally wreak havoc. They appear to have a clearer perception of erotic desire than does Uriel, perhaps because they observe their sister, Bat-Ammi, and her physical maturation. The older Bat-Ammi tolerates Uriel and upbraids him for not standing up to her brothers. As a result of her attention, he becomes infatuated with her and imagines marrying her, though his attraction remains childish. He primarily views her as a means to possess her bus driver father's chambered coin changer (113/98). Uriel laments that Bat-Ammi inexorably grows older; he would like to arrest her development (89–90/78). Here again Uriel's immaturity, indeed his resistance to maturity, is emphasized.

The Grill boys, despite their apparent burgeoning sexuality, which is noted explicitly at the expense of Uriel's lack of sexual development (118/102), are no more generative than his. Their anarchic energies are directed towards whim rather than to any fruitful end. Unlike Uriel, they do not parrot an ideology, adhere to the clichés of the *yishuv*, or appear to be much concerned with the struggles of the Underground. Uriel's affected seriousness of purpose is of course betrayed by his storybook fantasies of kidnapping the High Commissioner (114/99). The Grill boys make no pretense of their mischief. Their games are not in the service of the struggle for decolonization or for the greater glory of the Jewish nation. Instead, they gleefully abuse Uri, torment their parents, and run off to the wild reaches abutting Tel Arza to hunt for a "leopard" [ברדלס]. Though the Hebrew term *bardales* is typically understood to refer to a "cheetah," translator Nicholas de Lange, again presumably with Oz's agreement, settled on "leopard." Both types of large cats were rare in 1940s Mandate Palestine and only leopards still (probably) exist in the Judean desert today.

Uriel's mother naturally considers the leopard to be a collective delusion or "everybody's nightmare" (118/103). The Grill boys will never catch the leopard, for it does not really exist. But her son believes with childish innocence in the beast's lurking presence. He imagines that he will "follow the leopard beyond the mountains to the forests of leopards" (118/103) and will even sweep Bat-Ammi away from her family and make her his queen among the "forests of the leopards" (119/103). Visions of the creature insinuate themselves into Uriel's thoughts and yearnings. The mysterious, titular "Mr. Levi," a fugitive Underground operative, arrives at the Kolodny home to hide from the British. In Uriel's imagination, this shadowy "Mr. Levi" at first resembles a familiar shopkeeper. Soon Uriel comes to believe that beneath his alias there lurks yet another man, an attractive "lean leopard youth" (122/105) and hero of the Underground. For Uriel, the leopard stands as an index of power and the ability to transform the self to wield a vitality that is both militarized and sexualized. While the Grill boys roam the empty lots of Tel Arza hunting an incorporeal leopard, the British conduct house to house searches in Tel Arza for the leopard-like "Mr. Levi." Neither the British nor the Grill brothers find what they seek, but against this backdrop of events Uriel begins to envision his own maturation.

The morning after "Mr. Levi's" furtive sojourn at the Kolodnys', Uriel asks his parents where their nocturnal visitor has disappeared to. His parents maintain that "Mr. Levi" was only a figment of the boy's hyperactive imagination. They stubbornly withhold the truth from Uriel, insisting that he suffers from a "slight temperature," which they attribute to his pubescence—a sign that they perceive their son's dawning physical maturity as a kind of pathology, telling him: "It's your age" (128/111). Uriel responds to their obfuscations with frustration and tears. He recognizes for the first time that he has been deceived by the adults whom he trusts and emulates. His parents have just been humoring him. Ephraim has only let him tag along as a mascot. Nehamkin alone has been sincere, but the doddering poet suffered an unspecified attack during the night and has been admitted to a hospital, and presumably faces mortality. Uriel disconsolately concludes: "There had never been a leopard in the Tel Arza woods" (129/112). Here Uriel achieves the disenchanted awareness of the narrator, the adult Uriel. As in Shabtai's "A Private and Very Awesome Leopard," the child focalizer's disillusionment has been relayed by the adult narrator. Likewise, the covert narratee has matured from being a child to an adult. The cat is now out of the bag.

Uriel recognizes that exotic beasts from afar cannot infiltrate his dreary world, and he reluctantly understands that though adults may arrogate power to themselves by virtue of their maturity, their imagined leopard-like "strength, flexibility, and nobility" is accompanied by less desirable feline qualities: deceit, secrecy, betrayal, lust. Uriel's abandonment of his fantasies marks his entrance into the adult world, an adult world in which the child will transform to possess both positive and negative feline characteristics. Paradoxically, once he abandons the childish fantasy of a leopard prowling Tel Arza, he himself becomes a kind of leopard—a boy on the cusp of militarized and sexualized maturity. The boy can, and inexorably must, change his spots. And with Uriel's expulsion from childhood's garden, time begins to resume its course. In the last paragraph of the story, morning dawns and the Jewish new year signals its approach. The narrator concludes the story with an inversion of the timeless "once upon a time" with which he began his tale: "what has been has been, and a new day is beginning" (130/113). Time's arrow is no longer paused in flight. Soon Uriel will complete his transformation into the adult narrator.

Panther in the Basement, like *Mr. Levi*, deals with the waning days of the British Mandate and the *yishuv*'s anxieties on the eve of independence. The narrative similarity suggests that the Mandate was a virginal period of Jewish nationalism; independence marks a coming-of-age and transition to disillusionment. *Panther in the Basement* has typically been considered a young adult novel in reviews and in journalistic interviews with the author. While the novel bears some hallmarks of young adult fiction, the first Hebrew edition of the novel does not contain paratextual markers indicating this—unless one considers the reproduction of sketches by artist Anna Ticho as particularly appealing to a teen audience. Nor do the sophisticated narrative dynamics, thematic concerns, and digressions on history and memory indicate that the novel conforms to the young adult genre, as does the more simplified presentation of these elements in Oz's earlier novella *Soumchi*. Most reviewers and critics have failed to recognize that Oz's playful subversions of popular fiction and culture cut deeper than typical young adult fiction.[6] Scholar Gilead Morahg has, however, noted that *Panther in the Basement* emerges as a "searing indictment of conventional thinking," and is in essence a "parody for adults"—a parody of the sloganeering, ideological clichés, and popular culture promulgated by *yishuv* society in the 1940s and 1950s, which aimed at inculcating its nascent citizens with a nationalist and militarist mindset.[7] The retrospective first-person narrator, an adult version of the child focalizer, has broken free of such conventional thinking.

As a child, the narrator bore the nickname of "Proffy," short for "professor." Readers never learn Proffy's given first name, but he shares a last name with Uriel Kolodny. Like Uriel, Proffy also lives in the vicinity of Tel Arza. He too is the precocious only child of a scholarly father and unhappy mother whose tense relationship enervates the household. The adolescent Proffy, in similar fashion to his doppelganger Uriel, acts out imaginary battles against Jewish oppressors past and present, indulges in apocalyptic revenge fantasies, feuds with bullies, finds himself slandered in neighborhood graffiti, and slips into chaste daydreams about an older woman. There is ample reason to conclude that Uriel and Proffy are intertextual clones, although the narratives avoid making this explicit.

Ungenerous readers might conclude that in *Panther in the Basement* Oz was at an imaginative impasse or engaged in a lazy recycling of features from one text to another. However, my more charitable reading of this generally overlooked novel finds Oz studiously adopting Shabtai's double-voiced narrative technique of retrospective narration—adult narrator in counterpoint to child-focalizer—and gradually refining this technique over a period of approximately thirty years, from novella, to short novel, and finally into the extended memoir-novel hybrid of *A Tale of Love and Darkness*. Shabtai did not, of course, invent the technique, and Oz could have turned to any number of first-person retrospective models drawn from well-known works of world literature (e.g., "The Egg" by Sherwood Anderson—an author whom Oz especially valued, Charles Dickens' *Great Expectations*, or Harper Lee's *To Kill a Mockingbird*). That "A Private and Very Awesome Leopard" seems to have captivated Oz-the-teacher and Oz-the-writer suggests that he found in Shabtai's story an especially apt deployment of the first-person retrospective narrator technique, one that comments on a unique Israeli reality: a child of the Middle East who grows up with his country. Conceiving of Oz's work diachronically not only brings his practice of craft into focus, but also allows readers to see the (implied) author stalking his prey—a definitive portrait of the artist as a young boy. Such a continually reworked portrait suggests the development of a supra-textual implied author.[8] Perhaps a diachronic approach even allows readers to see how the real Oz created a layered self-mythologization of his origins, one that illuminates the calamitous European Jewish past in parallel to the author's fraught Israeli present.

Published just one year before the essays collected in *The Story Begins*, Oz's *Panther in the Basement* begins with the adult narrator voicing a statement that might equally well have applied to the author himself: "I have been called a traitor many times in my life" (1/7). This seemingly direct declaration marks the overture of the novel's first-person retrospective narration. The introductory sentence does not call forth an enchanted time or space, as we saw in the first sentence of *Mr. Levi*. However, the novel's beginning does play other tricks. For readers who know anything about Oz, this first sentence blurs the identification of the real author with his narrator persona. Oz's activism for Peace Now and other liberal-left causes in Israel means that he has often been accused of betraying Zionism by those aligned with the political rightwing. That the novel appeared shortly before Yitzhak Rabin's assassination at the hands of an ultranationalist who considered the prime minister a "traitor" endows the retrospective narration a curiously prospective quality. Readers across the political spectrum may suspect that a strident author is being coy and hiding behind a charming narratorial persona in *Panther in the Basement*.

As with "Mr. Levi," no narratee is explicitly addressed by the narrator. The adult narrator may even be addressing himself throughout the novel, as if writing a confession. The indistinct narratee and the slippage of identity between Oz-the-author and his novel's narrator, to whom the author bears more than a passing resemblance, encourages readers to erroneously believe that the narrator (or author) addresses them directly. In other words, much as the author/narrator distinction is blurred, so too is the reader/narratee border effaced. A similar dynamic obtained in *Mr. Levi*, as previously noted.

The narrator's opening words in *Panther in the Basement* immediately raise questions of reliability. To what degree should the narratee and his reader-proxies trust a narrator accused so "many times" of betrayal?— especially if the persona of narrator and author have been purposefully confounded. Perhaps the suggested conflation of author and narrator is just another in a series of these betrayals? Then again, by admitting that the charge of being a traitor has repeatedly been leveled against him, the narrator may be seeking to place himself beyond reproach. He thus appears open-handed, honest, sincere simply by virtue of making his disclosure. The narrator has only "been called" a traitor; he does not state that he is in fact a traitor. The narrator confesses to nothing save the act of confession itself. Nonetheless, that confessional mood enjoins a conspiratorial intimacy with the textual narratee and the metanarrative reader. Perhaps, then, the narrator is a double-dealer after all. As with the first sentence of *Mr. Levi*, the opening line of *Panther in the Basement* conceals vertiginous equivocation and ironic twists and turns.

The next sentence continues: "The first time [I was called a traitor] was when I was twelve and a quarter and I lived in a neighborhood at the edge of Jerusalem" (1/7). The narrator's voice directly channels the idiom of childhood in this second sentence. Only children indicate their age by quarters. (Readers attuned to Oz's biography will note that his troubled mother committed suicide when young Amos was about the age of his protagonist.) In this second sentence readers also encounter a rapid shift between the present of the narration and the boyhood past that will mark the action of the novel. Long passages that present Proffy's focalization are interrupted by the narrator briefly commenting on his own tale and by extension making observations generally true of the real world: "But why did I lock my bedroom door on the inside that night? Even now, more than forty years later, I don't know. [. . .] (There are all manners and degrees of not knowing. Just as a window can be not just open or shut, but half open, or one part can be open and the rest shut, or it can be open just a crack . . .)" (132/140). The shifts in time afforded by the first-person retrospective narration compress the *yishuv* of 1947, the time of the action, with 1990s Israel, the time of the narration, much as ancient Jerusalem and Mandate-era Jerusalem were contiguous in space-time in *Mr. Levi*.

Proffy, like Uriel before him, possesses only partial knowledge of the adult world. His perception is characterized by a naïvety that provides for dramatic irony. Proffy mistakes the panting and laughter that accompany sexual activity between his older neighbor, Yardena, and her boyfriend for the groans and sighs of a wounded Underground combatant (133–34/141–42). Readers, and the narrator, understand far more about what went on next to Proffy's bedroom that night, but Proffy remains an innocent pre-adolescent. His "fall" to adulthood, and with it the arrival of carnal knowledge, exists only on the horizon. Like Uriel, Proffy does not yet possess generative potential. His lack of potency is mirrored not by a figure of senescence like Mr. Nehamkin, but by an asexual British soldier, Sergeant Dunlop, who speaks an archaic Hebrew similar to the old poet's biblically infused tongue. Dunlop's inflated diction, his ponderous gait, asthmatic breathing, and shambolic bearing present him as a dreamer, a man-child suitable to befriend the lonely child-man Proffy. To the adult narrator, Dunlop appears in retrospect like a man bewildered at finding himself in "a bus station in a strange city" (78/85). In *Mr. Levi*, Nehamkin possesses only a past; he is of a different time. In *Panther in the Basement*, Dunlop is a misplaced invader; he is of another place, cast out of "perfidious Albion" to live as an alien in 1940s Jerusalem (22/27).

The brief and uneasy association between Proffy and Dunlop sets the stage for accusations of Proffy's treachery. The boy convinces himself that he accepts Dunlop's friendship only in order to spy on the British for the Underground, or rather, for the neighborhood boys' parody of Zionist paramilitary organizations they call "Freedom or Death" (22/27). He will be a double-agent, Proffy resolves, but his affection for Dunlop means that he betrays himself. Instead, he has befriended the colonial enemy, at least according to his "frenemies" in "Freedom or Death": Ben Hur and Chita Reznick. These boys are the ones who call him a traitor. The acknowledged leader of the trio, Ben Hur, bears the name of the hero from famous film spectacles (1925; 1959) based on one of the most popular novels of the nineteenth century, Lew Wallace's *Ben-Hur* (1880). Note also that Chita, the subservient lieutenant to Ben Hur, bears a nickname that is homophonic with "cheetah." The name "Chita" may point either to the predatory cat, or to Tarzan's chimpanzee sidekick in the popular action film series (1932–1948). Given the novel's frequent mention of films, these character names are significant. Thanks to Ben Hur and Chita's persecutions, Proffy comes to learn that despite his cinema-inspired fantasies, he is in actuality no military hero, no stealthy secret agent, no "panther in the basement" ready to pounce on his prey.

In addition to the probable references to the Tarzan films, the narrator mentions several other movies throughout the novel. None of the titles refer to real movies, but rather are composites evocative of Hollywood cinema of the 1940s. These films, as much or more than the biblical tales of Jewish heroism Proffy absorbs at school and home, are the models for the boy's ideal adult self. He wishes to be tough like Humphrey Bogart (45/49) in a war picture, brave like Gary Cooper in a western (65/72), and implacable like Tyrone Power in the spy thriller "Panther in the Basement" (48/53). As in *Mr. Levi*, the motif of a great cat indexes attributes that the boy focalizer equates with masculinity and that he desires to attain for himself: muscularity, stealth, dignity, prowess, charisma. The retrospective narrator, however, ironizes Proffy's juvenile attraction to such qualities because the boy extracts these characteristics from the fantastic plots that flicker in black-and-white on the big screen of the Edison Cinema. These movies create fictional "once upon a time" story-worlds that Proffy imaginatively inhabits within the frame setting of the novel's drab and dusty Tel Arza. Certainly, these heroic figures are far more appealing models of manhood to Proffy than his father's emotional distance, pedantry, absentmindedness, and emasculation. For Proffy, the only adulthood worth emerging into is one that promises passion and virility on the model of the silver screen. Of course, those models are just empty fantasies, as the adult narrator discloses.

Panther in the Basement's retrospective narrator sounds a somber coda to this promised vision of adulthood. The narrator concludes by maintaining that his "story [. . .] comes from darkness, wanders around, and returns to darkness" (146/154). Perhaps the narrator suggests that the adult surfaces from childhood much like we emerge from a movie theater in the daytime: blinking into the harsh glare of maturity and sometimes unsteady on our feet. Afterwards, the adult vainly circles for his allotted time beneath the sun, before eventually merging back into the shadows to lick the wounds of old age. The darkness the adult narrator refers to is at first the distant past of childhood, and later the dimly perceived future that only promises decline. But "darkness" also alludes to the murky shadows of a particular imagined place, the "basement" of the film-within-the-novel "Panther in the Basement," and naturally to the novel's title itself.

The "basement" in the film's and novel's titles, like the cellar and its many hiding places described in *Mr. Levi*, serve as metaphors of subconscious desires and fears that are discarded, repressed, or concealed in childhood yet mark one for life.[9] The "darkest darkness" of the young Amos's cramped hiding place, evoked in a vivid scene of fairy tale terror from *A Tale of Love and Darkness*, functions in a similar way (227/264). The subterranean sites plumbed in childhood by Uriel, Proffy, and young Amos serve to form and to deform the adult.[10] Such episodes accumulate, as Nitza Ben-Dov evocatively puts it, to a "historiography of pain" (246). From these dim foundations there emerges the ungainly young man, no longer a child, who now possesses an appetite for self-assertion. That Oz-the-writer adopted his "power"-ful surname during his teenage years should therefore come as no psychological surprise.

Oz's retrospective narrators in *Mr. Levi* and *Panther in the Basement* look backward fondly on the last years of childhood innocence, years that just so happen to coincide with the final days of the British Mandate, before Israel's independence is borne of armed conflict. Individual innocence is thus equated with a prelapsarian national identity. In using the technique of first-person retrospective narration in his fiction, and later in passages of his memoir-novel *A Tale of Love and Darkness*, Oz the author expresses a diffident longing to return to an age of heroic fantasy that preceded the Eros of love and Thanatos of warfare, and of course the tragic circumstances of his own family. Or maybe Oz never left childhood in the first place: forever remaining the polite, awkward, and precocious boy who stood aloof from his peers, who played with words, and who forged heroism out of games with buttons, matchsticks, pins, and colored threads. Readers today may want to hearken once again to the uneasy synthesis between boy and man that several of Oz's earlier narrators reveal in order to fully appreciate the darkness from which his masterwork emerged, and to which it returned.

Notes

1. The author wishes to acknowledge the assistance of Maya Arad and Matan Hermoni.

Throughout this essay, references to English editions are provided first; references to the Hebrew original follow.

2. Oz refers to the character as "Pinek." In the English translation of the story, the uncle's name is rendered as "Fink," which of course hints at his character. The Hebrew reads [פינק].

3. The first pages of Oz's *To Know a Woman* (1989) describe a predatory feline figurine that bears the imprint of many of these same characteristics.

4. Bartana notes similar connections.

5. Balaban notes Oz's common use of shifting narrative perspective in *Between God and Beast* but does not delve into its mechanics, see p. 22.

6. Hever is one of the few critics to highlight Oz's debt to popular fiction in his review of the novel.

7. See Morahg, p. 20. Kaplan has noted similarities between elements of Oz's novel and Yigal Mossinson's "Hasamba" series, p. 138.

8. Mazor similarly suggests this in *Somber Lust*, see p. 120.

9. Balaban discusses Oz's use of Jungian motifs at length in *Between God and Beast*, but he does not treat the specific spatiality of this imagery.

10. Other childhood psycho-sexual cellars that appear in retrospective or quasi-retrospective narratives by Jewish American or Israeli writers include, for example, David Grossman's *See Under: Love*, Henry Roth's *Call It Sleep*, and Philip Roth's *The Plot Against America*.

Works Cited

Balaban, Avraham. *Between God and Beast: An Examination of Amos Oz's Prose.* Pennsylvania State UP, 1993.

Bartana, Orzion. "Open Letter to Amos Oz." *Moznayim,* no. 2, Nov. 1995, pp. 16–18.

Hever, Hanan. "On *Panther in the Basement." Haaretz,* no. 138, 18 Oct. 1998, pp. 20–21, 41.

Kaplan, Eran. "Amos Oz's *A Tale of Love and Darkness* and the Sabra Myth." *Jewish Social Studies,* 14.1, Fall 2007, pp. 119–43.

Mazor, Yair. *Somber Lust: The Art of Amos Oz.* Translated by Marganit Weinberger-Rotman. State U of New York P, 2002.

Morahg, Gilad. "The Strength of Clichés." *Iton 77,* no. 220, June 1998, pp. 20–21, 41.

Oz, Amos. *A Tale of Love and Darkness.* Translated by Nicholas de Lange. Harcourt, 2004.

———. "From Tnuva to Monaco." *The Story Begins.* Translated by Maggie Bar-Tura. Harcourt Brace & Co., 1999, pp. 104–12.

———. "Mr. Levi." *The Hill of Evil Counsel.* Translated by Nicholas de Lange. Harvest Books, 1991, pp. 61–130.

———. "The Hill of Evil Counsel." *The Hill of Evil Counsel.* Translated by Nicholas de Lange. Harvest Books, 1991, pp. 5–54.

———. *Panther in the Basement.* Translated by. Nicholas de Lange. Harvest Books, 1995.

Shabtai, Yaakov. "A Private and Very Awesome Leopard." Translated by Dalya Bilu. *Uncle Peretz Takes Off.* Overlook Press, 2004, pp. 143–69.

Chapter 10

Tilling the Soil of National Ideology

Oz and the Hebrew Environmental Imagination

Eric Zakim

Years ago, I delivered a preliminary version of this paper at a conference on Amos Oz at the Ben-Gurion University of the Negev in Beersheba, Israel—with Oz in attendance. I naively thought that a university conference, even where the writer might be employed, would want to promote a critical perspective of his work. This conference, however, was much more celebratory than scholarly. Because of that, I like to think, my paper did not garner a lot of praise or much reaction at all.

Oz took pity on me, both for the lukewarm reception of my talk by the audience and because, in the immediate aftermath, Gershon Shaked—as was his wont—had decided to recite to me all the errors of my ideological ways, in an insistent, yet friendly way. Oz must have seen this and, coming up to us, interrupted Gershon's harangue to tell me how much he appreciated my paper, even though it was a bit complex to take in in one hearing. He invited me to send him a copy so he could go over it more thoroughly. He left and Gershon gave me a knowing look, as if to say, "Good going." I don't think that Oz understood that the harangue was a practiced dynamic between Gershon and me, which he enjoyed repeating a few more times at that conference alone.

I never sent the paper, but I saw Oz a couple of years later at Duke University, where I was then teaching. He was on an American speaking tour, and I caught up with him at the campus bookstore where he was signing copies of the latest English translation of one of his books. I meekly approached holding an early hardcover edition of *Artsot ha-tan*, his first collection of short stories from 1965 and a rare volume, especially since he rewrote the stories in the mid-1970s. I had barely reminded him of my presence in Beersheba when he blurted out that, yes, he remembered, I had spoken about "Derekh ha-ruah" ("The Way of the Wind"). He then generously inscribed my book and asked me where I had found it.

Later that evening there was a donor dinner with Oz. As an assistant professor, I was invited but seated a bit to the side. Oz arrived and came right over to sit next to me. We chatted as if old friends in a sea of strangers. The refuge—for him and for me—of casual Hebrew conversation at this stifling institutional event came to an abrupt end when he was anxiously summoned by a senior Jewish studies professor to work the room, and I was scolded for monopolizing his attention and having the temerity to speak Hebrew at such an event.

I heard Oz speak publicly on later occasions, and he always seemed quite comfortable on a large public stage, which was also a consistent metaphor he used to describe being an Israeli Jew—as opposed to the passivity of sitting in the "audience" of the diaspora. I never liked this conceptual division, which always came across to me as more than a bit haughty—like both Shimshon and Gideon in "Derekh ha-ruah"—and so I was surprised and heartened to discover a more personal side to Amos Oz.

The story of modernism has always involved a retreat from nature, beginning with the growing abstractions in European painting and lyric poetry at the end of the nineteenth century, to the defamiliarizing enlargements of natural objects in early cinema of the twentieth—for instance, the films of Jean Painlevé—or the outright hostility to "nature," as it might be used to justify the hegemony of diatonic harmony, in the non-tonal music and theoretical writings of Arnold Schoenberg. Modernism's suspicion of nature was a suspicion of idealism, of a world that would present itself as self-evident—a totality—and yet alienated from the interior life of the individual. Consistently, within the dialectics of modernism, nature's idealized and unwavering objectivity presented itself in contradistinction to the true subjective core of the psyche. And in the anxiety of a modernism centered on the frail position of the self in the world, nature as such retreated from the aesthetic experience of interiority. Georg Lukács, early in the twentieth century, in *The Theory of the Novel* from 1916, diagnosed in modernist fashion the perceived lie of nature, which for him is a "world of convention, a world from whose all-embracing power only the innermost recesses of the soul are exempt."[1]

American and European modernism would thus fall back from representations of landscape and environment, retreating into both the self and the city as the harried sites of expression. Impressionism and Expressionism in the visual arts would evolve into Abstract Expressionism in the 1950s, which gave up all semblance of figuration. The lyricism of Symbolism and Imagism receded before the harsher neologistic poetics of Futurism and automatic writing, which both sought to rid convention from poetry and prose, and thus mine ever deeper the dark caverns of the soul. Even Schoenberg's radical atonalism (a term he never liked) was almost immediately attacked as too conservative and tradition-bound, and concert music after the Second World War aspired after forms ever less connected to conventional organization and sonorities.

Hebrew modernism, of course, would follow a different path, even if it too was caught within the dialectics of nature and self. But the political exigencies of Zionist settlement (based as it was on a newfound confidence of self and action in the land) in a historically alienated place, Palestine, would present to Hebrew modernist creativity a different set of requirements for engaging with nature and reconceiving it within the context of Jewish history. Thus, even a modernist poet like Avraham Shlonsky, who revered and mimicked Russian Futurism, and published translations of Vladimir Mayakovsky's revolutionary and esoteric metapoetic programs in the popular Hebrew press of Palestine in the early 1920s, produced enduring evocations of the Palestinian landscape, as it might be reflected in the pioneering endeavors of the Jewish settlement community working to redeem the land for a specific political future. Indeed, Hebrew modernism, we might say, seemed free of the restrictions of an always already conventionalized conception of nature—since the *dispositif* of place, nature, and environment had not previously existed within a Hebrew framework. For the political requisites of Zionism, the dialectics of nature and self—the ubiquitous frame of modernism—were easily replaced by what seemed the more urgent tension between collective and individual, which still holds sway in most analyses of Israeli culture. After all, the Zionist entry into the modern world always promised to negotiate precisely that dialectic between individual aspiration in the era of enlightenment and Cartesian self-certainty, on one hand, and the traditions of a community-bound understanding of identity, on the other.

Within that sort of cultural dynamic, the aesthetic and political changes that the Statehood Generation writers effected in Israel in the early 1960s—especially those of the leading prose writers of the movement, Amos Oz and A. B. Yehoshua—have always been commonly understood within specific modernist terms, terms that reproduce and reify an understanding of modernism that is constrained by a Zionist perspective of the world. Over and against the collectivism of the Palmach Generation, which dominated cultural production in the country at the time of independence and through the 1950s, Oz and Yehoshua focused on individuals and their psychological states, in a prose style that experimented with interior depiction. The national allegory of the heroic figures of the Palmach (Moshe Shamir's Uri, for instance) was replaced in the 1960s by the psychologically fraught protagonists of these younger writers, who concentrated on interior experience and the frailty of the psyche.

Like most literary revolutionary movements, the Statehood Generation's continuities with their predecessors might have been stronger than any imagined break. Oz certainly inherited a mantle from S. Yizhar, who with Shamir defined the literary ethos of the Palmach Generation, which included a new focus on the individual, in the form of Israeli youth. In 1962, the critic Robert Alter wrote about the "inevitable movement of rebellion by the younger writers against the tastes, standards, and objectives of their immediate predecessors."[2] He was actually referring to the previous break between the Palmach Generation and the "older literary generation," a break that sought to give voice to a new, specifically Israeli reality. And that meant abandoning the "publicistic" writing of a Hebrew literature informed by Ahad ha'Am's insistence on national writing.[3] Yizhar gave voice, then, to the young men and women who formed Israel's first adult generation and who had fought in the War of Independence in 1948. But the literary experiment fomented by the Palmach Generation had its limits. While Yizhar's characters questioned the political assumptions of their elders and vocalized the moral quandaries of the young state, his Hebrew style, let alone the style of Shamir, remained descriptive and distanced. "Interior monologues" and "lengthy discussions" characterize Yizhar's early magnum opus, the *Days of Ziklag*, according to Alter, as well as his other stories about the War of Independence. In Yizhar, the individual begins to appear, but remains the object of a writing that would narrate and describe. The individual gives voice to moralistic questions and political rumination, but the affective state of emotions, urges, and desires remains beyond the focus of the Palmach Generation's engagement with the young voices of its age.

The Statehood Generation writers, Oz and Yehoshua in particular, pushed the depiction of interiority of their protagonists into the realm of psychological realism, where inner feeling, anxiety, and fear become the focalized object of the narrative. The context for these interior states remains the collective experience of the young nation, but moralistic and political questions—the questions of national action and individual complicity in these actions—fall away; indeed, in Oz and Yehoshua, political action and individual ennui become the product of a misapprehended relationship between the self and the collective. While Oz and Yehoshua delve inward in their narrative invocations of interior states, the condition of the individual remains driven by their place against the expectations of the national collective.

Lost within a critical analysis mired in the opposition of individual and collective, however, is the place and function of nature—the *land* of Israel—as shaping the actors who would perform within and on it. As national writing gave way to psychological realism, lost too were the explicit politics of the generation (the relation of thought and feeling to action), a question that has led to several decades of critical commentary trying to locate those politics within the psychological depiction of the individual. However, the enduring legacy of Oz's writing—that is, the shift from previous Hebrew writing—might best be understood within a different, environmental challenge proffered by the Statehood Generation, especially Oz's early stories collected in the volume *Artsot ha-tan* (*Where the Jackals Howl*). Instead of viewing nature and environmental description as a backdrop in literature and art, a critical reading sensitive to issues of place suggests that foregrounding the way literature represents landscape and nature reveals an environmental ideology that places form and content within the context of action within the surrounding world—a mode of reading that would tease out, what is called in Anglo-American criticism, the environmental imagination.[4]

By reading land in the forefront of the text, by seeing how environmental description shapes the contours of character and plot, form, and content, we can see how meaning in cultural production is derived from an encounter with the environment itself. The importance of the

questions raised by an environmental reading lies not just in how they
investigate generally the relations between poetics and ideology, or in how
they might begin to unearth the particular poetics of a Zionist ideology.
Rather, this conflict needs to be read beyond the atmospheric background
that is the traditional trope of nature depiction in prose writing. The
environmental imagination in the Hebrew context does not lead to evocative description and Romantic figuration—to a contemplation of veracity
of realistic depiction in the landscape, as it has in the Anglo-American
literary tradition. Instead, the Hebrew environmental imagination seems
completely bound up in a modernism of interiority and shows the ways
that a Zionist reinvention of the individual was dependent on a particular
understanding of the environment. In this, Hebrew modernism hearkens
to Theodor Adorno's refusal to see the defined outlines of a phenomenological dialectics of self and nature. Over and against a separation
between objective knowledge (nature) and subjective projection (what
Adorno called history), Adorno might indeed outline a specific way of
reading environmental writing when he objects in the 1930s to the naïve
objectivism in Heidegger. For Adorno, each side of a dialectics—self and
nature, subject and object—inflects and informs the other. His criticism
follows from Lukács, who anticipates a phenomenological celebration
of nature as object when he writes about the idea of nature as interior
projection—"second nature," as he calls it. As nature loses its romantic
objectivity—the way it stands apart in a sublime contemplation of the
environment as natural object—it becomes contingent on those aspects
of the individual that modernism most cherishes: the interior psyche.
Nature, Lukács writes, "bereft of its 'senseless' autonomous life as well of
its meaningful symbolism, becomes a background, a piece of scenery, an
accompanying voice; it has lost its independence and is only a sensually
perceptible projection of the essential—of interiority."[5]

Throughout a cultural history of the Zionist settlement of Palestine,
echoes of Lukács seem to resound: the poetic iterations of the land—of
what might be called Palestine or Israel or the Middle East, each phrase
with its own set of values and assumptions—become the locus for political struggle and the site of ideological contestation.[6] Through the very
language used to name the space we live in—from the proper names of
geo-political organization to the seemingly neutral vocabulary of *svivah*
in Hebrew or "environment" in English—we can hear the difficulties of
fixing attitudes toward the land. The physical place—the environment, our
surroundings—easily recedes into subjective projection once language inter-

venes in its representation and expression. Even the denotative meanings of these words that signify the physical world lack clear fixity. Heidegger presented this problem in explicit terms when he wrote, "Environment is a structure which even biology as a positive science can never find and can never define but must presuppose and constantly employ,"[7] but then sought an answer to science in the certainties of the subject position. Heidegger and other phenomenologists, Maurice Merleau-Ponty, for example,[8] would rely heavily on the interpenetration of self and nature in a denial and reversal of Cartesian norms that guided an Enlightenment understanding of the separation between subject and object. The words that signify nature—*svivah*, environment, surroundings—always already seem to slip through the tightly woven network of meanings fixed in linguistic communities and national cultures and refer to what seems the most real of things, on one hand, and yet as signifiers lack—to borrow and corrupt a term from T. S. Eliot—a definite objective correlative. If we refuse to presuppose a physical space and begin to ask what types of linguistic projections are made when we define and discursively organize the environment (through poetry, law, art, prose, photography, even agriculture) then what can we discover about the influence of political fantasy on individual perception? What are the assumptions we make when we talk and write of the environment?

As a description of modernist modes of projection onto the environment, Lukács might be describing with uncanny precision a Zionist relation to the land, one that Oz will take up in the 1960s, but which had a much older history within the Zionist movement, reaching back at least to the Second Aliyah and pastoral socialism of the early Zionist pioneer A. D. Gordon. Despite Oz's admiration for Gordon as a naturalist, his reflexive projections into the environment were really a move toward physical manipulation of nature. This is certainly why Gordon's philosophy on a Zionist return to nature was centered almost exclusively on labor. While Gordon may be the closest that both Zionism and Modern Hebrew come to pastoral philosophy, even in such works as *Ha-adam veha-teva* (*Man and Nature*), the relationship Gordon envisions for the new Jew is less a person's individual commingling with an independent natural environment, as in Thoreau or Emerson or any of a long line of American and British pastoral writers and philosophers, than with a very human-oriented exploitation and colonization of the land. Certainly, the years intervening between the height of Anglo-American pastoralism and Gordon's Zionist nature ideology go a long way toward explaining the shift from nature within an objectivist world view to nature as subjective projection. While Gordon appears during the waning of Hebrew's belated Romanticism at the early part of the twentieth century, modernism's intense obsession with individual experience already held sway across Europe and had captured much of the imagination of the young idealist settlers working alongside Gordon in the fields of Kibbutz Degania.

For Gordon, despite his guru-like trappings and spiritual rhetoric, there actually exists *no* metaphysical connection between man and nature, but rather only a hyper-physical bond that is completely androcentric. Nature becomes the fantasized vision of a reconstructed, reunified Zionist psychology. Despite the rejection of European bourgeois existence, for Gordon the relation between man and nature is still one of competition even though man must shed the urban, unnatural existence of the diaspora (*galut*). As Gordon remarks in 1911 in one of the core essays that make up his volume *Labor*:

> There is only one way that can lead to our renaissance—the way of manual labor, of mobilizing all our national energies. . . . We have as yet no national assets because our people have not yet paid the price for them. A people can acquire land only by its own effort, by realizing the potentialities of its body and soul, by unfolding and revealing its inner self. This is a two-sided transaction, but the people comes first—the people comes before the land. . . . Our people can be brought to life only if each one of us recreates himself through labor and a life closer to nature. This is how we can, in time, have good farmers, good laborers, good Jews and good human beings.[9]

The rhetoric here is strangely market-oriented and liberal, a tone that was used as well by the Hebrew poet Hayim Nahman Bialik a decade later in writing about national coalescence through language.[10] I call it strange because writing about nature has typically been *anti*-modern and *anti*-liberal, and the call to collective sacrifice through national labor and closeness to nature would hardly seem to correspond to the transactional imagery that Gordon evokes. But through the call to labor and the competitive spirit of the relationship to the environment, Gordon and Labor Zionism set the ground not only for the colonization of the land, but a colonization legitimized by the discourse of interiority that would save the land from an indigenous population that did not share the same philosophical values, that perhaps did not share the same interior experience.

On the outside, in particular the outside of visual image and figuration, we do see an exalted, idealized representation of the environment, especially in a pre-war era of settlement expansion and political optimism. And so, the landscape and the native appear as Orientalized fantasies, whether in the early Palestinian stories of Moshe Smilansky or the painted landscapes of Nahum Gutman. But while both invoked carefully adapted modes of Oriental representation from European precursors, they each placed modernist limits, we might say, on how far they might identify with this place and its indigene as independent objects. Thus, in the political realm, the members of the self-defense militia, Hashomer, might take on the sartorial accoutrement of the Bedouin and ape an idealized version of the Arab, but self-defense was, after all, aimed *against* that same indigene. In Smilansky, the limits of identification are similar and while his lightly disguised, reflexive narrator, Hawaja Musa, might take on an Arabic moniker and work alongside the native Arab in the fields—*his* fields, it should be noted—there's the unmistakable sense in the stories that the Arabs simply don't get it—the "it" being the symbiosis between the consciousness of the new Jew and nature itself.

Literature, or writing more generally—more so than visual imagery—established an environmental *dispositif*, in Foucauldian terms, within the Zionist movement: a political mode of thinking about Palestine as integrally and "naturally" linked to the fate of the Jewish community. Although those ideals began to weaken in the 1980s—albeit for most in Israel they still form the ideological basis for legitimizing Jewish political control in the country—the initial challenge and awareness of the contradictions of that discourse on nature began to appear in the Statehood Generation of the early 1960s, in the stories of Oz and Yehoshua. In Oz's "Derekh ha-ruah" ("The Way of the Wind"),[11] for instance, the natural environment plays an important role in defining meaning in the text, explicitly problematizing a dissonance between the land and its ideological conception, even as it seems to hover atmospherically in the background. Indeed, Oz, especially in *Artsot ha-tan* (*Where the Jackals Howl*), his first book of short stories from the early 1960s, might be one of Israel's great crafters of landscape imagery, and certainly the best of his generation going back to S. Yizhar. In that, both Yizhar and Oz use dissonance in nature representation—

especially as it can be applied to the colonization and suppression of the Arab—as a way to introduce critical elements into their writing.[12]

Yizhar and Oz were both aware of the affinities their writing shared,[13] and it is instructive to consider Oz as inheriting many of the same writerly sensibilities. But then, the differences might be even more useful to analyze, especially in their approaches to depicting action within the land. Yizhar's protagonists, especially in his two most famous stories, "The Prisoner" and "Khirbet Hizeh," both from 1948–1949, have a certain inert quality: they cannot act with any sort of confidence and decisiveness. Others act, but mostly in crass, unthinking, and morally transgressive ways. Yizhar seems to assert that thinking thwarts action, arrests it, and paralyzes the Jew from acting in the land. The land is seen in contrast to the Jewish actors engaged upon it. In the case of "The Prisoner" the Jewish soldiers of the home guard are described visually in geometric opposition to the contours of the land: the home guard soldiers try to traverse the landscape but can only clash with the natural lines of the hills they cross on foot. In "Khirbet Hizeh," inaction is more pronounced: the soldiers constantly *look at* but can never act in the landscape, except through violent intrusion. In the terms of Gilles Deleuze, Yizhar's characters seem mired in the inaction of the optical-image; they have become alienated from action *within* the diegetic frame. Deleuze developed the term *optical-image* to describe a form of alienation cinema after the Second World War, as opposed to the way characters before the war, in what he called the movement-image, were able to act within the frame of the represented world. Deleuze's distinctions for cinematic history have strong resonance to the evolution of Hebrew culture in Palestine-Israel over the same decades of the twentieth century (indeed, a history of cinema maps quite neatly onto a history of Zionism and modern Hebrew writing), and the challenge of Yizhar's writing lies in how the optical-image would critique a Zionist political belief in Jewish action in the landscape of Palestine.

Oz's mode of representing action in the landscape does something different. If Yizhar's characters are mostly inert and ineffectual in acting in the world, Oz reimbues action into the scene—but it goes awry. If in Yizhar sight and seeing are the principal means by which characters take in place—but always at some distance—in Oz distance has disintegrated in favor of a union of consciousness and environmental action, but the dominant mode of understanding becomes misapprehending of the scene, of the land, and of the environment. Between the movement-image and the optical-image action falls away—and that seems to be Yizhar's message in his 1948 stories. By the early 1960s, at least within Oz's stories, action returns, but it is misapprehended and misdirected. If "Derekh ha-ruah" refers to *Kohelet* (Book of Ecclesiastes), then it must be ironic, since *Kohelet's* lesson of modesty and nothingness (*hevel*) before the inexorable processes of nature are grossly misunderstood by characters preoccupied with gazing at their own navels—in a literature of interior verisimilitude and self-knowledge. In *Kohelet* 11:5, the direct message of the verse emphasizes the ignorance of humans in knowing the inner workings of life or the world.

For Oz, no story and no characters better illustrate these processes of misperception and ironic self-misunderstanding than Shimshon and Gideon in "Derekh ha-ruah." Nature description frames the story, and the very role of nature as an inexorable process gives the story its lasting image: against the harshness of the *khamsin*—the dry, hot desert wind—on this Independence Day sometime during the late 1950s or early 1960s (the story is dated 1962), the trivialities of human existence—the life and death of any particular individual—seem of little consequence. Nature description and its role in characterizing the story ties into the allusion in the title to *Kohelet* and a philosophy of the dialectical (and oftentimes harsh) force of nature that makes our petty worries and anxieties seem rather senseless.

A general nature philosophy drawn from the oppositions expounded in *Kohelet* might describe the overriding architectonic structure of this story that begins with daybreak and ends with the evening's moon. But then, the specific oppositions represented by the two main characters, Shimshon and his tragically fated son, Gideon, seem all the more ironic and downright foolish. For while Gideon the paratrooper who jumps out of an airplane and becomes suspended upside-down in air (caught in high-tension wires) might thus represent the semiotics of some sort of diasporic *luftmensch* in both physical and mental orientation, it is when we apply the opposite value to his father, the *vatik* of the kibbutz, the socialist founder from the mythical immigration of the socialist Second Aliyah (1903–1909), who seems in every way the quintessential Israeli salt-of-the-earth type, that we begin to see how the role of nature in the story highlights all the contradictions and ironies in these artificial Zionist oppositions.

Shimshon, that ideal old-timer and movement founder, a leading ideologue of his socialist party, splits his workdays on the kibbutz between his political work and his tending the communal gardens. Even though Shimshon seems more in touch with the earth than his paratrooper son—a

founder of the kibbutz, of the state, with all the gravitational heaviness
and rootedness that the word founder confers—nature is something to
control, for Shimshon, something that comes under the collective authority
of the kibbutz community, something he will tend and manipulate. The
environment is a place for his personal exploitation and for an affirmation
of self-worth and self-righteousness. Action in the land redounds to his
favor. Nature and politics thus represent not two different sides of the one
man—his flesh and his spirit, to put it again in the terms of *Kohelet*—but,
in terms that echo a Labor Zionist sentiment, nature and politics are intertwined and interdependent. Or, to put it in Lukács's terms, the interiority
of politics constructs nature as Shimshon would have it, as "second nature."
Shimshon's closeness to the land confirms for him the same prescience
he exhibits in his political work. From our first glimpse of his character,
which comes to us through his own perspective—through the inaction of
the optical-image (he might indeed be a Yizhar-ian character)—we understand this arrogance: "Already yesterday Shimshon Sheinbaum foresaw with
confidence that the *khamsin* season was fast approaching. Hence as soon
as he woke he quickly stuck his head out the window. With a sense of
quiet satisfaction the father of Gideon Shenhav noted the accuracy of his
assessment" (43). Shimshon is certainly no Thoreau. To encounter nature
and (fore)see the weather, he sticks his head out the window.[14] He leaves
his mark on the environment not because of his awe for the power of
the natural sphere, but because of the way his generation controlled and
transformed everything around them.

In the dream that Shimshon is constantly struggling to remember
throughout this Independence Day (and here the critique of modernism
begins to creep into the story because of Shimshon's inability to control
his own inner life), in the dream that expresses the character's psychic
anxieties, the Lukácsian unity of place and interiority begins to disinte-
grate. Shimshon narrates:

> Let's struggle with the thought and organize the memory in
> a systematic way. The dream was becoming clearer. It seems
> that the dream began with an ugly, shouting woman. An ugly
> woman knocked on the door and announced to Shimshon that
> it was necessary for him to hurry to where the scandal was.
> Her message was expressed in broken language. I had to do a
> lot of inferring, following her to the lawn behind the dining
> hall. The scandal was indeed terrible. Without telling anyone,

the grounds workers had fashioned a pool in the middle of
the lawn. It teemed with elegant goldfish. A crude individual
stood there stupidly slapping himself on his cheeks. A tall boy
was filling the pool with a hose. The black hose poked through
from between the thin knees of the boy. I suggested that he
run and bring a chess board so that I could teach him a nice
trick. It seems that my intention was to divert his attention.
The boy replied with a lewd wink and promised excitedly that
naked women will be coming to dip into the pool. I warned
him that that would detract from the parachuting demonstration. He winked again and said mockingly that when Gideon
falls into the pool we'll have to set him up with some gills.
I walked along the hose in order to find the faucet and stop
the flow of water. It turned out that the hose skirts the edge
of the lawn and returns to the pond to suck water out of it.
A matter of nonsense (*Inyan shel hevel*). (45)

Shimshon's dream is a fantasy of control and competition. Or rather, the
dream reveals the modernist impulse for what it is: the disclosure of desire
and not the self-delusion of action in the land for its own sake. The free
indirect mode of narration mimics the way the medium—the environment,
the narration itself—would refuse to identify with the desires of the Zionist
who would act within it. It simply falls away, as if emphasizing the divide
between protagonist and the mechanisms that would control the narrative
or the represented environment. The environmental message of the story
might be contained in the fact that only nature itself seems capable of
acting within the landscape and figuring the narrative, as in the natural
descriptions that open the story, which then oscillates between an active
nature and the two rather passive human protagonists.

The inability of the narrative to sustain a stable mode of narration
echoes the tensions of individual action in the land: both Shimshon's
inability to tame and control the garden, and Gideon's ill-fated attempts
to make nature reflect his will to overcome his Oedipal anxieties. Nature
does not actually figure in the dream as such, but we are reminded clearly
that the environment is man's plaything—at least within man's hidden
desires—an arena for competing claims to ownership and authority, and the
product of the projection of a psychological fantasy, one that is specifically
masculine. Otherwise, the land and nature start to threaten the deepest
part of Shimshon's psyche: his masculine sexual prowess. Competition to

control nature becomes a struggle for the control of the self. The garden must be tended, and any errant irrational urge, any individual desire to realize *natural* desire, must be quelched in favor of the imposition of a modernist rationalism, of the grid itself, through the image of the chess table—a clear reference to the ubiquitous propagandistic images of well-tended checkered fields, going all the way back to the origins of the Jewish National Fund at the beginning of the twentieth century.

Meaning in the language of the story, then, occurs through both Gideon's and Shimshon's misapprehending of nature, their inability to understand how one's modes of expression and the discourse one uses create very real results in the physical realm: how their projections of a personal control of the environment might clash within a decentered, selfless space. We could make the same critique about Oz's story "Navadim va-tsefa" ("Nomad and Viper"), also from *Artsot ha-tan*. Just as Shimshon Scheinbaum devotes his labors to figure nature as he would have it, and thus suppress anything wild—"Scheinbaum's small harsh eyes always picked out the wild growth"—Geula in the story "Navadim va-tsefa" imposes an alternate fantasy of wildness on the forest and cathects a closeness to nature onto the Arab (à la Gutman), only to have that fantasy completely stifled by the savage's utterance of the unexpectedly civilized line: "*Ma ha-sha'ah?*" (What time is it?). Not only does the indigene speak, but measured objectivity—albeit, itself an artifice—thwarts the fulfillment of interior fantasy to take over the natural space. This is a wonderful scene: Geula runs through the forest lost in an atmosphere of primal fantasy about the eroticism of physical sense. And when she stumbles on the Arab—who suddenly and frighteningly appears from the shadows, one with the irrational sensuousness of the land, at least from *her* perspective—when she sees him, we are taken in by her projections of dark eroticism and actually expect the rape that becomes the fantasized catalyst for action within the text. But then, when the Arab deflates the fantasy and asks for the time, he not only betrays a banality in face of the heightened symbolic projections Geula has placed on this natural space, but actually achieves a much greater subversion by reversing the usual east-west dialectic of western rationalism and eastern eroticism. The banality of the Arab's question is quite hilarious and politically tragic since it shows how much control over nature resides in the hands—and fantasies—of the colonizing power.

Geula, whose name ironically and comically means "redemption" in English, mirrors Shimshon's fantasy projections, especially as they would then have real effects in the environment, either in the tending of the garden or in the violent accusation against the Arab. However, the comical inversion of the utterance in Geula's encounter with the Arab refers mostly to Gideon's ill-fated attempt to control his own actions within the environment, which leave him clownishly inverted and entangled high above the ground. Gideon, the paratrooper, tries to cathect desire onto nature by pulling the ripcord of his second chute, thus individuating himself as out-of-step with the other jumpers—in a moment of Oedipal competition that plays out appropriately enough in the environment. But the arrogance of self-directed desire—the impulse to express the self at all costs—tragically runs up against a competing nature, which would not easily yield to the interiority of self-centered fantasy, and Gideon tragically drifts into electrical high-tension wires.

In "Derekh ha-ruah," finally, it is the character of the wild boy, Tsakhi, who acts to disrupt the seemingly oppositional structure represented by Shimshon and Gideon. Tsakhi's presence—untamed, undisciplined, inattentive to any civilizing authority—is, in fact, far more disturbing than Geula's deflation in "Navadim va-tsefa." For while the Arab's rational discourse might momentarily invert the expected hierarchy of control and thus break the erotic fantasy, the disruption is easily contained and even itself inverted within Geula's fantasy: the rational disturbance becomes itself ironically transgressive and is violently eroticized into the story of the rape. Tsakhi, though, destroys the opposition of father and son not through any specific actions but through his very existence, and thus is a more permanent force: he's the illegitimate child, the uncontrollable element in the community who will destroy Shimshon's dialectical projections of Zionist history. In Freudian terms, he's the id run wild. Instead of the desired synthetic rationalism that Shimshon predicts for the third generation, Tsakhi's primal wildness and closeness to nature represent the very breakdown of a control over nature and history by the political subject, the destruction of the planned succession through the dialectic, the final efficacy of a nature that cannot be disciplined. In Marxist terms that Shimshon might himself understand, Tsakhi represents immediate and noncontingent objectivity, existing outside of any dialectical determination—and that just shows, in contrast, how caught both Shimshon and Gideon are within the same conceptual structure.

While I have tried here to present the framework for a possible reading of "Derekh ha-ruah" that acts out an environmental critique of Labor Zionism, I do not believe this was necessarily the focus of Oz's writing project, and I would be remiss to imply a conscious critique of a

Gordonian labor philosophy in these stories. In fact, ten years after *Artsot ha-tan* was first published, Oz declared his strong admiration for Gordon in terms that emphasize the psychological polemic of Gordon's ideology, that is, the need to invent a new Jewish psychology within the Zionist settlement (the *Yishuv*).[15] In this context, we might then understand why Shimshon's environmental anxieties receive their expression precisely in a dream that is replete with sexual imagery and, by implication, a Freudian psychological lexicon of symbols. Oz's rejection of a scientific socialism that is cut off from the inner life of men and women happens in the sudden bifurcation within Shimshon's mind between dream and political work. It isn't the environment Shimshon struggles with, any more than does Gideon to get himself down, out of the air. Instead, each struggles with their own inner demons, and it is this interior realm in which the story takes place. Nature remains always a reflection and projection of this inner psychology. While scientism might have to be debunked in the story, and shown to have a pitiless and unfeeling face, the narrative reverts to a modernism of interiority, and the spaces of meaning here are all finally subjective fantasy.

The dream, therefore, both clues us into the environmental competitiveness of a Labor Zionist philosophy and marks the limits of that critique. By locating the moment of ecocritique in a psychical disturbance, the story does little to undermine the Gordonian emphasis on psychology and fantasy in the landscape. Thus, nature, even in critique, remains bound to Zionist categories: of the Bible, which, through *Kohelet*, reinforces the timelessness of the landscape and the connection to some ancient past; of Orientalism, especially when we realize that the positivist description of the *khamsin*—indeed the word itself—is merely a Zionist invention, a projection of Arab closeness to the land, a phantasmagoria of Jewish nationalism. Labor and working the land remain mixed up in a projection of the self *onto* the land, in what we might call an eco-orientalism. Within the dream, the control of discourse never falls outside of Shimshon's mental struggles. He is ever confined within the spaces he sets up for his thinking. Whether it's about politics or about the kibbutz landscape, his thoughts always emanate and are projected from the confines of his study or, as in the dream, from his bedroom, all enclosed and artificial spaces. Nature forever remains a fantasy and divorced from the quotidian lives of these characters. And this attitude, finally, is echoed by the story itself which might present us with the tragedy of psychological hubris, the *hevel* of *Kohelet*, but which still relegates nature to a fantasy projection, a haughty romanticized biblical power that, in the story's own diptych between the nature description and human story, can only occupy the poetic realm of the high registers of landscape imagery completely cut off from the banalities of the prosaic everyday.

Despite poetry's position as the more important genre throughout most of modern Hebrew literary history, there is something curious—and even suspicious—about the inability of the land to be depicted prosaically. Oz elevates nature linguistically to a poetic realm whenever he needs to describe it. A similar comment can be made about other literatures, and the reasons may be more semiological than linguistic. Lukács noticed this too and valorized poetry as a mode for writing about nature: "Lyric poetry can ignore the phenomenalization of the first nature and can create a protean mythology of substantial subjectivity out of the constitutive strength of its ignorance." But lyric poetry cannot break free of the inexorable connection between nature and interiority: "At the lyrical moment the purest interiority of the soul, set apart from duration without choice, lifted above the obscurely-determined multiplicity of things, solidifies into substance; whilst alien, unknowable nature is driven from within, to agglomerate into a symbol that is illuminated throughout."[16]

For Lukács, it seems, the interiority of the soul might only find its expression in the way nature coalesces as a symbolic presence within subjective expression. But perhaps that sort of unity between nature and symbolic expression was not Oz's goal in the story. Shimshon is no romantic and seemingly unmoved by lyrical expression of nature's unknowability. This might be the reason for Oz's urge to wrest nature from poetry and create a prosaic depiction of the environment that would clarify its secondary role to interior depiction. In 1975, when Oz rewrote the story,[17] the competition and contrast between poetry and prose seems to lie at the heart of the changes he made, which focus primarily on the depiction of nature. The new language serves actually to flatten the story, to take away the Biblical awe in the depiction of the environment and make nature a background element—to frame the environment in the control of character and thus to de-emphasize the critique of Zionism. The changes emerge from the very first sentence—"*Yomo ha-aharon shel Gid'on Shenhav nifkah be-zrihat-shemesh martitah*" (Gideon Shenhav's last day opened with an awe-inspiring sunrise)—which serves throughout the story as a repeated trope of the ultimate power of nature, and which alludes to the fire and brimstone spirit of the Old Testament by placing subjective power in the day to cause a physical response: *martitah*–to make shudder, to make quiver.

In 1975, Oz changes the trope to: "*Yomo ha-aharon shel Gid'on Shenhav niftah be-zrihat-shemesh nehederet*" (Gideon Shenhav's last day opened with a marvelous sunrise). Lexically, the changes are minor, but the shift from *nifkah* to *niftah* emphasizes the rejection of poetic anthropomorphism, as does the morphological change from the verb, *martitah*, to the adjective, *nehederet*. The subject position of the day loses its power to act. Nature becomes, to quote Lukács once again, "bereft of its 'senseless' autonomous life as well of its meaningful symbolism, becomes a background, a piece of scenery, an accompanying voice; it has lost its independence and is only a sensually perceptible projection of the essential—of interiority."[18]

Perhaps the reduction of the poetic discourse of nature description to a more prosaic and spoken register indicates a newfound ideological comfort and confidence in the story. In this context, the changes can be compared to the cleaning up of the dream in the 1975 version, and the erasure of all of its more explicitly sexual elements. Indeed, in the new version, the dream is nicely framed by Shimshon's ideological work, his contemplation of dialectical matters. And while this certainly can be read ironically, the new dream, *without* Freudian symbolic fantasy, becomes little more than an expression of political competition and not the explosion of deep structural ideological anxiety. If, in the first version of the dream and story, competition was the name of the game, then in the second, control has been achieved and power has already been awarded to the ideological victor, Shimshon.

Let's focus for a moment on the very end of the dream in the 1975 version: "Puff and nonsense [*hevel u-re'ut ruah*]. Done. The ideological platform of the Poalei Zion Movement must be understood without any dialectics, it must be taken literally (*peshuto ke-mashma'o*); word for word." Not only does Shimshon's political work now get the last word and frame the dream, but the construction of the dream narrative itself points to the extraordinary erudition of the character himself. While language in 1965 was more fungible, ironically, even in the stiltedness of high poetic registers and an antiquated syntax, here in 1975 language loses a flexibility that would be independent of the controlling consciousness.[19] Thus, the nature description is no longer set apart, no longer is expressed as anthropomorphized competitor, on both a thematic and formal level, to the character of Shimshon. The diptych between human activity and the natural realm, where neither side completely controls its own textual boundaries, is reduced to the monolingual expression of human control.

The text closes in on itself and no longer allows disruption and interpenetration from without.

The political implications of this formal transformation move from critique to something more acquiescent, just as in the summer of 1982 in *The New York Times Sunday Magazine*, Oz published quite a nostalgic piece about Labor Zionism, lamenting how the pastoral utopia of years past had been trampled by later immigrants to Israel.[20] There is a certain dissonance between what Oz published in English during the first summer of the Lebanon War and what he published in Hebrew later in the autumn,[21] a dissonance that seems to rehearse old Zionist anxieties about not airing internal grievances to the outside world. How else to understand how language and audience might have such a radical effect on Oz's message? I have my suspicions that the dissonance might only be aural, and on some other plane we would find important consonances among his different stances. However, in terms of the rewriting of "Derekh ha-ruah," the turn to nostalgia and the defense of a historical ideology seems to have caused a leveling off of the narrative, to the point where any type of dialogic cacophony has been squelched and instead a linguistic monolith disempowers the critical nature of the intra-textual diptych.

The stakes in all this reading about nature and the imposition of human design can perhaps be summed up best by a childhood story an Israeli friend once told me. During a school outing into nature, she and her classmates were walking somewhere in the Galilee accompanied and guided by a young man working for a long-forgotten educational organization. At one point they ascended the crest of a gentle hill from where they had a wonderful view of the surrounding countryside. Not too far distant, as is typical in the Galilee, lay two villages, one Arab and one Jewish. The guide pointed out the two to the children and remarked about how the Jewish settlement is neatly ordered, the houses all built in rectilinear precision—to each other and within themselves—and about how the Arab village grew haphazardly with curved streets running every which way, each house different, with little obvious regard to its neighbor. Then, the young man asked the students which system was better, which village more perfectly designed. Much to the dismay of my friend, who in her heart of hearts already knew the answer—it was obvious, she would tell me, after growing up so many years in the Israeli educational system—the guide pointed to the Arab village and said, "That one, because it's more organic."

The remark is not without its own ideological difficulties and inner contradictions; indeed, I offer this story in order to show the complexities and multi-dimensionality of nature as an object of ideological projection. It is the shock of my friend's reaction as her ideological suppositions were inverted that is of importance, and not any truth content in the guide's analysis. The reversal of expectation engendered by this simple remark demonstrates the depths of the assumptions we bring to a contemplation of our surroundings.

In this context, we might do well to reread Foucault on the new nature of fantasy in a technological age. Writing of Flaubert and the experience of the fantastic in the nineteenth century, which he saw coming from the discovery of new imaginative space in texts, Foucault identifies a modern, technologically driven ideological discourse that seems to apply as well to contemplation of the environment in our scientific age: "[The] domain of phantasms is no longer the night, the sleep of reason, or the uncertain void that stands before desire, but, on the contrary, wakefulness, untiring attention, zealous erudition, and constant vigilance. . . . The fantastic . . . evolves from the accuracy of knowledge, and its treasures lie dormant in documents."[22] The complex elision between text and nature, between representations of knowledge and their impact on the physical environment surrounding us, implies an important critique for all discourses that claim to know what constitutes a natural space.

Notes

1. Lukács, Georg. *The Theory of the Novel*. MIT Press, 1971, p. 62.

2. Robert Alter published his assessment of generational tension in Hebrew literature, in a discussion of the 1962 republication of Sholom J. Kahn's anthology of Israeli writing, *A Whole Loaf*, from 1957; "Israeli Writers and Their Problems" appeared in *Commentary*, vol. 34, no. 1, July 1962, p. 20.

3. Alter, 22. Alter's use of the term *publicistic* literature refers generally to modern Hebrew writing's connection to Russian literature, especially the publicistic style of polemical writing in Russia in the late nineteenth century, and into the twentieth. The opposition of individual and collective infected narrative stylistics, which took from Russian the notion of a specifically publicistic—that is, public, social, and political—mode of expression in imaginative literature.

4. The study of the environment in the context of the humanities began in the mid-1990s as a reaction against the relativistic uncertainties of post-structuralism. The environment in Anglo-American criticism seemed to offer an uncon-

tingent object of study. Jay Parini, writing about the trend in *The New York Times* in 1995, announced the critical aims of the new trend quite explicitly beginning with his title: "The Greening of the Humanities: Deconstruction Is Compost. Environmental Studies Is the Academic Field of the '90s" (29 Oct. 1995). Laurence Buell had published that year an important work in the field: *The Environmental Imagination: Thoreau, Nature Writing, and the Formation of American Culture.* Harvard UP, 1995. Buell's corpus includes *The Future of Environmental Criticism* (Blackwell, 2005) and *Writing for an Endangered World: Literature, Culture, and Environment in the U.S. and Beyond* (Harvard UP, 2001). Important collections of essays include Cheryll Glotfelty and Harold Fromm, *The Ecocriticism Reader: Landmarks in Literary Ecology* (U of Georgia P, 1996) and Greg Garrard, editor, *The Oxford Handbook of Ecocriticism* (Oxford UP, 2014). In the fields of history and environmental philosophy, the works of David Cronin (*Uncommon Ground: Toward Reinventing Nature* [Norton, 1995]) and David W. Orr (*Hope Is an Imperative: The Essential David Orr* [Island Press, 2010], which includes many of his articles from the 1980s and 1990s) also gained prominence in the mid-1990s and helped spread ecocritical thinking throughout the humanities. Since the 1990s, ecocriticism and environmental thinking in the humanities have exploded as a field, especially in the wake of raised public consciousness of human-induced climate change and global warming.

5. Lukács, p. 63.

6. I have in mind a generalized reading of Foucault's ideas of culture and power. Edward Said differentiates between two phases in Foucault's development of his ideas on culture and power. For a subtle reading of the effects of power in cultural discourse, see Foucault's *L'Ordre du discours* and *L'Archéologie du savoir.* For what Said calls a "hypertrophied" vision in the later works of Foucault, see *Surveiller et punir* and *L'Histoire de la sexualité* (from "Foucault and the Imagination of Power," in *Foucault: A Critical Reader.* Edited by David Conzers Hoy. Oxford, 1986). While Said's analysis seems too schematic and simple—and perhaps, as well, tinged with a certain anxiety of influence—what binds both Foucault's projects and Said's analyses of imperialism and culture is the notion of "savaging . . . limits and reifications," that is, the expansion of textual and cultural analysis until social discourse is seen as a conduit and tool for the expression of political control and power. For a less Foucaultian analysis of the political history of Israel's naming of places in the land, see Meron Benvenisti, *Sacred Landscape: The Buried History of the Holy Land Since 1948* (U of California P, 2000).

7. From *Being and Time*; quoted in Lawrence Buell, *The Environmental Imagination* (Harvard University Press, 1995, p. 1).

8. See his *Phenomenology of Perception.* Translated by Colin Smith. Routledge, 2002.

9. Gordon, A. D. "Some Observations." (Hebrew), *Nation and Labor.* Tel Aviv, 1957, p. 128.

10. See H. N. Bialik's essay, "Hevleu lashon." (Language pangs), in *Divrei sifrut*. Mosad Bialik, 1965, pp. 6–18. For a discussion of this essay, see Kronfeld, Chana. *On the Margins of Modernism*. U of California P, 1996.

11. *Artsot ha-tan* [*Where the Jackals Howl*]. Sifriat po'alim, 1965. No translation was ever published of this edition of the stories.

12. See, for instance, Yizhar's story, "*Ha-shavui*" [*The Prisoner*] in *Be-terem yetsiah* (Zemorah-Bitan, 1991), especially the opening paragraph, which sets the scene and creates expectations of the ineptitude of the civil guard unit sent by the Israeli command to capture an Arab at all costs.

13. A note on Yizhar's talk in Beersheva in 1997.

14. The matter of where one does things is not a trivial consideration for Thoreau. During his time at Walden Pond, his thoughts about engaging the seasons and describing them was dependent on a physical closeness to the outdoors, and not just the proximity of his cabin: "each page . . . should be written in its own season & out of doors or in its own locality wherever it might be" (from his journals; quoted in Buell, *The Environmental Imagination*, 131). Sticking his head out the window was not enough.

15. Gordon ha-yom, A. D. (A. D. Gordon today), in *Ba-or ha-thelet ha-azah* (Sifriat ha-poalim), 1979, pp. 175–76.

16. Lukács, p. 63.

17. Tel Aviv, 1976.

18. Lukács, p. 63.

19. In these few sentences are embedded three separate textual references: 1) to *Kohelet* itself, in "*hevel u-re'ut ruah*" ("*hevel*" [nonsense] concludes the 1965 dream, but in 1975 the full phrase appears as a static collocation that invokes the alluded-to text as a set object); 2) to Rashi, in *peshuto ke-mashma'o* (literally) (a neologism that ironically does not seem to signify clear meaning); and 3) to Shakespeare's "The Rape of Lucrece," in *hevel u-re'ut ruah*: " 'What win I, if I gain the thing I seek? / A dream, a breath, a froth of fleeting joy."

20. In his essay "Has Israel Altered Its Visions?" Oz writes: "Jewish youths sick and tired of the stifling atmosphere of the Jewish petite-bourgeoisie of Eastern Europe embraced Tolstoy's prescription of going back to the land, mingling with the peasants, enlightening them and being healed by the pure simplicity of rural life. . . . Sadly enough, they couldn't wrap the Arab peasantry in Tolstoyan lovingkindness because of the language barrier and other reasons. . . . Those early Zionist Socialists were simultaneously drying the swamps and arguing about the social, political, ethical and theological significance of each of their actions" (in *Israel, Palestine, and Peace*. Harcourt Brace, 1994, p. 7). Later in the same essay, Oz continues: "As for the North African Jews, and many of the Central Europeans, they brought with them the attitudes of a French-inspired middle class—conservative, puritan, observant, extremely hierarchical and family oriented, and, to some extent, chauvinistic, militaristic and xenophobic" (13). Of the myriad conceptual

and historical errors Oz commits in just these few lines, the implications of his stereotyping posit onto Zionist history a monolithic and utopian apparatus that is, at best, racist and political naive.

21. I am thinking most particularly about *Po va-sham be-Erets-Yisraʼel bi-stav 1982* (*Here and There in the Land of Israel*, Autumn 1982) (Keter, 1983).

22. Quoted in David Halperin, "Forgetting Foucault: Acts, Identities, and the History of Sexuality." *Representations*, 1998, p. 93.

Chapter 11

On Eternity

Homelessness and the Meaning of Homeland

LIAM HOARE

Often around 5 or 6 o'clock I see an elderly woman on the kibbutz sitting on a bench, singing to herself, and I don't know what she sings, because it's Polish. And I think to myself: That woman 45 years ago must have been a romantic girl with braids sitting by a stream somewhere in Poland singing a Hebrew song about Jerusalem. And everything I write is just a footnote or commentary on that scene.

—Amos Oz, 1978[1]

1

On Amos Oz's writing desk, whether in his study in Arad or apartment in Tel Aviv where he resided until the end of his life, there were always two pens—ordinary ballpoint pens, which he swapped out every three weeks or so. One pen was blue; the other, black. "I never mix them up," Oz told *The New York Times*'s then-Jerusalem correspondent Ethan Bronner in 2009.[2] "One is to tell the government to go to hell. The other is to tell stories." One pen was for his essays and columns; the other, his novels and short stories—symbols of a bifurcated writing life.

The two forms served entirely different purposes, as Oz explained
to *The Paris Review* in 1996. His essays and columns—the political as
opposed to literary ones—derived from a place of rage and a sense of
injustice, as punchy articles written for the Israeli press during the 1982
war in Lebanon like "Hitler's Dead, Mr. Prime Minister," "Where Can We
Hide Our Shame?" and "On Wonders and Miracles" (later collected in
The Slopes of Lebanon) indicate.[3] They were written quickly and passionately. While a good day's work on a story might end with half a page of
prose—and sometimes just a sentence or two—Oz tended to write his
essays in six or seven hours in a single burst of creative energy. Perhaps
the key distinction, however, is that his essays were written from a place
of certainty and with an intent to argue and persuade:

> I can write an article only when I agree with myself one hundred
> percent, which is not my normal condition—normally I'm in
> partial disagreement with myself and can identify with three
> or five different views and different feelings about the same
> issue. That is when I write a story, where different characters
> can express different views on the same subject. I have never
> written a story or a novel to make people change their minds
> about anything—not once. When I need to do this, I write an
> essay, or an article.[4]

This distinction between the essay and the story, certainty and ambiguity,
one perspective or multiple ones, is perhaps clearest in Oz's work when
it comes to the subject of home. His essays from 1967's "The Meaning of
Homeland" collected in *Under this Blazing Light* through to "Dreams Israel
Should Let Go of Soon" published in *Dear Zealots* are clear and consistent
as an argument for and a defense of Oz's particular kind of Zionism which,
as I shall describe, was a secular and humanistic one which recognized that
the Israeli-Palestinian conflict was a struggle between right and right and
a war between two victims and that any political solution thereto was one
which had to recognize that Palestine was a land twice-promised. Neither
the occupation nor the failings of one government or the next invalidated
the original conceit, the Zionist dream, which Oz called "wonderful and
awesome" (*The Slopes of Lebanon* 191). "If there had been no Zionism,
six and a half million would have been dead rather than six million, and
who would have cared?" Oz told *The New Yorker* editor David Remnick

in 2004.[5] "Israel was a life raft for a half-million Jews." In a similar mode, Zionism, Oz pronounced in a 1983 lecture, was "the best and straightest idea to have sprung from the twisted Jewish mind in two thousand years. That is my opinion, despite everything we have done and everything that has happened to us" (191). That which Jews were able to accomplish in Palestine, Oz wrote in 2015, "is far less and yet far more than what my parents and their parents ever dreamed of" (121).

Yet Oz, of course, did not write *Exodus*. "I am fundamentally a Jewish writer," Oz said in a 1978 interview. "But I am a Jewish writer in the sense of writing forever about the ache to have a home, and then having one, aching to go away thinking that this is not the real one" (Oz and Wirth-Nesher 312). From the very beginning, with short stories like "Where the Jackals Howl," novellas like "Late Love," and novels such as *Elsewhere, Perhaps*, Oz's works were shot through with doubt and uncertainty, restlessness and unfulfillment. His well-intentioned yet tragicomic men and dreamy, melancholic women live in a kind of ambiguous, often discontented, and sometimes disturbed state, fighting against the land and the elements, haunted by the ghosts of Jewish history, and bedeviled by violent dreams. *Fima*, a novel to which I will later devote some attention, is entirely about the central character's search for a certain equilibrium, for a moment's inner peace, for an end to his feeling of homelessness, only to discover that such a condition is unachievable. The Jewish people had nowhere else to go other than the Land of Israel, Oz said in his final public appearance before his death. The homeland was a necessity, but to have a homeland is one thing but to feel at home is quite another.

2

"I am a Jew and a Zionist" (79), Oz declares in the opening passages of his 1967 essay "The Meaning of Homeland," published in the pages of *Davar*. This keystone piece articulates most clearly what Oz meant by "Zionist" and by extension "Zionism" and, written around the time of the Six Day War, reflects on a number of other terms essential to the debate such as "Jewishness," "homeland," "national right," and "peace." The Zionism expressed in "The Meaning of Homeland" is clearly as much about that to which it is opposed to as the principles in which it is grounded. It is muscular and uncompromising, secular and humanistic—a Zionism at the center of which stood not a land but a people, yet at the same time one that recognized that the land was in some way inherent to the wide arrays of dreams invested in the Zionist idea.

Oz's Zionism was, in the first instance, a rejection of the idea that one could live as a Jew in the Diaspora. The Diaspora in "The Meaning of Homeland"—and by the Diaspora, Oz meant Europe—meant to live as a national minority and exist not as a fully realized individual or people but rather as "a fragment of a symbol in the consciousness of others" (81). Jewish peoplehood and self-determination, to be a Jew in a Jewish state, saved Jews from that fate: "Being a Jew in the Diaspora means that Auschwitz is meant for you. It is meant for you because you are a symbol, not an individual. The symbol of the justly persecuted vampire, or the symbol of the unjustly persecuted innocent victim—but always and everywhere, you are not an individual, not yourself, but a fragment of a symbol."[6] In July 1967, in the aftermath of the Six Day War, The Movement for the Complete Land of Israel launched itself on the national scene.[7] The great Hebrew poet Natan Alterman, the Nobel Prize-winning novelist Shai Agnon, Uri Zvi Greenberg, Haim Gouri, and Moshe Shamir were among its prominent members, opening up a schism in Israel's writerly community. Their manifesto argued in part that "just as we are not permitted to relinquish the State of Israel, so we are commanded to maintain what we have received from its hands: the Land of Israel. We are hereby loyally committed to the wholeness of our land and no government in Israel is entitled to relinquish this wholeness" (Rapoport).

Oz—along with A. B. Yehoshua and Yehuda Amichai—sharply disagreed. "The meaning of homeland" is in a sense a repudiation of The Movement for the Complete Land of Israel's tendential view. Labor Zionists and adherents of A. D. Gordon of course believed in an inherent connection between the redemption of the Jewish people and a renewal or rehabilitation of the land—that, as Oz once wrote of Gordonian Zionism, human nature could be gradually improved through a certain intimacy between people and "a renewal of links with the old elements: the soil, the cycle of the seasons, tilling the soil, 'mother nature,' inner rest" (117). Yet Oz was not one to believe that the Land of Israel was, to borrow a formulation from Avraham Yoffe, a "living creature." "It is we who are living creatures. The land is not," Oz told Yoffe at a symposium in 1982. "The land is our place, a place without which we would surely be different people. This makes it an important place for us, but not a living creature" (193). The distinction he made was an important one. The role of Zionism,

Oz argues in "The Meaning of Homeland," is not to liberate a land but rather a people; "the word 'liberation' applies to people, not to dust and stone" (83). Oz believed in a Zionism that had to be honest with itself, that eschews what he would later term *reconstructionitis*, and come to terms with "both the spiritual implications and the political consequences of the fact that this small tract of land is the homeland of two peoples fated to live facing each other, willy-nilly, because no God and no angel will come to judge between right and right" (101–02):

> The results of the recent war have placed Zionist ideology before an urgent and fateful choice: if from now on the current which has flowed within Zionism almost from the beginning, the current of nationalistic romanticism and mythological delusions of greatness and renewal, the current of longing for a kingdom and blowing rams' horns and conquering Canaan by storm, the national superiority complex based on military enthusiasm in the guise of crude biblical nostalgia, the conception of the entire State of Israel as one giant act of retaliation for the "historical humiliation" of the Diaspora—if that trend prevails among us, then the Middle East is fated to be the battleground of two peoples, both fighting a fundamentally just war, both fighting essentially for their life and liberty, and both fighting to the death.[8]

Oz's Zionism was, then, a rejection of its most backward-looking, maximalist, expansionist, and revanchist tendencies. Until the end of his life, in essays like "Dreams Israel Should Let Go of Soon," he warned that without two states in the Land of Israel, there would soon be one—and that state, he believed, would be an Arab as opposed to a Jewish one, as his domestic political opponents desired. For the very same reason that he rejected life in the Diaspora in 1967, Oz rejected bi-nationalism, multinationalism, or a single Arab state in Palestine. He did not wish to live as a Jewish minority, no matter the ruler or the nature of the state: "I insist on the right of Israeli Jews, like any other people, to be a majority, if only on a tiny strip of land" (97). The principle of Jewish statehood, of Jewish self-determination, remained paramount. Better, for Oz, to have a state and some of the land than all of the land without a state. And yet the state and the people could not exist without the land. This was not a sentimental view—as I have argued elsewhere, Oz was staunchly opposed to sentimentality in politics—but rather a practical and realistic one.[9] Oz also believed strongly that a Jewish state could not exist anywhere else save the Land of Israel: "the Israeli Jews are in Israel because there is no other country in the world which the Jews, as a people, as a nation, could ever call home. As individuals, yes, but not as a people, not as a nation" (5). The Zionism of the kibbutz, the Zionism of the secular, humanistic left, was but one current within Zionism, an idea which Oz often in essays and speeches called a spectrum of dreams, visions, and masterplans encompassing those who wished to transplant the manners and customs of the Austro-Hungarian Empire to the Land of Israel all the way to those *kibbutznikim* on the far-left who believed they were more Marxist-Leninist than Stalin himself. In his final speech delivered in July 2018 at the University of Tel Aviv,[10] Oz explains that while Zionism was diffuse and diverse all those who called themselves Zionists or in a sense became Zionists by emigrating to Israel before or after its founding were united by a common belief: the Jewish people had nowhere else to go.

3

The Jewish people had nowhere else to go, and yet from the opening lines of *Where the Jackals Howl*, as a blast of wind from the sea pierces the heatwave that had been suffocating the kibbutz, the land itself is a kind of oppositional force, uncaring, without mercy, a source of insecurity and uncertainty that seems to reject the very presence of those who would try and master it. Oz writes in the richly descriptive early passages of *Elsewhere, Perhaps* of an "enmity between the valley, with its neat, geographical patchwork of fields and the savage bleakness of the mountains" and the kibbutz as a kind of "negation of the grim natural chaos that looks down on it from above" (11–12); and "We cannot conceal our modest pride at the marked contrast between the cultivated plain and the grim heights, between the blooming valley and the menacing mountain range, between the confident optimism below and the unruly glowering presence above" (*Elsewhere Perhaps* 14). In this novel, the land is a harbinger of danger. It lays in wait, broodily, as if preparing to strike back. The burning heat of the day scorches the earth; the encroaching cold of winter causes the kibbutz's irrigation system to fail. Elsewhere, in the story "A Hollow Stone" members of the kibbutz go out in the fields to assess the damage caused by a storm, one which has wiped away their crops, unrooted saplings, shorn the palm trees of their crowns, and lifted the corrugated iron roofs of the sheds and barns, carried away on the wind (*Where the Jackals Howl*). And this is to say nothing of those who were there before the settlers and pioneers arrived to turn over the soil, to begin anew. In "Where the Jackals Howl," the character of Matityahu dreams of "hordes of thin, dark people" streaming down the mountainside and sweeping across the fertile valleys, "racing over the ruins of deserted villages without a moment's check" (17): "In their rush toward the sea they drag with them all that lies in their path, uprooting posts, ravaging fields, mowing down fences, trampling the gardens and stripping the orchards, pillaging homesteads, crawling through huts and stables, clambering over walls like demented apes, onward, westward, to the sands of the sea."[11] This sense of pervasive threat and enmity is made even more explicit in "Nomad and Viper," in which a passing caravan of nomads disturbs and upends kibbutz life, an incident that ends with a group of young men crossing the kibbutz boundary, armed, heading off into the wadi in search of their quarry. "Excitement was dilating our pupils. And the blood was drumming in our temples" (38). In one of Oz's later stories, "Deir Ajloun" from *Between Friends*, the character of Yotam, frustrated by his inability to leave Kibbutz Yekhat, walks moodily and contemplatively around the overgrown ruins of a depopulated Arab village nearby the kibbutz—a reminder of those who once worked the land before the kibbutznikim arrived. "What he wanted more than anything was to remain sitting there among the ruins of Deir Ajloun, on the edge of the blocked well, to sit there utterly still, his mind empty of thoughts, and to wait" (167). Of course, the recurring enemy of the kibbutz in *Where the Jackals Howl* is the titular creature itself. Oz writes self-deprecatingly in *The Same Sea* that in the "bad old days of his youth," he would "run away at night to be all alone in the reading room on the edge of the kibbutz where he could cover page after page with jackals' howls" (41). So it is that jackals encircle the kibbutz in the gray light of the autumn night, out of sight, "their paws gliding over the turf, scarcely touching the ground" (9). Man and jackal are engaged in a struggle of life and death: to ensnare and avoid being ensnared. In "Where the Jackals Howl," Oz describes in bloody, visceral detail the moment a jackal tentatively, "soft as a viper," approaches a piece of forbidden fruit with its jaw, only to have the cold steel trap snap shut upon him, "with a metallic click, light and precise" (10). Seized by despair, with a frantic leap, the jackal tries to free himself from the trap. Pain rips through his body. "The sound of his wailing rose and filled the night" (10). And then he was gone.

The jackal is often rendered as a symbol of a threat posed to the kibbutz in the 1960s, a time of generational conflict between fathers and sons, those who had founded the kibbutz and those who would inherit it, but there is more to it than that. The jackal—akin in some ways to the nomad—is the image of a kind of eternal threat. The jackals posed a danger to generations of farmers and workers before the pioneers arrived in the Land of Israel to turn the soil over and renew the days of old. The jackal, moreover, is a threat that replenishes itself. It is an uncurable curse. "Generations of jackals," Oz writes, have come and gone "but the young ones follow the lead of their fathers, and nothing is changed. In every generation the gray open spaces are filled with night after night with sounds of wailing and jubilation, with cries of impiety, malice, and despair" (69). The jackal is an existential threat to kibbutz life that no man has yet overcome: "The jackal pack . . . gave a laugh. Their laughter ran through the empty streets of the night, . . . and like a monkey the laughter climbed the gutters of the house and penetrated inwards in a thousand jagged splinters. When the kibbutz was founded, we believed that we really could turn over a new leaf, but there are things that cannot be set right and should be left as they have been since the beginning of time."[12] In profiling Oz for *The New Yorker*, Remnick visited him at his then-home in Arad. Together with Oz's wife Nili, they went on a desert ramble. " 'The landscape here is no different than it was in the time of the prophets and Jesus,' Oz said along the way. The hills are bare, but there are wolves, desert hares, jackals. There are Bedouin camps, oases. Oz takes his walks here to clear his mind . . . , to 'keep perspective on eternity.'" "So much of what I have to tell has to do with the open," Oz later reflected in that profile, "the desert, the field, a kind of arid mountains around Jerusalem" (Remnick), and indeed, from these earliest short stories through to works like *Don't Call It Night* and *Between Friends*, nature and the landscape have been used to denote something timeless, unchanging, in contrast to the actions and follies of man: their broken relationships, their aimless state, their failing political and sociological experiments. "There are things that cannot be set right and should be left as they have been since the beginning of time" (Oz 83). Or, as "Where the Jackals Howl" closes: "The path of the seasons is well trodden. Autumn, winter, spring, summer, autumn. Things are as they have always been. Whoever seek a fixed point in the current of time and the seasons would do well to listen to the sounds of the night that never change. They come to us from out there."[13]

4

In January 2016, I interviewed Oz over coffee in his study in his home in north Tel Aviv for a feature published in *The Forward*.[14] One wall of the room was lined with books: floor to ceiling, end to end. Upon his writing desk, which faced views northward along the Mediterranean shoreline in the direction of Herzliya, was an old laptop computer, piles of papers, and some of the latest translations of his final novel, *Judas*. The conversation was wide-ranging, a literary summing up or stocktaking. Towards the end of our interview, we were discussing the subjects of his novels, and in particular, why Oz at the end of his writing life had taken to returning to the places in which he had, in a sense, started out: Jerusalem and the kibbutz. I put it to Oz that various Israeli authors from Aharon Appelfeld to David Grossman had made it their business to write about the Holocaust. Oz had touched upon this subject in *Touch the Water, Touch the Wind*, but generally his subject is considered to be Israel and Israeliness: its towns and cities, land and people. As I unwound the flawed premise of my question, Oz stopped me in my tracks:

> Be careful there, my friend. Aharon Appelfeld wrote about forty or maybe forty-five novels. The word "Holocaust" is not mentioned once in any of his works, ever. There are no concentration camps, no gas chambers—not even once. Never. There are hard labor camps, there are Nazi torture chambers, but there are not immediate descriptions of mass murder. None. (As far I remember, I may be wrong.) If there are some executions, they always happen on the margin or in the background—they are not in the front of the story. Whereas, on the other hand, a novella which I wrote many, many years ago called "Crusade"—the first one to be translated into English— set in the eleventh century could not be understood without the Holocaust in the background. Even *A Tale of Love and Darkness* would have been a completely different tale where it not for the fact that my parents fled by the skin of their

teeth, in the nick of time, from Europe to Jerusalem, and
by the fact that so many relatives were murdered in Europe.
It would have been a different tale. Maybe they would have
lived a different life. So it's not that simple. You don't have to
actually tell the story of death camps or the story of ruined
Jewish small towns in eastern Europe or the stories of fleeing
refugees or the stories of executions in order to relate to this
most significant event in my life—more significant than the
creation of the State of Israel.[15]

He was right, of course. Because of Oz's direct political engagement
through organizations like Peace Now, because of his identification with
the kibbutz and Labor Zionism through his life and stories, because of
the way native-born Hebrew novelists of his generation challenged the
literary establishment with their unadorned, colloquial language, because
of his essays which articulated, as I have argued, a very precise secular
and humanistic form of Zionism, and because of works like *A Tale of Love
and Darkness* in which he helped write the story of Israel's birth—because
of all these things, Oz is oft considered one of the most Israeli of Israeli
writers. He "embodied every captivating quality, be it real or imagined, of
the mythological *sabra*: he was brilliant yet humble, sophisticated and self-
aware but not neurotic, highly idealistic but also tolerant and pragmatic,"
the New York-based Israeli novelist Ruby Namdar has written. "Even his
casual good looks reflected the fantasy of the ultimate sabra, the golden boy
of the kibbutz, and the Zionist dream."[16] Nevertheless there remains a gap
between perception and reality. Oz, as we also discussed in my interview
with him, grew up in Jerusalem in a Revisionist Zionist milieu of a sort
that no longer exists—secular, in contrast to the fusion of nationalism with
east European mysticism that Menachem Begin embodied, but one that
combined an emotional form of nationalism with liberalism, pluralism,
and certain progressive values. "My family was very, very progressive
on minority rights, on women's rights, on many issues which are today
associated with the liberals on the left. All of this is part of my childhood
heritage, my family heritage" (Oz), Oz told me.

It was a hawkish environment, one in which Oz spent his days
writing "ecstatically chauvinistic little poems about heroism and dying on
the battlefield, about the glorious history of the kingdoms of David and
Solomon which we are soon going to restore" (Oz). It was also a deeply
European milieu: of European ideas like liberalism and nationalism,

European languages, and European history; European dreams, European nightmares, and European authors. Oz, we know from his work, was influenced by Israeli writers like S. Y. Agnon and engaged by the work of S. Yizhar and Yaakov Shabtai, but to browse a collection of essays like *The Story Begins* is to observe names like Gogol, Kafka, and Chekhov, not to mention Tolstoy, Dostoyevsky, and Thomas Mann.[17] The Holocaust and the milieu in which he was raised leaves a deep impression on Oz's novels. In one sense, the aforementioned conflict between man and nature in his earliest stories is a manifestation of a clash between the dreams of certain European Jewish immigrants for the Land of Israel and its realities, that Jerusalem was not the city of which his parents and grandparents dreamt. "My father used to say from time to time that one day . . . Jerusalem will evolve and develop into a real city," Oz told NPR's Terry Gross in 2004.[18] "Over the years, I learned that when my father . . . meant a city with a river in the middle, bridges across the river and dense forests round-about—Europe, the promised land from the promised land." Jerusalem in *My Michael* or *The Hill of Evil Counsel* is a haunted city of stone and rusted iron railings, a backwater, an endangered outpost enveloped by hills which cry out at night with wild sounds. It is a city of mystics and peddlers and wild dreamers who themselves resemble characters from a Bulgakov novel, walking down deserted, airless streets carrying a large sack yelling, "Pri-mus, pri-mus" (*My Michael* 60). There are those in Oz's Jerusalem stories who cling to violent, fiery slogans and visions for Israel's future and those whose lives were transformed not by their immigration to the Land of Israel but that which came before it. They have moved to a new homeland only to discover that one cannot leave behind the ghosts of the old one. Hannah Gonen observes of her mother "All day she shuts herself up in a small room on the edge of the kibbutz reading Turgenev and Gorki in Russian, writing me letters in broken Hebrew, knitting and listening to the wireless" (*My Michael* 7). Hannah herself is a child of Jerusalem, one beset by depression, hysteria, and mania. When characters like Hannah dream, they dream of Europe, of gushing rivers, snowy peaks, and the sound of horses' hooves:

> Sometimes at night I see a bleak Russian steppe. Frozen plains coated with a crust of bluish frost which reflects the flickering light of a wild moon. There is a sledge and a bearskin rug and the black back of a shrouded driver and furiously galloping horses and wolves' eyes glowing in the darkness round about

and a solitary dead tree stands on the white slope and it is
night within night on the steppe and the stars keep sinister
watch. . . . The dead tree which stands all alone on the slope
on the steppe is not there by chance, it has a function which
on waking I cannot name.[19]

Europe and the Holocaust are always there in the early works: inform-
ing the work either as a manifest theme or a subterranean current. In
"Late Love," written in 1970 and printed in *Unto Death*, Shraga Ungar
lives in a small apartment in a housing development in Tel Aviv where
damp blossoms upon the walls and the floors slope towards the center
of the room. He works as a traveling lecturer for the Central Committee,
traveling from kibbutz to kibbutz holding lectures on Russian Jewry. The
subject, and the notion that there is a "Bolshevik plot to exterminate the
Jewish people as a first step towards the dismemberment of the whole
world" (74), consumes him. No Jew is safe: from Ukraine to the Jezreel
Valley. Fading, aging, restless and sleepless, Ungar speaks of the "sinister,
suffocating nights" (83) in Tel Aviv. "Spare a thought for the flavor of the
nights here in Tel Aviv," he commands:

> There is no other city in the whole world . . . where so many
> people dream such terrible dreams every night. . . . Just sit
> down at night, if you please, along on the balcony. . . . You
> will surely hear, through the open bedroom windows, how this
> whole Jewish city cries out in sleep. It is the sound of night-
> mares . . . , of horrors past and horrors yet to come. . . . The
> Jewish people . . . are totally unable to withdraw from the
> game once and for all. Did we really hope to take a refuge
> here and build a new land and pretend to be a Bulgaria or a
> New Zealand? . . . All the anger, all the misery, all the enthu-
> siasm, all the hysteria, all the madness in the world, all the
> revolutions and ideologies and complexes and suffering and
> horrors, everywhere are all directed against us.[20]

In *The Jewish State*, Herzl famously posits that antisemitism exists where
Jews lived among Gentiles in perceptible numbers, and thus, by transferring
Jews out of the Diaspora and into a Jewish state as "free men on our own
soil" where they could "die peacefully in our own homes" (99), antisemitism "would stop at once and forever," for the creation of a Jewish state

would be "the conclusion of peace" (98). Ungar believes, meanwhile, that only by devising and constructing a mechanical device of some sort, one large enough to transport to the entirety of the Jewish people into outer space, far away to another galaxy, could they at last be at rest and achieve a final perfect peace. Perhaps. Here on Earth the idea of overturning the Jewish condition, of escaping antisemitism, was an illusion—even in a Jewish state. "So it has been in every generation gone by," Oz writes, "so it will be in every generation to come" (121).

5

Following his death in December 2018, one of the most perceptive tributes paid to Oz was that of German author and literary scholar Stefana Sabin writing in the Swiss *Neue Zürcher Zeitung*.[21] For Sabin, Oz did not write in order to merely depict the Israeli reality as if he were some sort of stenographer or anthropologist but in order to trace the emotional entanglements, loves, and sufferings, and thus the psychosocial, psychological, and emotional patterns of Israeli lives. His novels captured a kind of "precarious reality," Sabin argues, in which there is a symbiotic relationship between the "inner turmoil" of his characters and the "existential threats" they face, whether that be, as I have also outlined, metrological, animal, or human; the seasons, the jackal, or the nomad. Behind this depiction of what Sabin calls an "everyday life that was actually unlivable" was a reckoning with Zionism itself: that by having his characters' inner lives shaped by existential danger and emotional peril, Oz "succeeded in capturing the most intimate facets of the human psyche and portrayed his characters as imperiled, unstable, homeless figures. This is one reason why Oz's characters have more to do with the *Luftmenschen* of Yiddish folklore than the Zionist ideal of the new Hebrew" (Sabin).

In no work of Oz's is this sense of peril, instability, and homelessness more palpable and the influence of Diasporic forms of storytelling more apparent than in *Fima*, a novel that opens with its eponymous hero awakening from a terrible, haunting dream "overcome by the feeling that he was here by mistake, that he ought to be somewhere completely different. But what the mistake was, or where he ought to be, he did not know this morning. In fact he never did" (4). This is the essential subject of *Fima*: the sense of place, of groundedness, of feeling at home. Efraim Nisam lives a chaotic, disordered, and directionless life. He is, as Michael Silverblatt evocatively described him, "a Hamlet of indecisive conscience, suffering a kind of paralysis that could have been said to have been brought about by an inability to know what to do" (Oz) about the state of the world, in this case Israel's treatment of the Palestinians. To read the novel more broadly and perhaps more accurately, Fima is indecisive and paralyzed by an inability to know what to do about the state of the Jewish people and his feeling of homelessness in an era of statehood.

Fima lives alone in a grotty apartment in Jerusalem with cockroaches that feed off of discarded scraps of food in his kitchen. He is a product of his environment, in a certain sense. *Fima* is a Jerusalem novel and Jerusalem, in Fima's words, is a city of "longings and madness. A refugee camp, not a city" (252). Fima is a restless, rootless character to the extent that Jerusalem is a city that attracts them, an ancient city built upon rocky hills that has outlasted peoples, religions, ideologies, leaders, zealots, and prophets. Thinks Fima: "Once upon a time kings and prophets, saviors, world reformers, madmen who heard voices, zealots, ascetics, and dreamers walked around Jerusalem. And one day in the future, in a hundred years or more, new men, totally different from us, would be living here" (216). He is the son of a factory owner, a libidinous man like his son yet one whose traditional views on other issues, political or religious, clash with Fima's more secular, dovish, and conflicted outlook. He is deeply and perhaps uncomfortably involved in the life of his ex-wife's son, taking on a fatherly role as if he were the father himself. He works part-time as a receptionist in a gynecologist's office—perhaps the only example of order in his life. Though something of a schlub, he arouses a curious sympathy in his female friends and possesses a certain sexual attractiveness, even if his sexual encounters are less than satisfactory. In his head are the solutions to all the country's ills, if only he could get someone to listen. He is a poet who can no longer write poetry. He has a taste for and is shaped by the heroes of nineteenth-century Russian literature. He driven philosophically by the search for the so-called Third Condition: a kind of equilibrium, a perfect peace, a "grace that can only be achieved by renouncing all desires, by standing under the night sky sans age, sans sex, sans time, sans race, sans everything" (282); what Oz described in a 1994 interview[22] as "a mystical Jewish condition" in which "all the conflicts, contradictions, and disagreements in the world could be harmonized—not resolved," in which "everything could be reconciled with everything else." Fima is, therefore, in part a product of the archetypes of nineteenth-century Russian literature: of Gogol and Chekhov, of Tolstoy and Dostoyevsky. "Not only does Mr. Oz strive toward a Chekhovian compassion for his characters, but his novel depends—as many Chekhov stories do—on making us believe in the possibility of last-minute grace," Francine Prose observes of *Fima*.[23]

He is also related to Gregor Samsa of Kafka's *Metamorphosis*, a novel which, as Prose too notes, begins with the protagonist "only just awakening from bad dreams of his own." Of course, Fima cannot be understood without reference to certain Jewish mystical traditions and methods like the Kabbalah, especially when it comes to his philosophical inquiries (and here, I cannot help but note the similarity between Oz's Fima and Goldman from Yaakov Shabtai's *Past Continuous*, another mercurial, directionless figure who commits suicide "just when it seemed to him that finally, thanks to the cultivation of detachment and withdrawal, he was about to enter a new era" (3) in part by means of his translation of the *Somnium*, a seventeenth-century work in Latin by the German astronomer Johannes Kepler on which Goldman had spent the better part of a lifetime working and never finished.) Yet while Goldman is rooted in Tel Aviv, Fima can be seen as a Diasporic figure in an Israeli setting, a character drawn from the Yiddish tradition of the *schlemiel* and the *schlimazel*. As Fima himself says at one point in the novel, they are eternal and immortal archetypes from Cain and Abel to Rabin and Peres. "Hand in hand they wander from country to country, from century to century, from story to story" (64). Here, they have wandered into Oz's *Fima* in the guise of a central character who would not feel out of place in the pages of a Diasporic novel like Saul Bellow's *Herzog*.

As Sabin suggests, there is an inherent relationship between the unmooring of Fima and the political context in which he lives, that of the First Intifada by which Fima is animated and consumed, driven to writing fiery op-eds for national newspapers, which he sometimes though rarely has the determination to finish. His quest for the Third Condition is in part a response to the occupation and the Intifada, to its maddening cycle of violence, to the breaking of bones, and to the placing of Israeli Jews in the role wielding power over another powerless people:

> He was thinking: In the middle of the day, in broad daylight, in the middle of Jerusalem, they're already walking around with guns in their belts. Was the sickness implicit in the Zionist idea from the outset? Is there no way for the Jews to go back onto the stage of history except by becoming scum? Does

every battered child have to grow up into a violent adult? And
weren't we already scum before we got back onto the stage of
history? Do we have to be either cripples or thugs? Is there
no third alternative?[24]

So too, inescapably, is Fima unmoored by European Jewish history. "What
Hitler did to us didn't finish in 1945," he contemplates in front of the
bathroom mirror, "it still goes on, it seems it always will": "Underneath this
whole state, a hidden insanity is simmering. Three times a week our long
arm catches the murderers in their dens. We can't get to sleep before we
have inflicted a little pogrom on the Cossacks. Every morning we kidnap
Eichmann and every evening we nip Hitler in the bud. In the basketball
we defeat Chmielnicki and in the Eurovision we avenge Kishinev. And
what right do I have to interfere?"[25] Following a particularly intense debate
over the telephone with his father, Fima, having hung up the phone in
order to chew a heartburn tablet and take his broken radio down to the
repair shop at the mall, is suddenly gripped by the image in his mind's
eye of the "frail, myopic East European Jew wrapped in a prayer shawl,
wandering in a dark forest, muttering biblical verses to himself, hurting
his feet on the sharp stones, while softly and silently the snow fell, a night
bird gave a sinister shriek, and wolves howled in the darkness" (169). The
political, historical, and familial threads of his life get tied together in
the novel's final revelation: a sense that exile is, for Fima, an inescapable
condition and that, by extension, a home cannot be found even in an era
when the Jewish people have one. *Fima* is a largely plotless novel, which
appears to have been constructed in the form of concentric circles, but
sprinkled throughout the text are doubts, questions, debates, and arguments
that, given the novel's endpoint, shape the book and give it a sense of
forward motion. "I sit writing articles as if there was somebody listening.
Nobody's listening and everything seems lost. What's going to become
of us all, Nina?" Fima asks. "Do you know?" (179) Later: "The question
was, where could be move along to? What should he be doing? Wasn't
the truth that he hadn't even begun? But begun what? And where? And
how?" (207) Alone in his father's empty home in Rehavia, Fima fights
back tears of longing, longing "for what might have been and was not,
and never would be. There came into his head the words 'his place does
not know him'" (285). The death of Fima's father is the hinge event that
leads to the novel's denouement. Fima is free, and yet, he is not, because
he never can be. "All these years," Fima contemplates, going through
the rooms of his father's apartment, his possessions, his contents of his

refrigerator, "he had ached to find a place where he could feel at home and he had never managed to, either in his own flat, at the gynecology clinic, at his friends', in his city, his country, or his time" (296). Maybe, Fima thinks, this was an impossible dream from the start, a self-defeating wish, one that lay beyond his or anyone else's reach:

. . . And he said to himself:

'Right. Exile.'

And he added:

'So what?'

Shakespeare's King Richard vainly offered his kingdom for a horse. Whereas Efraim Nisan, close to three in the morning, was ready to exchange the whole of his legacy for one day, one hour of total inner freedom and of feeling at home. Although he had a suspicion that there was a tension and perhaps even a contradiction between the two, which could not be resolved even by [those] who would be living here in our place in a hundred years' time.[26]

In the character of Fima, we can glimpse the woman sitting alone on the bench of the kibbutz, singing a song to herself in Polish. In Fima, we see the exile aching to have a home of his own, receiving one, and remaining nonetheless unsatisfied, believing that this cannot be it and that the real, true home must lay elsewhere. In Fima, we see the author in a state of partial disagreement with himself. In Fima, we see the difference between the essay and the novel, between certainty and uncertainty, between homeland and homelessness, between here and eternity.

Notes

1. Oz, Amos, and Hana Wirth-Nesher. "After the Sound and the Fury: An Interview." *Prooftexts, vol.* 2, no. 3, 1982, pp. 303–12.

2. Bronner, Ethan. "Amos Oz, Approaching 70, Sees Israel With a Bird's Eye View." *The New York Times*, 12 Apr. 2009. Accessed 16 Dec. 2020.

3. Oz, Amos. *The Slopes of Lebanon*. Translated by Maurie Goldberg-Bartura. Mariner Books, 2012.

4. Guppy, Shusha. "Amos Oz, The Art of Fiction No. 148." *The Paris Review*, no. 140, Fall 1996. Accessed 16 Dec. 2020.

5. Remnick, David. "The Spirit Level." *The New Yorker*, 1 Nov. 2004. Accessed 21 Dec. 2020.

6. *Under this Blazing Light*, p. 81.

7. Hoare, Liam. "Natan Alterman or Amos Oz? The Six-Day War and Israeli Literature." *Fathom*, Spring 2017. Accessed 16 Dec. 2020.

8. *Under this Blazing Light*, p. 100.

9. Hoare, Liam. "The Unshakeable One." *Tel Aviv Review of Books*, Winter 2020.

10. Oz, Amos. *Die letzte Lektion*. Translated by Anne Birkenhauer. Suhrkamp Verlag, 2020.

11. Oz, Amos. *Where the Jackals Howl: And Other Stories*. Translated by Nicholas de Lange and Philip Simpson. Vintage, 2005, pp. 17–18.

12. *Where the Jackals Howl*, p. 83.

13. *Where the Jackals Howl*, p. 20.

14. Hoare, Liam. "Amos Oz Looks Forward—and Back." *The Forward*, 28 Dec. 2018. Accessed 21 Dec. 2020.

15. Amos Oz, Interview with Liam Hoare. "Amos Oz Looks Forward—and Back." 4 Jan. 2016.

16. Namdar, Ruby. "The Wizard of Words and the Baggy Monster: Rereading Amos Oz's *A Tale of Love and Darkness*." *The Jewish Review of Books*, Fall 2020. Accessed 18 Nov. 2020.

17. Oz, Amos. *The Story Begins: Essays on Literature*. Translated by Maggie Bar-Tura. Harcourt Brace & Company, 1999.

18. Amos Oz, Interview with Terry Gross. "Growing Up in Israel: Writer Amos Oz." NPR: 1 Dec. 2004.

19. Oz, Amos. *My Michael*. Translated by Nicholas de Lange. Vintage, 2011, p. 17.

20. Oz, Amos. *Unto Death*. Translated by Nicholas de Lange. Fontana Books, 1977, pp. 120–21.

21. Sabin, Stefana. "Er lachte unter Tränen." *Neue Zürcher Zeitung*, 29 Dec. 2018, p. 40.

22. Amos Oz, Interview with Michael Silverblatt. "Amos Oz." KCRW: 24 Jan. 1994.

23. Prose, Francine. "The Man Who Loved Chekhov." *The New York Times*, 24 Oct. 1993. Accessed 28 Dec. 2020.

24. Oz, Amos. *Fima*. Translated by Nicholas de Lange. Vintage, 2002, p. 86.

25. *Fima*, p. 224.

26. *Fima*, p. 297.

Works Cited

Bronner, Ethan. "Amos Oz, Approaching 70, Sees Israel With a Bird's-Eye View." 12 Apr. 2009. *The New York Times*, 16 December 2020. <https://www.nytimes.com/2009/04/13/books/13oz.html>.

Guppy, Shusha. "Amos Oz, The Art of Fiction No. 148." *The Paris Review*, vol. 140, 1996.

Herzl, Theodor. *The Jewish State*. Penguin Books, 2010.

Hoare, Liam. "Amos Oz Looks Forward—and Back." 28 Dec. 2018. *The Forward*, 21 Dec. 2020. <https://forward.com/culture/332134/amos-oz-looks-forward-and-back/>.

———. "Natan Alterman or Amos Oz? The Six Day War and Israeli Literature." *Fathom*, Spring 2017. 16 Dec. 2020. <https://fathomjournal.org/1967-natan-alterman-or-amos-oz-the-six-day-war-and-israeli-literature/>.

———. "The Unshakeable One." Tel Aviv Review of Books 2020, 2020.

Namdar, Ruby. "The Wizard of Words and the Baggy Monster: Rereading Amos Oz's *A Tale of Love and Darkness*." Fall 2020. *The Jewish Review of Books*, 15 Oct. 2020.

Oz, Amos. Interview with Michael Silverblatt. Amos Oz. KCRW. Santa Monica. 24 Jan.1994.

———. Interview with Terri Gross. Growing Up with Israel: Writer Amos Oz. NPR. 1 Dec. 2004. 23 Dec. 2020. <https://www.npr.org/2019/01/04/682168487/remembering-israeli-author-and-peace-activist-amos-oz?t=1608718064819>.

———. Interview with Hana Wirth-Nesher. "After the Sound and the Fury: An Interview." *Prooftexts* 2.3, 1982, pp. 303–12.

———. *Between Friends*. Translated by Sondra Silverston. Chatto & Windus, 2013.

———. *Dear Zealots*. Translated by Jessica Cohen. Chatto & Windus, 2018.

———. *Die letzte Lektion*. Translated by Anne Birkenhauer. Suhrkamp Verlag, 2020.

———. *Elsewhere, Perhaps*. Translated by Nicholas de Lange. Penguin Books, 1979.

———. *Fima*. Translated by Nicholas de Lange. Vintage, 2002.

———. *How to Cure a Fanatic: Israel and Palestine: Between Right and Right*. Vintage Books, 2012.

———. *My Michael*. Translated by Nicholas de Lange. Vintage Books, 2011.

———. *The Same Sea*. Translated by Nicholas de Lange. Vintage, 2002.

———. *The Slopes of Lebanon*. Translated by Maurie Goldberg-Bartura. Mariner Books, 2012.

———. *The Story Begins: Essays on Literature*. Translated by Maggie Bar-Tura. Harcourt Brace & Company, 1999.

———. *Under this Blazing Light: Essays*. Translated by Nicholas de Lange. Cambridge UP, 1996.

———. *Unto Death*. Translated by Nicholas de Lange. Fontana Books, 1977.

————. *Where the Jackals Howl: And Other Stories*. Translated by Nicholas de Lange and Philip Simpson. Vintage, 2005.

Prose, Francine. "The Man Who Loved Chekhov." 24 Oct. 1993. *The New York Times*, 28 Dec. 2020. <https://movies2.nytimes.com/books/97/10/26/home/oz-fima.html>.

Rapoport, Meron. "One Day, Two Declarations." *Haaretz*, 6 June 2007. <https://www.haaretz.com/1.4824451>.

Remnick, David. "The Spirit Level." 1 Nov. 2004. *The New Yorker*, 21 Dec. 2020. <https://www.newyorker.com/magazine/2004/11/08/the-spirit-level>.

Sabin, Stefana. "Er lachte unter Tränen." Neue Zürcher Zeitung, 29 Dec. 2018, p. 40.

Shabtai, Yaakov. *Past Continuous*. Translated by Dalya Bilu. The Jewish Publication Society of America, 1985.

Chapter 12

The Dialogic Encounter between New and Old

The Biblical Intertext in Oz's Fiction

Nehama Aschkenasy

The presence of the Hebrew Scriptures, and to some extent other ancient Hebraic texts, is evident throughout Amos Oz's body of works, starting in his early stories, such as "The Way of the Wind," "Nomad and Viper," "Upon this Evil Earth" and "Strange Fire," the novella *The Hill of Evil Counsel,* and continuing in novels such as *A Perfect Peace, Panther in the Basement,* and others.[1] Oz has also sprinkled his works with reminders of New Testament sites and narratives, such as in *The Hill of Evil Counsel* and in his final novel, *Judas.* Yet the predominant semantic and semiotic influence that animates Oz's fiction is undoubtedly the Hebrew Bible, amplified occasionally by allusions to midrashic sources or to modern Hebrew writers and poets. The Bible's presence may be overt or hidden; it may be a deliberate authorial decision or triggered in the Hebrew reader by the sheer biblical aura that modern Hebrew retains.[2] It ranges from a striking, isolated phrase echoing biblical idiom, or a name of a site, intimating ancient realities, to full blown dramatic personae and actions that appear to reenact ancient prototypes. In several stories the biblical precedence is woven into the very fabric of the narrative and provides an extensive intertextual underpinning that scaffolds the entire tale, both its dramatic action and the ideological discourse that drives it. Often, the biblical intertext functions as the protagonist's unconscious that stores memories from a collective past, or from a familiar master text, woven into and interacting with present-day events. In such cases, the biblical protagonist serves as more than an alter ego for the modern character, a literary strategy, but as the latter's ancient or buried self, not in the clinical sense of a personality disorder but as a personal or cultural anamnesis.

Embedding an earlier text in a modern one, especially from the two pillars of Western literature, Greek mythology and the Bible, seen as reservoirs of prototypical human situations of enduring cultural and psychological relevance, has been common in the history of European, English, and American writings. As for a Hebrew writer like Oz, burying the ancient tale in a contemporary Israeli narrative is both an artistic-aesthetic evocation of the primary monomyth as well as a cultural-political statement stemming from the writer's understanding of his social and cultural responsibility in evaluating the major grand story behind the modern Zionist state. Since Zionism wrested the ancient Jewish canon from its religious significance and converted it into the Hebrew national epic of return and secular redemption, the biblical underpinning of a contemporary story offers Oz an opportunity for a dialogic encounter between old and new: the old canon is examined with a skeptical, inquisitive modern eye while current geopolitical, nationalist, and ethical angst, and themes of betrayal, generational strife, womaan and land, conflicting territorial claims, confrontation between the "civilized" and "primitive," and unyielding ideological postures, are measured and tested against the ancient metanarrative.[3]

Oz's story "The Way of the Wind" (1962) exemplifies the broad array of the Bible's intertextual role in the writer's fictional orbit, beginning with its title that reverberates with multiple biblical echoes, and recalls the verse "As you do not know *the way of the wind*, or how the bones grow in the womb, so you do not know the work of God who makes everything" (Hebrew Bible, Ecc. 11.5). Oz clearly pays homage to the Bible's supreme poetic power to capture the human inability to fathom its own existence and the bleakness of human fate. And while it seems that Oz directs us to recognize the spirit of Ecclesiastes as dominant in his story, he engages in a subtle wordplay, itself a biblical technique, employing the multiple meanings of the Hebrew word *ru'ach*, which in the very opening of Genesis tantalizes the reader with its dual meaning of "wind" and "spirit." The very texture of this story is threaded with the manifold connotations of *ru'ach*; both a literal wind that has brought the young protagonist (entangled in his two parachutes that dangle from the electric cables above the kibbutz), to his tragic end, and also spirit, vanity, pride, mystery, emptiness, and death, the main themes in both Ecclesiastes and the present tale.

Readers of the story noted early that in addition to the explicit evocation of Ecclesiastes 12, the climactic scene in this story, in which Gideon, entangled in his parachute straps and is killed or kills himself in the presence of his father and "bastard" brother, is both a repeat and a reversal of the Akedah tale,[4] which runs through the entire story. In fact, the Genesis narrative, which underlies the entire story, provides the author with an opportunity to scrutinize his contemporary protagonists and their actions, while offering a devastating commentary, a midrash, on the ancient tale itself, a much-debated mainstay in Judaic literary and rabbinic tradition. The same is true of the Abraham-like stature of Shimshon Sheinbaum, whose hypocritical grandstanding is clearly deplored by the author, which serves to imply Oz's condemnation of Shimshon's biblical "double," Abraham. Indeed, once we realize the Akedah intertext, the story reads as if each protagonist follows the dictates of his ancient self, or his buried double, from the ancient canon. The zealot Shimshon Sheinbaum, a founding father of the kibbutz and an important force in the labor movement, is the modern analogue of the patriarch Abraham, founder of monotheism. Shimshon is first introduced not as one of the "founders," or "leaders," or "heads" of the labor movement, but as one of its " 'avot." In Hebrew tradition, while 'avot is grammatically the plural of the noun "father," or "forefather," it is more specifically an identification of the three Genesis patriarchs, the "Three 'Avot." Moreover, we follow both the Genesis Abraham and the modern Shimshon on their fateful days, respectively, from the moment they wake up, early in the morning.

Like Abraham in Genesis, Shimshon in Oz's story has two sons. Zaki, like the biblical Ishmael, is the illegitimate wild child, cast away by his father Shimshon, and never openly recognized as his son. Zaki is ugly and fierce but also brave, as he demonstrates at the climactic moment of the story, when he futilely attempts to save his older brother. Gideon, like Isaac, is his mother's only child, tame, gentle, and protected. Shimshon, a passionate Zionist and prolific writer of castigating, sanctimonious rhetoric, is self-centered and fiercely ambitious; like Abraham, he is the architect of the terrifying scene in which the bound son is about to be sacrificed. Shimshon has driven his poetry-writing, slightly effeminate son to join the paratroopers, though he knew full well that his son was unfit for this elite unit and that he chose it as a way of pleasing his disapproving father.

Gideon's Isaac-like predicament is displayed in the climactic scene of the tale when he chooses to perform an unusual feat to impress his intimidating, forbidding father, and instead, finds himself in grave danger when both his parachutes become entangled in the electric cables that run over the kibbutz skies. Both the biblical protagonist and his modern counterpart reveal a sense of foreboding, deeply buried under complete trust in the father, in Isaac's case, and hidden behind naive anticipation and excitement, in Gideon's case. The prolonged spectacle of Gideon's agony includes all the elements of the Genesis tale of the Akedah: we have the fanatic father, thinking less of his son's plight and more of his own image as the father of a cowardly son, the strapped son, about to become the victim of his father's zeal, the knife, and the sacrificial fire, in the form of the sparks spewed by the electric cables. To reinforce the intertextual presence of the Genesis harrowing scene behind the modern one, Oz borrows two key nouns from the Genesis text: in the critical ending of the story, Gideon the son is referred to several times as "*na'ar*," a boy or young man, which is how the angel refers to Isaac when he orders Abraham not to lay his hand on the "*na'ar*." Even more resounding with Akedah echoes is the noun used by Gideon when describing himself as "*yechidam*," his parents' "only" son, reminiscent of God's command to Abraham to take his "only" son (*yechidcha*) to Mount Moriah. Yet the modern scene is doubly excruciating since it is not only reminiscent of the older model, the first terrifying Hebrew example of a father ready to sacrifice his own son for the sake of his faith, but because each character seems to reenact a previous self, an anamnesis, buried within him and dooming him to repeat its destiny. At the same time, the differences between the old tale and its modern version make the latter more brutal and dramatically complex. The stark but dignified and wordless ancient scene, the collective anamnesis of the entire culture, resurfaces as a noisy and grotesque kibbutz scene, a public spectacle of horror and ridicule. Shimshon's apparent wish to see his son escape unharmed seems a reversal of his old double's intention to sacrifice his son, but this departure from the Genesis model in favor of the modern father is deceptive. It is Shimshon's behavior that finally seals his son's fate when his abusive language drives Gideon to thrash himself into the electric cable and die.[5]

The old tale of the foiled sacrifice thus returns as a modern tragedy in which the "sacrifice" is consummated, serving as a commentary on both tales, ancient and modern. Oz's story further implies that the tragedy occurring to the present-day protagonists was predetermined by the terrifying actions of the ancient patriarch. The ancient event, embedded in the people's collective memory, is seen as encouraging future fathers to sacrifice their sons on the altar of extreme ideas. The tragic ending of the modern story, in contrast with the miraculous rescue of Abraham's son, denounces both the biblical event and the modern one. According to Oz, the happy resolution of the biblical story has subconsciously implanted false hopes in Abraham's descendants, requiring of them almost inhuman heroism and fortitude with the promise of a reward that never materialized again. Oz highlights the cruelty and irrationality of both the ancient originator of the faith and the founders of modern Israel. The content of "faith" has changed, but irrational zeal and fanatic dedication have remained the same. Further, Oz seems to question the status of the ancient tale as the ultimate display of devotion and proof of Abraham's greatness. Shimshon's cruel behavior during the ordeal brings to light Abraham's mercilessness as well. In the biblical tale Abraham's brutal side is submerged under his unyielding, tenacious faith and God's praise of him; but when the near-sadistic Shimshon recalls for us the old patriarch Abraham, the image of the biblical protagonist looming behind the cruel kibbutz father becomes identified with the latter. At the same time, the more comforting elements inherent in the people's collective memory, in which the story of a father about to sacrifice his son is framed by the trial theme, and the zealot father is ordered by the angel to lay not his hand on his son, are absent in the modern tale, thus revealing the Israeli generational conflict as even harsher and more brutal than the biblical prototype, and contemporary reality as truly tragic.

In an interesting twist, Shimshon's internal rhetoric serves also as articulation of the inner thoughts of his earlier, buried self, Father Abraham himself. The Bible denies us access to Abraham's inner reflections, but we are privy to Shimshon's hopes of leaving a heritage and building a dynasty, and to his determination that his party's ideological platform will always be "understood without any recourse to dialectics," it must be read literally "word by word," which we recognize as the traditional way of reading the Torah. We may say that if the figure of the fanatic forefather Abraham is the Labor ideologue's anamnesis, his past existence or alter ego, then the Genesis story as a whole function as the anamnesis, the past life, of Oz's text. The interaction between text and intertext works both ways, so that we are led to recognize what the intertext does to the text, but also what the text, in this case Shimshon's maniacal, stubborn dedication to an idea, does to the intertext, that is, Abraham's actions. Thus, the past text, infiltrating the modern text, is also highlighted, or magnified, or made more complete, in a sense, by the modern text.

Similarly, we may see in Dinah, Jacob's daughter, whose story of rape is narrated in Genesis 34, as the anamnesis of Geula, the central protagonist of "Nomad and Viper." In both the biblical and the modern tale, the woman leaves a safe environment, meets a stranger, and has a sexual experience with him. Before she leaves the residential area of the kibbutz for the open fields, Geula's inner voice keeps telling her to "go out" (*latzet*). Oz uses the same Hebrew root for the infinitive "to go out" as the Bible. While the biblical text itself does not elaborate on this verb, Jewish commentators focused on the sexual meaning of the verbal construction "*vatetze*" ("went out"), which they thought illuminated Dinah's sexual motives.[6] In both cases, the woman's departure from her community is linked to a bloody act of revenge perpetrated by the heroine's male compatriots, Dinah's brothers in Genesis, and Geula's fellow kibbutzniks in Oz's story. In both tales, the woman's encounter with the "other," the act of rape (whether real or imagined), and the violence that follows point to geopolitical and territorial conflicts between the previous inhabitants of the land and its invaders, and to the tragic clash of tribal and national purposes. The close identification of woman with land since ancient times has made the act of rape the psychological and literary correlative of any event that marks the invasion of a land and the collision of opposite cultures. A modern precedent, which might have inspired Amos Oz's own story, is E. M. Forster's *A Passage to India*. Both Geula and Forster's Adela Quested belong to the dominant culture, yet each woman's encounter with the native other shakes her sense of identity and sends her reeling into a muddle of emotional and sexual turmoil, leading to a false accusation of rape and a social upheaval following it.

The analogy with the biblical precedence continues when Geula, like Dinah, is ultimately seen as directly responsible for the bloody vendetta that follows her encounter with the stranger. In Dinah's case, the brothers massacre the whole city of Shechem to rescue their deflowered sister. In Oz's tale, the woman's connection to the retaliatory action that is undertaken by the hotheaded kibbutz members is less direct and more complex, yet clearly established in the story. Geula's fabrication of a sexual attack is tied to the sexual and the national aspect of Oz's story. In terms of Geula's sexual frustrations within a male community that finds her undesirable, the invented sexual attack gives comfort to the girl's injured feminine pride. As to the political undertones, the nomad's imagined attack eases a collective conscience that is not at peace with seizing a desert land that has an indigenous population. The nomads who close in on the kibbutz borders are a reminder of the primitive, uncultivated state of the land; the kibbutz fences are artificial dividers, underscoring that the kibbutz is an enclave of rationality and culture in an uninviting and hostile desert terrain. The invented attack by the nomad gives moral justification to revenge, at least in Geula's mind. At the end of the story, Geula, who was expected to dissuade the young kibbutzniks from violent action, lies passively in the open field, immersed in self-destructive hallucinations, while her friends go out to take revenge.

In juxtaposing the "civilized" kibbutz community with the nomadic, "primitive" Bedouins it appears at first that "Nomad and Viper" is structured along the Levi-Straussian antinomies of civilization and barbarism, European and native, literacy and orality, or history and non-history, to which the entire kibbutz community seems to subscribe.[7] The opening chapters juxtapose the "we" or the "I," speaking mostly for the collective voice, with "them" (21); Geula herself does not occupy center stage until the third chapter of the story. The members of the kibbutz are united by a vision of their historical destiny fused with ideas of progress and brotherhood (25). Their attitude is rational and humane: "A whole population . . . could not simply be abandoned to the horrors of starvation" (21); they occupy the "settled land," provide care for their animals, and grow excellent crops. Their society is egalitarian, liberal, and democratic; but they insist on lawful conduct on the part of the Bedouins: the stolen property must be returned, and the pilfering stopped (26). The Bedouins are the opposite of the kibbutz community: they are nomadic, have no hygienic or sanitary habits, are at the mercy of the elements (most of them are half-blind), and they show no consideration for fences, boundaries, and laws. The ceremonial meeting between the kibbutz members and the Bedouin elders is a tragi-comic scene of miscommunication, cross purposes, and parodic exaggerations (23–26). According to some members of the kibbutz, the only language the nomads understand is that of violence, not of rational verbal discourse (26). In their great susceptibility to the famine, the nomads are not only "savage," as opposed to Levi-Strauss's "scientific," but also recall the predicaments of the region's residents in biblical times. Ironically, the nomads are biblical in other ways as well: they look like frozen statues from antiquity and their sheep appear "rooted in the parched soil" (22). The political and economic power is clearly with the kibbutz community; they set the rules, own property and tools, and are the masters of the land. Yet the Arabs' presence, with their drumbeats and singing at night, threatens the veneer of modern civilization and brings out the primitive in the kibbutz members.

Geula's name and initial introduction intensify the Levi-Straussian dichotomy and at the same time further clarify the network of metanarratives underlying the kibbutz culture. Geula's name (meaning "redemption") reverberates with biblical significance (a major issue in the Bible is the redemption of the land, of the woman, and of the blood) as well as with the Zionist idea of political redemption and the socialist ideology of the redemption of the Jewish psyche through physical labor. Geula embodies the ideals of enlightenment and progress: she is the voice of culture and moderation in the kibbutz, an avid reader, and a "merciless critic" (28). In her encounter with the nomad, Geula tries desperately to maintain the antinomy of savage vs. culture. He is half-blind, needs her to establish the time of day, and lets out a "terrifying, savage screech," while she owns a watch, acts condescendingly, and mockingly accuses him of stealing (32). The intellectual and cultural supremacy of the Israeli metanarrative is implied in the meeting with elders of the Bedouin tribe earlier in the story and Geula's traumatic encounter with the single Bedouin. The kibbutz leader makes a token gesture of respect toward the Bedouins, suggesting the educational advantages for the kibbutz children of exposure to the Bedouin encampment; but his condescension is obvious. And Geula's fleeting moment of intimacy with the Bedouin is humiliating and distressing to her because she sees in it her involuntary surrender to the irrational and to uncontrollable sexual desires; it triggers her descent into madness and eventual suicide.

Yet Oz has actually written a counter-story to the biblical tale as well as to the Zionist grand narrative, which assumed that the natives would come to appreciate the economic and technological advantages offered to them by the Zionist enterprise. While he has adopted the contours of the Genesis tale of Dinah, Oz transforms it in a major way by foregrounding the woman, who in Genesis is silent and mostly absent, and recording both her social and internal voices; he has also converted the rape into an imagined attack. Oz further reshuffles the hierarchy in the story by bringing to the fore another seemingly marginal element—the single Bedouin together with the tribe and its leaders. Levi-Strauss's binary opposition between savage and cultured collapses when the Bedouin elder phrases his elaborate, courteous remarks "in careful, formal Hebrew" while the kibbutz secretary Etkin insists on replying in "broken Arabic." On the

face of it, their exchange suggests that the oppressed "other" has assimilated into the master culture: by knowing Hebrew so well, the Arab has
acknowledged the dominant language. But it soon becomes clear that the
Arab's knowledge of Hebrew is a tactic for survival, not an admission of
defeat or inferiority. His insistence on using Hebrew rather than Arabic
may be understood as his exclusion of the Israeli from his own linguistic
territory. In the same vein, Etkin's invitation of the tribal children to the
kibbutz is ignored by the Arab elder, who thus implies that the visit would
not result in any benefits to them.

Further, the kibbutz community's discourse of law, morality, and
ideology (the "brotherhood of nations" is the "cornerstone of our ideology"
[25]) fails as well, not because of the tribal head's lack of understanding,
but because he insists on the validity of his own point of view that "boys
would be boys and the world was getting steadily worse" (25). The Zionist
meta-discourse of enlightening and advancing the "uncivilized" is proven
to be untenable. The Bedouin will neither be suppressed nor assimilated
nor integrated into the inevitable march of history. The Levi-Straussian
antinomy further disintegrates when we realize that the frontiers separating
the "savage" from the "cultured" are tenuous and blurred, in spite of the
fact that both Geula and the kibbutz family at large are firmly ensconced
within this binary conception. While the half-blind nomad starts as the
completely alien "other" of the rational Geula, he quickly becomes a man
to her: "He was alive and warm. . . . He was unlike any man Geula had
ever known" (31). She responds to him as a woman and bashfully fastens
the top of her blouse. He seems more polite and articulate in his courtship
of Geula than any man of her own group. He appears to understand her
sexual agony, drawing a "long caress on the air"; his Hebrew "exuded a
rare gentleness" (30) and, unlike her other male friends, he compliments
her on her appearance (32). Geula agrees to have a cigarette with him
and later asks for another one. The erotic nature of their smoking, and
of the sensually laden silences, is undeniable; for a moment, Geula sees
in the Bedouin her double, a reflection of her own pariah status as an
unattractive woman in the kibbutz. It is Geula's watch, signifying a return
to linear history and civilization, that makes her slip back to her previous
role and recast the Bedouin in his previous role.

The story's ending further interrogates the exact identities of the
savage and the civilized. The savage act of rape, the only justification for
violent retaliation, did not in fact occur. In the last kibbutz meeting, Etkin
advocates moderation and calls for putting an end to the ancient biblical

feud between Cain and Abel. When the militant young men win the day,
Etkin twice calls them a "lynch mob" (37). The Bedouin's transgression is
described as no more than "a little stealing" while the kibbutzniks' actions
are called "violent" several times (37). The kibbutz meeting is not democratic
but chaotic and it results in the suppression of "the right to speak" (37).
The zealots' retaliation is the last attempt to silence the "savage." But the
"local discourse" (to use Jean-François Lyotard's term [8]) of the Bedouin
tribe, not inscribed in books or written documents, seems as valid as the
Israeli narrative. At the same time the biblical and Zionist metanarratives
are cut down to size, reduced from a grand story-as-history that could
eventually swallow up the inferior "small story," to a local, communal story
that is one among many others. At the end, the Zionist metanarrative is
shaken, just as Geula's calm rationality and sense of justice, as well as the
kibbutz community's romantic idealism of the brotherhood of man, have
been disrupted.[9] Further, the biblical precedent, while potent artistically
and imaginatively, is presented as a non-model pedagogically because it
encourages the colonialist impetus and tribal violence. Yet its presence is
undeniable, so much so that the entire Dinah episode in Genesis functions as the deep-seated collective ancient memory, the anamnesis, of the
present-day protagonists and their actions.

In the figure of Lily, the central figure in "Strange Fire," Oz has strung
together biblical elements from the Genesis story of Eve's affiliation with
the serpent, the yearning for pagan cult exhibited in the Leviticus tale of
the sons of Aaron offering a "strange fire" to God, Proverbs's verses on the
dangerous and alien "strange woman," and later Hebraic myths regarding
the figure of the demonic Lilith, the seducer and killer of men. The legendary Lilith is undoubtedly the cultural and mental anamnesis of the central
character, Lily, who during the day is an ordinary Jerusalemite mother of
a young woman about to get married, and a diabolical being, inhabiting a
dark, alien reality at night. The quote from Berdichevsky's story "Hiding
in the Thunder," which serves as epigraph for Oz's story, pictures night
as a primordial force that brings out the beast in man, his carnal desires,
which can lead man to his grave.[10] The story itself starts in a mundane
scene, when two scholars, both rather uninspiring and lackluster, discuss
questions of good and evil in an academic, abstract fashion. But even
before the perverse Lily comes into the scene, the streets of Jerusalem at
night are portrayed as the physical and moral battleground of the forces
of good and evil, represented by the "birds of the day" and the "birds of
the night." Lily inhabits both the ordinary reality of modern Jerusalem

with its scholars, students, and young couples planning their future life and the sphere of evil, chaos, and madness that takes over the streets of Jerusalem at night. Lily's buried self is an owl, the bird Lilith, one of those night creatures who are messengers from the subterranean sphere of chaos and madness (113). As a nocturnal creature, Lily Dannenberg evokes the darkness of the night, *Lailah,* even though she is named after a white flower, and a modern incarnation of the mythic Lilith, Lily is a threat to a young man (her future son-in-law), and to a young woman about to be married (her own daughter). Lily's affinity with Lilith is further made clear when the taxi driver calls her "Queen of Sheba," reminding us that the images of the Queen of Sheba and Lilith merged in the popular imagination and that several early legends contended that the Queen of Sheba was actually Lilith who came to seduce King Solomon. Lily also recognizes in herself the biblical serpent lurking among the trees in the garden: "Pity I'm not there among the trees in the garden, secretly watching him, enjoying the expression" (69).

While at night Lily turns into Lilith, in her domestic, everyday life she also embodies other ancient precedents, especially the biblical "strange woman" and, more subtly, the pagan "strange fire" that Aaron's sons offered God. As such, Lily is a modern incarnation of the old yearning for the alien and foreign, even in the face of the Holocaust and the promise of Zionism. a frequent theme in Oz's works. While she appears to be an integral part of the Jerusalem community, she is the social "other" who thinks in the German language and finds the Hebrew inadequate for expressing the profundities of existence. In her cultural otherness Lily is reminiscent of other female protagonists in Oz's writings (such as Hannah in *My Michael,* Ruth in *The Hill of Evil Counsel,* and Oz's mother Fania, the protagonist of his biography, *A Tale of Love and Darkness)* who are contemptuous of the ordinary people who surround them and their dull, humdrum existence. Therefore, Lily's attempts to escape what she sees as a confining, provincial environment are not depicted without sympathy; and the male admiration for her is seen as well-founded.

That Lily's buried self is diasporic in nature becomes clearer when, under her hypnotic powers, the sedate scholar Elhanan Kleinberger, universally known as the zealous admirer of the Hebrew language, resorts to his hidden passion, which is composing love poetry in the German language (134). Kleinberger now surrenders completely to the spirit of the "strange fire" that overcomes him; he despairs of creating his own magic words and, appropriately, settles down to read a study of demons and

ghosts in ancient ritual. Elsewhere I focused on Lily's demonic nature "as
the embodiment of the male's primordial fear of women."[11] Yet in addition
to this critical feature, it appears that Oz employed the biblical intertext
to bring out Lily's other buried self, that which retains warm memories
of another culture and life. She is the keeper of the cultic, pagan "strange
fire," which persisted in the Hebrew people since biblical times, translated,
in the context of the early Israeli reality, to the modern Jewish self, craving
assimilation and yearning for alien vistas and cultures.

Lily has much in common with Ruth, the central figure in the novella
The Hill of Evil Counsel, which alludes, by virtue of its title, to the story
of Judas Iscariot's betrayal of Jesus. By naming the location from which
the modern Ruth deserts her family, the same place where a colossal and
history-changing event happened, Caiaphas and Judas plotting against
Jesus, Oz makes it clear that for the child Hillel, his mother's betrayal is
as momentous as the ancient event. Yet the story in its entirety reads as an
inverted version of the biblical tale of Ruth the Moabite, displaying a tragic
discrepancy between the biblical Ruth, a model of familial and national
loyalty, and her modern namesake, who becomes a traitor to her family
and people.[12] The tale takes place during the waning days of the British
mandate, a time of heightened Jewish nationalism, while Ruth remains
steeped in the Polish culture and landscape of her childhood, and unable
to identify with the explosive reality of a country and a people about to
be reborn. Hillel, the impressionable young son of Ruth and Hans Kipnis,
suggests the biblical underpinnings of the tale, and fervently wishes for
the return and repetition of the glorious days of old.

Ruth's biblical "self" is a combination of Jezebel, the epitome of evil,
treachery, and foreignness, and Ruth, the paradigm of loyalty and commitment. The image of Jezebel is recalled by the family's boarder, Mitya,
himself a character out of the biblical text, who laces his language with
prophetic rhetoric. Hillel, however, envisions himself as the young man
from the family of shepherds who became king of Israel, thus assigning
to his mother the role of the ancient Ruth, ancestress of the illustrious
King David. We know that Hillel is associated with none other than King
David, the founder of the royal dynasty, when his father playfully calls
him "king Hillel the first." Though for Hillel the mother is a modern Ruth,
it soon becomes clear that the contemporary Ruth is the direct opposite
of her biblical model. In a reversal of the idyllic old tale, the latter-day
Ruth betrays her son and her husband, as well as her people and their
historical memory, by running away with a British admiral, thus casting

her lot with a dying, corrupt empire. Biblical Ruth leaves an immoral, decaying society and ties her destiny to that of a young, future-oriented culture and religion. But Ruth in Jerusalem of the pre-statehood years prefers to turn her back on the emerging society and regress in time, as well as in morality, by leaving the new Jerusalem and its revived national spirit for the decrepit embodiment of a fading empire.

The inverted biblical analogy runs through the entire novella. Just as the ancient Ruth's acceptance into Israelite society occurs during the period of harvest celebration, the contemporary Ruth's betrayal takes place during the May ball at the house of the British high commissioner. The Book of Ruth is a spring tale and Ruth the Moabitess is forever associated in the Hebraic memory with spring season, while Hillel's mother's beautiful smile is "autumnal." The biblical Ruth is a foreigner who embraces the Israelite culture, while the modern Ruth is a Jewish woman who yearns for foreign men and alien landscapes. Significantly, the beloved boyfriend of her Polish childhood, with whom she recited Polish poetry, was named Tadeusz, after the mythic national hero commemorated in an epic poem by the same name.

Paradoxically, while Ruth in Oz's novella betrays the biblical spirit, she also embodies it. She is a locus of passion and romantic yearnings, a larger-than-life figure of remote beauty and charm, infecting the men around her with inflated biblical rhetoric, crazed passions, and mythic visions. In her son's eyes, too, Ruth embodies the biblical spirit, and her departure diminishes the lives of all the men in her orbit. But the novelist sees her exit as necessary for the restoration of normalcy and equilibrium to life. Even Mitya the boarder, who rants and raves in biblical pomposity, calms down and settles into a mediocre existence, shedding the mantle of the angry biblical prophet. Tragically for Hillel, the new Israeli reality, cleansed of unhealthy and dangerous romantic yearnings, can establish itself only when his mother finally leaves, taking with her the illusory magic of both foreign and ancient Israelite landscapes.

The analogy between the modern Ruth and her biblical counterpart illuminates the tragedy of the assimilated pre-holocaust generation, which failed to espouse its own true heritage while yearning for the foreigner who rejected it. Yet it also questions the validity of Zionist expectations to duplicate in modern times the glamour of the ancient Davidic kingdom. While Oz may view the removal of the biblical element as healthy and necessary, he also casts a dubious eye at the biblical Ruth, paradigm of loyalty and selflessness, and at the advisability of holding her story up as a model for modern times. If miracles and happy endings ever occurred, they belonged to the pages of the Bible, but under the harsher light of modern everyday existence they appear remote, naive, and even unbelievable. In fact, in this tale Oz condemns all romantic grand visions that wreak havoc on people's lives. Ruth the mother is wedded to the myths of the Polish nation, her young child, to the romantic biblical myth of the heroic King David, Mitya the boarder, to the prophets' rhetoric of outrage and their utopian vision of a moral society, and the British administration in Jerusalem, to the colonialist grandeur of the of British Empire. Hillel's chance encounter with the grotesquely smiling skull of a Turkish soldier evokes another faded empire, exemplifying the terrifying face of grand historical and nationalist ambitions.

In the novel *A Perfect Peace*, Oz again juxtaposes the biblical scene with modern reality, yet he highlights instead the parodic discrepancy between the biblical heroes and their hapless, present-day incarnations. The three main protagonists, Yolek, Yonatan, and Azariah, are comic, lackluster counterparts of the mythic heroes Saul, Jonathan, and David, respectively.[13] The ailing Yolek, the kibbutz secretary, is out of favor with the labor party's leaders, and feels defeated in his attempts to establish a dynasty. His son Yonatan refuses to follow his father's footsteps in the kibbutz hierarchy and is about to leave the kibbutz and abandon his childless wife. Yolek reluctantly shifts his affections from his son to the guitar-playing newcomer, Azaria. Yolek is thus the modern-day version of the tragic King Saul, who fell out of favor with God and failed to establish a dynasty. Yonatan, lacking his father's political aspirations and refusing to fulfill the latter's ambitions for him, yet still performing courageously on the battlefield, is the modern counterpart of King Saul's heroic son Jonathan. We remember that the latter is described in the Book of Samuel as brave and honest, fighting side by side with his father to the bitter end, yet not ambitious enough to succeed his father the king and willingly ceding the throne to David. Azaria Gitlin, a poor, slightly built stranger who feels inferior to the kibbutz-reared Yonatan and craves to become securely ensconced in Yolek's family, is the country-boy David, who infiltrates the king's court and his inner circle and takes them by storm. Like his biblical precursor, Azaria hypnotizes people with his romantic rhetoric, his guitar playing, and dreams of glory.

The biblical analogy ties modern Israel with the ancient kingdom while expanding the novel's dimensions chronologically and thematically; it impels us to view the battling protagonists within a larger historical context and swing our perspectives back and forth. The ancient drama of the tragic first king of Israel, his doomed son who died while fighting for his people, and the charismatic shepherd who has assumed Messianic proportions in our collective imagination, is here both imitated and cut down to size. Yolek is a comic king Saul; his fate is not as bleak as that of his precursor, and his illness is physical, not mental. There is no sense of darkness and doom hovering over Yolek as it did over Saul. His tragi-comic letters to Prime Minister Eshkol and to his old antagonist Benya, which he writes but never mails, are reminiscent of the letters that Bellow's Moses Herzog sends to numerous personalities, dead and alive. Yolek's letters seem angry, but they do not transmit the sense of defeat and hopelessness that controlled Saul towards the end of his life. In fact, in spite of Yolek's fury and his many grievances against the veteran Israeli leaders as well as the new generation, there is an underlying energy in his words, a lust for life and action, an optimism that things can be corrected and repaired. His deep faith in the Zionist idea and its modern, secular interpretation and his dedication to the realization of the socialist utopia remain intact. His poor physical health and disaffected view of present-day Israel as a "poor man's America" have not dried up his stamina and vitality. Yolek will eventually succumb to his illness, but he will be remembered not as a failed, maniacal leader, but as an admired kibbutz founder and a beloved father and husband.

Yonatan, Yolek's son, both resembles and departs from his biblical model. First, he lacks his biblical namesake's magnanimity and fierce loyalty; what is more, he does not admire Azaria the way Jonathan did David. And while he performs admirably on the battlefield, like his biblical prototype, Yonatan is a reluctant and skeptical hero who constantly questions the meaning of heroism and courage. In fact, Yonatan's view of war is decidedly unheroic and lacking in any epic glamour. He wonders at the discrepancy between the dehumanizing panic of war that reduces a mature man to a crybaby, the mindless chaos, the stench and filth of the battlefield, on the one hand, and the glamour of the same experience when described in the military magazines and award ceremonies. His story ends with none of the tragic or heroic halo that defines the biblical Jonathan's death. His suicidal journey to the romanticized ancient city of Petra does not end in disaster and is devoid of epic glamour. Yonatan returns home humbled and resigned, and his redemption is not depicted in grandiose terms, but in language that conveys the mundane and imperfect nature of man and the limits of human reach.[14] Azaria, King David's counterpart, is far from being the heroic version of the ancient king. Rather, he is a metamorphosed, latter-day David, a curious and somewhat ludicrous blend of the mythic, romantic young warrior from Bethlehem and the persecution-ridden ghetto Jew. He is David writ small, remolded into humbler proportions by two thousand years of Diaspora experience.

The biblical precedents cast a formidable shadow that pressures and burdens their diminished reincarnations. Yet Oz does not denigrate these moderns who are unable to measure up to their larger-than-life forebears. It is true that the comparison with the biblical models de-mythicizes the modern, unheroic personalities. But the discourse with the biblical model goes both ways. The presence of the biblical landscape and its legendary characters de-glorifies the modern personalities, but the contemporary text questions some of the biblical myths. Underneath the glamour and bravado associated with Davidic times, Oz perceives a current of bloodthirstiness, cruelty, and immense suffering. In opposition to Ben Gurion's glorification of the biblical era and his wish to repeat it in modern Israel, Oz believes that the biblical arena is too stark, uncompromising, and ferocious to alleviate the existential anguish of his modern protagonists. Measured against modern, humanistic values, the biblical world is found wanting. The phrase "biblical cruelty" is repeatedly echoed in one of Yonatan's nightmares, signifying the most harrowing form of savagery. Oz is thus pleading for the distancing of the biblical model from modern Israel as necessary for the country's well-being, implying that in attempting to emulate their ancient ancestors Israelis are undertaking an insurmountable task that will only end in insecure individuals bewildered about their identity and heritage. Yonatan's constant questioning of the concept of heroism, which he finds shallow and empty, his brutally honest assessment of himself as cowardly and reluctant to perform his military and familial duties eventually win our respect. However uneasily he carries his country's destiny on his shoulders, Yonatan will in time reconcile himself to his kibbutz duties and role in his country's life and overcome despair and total nihilism. Yonatan is not heroic, because heroism is an illusion, not because he is a coward, and thus the Bible's admiring recounting of its protagonists' valor is questioned. Within the limits of human possibilities Yonatan emerges as a worthy young man, aimless and searching at first, but finally coming to terms with the boundaries of his own existence.

In *Panther in the Basement* two opposing biblical personalities serve as the boy Proffy's "doubles," or his deep-seated earlier selves: the "defeatist" prophet Jeremiah, on the one hand, and the heroic King David (alternating with a warrior in King David's circle) on the other. But it appears that the more powerful model for Proffy the boy-narrator is that of Jeremiah. Called a traitor by his friends for associating with the kindly British sergeant, Proffy is in many ways the reincarnation of the prophet Jeremiah, who during the siege of Jerusalem preached surrender to the enemy and was accused of treason by his contemporaries. By sympathizing with the prophet and seeing in his predicament a mirror of his own, the child Proffy is an anomaly among his schoolmates, because in pre-State Palestine and the early years of Israel, school children were taught to see Jeremiah as a traitor and identify with the heroes of the Bible.[15] Proffy's own Bible teacher criticizes the tormented prophet for failing to uplift the national morale during the siege of Jerusalem: "In Mr. Gihon's view, when the enemy is at the gate, the duty of the prophet is to raise the people's spirits, to unite their ranks, and to pour out his wrath on the foe outside the walls, not on his brethren inside" (139). Preoccupied with the prophet's tragic dilemma, Proffy creates a parallel between himself, sneaking through the streets of Jerusalem on the eve of national independence, to secretly meet his British "friend," and the prophet Jeremiah, walking through the same alleys on the eve of the Babylonian's invasion, advocating surrender to the enemy. Jeremiah thus becomes not only a mirror of Proffy's dilemma, but his ancient anamnesis, "I have been called a traitor many times in my life" (1).

It is a measure of Oz's ongoing dialogue with the Bible that he has Proffy, as close a mirror of himself as he has ever come to in his fiction, choose from the biblical model to grapple with his own dilemma regarding patriotism and treachery, rather than draw from the authentic models from this era. Oz undoubtedly had numerous occasions during his childhood in Jerusalem to watch the leaders of the pacifist organization "Brit Shalom" ("Covenant for Peace"), such as Professors Yehudah Magnes, Martin Buber, and Ernest Simon, marching through the streets of the city, advocating appeasement of and accommodation toward the Arabs. Pointedly, in this novel the nation's claim for the land moves from adherence to the Messianic metanarrative which, like many other grand narratives has been rejected in the postmodern climate. In *Panther in the Basement*, Proffy's father, a moderate, unassuming person who nevertheless supports the underground, gives Proffy the best justification for a Jewish country. He tells Proffy of a violent act against himself and his own father in their hometown in Poland when he was a child (145). The father's Zionist conviction is based not on the biblical grand story, but on a personal experience of persecution.

As Oz's writings become more confessional or autobiographical his dialogue with the Bible becomes both more personal and more conciliatory. From the overarching metanarrative, associated with the colonialist enterprise in the postmodern mind and commanding a national, collective response that suffocates the individual, the ancient canon may be seen as a comforting text with which one can identify in difficult times. Oz's early gallery of biblical personalities consists of a zealous father, exaggerated, inflated heroes, or models of loyalty impossible to imitate, thus reducing the modern characters either to ludicrous pretenders or treacherous individuals. By contrast, the older Oz finds kinship with the sympathetic and tragic personality of the prophet Jeremiah. A further wrinkle in Oz's continuing discourse with the biblical models occurs in the writer's autobiography that reads like fiction, *A Tale of Love and Darkness*. Generally, Oz's depiction of his real-life mother Fania is reminiscent of his portrayal of other enchanting but treacherous female figures in his fiction, replete with embedding from the Bible, modern literary images, and mythic archetypes. Among these multiple intertexts in this work it is interesting to point out how the figure of the biblical Abraham, the zealot founder of the faith, metamorphoses from a powerful and appalling patriarch to a helpless, tragic mother.

This happens when the young Oz imagines how he would have prevented his mother from committing suicide; in the translation, the sentence reads as follows: "If I had been there with her in that room. . . . I would certainly have tried my hardest to explain why she mustn't. And if I didn't succeed, I would have done everything possible to stir her compassion, to make her take *pity on her only child*" (537; emphasis added). The Hebrew of the last phrase reads " *'al benah, 'al yechidah*" (on her son, her only son) and its most immediate association is God telling Abraham to take "your son, your only son," with a change in gender from the masculine to the feminine. In addition, this phrase in Hebrew is in fact a direct lifting of a verse from Bialik's poem "Levadi" ("By Myself") in which the Shechinah is seen as the mother bird unsuccessfully trying, with her failing wings, to protect her son, the last student in *beit hamidrash*, (the Synagogue and House of Learning) the metaphoric "*gozal*," (chick or little bird). The biblical connotation paints the mother abandoning her young child as the ferocious Abraham sacrificing his son, but the figure of the ruthless patriarch is mitigated and softened by being merged with that of the Shechinah as the mother bird, loyal and loving, yet inadequate and broken mother figure. Behind the merciless mother who abandons her young, fleetingly evoking the ruthless Genesis father, is the sick, helpless mother, pitiable rather than cruel. Thus, while the explicit association of the mother with Abraham is condemning, the additional intertext already begins to exonerate the mother: like Bialik's Shechinah she was quickly losing ground, unable to help her son or herself. Further, the bird at the center of Bialik's poem ties in with another poetic trope that runs through the autobiography in connection with the mother: the image of the bird Elise, who follows Fania in her doomed journey to Tel Aviv and witnesses her last moments. Elise calling Fania in vain to wake up from her final sleep reminds us of the angel of God who tries—and in the Genesis case succeeds—to foil the cruelty toward the young son. In this instance Oz has cobbled together several intertexts that ultimately soften Abraham's ferocious figure.

We know that Amos Oz was an admirer and astute reader of the works of S. Y. Agnon, the master practitioner of the intertextual mode, and therefore a brief comparison between the different functions of the biblical material in their works is of relevance.[16] In Agnon's works the scriptural intertext is inseparable from a dense network of Judaic master texts, discoursing with and commenting on each other. The prototypical Agnon narrative is an artistic masonry, a multi-tiered structure welding biblical idiom and patterns with other layers of the Judaic literary heritage; it therefore reads, as Gershon Shaked has pointed out, "as if" it is in itself one of those "sacred" or "semi sacred" texts.[17]

By contrast, in Oz's works, the biblical element, though occasionally interlaced with postbiblical and modern Hebraic vocabularies as well as mythic archetypes, is usually more distinct and sharply defined, unencumbered, so to speak, by generations of commentaries. It is the ancient parallel of present-day reality, the admired yet challenged age-old epic refashioned into a secular, powerful national story that buttresses the Zionist enterprise and also mirrors and informs current events. The scriptural presence provides Oz with a vehicle to confront both his own demons in his journey into his personal history and the Israeli meta-narrative, a fusion of the biblical grand tale and the modem one. The biblical intertext in Agnon, tightly interwoven into the entire spectrum of Judaic sources, is a way for the writer to immerse and integrate his stories into the time-hallowed continuum of the Judaic literary tradition. For Oz, it is a tool to uncover the national psyche, and probe, and often challenge, its geopolitical positions and ideological foundations. As with other Israeli writers, Oz's fiction and his public activities reveal the extraordinary symbiosis between a writer and the Israeli public at large. His works, even to his last novel *Judas*, are fundamentally within the larger Zionist idea, not aligned with the post-nationalist and post-Zionist theories that pervaded the Israeli culture and writings in the last decades of Oz's life.[18] In addition to being an enduring archetypal story magnificently told, the Bible for Oz is a form of a Zionist manifesto, and he wrestles with it, just as he does with Israeli politics and society, with combativeness and reproach, but also as a source of solace and comfort. In the final analysis, Oz's engagement with the Bible reflects his relationship with his homeland and its people, disillusionment and harsh criticism together with fierce loyalty and awe.

Notes

1. References are made to the following editions: The first four stories are from *Where the Jackals Howl and Other Stories*, translated by Nicholas de Lange and Philip Simpson (Harcourt, 1981); *The Hill of Evil Counsel*, translated by Nicholas de Lange (Harcourt, 1978); *A Perfect Peace*, translated by Hillel Halkin (Harcourt, 1985); *Panther in the Basement*, translated by Nicholas de Lange (Harcourt, 1997); and *A Tale of Love and Darkness*, translated by Nicholas de Lange (Harcourt, 2004).

2. While contemporary scholars of the intertextual activity, such as Julia Kristeva and others, posit that the reader is the ultimate authority regarding the intertextual signification of a text, my approach is similar to that of Michael Riffaterre, who suggests that intertextuality is mostly an intentional sign within the text, yet the reader's own intertextual connections, unknown to the author, may also be valid. See, Kristeva, Julia. "'Nous Deux' or a (Hi)story of Intertextuality." *Romanic Review*, vol. 93, Jan.–Mar. 2002, pp. 7–13 (8). On Riffaterre's theory of intertext see Orr, Mary. *Intertextuality: Debates and Contexts*. Polity, 2003, pp. 37–40.

3. Oz's search for ancient myths of enduring cultural and psychological relevance, deep-seated in the collective Western consciousness, goes beyond the Bible, as Abraham Balaban has shown in his study, which uncovers strong Jungian and mythic elements in Oz's tales. See *Between God and Beast: An Examination of Amos Oz's Prose*. Pennsylvania State UP, 1993.

4. See Gertz, Nurith. *Amos Oz: A Monograph* [Hebrew]. Sifriat Po'alim, 1980, pp. 93–116. See also Weinman's article cited in the next footnote.

5. For a reading that interprets Gideon's last moment as suggesting as well the image of Jesus on the cross, see Weinman, Aryeh. "Overtones of Isaac and Jesus in Modern Hebrew Narrative." *Hebrew Studies*, vol. 56, 2015, p. 378.

6. Genesis Rabbah. Soncino, 1961, vol. 2, pp. 735–36.

7. See Levi-Strauss, Claude. *The Savage Mind*. Chicago UP, 1966.

8. Lyotard, Jean-François. *The Postmodern Condition: A Report on Knowledge*. Translated by Geoff Bennigton and Brian Massumi. Manchester UP, 1984, pp. 37, 41.

9. Postcolonial literature typically reverses an earlier, canonical model, which accepts hierarchical thinking and shows how the Western person improves on nature and advances the native. See Clowes, Edith W. "The Robinson Myth Reread in Postcolonial and Postcommunist Modes." *Studies in Contemporary Fiction*, vol. 36, no. 2, 1995, pp. 145–60.

10. For more on Oz's debt to Berdichevsky's story, see Holtzman, Avner, and Chaim Seymor, "Strange Fire and Secret Thunder: Between Micha Josef Berdichevsky and Amos Oz." *Prooftexts*, vol. 15, no. 2, May 1995, pp. 145–62.

11. In *Eve's Journey: Feminine Images in Hebraic Literary Tradition* (U of Pennsylvania P, 1986; rpt. Wayne State UP, 1998; rpt. U of Pennsylvania P [book and eBook], 2015), p. 71.

12. Commenting on my reading of this novella in *Eve's Journey*, Oz wrote me in a letter dated 25 February 1987 expressing his pleasure that I uncovered the biblical model in my discussion and confirmed that he had indeed meant for the mother Ruth to evoke the biblical Ruth.

13. In an earlier letter, dated 2 December 1986, Amos Oz responded to my review of this novel in *Midstream,* when it first came out in English translation, confirming that it was his intention to create an analogy between the modern story and the biblical tale of Saul, Jonathan, and David and specifically pointing out the following observations that I had made: the biblical underpinnings of the story, the theme of "biblical cruelty," which was meant to oppose Ben Gurion's promotion of the Bible as the national, heroic epic, and the conciliatory tone towards the fathers' generation, especially in comparison with the story "The Way of the Wind."

14. On the function of the desert as landscape and trope in this novel, see Omer-Sherman, Ranen. "'A Disgrace to the Map of Israel': The Wilderness Journey of the Citizen-Soldier in Oz's *A Perfect Peace.*" *Journal of Modern Literature*, vol. 27, no. 1, Winter 2004, pp. 97–114. On the polarity of desert/ kibbutz as a correlative of Yonatan's inner turmoil, see Omer-Sherman, Ranen. "Zionism and the Disenchanted: The Plight of the Citizen-Soldier in Amos Oz's *A Perfect Peace.*" *Middle Eastern Literature*, vol. 8, no. 1, Jan. 2005, pp. 53–71.

15. Anita Shapira quotes an article by the scholar and pedagogue Ernest Simon who complained about this very tendency in Israeli schools, citing the attitude to Jeremiah in particular; see *Power and Land, The Zionist Resort to Force, 1881–1948* (Oxford UP, 1992), pp. 258–59.

16. Reflected in his study, *The Silence of Heaven: Agnon's Fear of God*, translated by Barbara Harshav (Princeton UP, 2012).

17. *Panim 'aherot biezirato shel Shai 'Agnon.* Hakibbutz Hameuchad, 1989, p. 12.

18. In the past two decades or so, Israeli intellectual circles promoted a move beyond the Zionist metanarrative as a canonical form with the intention to release Israeli literary criteria from their Zionist/nationalist foundation. For more on these permutations, see Aschkenasy, Nehama. "Israeli Fiction: National Identity and Private Lives," in Fred Greenspahn, (ed.), *Modern Israel: New Perspectives.* New York UP, 2016, pp. 195–223.

PART 4

OZ AND THE OTHER

Mizrahis and Palestinians

Chapter 13

Oz's Contentious Journey

In the Land of Israel

ADIA MENDELSON-MAOZ

Amos Oz's book *Po va-sham be-eretz Israel: Be-stav 1982* (*In the Land of Israel*) is composed of ten chapters and an epilogue written between November 1982 and the winter of 1983 and originally published in the *Davar* newspaper. At the time of the first Lebanon war, five years after the rise of the Likud party, Oz travels throughout Israel and the West Bank and tells of his encounters with various peoples of Israel, among them Orthodox Jews, settlers, Mizrahim, Palestinians, and aging pioneers. When Oz died in 2018, Benny Ziffer, the editor of the *Haaretz* newspaper's literary supplement, wrote a provocative obituary entitled "The Leader of the White Tribe Has Died." Echoing the current atmosphere in Israel where identity politics continue to create rifts in Israeli society, Ziffer blamed Oz for being a representative of the Ashkenazi hegemony that is unable to understand the other sectors ("tribes") of Israeli society. This chapter confronts Ziffer's populist argument, not in the sense of a total negation of his claims, but rather by articulating the path Oz chose when he embarked upon his unprecedented wanderings to meet the "other tribes" of Israel.

In the Land of Israel has a distinctive quality and lasting significance for Israeli literature and culture. It provides a stark confirmation of what Baruch Kimmerling famously called "the end of Ashkenazi hegemony" (as he phrases it in the title of his book) and predicted major societal upheavals in Israel society that remain starkly visible today, almost four decades after it was published. However, the power of the book resides not only in the fact that it pinpointed these new fractures but that it also made a brave attempt to probe their sources by asking tough questions about Zionism, its mission and fulfilment. Throughout the book, Oz takes on the literary role of "Ha-tzofe le-beit Israel" ("the watchman of the house of Israel" [Ezekiel 3.16]), by crafting a new literary genre of essays in which writers purposely step out of their comfort zone to engage with others through a process that involves contemplating Israel as a nation and as a culture.[1] Along his literary journey, Oz never conceals his identity or his privileged status within the Israeli hegemony, nor his personal political and cultural vision. In that context, the question of the writer's empathy can be tricky, since although it may enable a better understanding of suffering, it is based on the assumption that people can fully assimilate the experiences of others. In contemporary criticism of the relationships between the developed and developing worlds or, in Oz's case, the relationships between center and periphery, empathy may be viewed as less desirable. In Dominick LaCapra's view, empathy may tap into the pleasure principle because one of its components involves achieving some kind of harmony (78). It also has an intrinsically paternalistic component whereby the wealthy and powerful feel good when they "understand" the suffering of the weak (see Andrew Gibson and Adia Mendelson-Maoz). Oz does not always understand the people he meets (and so Ziffer may be right in his observation, but not in his conclusion); nor does he pretend to manifest total empathy towards people whose history or views he does not share. Instead, he is unsparingly honest in the sense that he refuses to endorse an artificial or paternalistic empathetic gaze. Ultimately, he offers something more powerful—an attentive willingness to let them speak for themselves.

These critical qualities, Oz's ability to sense future currents in Israeli culture, as well as his ability to capture different voices in a discourse that does not praise or flatter but also does not condemn, turned *In the Land of Israel* into something of a transformative book in Israeli culture, as can be seen from its enthusiastic reception both then and now. *In the Land of Israel* directly inspired Grossman's *Ha-zman ha-tsahov* (*The Yellow Wind*, 1987) and *Nokhehim nifkadim* (*Sleeping on a Wire*, 1992). Nir Baram's *Ha-aretz she-me'ever la-harim* (*A Land without Borders: My Journey Around East Jerusalem and the West Bank*, 2016) must also be viewed as a scion of Oz's book.

Oz's ten chapters of conversations begin with the Geula neighborhood of Jerusalem where Oz grew up. In his childhood, the neighborhood was populated by a mixture of Eastern-European intellectuals, German and Austrian immigrants, revisionists and members of the Hagana, artists and scholars, who all lived together with the ultra-Orthodox. In 1982, when Oz returns to the neighborhood after years of living in Kibbutz Hulda, he notes that "all this is finished here" (20).[2] The heterogenic fabric so richly captured in *A Tale of Love and Darkness* has been replaced by Yeshiva students and Hasidim who moved either from the Mea Shearim and Sanhedria ultra-Orthodox neighborhoods of Jerusalem, or emigrated from Toronto, New York, or Belgium. Now all one sees are people dressed in black and throngs of children speaking Yiddish. The streets are papered with pashkevils (broadside notices in Yiddish) featuring heated debates between different ultra-Orthodox "courts" and Oz regards the transformation of the neighborhood as a step backward toward the Eastern European Jewish shtetl, before the Holocaust, before Hitler.

The most emblematic change is the transformation of Tachkemoni, the school Oz attended as a child, into a rabbinic school, whose teacher is proud of the level of education which consists almost exclusively of Torah study and does not teach science or history. When Oz asks how the school celebrates Independence Day, the teacher responds, "What's to celebrate here?" (13). Oz concludes that "Zionism was repelled from here" (14–15) a powerful statement he repeats at the start of several paragraphs to hammer home what he experiences as an unbearable outcome.

"Zionism has been repulsed" (9) from the Geula neighborhood, but Oz shoulders and internalizes the blame as "ours," as a result of Ben Gurion's concessions to maintain the "status quo." Oz explains the state of mind in that era, when people who believed in Zionism worked to build the State of Israel as a haven for the Jews who were persecuted in Europe, the ultra-Orthodox mentality could not be negated. But now we understand that this would result in annexing "region after region, and we will stand deaf and dumb, lest we find ourselves cast in the monstrous role of 'Hitler's successors'" (18).

Oz's point of departure is made explicit in this opening section: something went wrong with the Zionist enterprise he once knew and cherished. *In the Land of Israel* portrays people on the fringes of Israeli society, but its prime thrust is the relationship between the Israeli hegemony and the other groups that challenge it. Throughout the book Oz attempts to understands the roots of this change, revealing again and again yet another blind spot of Zionism that lays the groundwork for the debacle, and ultimately predicts, with sorrow and frustration, that his personal views will fade and be overrun by others.

The Invention and Decline of Israeliness

In *The Invention and Decline of Israeliness*, Baruch Kimmerling defines the Israeli elite as Ashkenazi, secular, socialist and Zionist, and claims that "Israel's hegemonic secular Zionist metaculture had declined, and a different social order had risen in its place. The appearance and persistence of a new system of competing cultures and countercultures and an escalating cultural war between them and the still dominant culture has accompanied the decline of the hegemonic order" (112). The decline of Israeli hegemony did not take place in one day. Although the formal watershed is widely understood to be 1977 when Begin and the Likud party replaced the long leadership of the Mapai in government, its actual beginnings date back to the 1950s and 1960s, specifically in groups that challenged the elite such as the Mizrahim, the National-Religious parties, and later the ultra-Orthodox. The unrest among the Mizrahim that include the 1959 riots in Wadi Salib in Haifa, and later in 1971 when the Mizrahi Israeli Black Panthers demonstrated against Zionism and the State, voicing rejection of the paternalist approach of the Ashkenazi hegemony and their prejudices toward the Mizrahim.

The 1967 War marked the ascension of the national political group that supports Religious Zionism. The territories occupied during the 1967 War encompassed major sites linked to the Jewish past associated with strong Biblical references such as Hebron, Nablus, Mt. Sinai, and the Western Wall of Herod's temple in Jerusalem, which fueled a messianic drive to establish a Jewish nation within these wider, presumably ancient borders. The subsequent events of 1977 were not only a repudiation of the Ashkenazi elite, but also a turning point when the delicate balance between a Jewish and a democratic state tipped in favor of the former. As Kimmerling puts it: "on the one hand, Machal [Likud] was able to overtly express ethnic discrimination for the first time, and on the other promoted 'Jewishness' instead of the Ashkenazi hegemony's 'Israeliness' as a common denominator" (*Ketz shilton ha-ahusalim* 16). This process of religion-ization not only strengthened the national religious groups but also enhanced the legitimacy of the ultra-Orthodox who began to stake claims on state institutions. Against this backdrop, alongside the Occupation and its impact in the 1970s and the 1980s, the Palestinians, both those living in the Occupied Territories and Palestinian citizens of Israel, responded by constructing their own identities.

Thus, *In the Land of Israel* captures a major moment of fragmentation in Israeli history. In the midst of the First Lebanon War, when the Sabra and Shatila massacre had ignited heated discourse on the ethics of Israeli military actions, Oz set out to meet the different "tribes" in Israel to discover what they thought about the past, the present, and the future of Israel. In the author's notes to the original edition, Oz states that his conversations were not designed "to be a 'representative picture' or a 'typical cross-section' of Israel at this time" (viii). In Oz's preface to the Harvest edition, in 1993, ten years after the original publication, he states, "I never intended to draw socio-ideological picture of Israel. This was a deliberate journey to the fringes [. . .] It was a journey among people of strong convictions, individuals inclined to exclamation points" (ix). Nonetheless, these remarks can be seen as a rhetorical device, since much of the book does indeed constitute an X-ray of Israeli society at that time and revealed new trends in Israeli culture that were only on the margins of mainstream Israeli culture when Oz made his journey, yet ultimately radically transformed the future, becoming its most formidable players.

Who Has the Power? Ashkenazi, Mizrahi, Arab

In the book's fourth conversation, Oz travels to Ramallah, a major Palestinian city in the West Bank, which today is the administrative capital of the Palestinian National Authority. The meeting took place more than a decade after the 1967 War and the Occupation of the West Bank, when the Occupation had become a fact on the ground that involved both economic collaboration with Israel and internal national Palestinian discord.

For Oz, who voiced his objections to the Occupation soon after the 1967 War, the 1982 visit was an opportunity to see what had happened to these territories years after the war. Oz talks to several Palestinians, including an elderly man, Abu-Azmi, who describes the relationship between Israel and the Palestinians as a power ploy:

> Before the '48 war, what did the Jews say? They said they wanted a peace and that's all.[3] Just give them a peace of their

own and they'd be happy and have done with it. They talked
pitifully. That was smart. The Arab had no sense then. They
told the Jews, We have the power [. . .] we have it all. The Jews
won't get a peace or anything else. Let them march into the sea.
Now it's the other way around. The Arab will tell you today
that he's pitiful, that he wants only to be given a peace and
nothing else, and the Israeli will tell him, I've got the power,
I've got it all—why should he give the Arab a peace. (80–81)

Naif, a younger Palestinian, presents a different version, suggesting that
"the Jews and the Arabs [are] like two people standing on a roof tight
together: if they don't want to fall off the roof together, they have to be
careful. They have no choice" (83). The combination of these two accounts
clearly reflects the complexity of the situation. The relations between the
two nations are like a seesaw: when one end goes up the other goes down.
The two nations have a history of suffering when down, but when they
are up they delude themselves into thinking that they are in no danger
of yet another imminent tilt. Abu-Azmi stresses that the powerful side
never agrees to compromise, since power intoxicates and corrupts. Hassan
and Naif both claim that the Jews are not bad people, but that the Israelis
are driven by a thirst for victory that makes them pursue pipe dreams.

This conversation targets the concept of power and the question of
identity. Throughout, the speakers do not use the terms "you" and "us"
but rather employ the third person by referring to "the Arabs," and later
"the Palestinians" ("don't write 'the Arabs.' Write 'the Palestinians'; that's
more correct"; 84), "the Jews," and "the Israelis." Later, in Oz's conversation in East Jerusalem in the office of the daily newspaper Al-Fajr, the
question of identity is again broached when Ziad states "there is an open
debate among us on the question of identity. [. . .] something like your
debate over who is a Jew" (158–59). Oz asks himself (and his readers)
whether he can compare the newspaper Al-Fajr (The Dawn) to the Zionist
Hebrew newspaper Ha-shahar (also meaning The Dawn) that was founded
a hundred years ago in Vienna by Peretz Smolenskin. The potential for
comparison not only draws on the identical name, but also on the historical notion of shaping the identities of people who aim to build their
nation. Thus, while Oz pretends to ask an innocent question, he clearly
knows the sobering answer.

In this exchange Ziad argues that if Yasser Arafat had tried to offer
peace and mutual recognition, it would have brought about a split and

greater conflict in the Arab street since some factions would have praised Arafat and others would have said he was a traitor. Ziad funnels this question back to Oz to inquire what would occur in the Israeli society if peace and mutual recognition with the Palestinian were on the table, and Oz reprises Ziad's comment: "There would be a split. There would be a great conflict" (161).[4] Oz appears to hint that the two nations are not so different but does not express full empathy or underscore the similarity. Oz's belief in Zionism does not negate the Palestinians' right to independence. Rather, in the name of Zionism, he believes that the Palestinians deserve their own state. As Jonathan Freedland commented, "He was firm that none of that contradicted a basic belief in Jews' right to a home of their own." However, this changed nothing for the Palestinian incarcerated in Ketziot prison who requested the *In the Land of Israel* but was told that Oz's book was banned under the category of "incitement material."[5]

In the second chapter Oz's visit to Beit Shemesh constitutes the framework for enlarging on discussion of the questions of identity and power raised earlier. Unlike the conversation with the Palestinians who formulated general definitions in the third person, here the two sides are designated in first person as "we" the people of Beit Shemesh, and "you" (Oz and those who think like him). Uzi Behar suggested that the Palestinians expressed themselves in the third person to avoid highlighting their defeat, whereas the Mizrahim perceive themselves as the winners who can take a stand in the first person. However, the conflict between "we" and "you" is no less trenchant when it comes to the Mizrahi-Ashkenazi clash. Oz's reflections begin with a stark admission: "It was almost twenty years since I had been in Beit Shemesh" (27). In an article written after the publication of the book, an anonymous author under the pen name of "Oriental Jew" commented acerbically on Oz's preface to this chapter: "He has not been in the town for twenty years, and now sees that many of the shanties that were constructed by the Amidar company in the 50s have turned into extravagant villas in the meantime. But the residents have also changed. Instead of those depressed immigrants, he encounters enraged people who have no fear to pass a fatal judgment on the past" (3). Hence, the theme of monumental societal change in the first chapter is equally evident here. Oz gazes at the city and the beautiful countryside around it. The "gloomy workers" (27) he once saw have turned into his invigorated political and cultural opponents, who not only have a great deal to say, but also have the economic and political clout to implement change.

When Oz first glimpsed it, the city of Beit Shemesh was a typical "development town" with a majority of North African immigrants. In the 1970s it was known as one of the bastions of the Likud party and Menachem Begin campaigned with a promise to invest heavily in the city. Oz's visit to the city takes place five years after their political victory, and the level of rage is still very high. The residents are convinced that the plan of the Labor government had been to turn the Mizrahim into permanent second-class citizens, servants of the elite. In their comments to Oz, they often blame him for what they see as his inability to internalize that the historical Mapai has been ousted, and that the Ashkenazi hegemony has yet to "realize that Begin is prime minister" (35), but in fact, they themselves are not entirely sure what this political victory has in store for them. In their view, which is still rooted in Israeli discourse to this day, power can be tricky, such that even though they have recovered their dignity (with Begin), they must never drop their guard, since "the real power is not in Begin's hands. You've got the Histadrut, [the main labor union] and you've got the newspapers and the big money, and you've also got the radio and the TV. You're still running the country" (37).

Their sense of enduring grievance, their uncertainty about the strength of their newfound political and social clout against the country's elite is strongly entwined with their view of the conflict with the Palestinians. This does not refer to borders or Israeli identity, but rather to economics and the issue of status. The people Oz encounters in Beit Shemesh view the 1967 victory and the Occupation as an opportunity to save themselves, since the Arabs can take their places as the servants and the cleaners. But if "they give back the territories, the Arabs will stop coming to work, and then and there you'll put us back into the dead-end jobs, like before" (36). This is again suggestive of the seesaw depicted by Abu-Azmi, but this time between two oppressed groups. Is this the nature of Zionist society, where, as in iconic Arik Einstein and Uri Zohar TV parodic sketch of the 1970s portraying the country's diverse waves of immigrants from 1882 to the present, in which there will always be an inferior group to do the country's "dirty" jobs.[6]

Who Is a true Zionist?

Perhaps the appearance of Gush Emunim was also a blow to the ego of the youth in the kibbutzim and the Labor movement: a part of society that had been accustomed to being regarded as the standard bearer, accustomed to being looked up to by the country, had then been swindled—it, the firstborn—by people who were masquerading in *their* sloppy army jackets, running around on hilltops with sub-machine guns and walkie-talkies, who had adapted the mannerisms and the slang of the kibbutz.

—Amos Oz, *In the Land of Israel*

Oz's concept of Zionist history and the grave mistakes made in the past that seep into the present and the future converge during Oz's visit to the settlement of Tekoa and his encounter with the residents of Ofra. As Oz describes it, the 1967 Occupation brought "the ecstasy over the Wailing Wall and Biblical sites in the West Bank, the talk of victory and miracles, Redemption and the coming of the Messiah" (132). While Oz and his friends in the kibbutzim were struggling to cope with the violence of the War and its outcomes in texts such as *Siah lohamin* (*The Seventh Day*),[7] changes took place on the ground. Gush Emunim was founded in 1974, as a pressure group to prevent territorial concessions after the War. Later, in 1977, the group initiated a movement to build settlements in the West Bank. As a member of the "Shalom Achshav" movement (Peace Now) founded in 1977, which viewed the settlements as a threat not only to a possible two state solution, but also to the very nature of Israel as a liberal and democratic state, Oz's visits to these settlements were bound to be fraught.

Three chapters in the book are dedicated to the enormous disparity between Oz's views and those of the settlers. Here again Oz does not hide his convictions or extend empathy. He comes to hear their view and to familiarize himself with them. His description of Tekoa portrays the diversity of the settlers (which can help account for the expansion of settlements to this day): he meets firebrand ideologists, individualists calling for a return to nature, and others who simply consider it to be an economic opportunity. He hears from Harriet who sees the situation as a holy war: "A war against all of Islam. And against the Goyim" (60), who is willing to hire Arabs as "hewers of wood and carriers of water" (71), as long as they understand who is the boss. He meets Danny who after visiting the Cave of Chariton (the Tekoa gorge) "was enchanted by the place and decided to stay" (60) and listens to Menachem's more pragmatic financial considerations that prompted him to invest in the area and set up factories (55–66).

Oz travels from Tekoa to Ofra, where he spends the whole weekend, and takes up Israel Harel's invitation to give a long speech on his worldview. In Ofra, the center of Gush Emunim, he meets Pinchas Wallerstein who was the chairman of the Mateh Binyamin Regional Council at the time, and one of Gush Emunim's most prominent leaders. Notably, his visit took place shortly after the massacre of Sabra and Shatila in Lebanon, and after Ofra publicly announced its support for the government; in the view of settlement officials, the massacre showed the extent to which Arab can hate and kill one another. As a settler named Sarah Harel grimly observes (without acknowledging Israel's own culpability in the atrocity), "If the Arabs are capable of doing something like that to other Arabs, what awaits us if we are trapped in a moment of weakness?" (119). Even as he gives voice to such views, Oz never wavers from his deep-seated rejection of the settlers and their ideology. However, his disappointment does not apply to the people as individual human beings, but rather reflects his realization that the root of their ideology derives from their interpretation of Zionism, acknowledging the settler's view that "Gush Emunim, from the day of its founding, has actually operated by classical Zionist techniques: another stake, another goat, another acre. [. . .] the story of Ofra begins in '75, with a handful of folks who settled it as a work camp in the abandoned Jordanian garrison" (111). While Oz is astounded to see what people who are driven by Zionism are capable of thinking and doing, when he delivers his lecture in Ofra, after the Sabbath has come to a close, he nevertheless employs the metaphor of the family to articulate the relationships between them: "Zionism is not a first name but a surname, a family name, and this family is divided" (128). Diverse voices and contested plans emerge from the consensual base that Zionism means "that it is good for the Jewish people to return to the Land of Israel" (128). This is the only chapter where Oz apparently feels he cannot remain silent. Moreover, he voices an uncompromising critique that illustrates the chasm between the settlers of Ofra and the vision of Peace Now.

Oz's heartfelt message to the settlers is the following: "You people are convinced that to relinquish Judea and Samaria would endanger the existence of the State of Israel. I think that annexation of these regions endangers the existence of the State of Israel" (128). This clash in objectives stems from two different worldviews. For Oz, the nation-state is a tool or instrument that saved the Jewish people from the Holocaust and provided them with a safe haven associating Jewish tradition and Western humanism. In contrast, the settlers fuel ideological passion steeped in religious isolationism and nationalism, and twist Zionism in the name of messianic rhetoric. "Zionism was not a matter of turning our back on the gentile worlds," Oz asserts. "On the contrary, it was born precisely out of the desire to return to the family of nations" (141). But "which family of nations? Cannibals? Murderers? Anti-Semites?" (141). With extreme arrogance, they cherish ideas that are inhuman and immoral and where everything is sanctioned as legitimate if it enters into the ritual of the Land of Israel.

Oz argues that their orientation constitutes a negation of Jewish values. In terms of the Palestinians, he states that "one who denies the identity of others is doomed to find himself ultimately not unlike those who deny one's own identity" (144). Oz's sharp denunciation expressed his overriding fear not only of the terrible price that the people of Israel would pay on the battlefield in combat for the messianic dream of the Greater Land of Israel but also the fear that these extreme and uncompromising ideological urges would constitute the seeds of the Jewish people's self-destruction, which would bring about yet another cycle of defeat and destruction.

Dear Zealots

Oz knew very well that such extreme views were not limited to the settler enclaves that support extreme manifestations of Zionist ideals and ultimately broadens his argument to encompass stereotypes of the Jewish people. Antisemitic stereotypes characterize the Jew as weak, miserable, humiliated, and effeminate. As Tamar Mayer, Anita Shapira, and others have explained, the Zionist movement aimed to change the image of the Jewish prototype by promoting the Sabra, the new prototype of the native-born Israeli Jew (Mayer 15). The Sabra was proud, undiscouraged by failure, typically gendered a man of action and of words, optimistic and cheerful, loyal to his friends, and instilled with a powerful sense of ideological commitment and national responsibility. The Sabra was the perfect warrior who was brave, devoted to his mission, and willing to sacrifice his life to protect the country and its people (Shapira 184). The Sabra myth defined Israeli masculinity for years. Oz himself, as he describes in A Tale of Love and Darkness, lived in a small "diasporic" apartment with his parents who failed to adjust to the new land, but knew that "somewhere, over the hills and far away, a new breed of heroic Jews was springing up" (4), and fiercely admired them. After his mother's death he is "too hurt and angry" (203) to mourn her, distanced himself from his familial origins by changing his last name in an attempt to fully claim the native Israeli Sabra identity. Forsaking Jerusalem, he embraces the agrarian heart of this Sabra territory—the kibbutz, effectively transforming himself.

There are two consequential conversations with farmers in *In the Land of Israel*. Toward the end of the book, Oz talks to Zvi Bachur from Bat Shlomo, and discovers his extraordinary life story and that of his wife who built their farmhouse with their own hands. Adhering to the ideal image of the Sabra and the Zionist mission to work the land, he gets up at five o'clock in the morning to begin his farm work: "This is already an Arab country [. . .] the Arabs are up and working and the Jews are still fast asleep" (209). Bachur views the younger generations of Israelis with a jaundiced eye. He criticizes the lures of consumerism, the shallow appeal of money, stocks, and diamonds, and says that everybody should roll up their sleeves and get to work.

The second farmer, Z., takes the image of the Sabra to troubling extremes, with a monologue full of hatred and violence. Z. is disturbed by any manifestation of what he regards as weakness that he invariably attributes to the lingering effects of the Diaspora. To abolish the *Zhid*, the prototype of the weak Jew, he is willing to adopt such an extreme stance that he ironically embraces the identity of a "Judeo-Nazi" (94), the very terminology with which Yeshayahu Leibowitz bitterly condemned the cruelty of Israeli soldiers towards Palestinians. Z. vows to fight like hell against anyone, to be mad and violent as mandated by the situation, so the Other would "realize that we're a wild country, deadly and dangerous to everyone around, awful, crazy, capable of suddenly going nuts because they murdered one of our kids—even one! [. . .] if we act like that, it means we're angry and desperate. And if we're angry and desperate, it means we've been the victims of injustice" (89–90).

Z. has no moral quandaries with the war in Lebanon. As a matter of fact, if he were in charge it could all have been taken care of in 1948. He also declares he is willing to take illegal steps for the cause and perceives any restraint as weakness. His attitude towards Oz's values is summarized as follows: "As soon as we finish this phase, the violence phase, step right up, it'll be your turn to play your role. You can make us a civilization with humanistic values here" (93). Z.'s view adheres to the adage that "when the guns roar, the muses are silent." He is willing to fight for a brighter era when the wars are at last over. Upon the book's publication, Z.'s anonymity and the brutality of his monologue made many wonder whether this chapter was even authentic since he is the only figure in the book whose name and location are concealed. Some Hebrew readers suspected that the figure of Z. was wholly fabricated by Oz. Amos Kenan, who wrote about the book soon after it appeared, related to the character of Z. as follows: "The character named Z. appears in Oz's book. Those who read it will understand. Fools will say that this character is fictional, that there is no such person. Anyone who knows this country knows this man exists. And the possibility of his being indicates that he exists" (Kenan).

Kenan does not explicitly address whether Z. is a real or fictional character, but instead uses Aristotle's definition of literature (versus history) by reasoning that if this type of character is possible, he should be included in this gallery. Oz was fascinated by this extremist and his ilk for years and in his 2017 book *Dear Zealots: Letters from a Divided Land* he discusses the roots and the manifestations of fanaticism: "More and more commonly, the strongest public sentiment is one of profound loathing—subversive loathing of 'the hegemonic discourse' [. . .] Sweeping, unmitigated loathing surges like vomit from the depths of this or that misery. Such extreme loathing is a component of fanaticism in all its guises [. . .] [multiculturalism] that began with an expansion of cultural and emotional horizons is increasingly deteriorating into narrower horizons, isolationism, and hatred to the other" (6–7). Oz's analyses of fanaticism and extremism were written more than thirty years after his original journey to the fringes of Israeli society. In that span of time, the fury had not dimmed, but in fact had become a flame. As Kenan insisted in his review of *In the Land of Israel*, Oz provides "a snapshot so right for the autumn of 1982 that it becomes a refined, polished thought, which absorbs the entirety of the snapshot of every possible situation, including those from beforehand, and those to come in the future."

Epilogue

What lessons can be learned from Oz's uneasy journey to the Land of Israel? The final chapter provides not one but three endings. The first is a placated look at the city of Ashdod as a manifestation of an ordinary city, with no myths or desires, with no great history, simply a place where decent people live. The second ending drew a full circle: the book starts in Jerusalem's Geula quarter, where Oz lived as a child, and ends in

Kibbutz Hulda, the place where Oz lived during the book's composition, an ideological haven where other people share his values. Yet there is a third ending, one not located in space but rather in time, in which he updates the reader on current events including the appointment of the Kahan commission to investigate the massacre in Lebanon, the murder of peace activist Emil Grunzweig at a Peace Now demonstration, the snow that fell into the newly dug graves of soldiers who died in the Lebanon war and on the soldiers who were still fighting, the court-martial of soldiers and officers charged with harassing Arab inhabitants in the West Bank, and lastly the angrily threatening letters that Oz himself received calling him a traitor.

As is well known, Oz's version of Zionism was staunchly liberal and secular. However, in both his fiction and nonfiction, Oz remained fascinated with the feverish politics of religious fanatics. Miron points out that this book is no exception as it aligns with the features of Oz's poetics such as "prophetic extremism, the destructive striving for absolute experiences, the rapid shifts from feelings of abysmal inferiority to illusions of prevailing power, and the mental and physical illness." This prompts Dan Miron to inquire: "Did the author not cast the transmission of his work's inherent landscape onto the Israeli reality that he described? Did Oz invent this fundamental illness of contemporary Israel, that appears in the book as it tosses in the feverish heat of disorientated greatness and a breaching of a strait towards a fictitious space?" (Miron 1). Clearly, there are connections between his fictional writing and this book, mainly in his eagerness to enable the voices of different, sometimes extremist, non-conformists to be heard.

In Oz's frank conversation with Shira Hadad (2018), he talks about the way he looks at people: "My whole life, I have lived the life of a spy. [. . .] I look at strangers [. . .] I hear what people say, steal parts of conversations and finish them. [. . .] my initial urge is the urge to guess what I would feel if I were him, what I would feel if I were her: what would I think? What would I want? What would I be ashamed of?" (*Mima asui ha-tapuah?* 13). In an essay in honor of Oz's 70th birthday, A. B. Yehoshua argued that although he understands Oz's statement that he has two pens—one for writing literature and one for writing political and ideological essays—he knows that these two are one and the same (Yehoshua). Oz's comments to Hadad suggest that in this book as well he situated himself as a silent observer who aims to enter the mind of others and see the world from their point of view. The core of each conversation is a monologue by an individual who describes his life and his views (Miron); Oz does not interfere, but rather listens, whether it is to the religious settlers in Tekoa, the angry Mizrahi Jews in Beit Shemesh, or the Palestinians in Ramallah. He manifests attentiveness, but eventually proves that fanaticism is never far away.[8] As noted earlier, Ziffer claimed that as a member of the "white tribe," Oz is unable to understand the other. This may be true, but it does not mean he needs to remain silent and shoulder the guilt of the hegemony's faults forever. Oz did what he could do by being unsparingly honest with himself and not offering the pretense of shallow empathy, instead aspiring to illuminate the "current tensions in the land of Israel" (Wisse 68).

Nitza Ben-Dov, who ably analyzes the endings of Oz's works, maintained that Oz himself is the protagonist who inserts his presence into the story, and uses the metaphor of "the morning after" to express Oz's constant recognition of the gap between ideologies and dreams and their realization (281–84). Yigal Schwartz asked, "Why does Oz [. . .] constitute such a powerful source of attraction and aversion?" (*Pulhan ha-sofer* 21), and claims that during the 1980s, and specifically from 1982 to 1991, Oz wrote "requiem books of eulogies for his world and his era, and prophesized, [. . .] alternative paths for the different peoples who would be the protagonists of the coming era." ("Ha-migdalor"). Ben-Dov's "the morning after" and Schwartz's "requiem" correspond to the reading suggested here. In other words, Oz reassessed the values of Zionism, and identified its darker sides: the Zionist decapitation of the image of the diasporic Jew can degenerate into aggressive military behavior; the ideology of making the land bloom, which later played a major role in the Occupation and settlement culture; the concept of integration that in fact led to segregation and outrage; the war of 1948 driven by the urge to find a haven for the Jews after the Holocaust that turned into the Palestinian trauma; the need to build a strong army to make Israel safe that morphed into the Occupation in 1967 and the Lebanon War; and the multifaceted relationship between Zionism and Judaism where the delicate balance between the definition of the state as both Jewish and democratic is often upset.

These matters form the heart of Oz's investigation, and this is what made many readers feel that the book captured their own thoughts. Menachem Brinker, in his essay on the place of the author in society, maintained that "for me, as for many readers of my generation, these essays [. . .] gave a perfect, enviable expression to what was stirring in our hearts, and even when they enraged us with one statement or the other, they challenged us" (321). The book itself attracted immense attention when it was published in 1983 and when the English version, which has a preface by Oz, came out. Eleven years after the book was published, the writer Eli Amir stated that "Israeli society did not settle any of its core problems: peace, borders, identity, culture, religion and state. [Oz's] writing of a social-political essay in a literary style that captivates the mind and heart, which nowadays is popular here and abroad" (35). In 2002, to celebrate twenty years since its first publication, Alon Hadar went to the city of Beit Shemesh to view the changes since Oz's visit and published his conclusions in *Kol ha-ir Jerusalem* magazine. In 2009, twenty-seven years after its publication, and timed to coincide with the 6th edition of the book, Uri Misgav repeated Oz's trip to meet the people (or their children) Oz dialogued with in 1982 and painted an insightful picture of their changing lives and communities ("Hiluch hozer"). The 2009 edition of the book in Hebrew includes an epilogue written by David Grossman (which appears in English for the first time in this volume). He defines the book as a beacon for society, declaring that:

> Its readers already know that the patient has not recovered since that time; rather, it looks like his illness has only become worse, and that at times his illness has turned into some sort of strange ideology. [. . .] The readers already know that several of the most extreme and preposterous inclinations expressed in these pages have become part and parcel of our everyday lives. A world view where force and paranoia and racism [. . .] to some extent characterize the ways of thinking and acting of large groups in the public and political space in Israel. [. . .] Every page in this book is frighteningly contemporaneous, and gives the feeling that the State of Israel is not moving forward in time almost, but is rather trapped in an eternal vicious circle, in which it is doomed to repeat the same mistakes again and again, experience the same disasters again and again. (Epilogue 193–95)

When visiting Tekoa, Oz relates to the prophet Amos. Unlike the residents who see their settlement as a realization of Amos's prophecies of consolation, the "return of my people Israel," Oz is afraid that other verses in the Book of Amos might also come to pass, such as the promise that "thy sons and thy daughters shall fall by the sword" (*In the Land* 72). Shortly after the book was published, Ilan Shainfeld suggested that Amos the prophet was a manifestation of Oz himself. Uri Misgav returned to this book after Oz passed away, claiming that "With an accuracy that is both depressing and admirable, Oz simply predicted contemporary Israel, which has been created in the image of Netanyahu" ("Ziffer tsodek").

In a revealing interview with Shiri Lev-Ari, Oz stated that he had a public duty to write. Yaffa Berlowitz discusses Oz's pervasive sense of duty in a study that positions his book within the genre of travelogue, travel stories, and their specific manifestations in Hebrew literature, from the first waves of immigrants to Israel who traveled far and wide to familiarize themselves with the landscapes (Moshe Smilansky, Josua Barzilai Eisenstadt, Yaacov Rabinovich), to the Palmach generation who discovered Israel as combatants. These travelogues played an ideological role but also raised acute questions of identity and belonging.[9] In a cursory sense, Oz's text can be seen as part of this tradition, but ultimately differs from it in terms of both structure and values. For David Grossman this book provided a new literary path he himself chose to take. He read the book when he was only twenty-nine, as the father of a child, after serving in Lebanon. Four years later, in March 1987, just before the first Intifada broke out, he himself went on a journey, and wrote *The Yellow Wind* (which he personally called "In the Land of Ismael"). The book was based on a series of columns that originally appeared in the weekly *Koteret Rashit* where he was traveling in the West Bank, interviewing Palestinian and Israelis, Arabs and Jews. "It seems to me" Grossman admits "that in those days, I didn't really understand how much the writing of *The Yellow Wind* was influenced by *In the Land of Israel*" (Epilogue 199). Later Grossman went to another journey among Palestinians living as Israeli citizens and in the Occupied Territories and wrote *Sleeping on a Wire*. These books of conversations have several parallels with *In the Land of Israel*: the attentiveness to the other's voice, the issue of comparisons between the Jewish people and the Palestinians and their inner soul-searching of Zionist ideology and Israeli society.

Ultimately, Oz's profound legacy was not acknowledged by Grossman alone, but strongly influenced the work of younger authors such as Nir Baram in *A Land without Borders*. In 2016, more than thirty years after Oz's book first came out, Nir Baram went on a trip in his book *A Land Without Borders*, a collection of interviews with people in the West

Bank, Gaza, and East Jerusalem. Like Oz before him, he mainly listens to the views of the people he meets that define the Israeli situation in the Territories. Baram was raised in a different era, but he too endorses the mission of Oz and Grossman in his investigation of the rift between the Zionist liberal legacy and facts on the ground. At the end of his book, Oz pleads for "patience," claiming that "there is no shortcut" (241); Baram is less optimistic and is concerned about the future. In his introduction he asks: "What will our future look like? What sort of country will be here? [. . .] I realized that [. . .] what has evolved in Israel over the past few years is a collective repression of the future" (10). Should we, the readers, adopt Baram's more pessimistic view or should we return to Oz's basic attentiveness and muster our patience before we judge the future of Israeli society?

Notes

1. While there are Yiddish and Hebrew authors who went on journeys around Jewish provinces and described what they have seen, these do not resemble Oz's text. Isaac Leib Peretz, for example, was sent by the Polish administrators on an expedition to check the condition of the Jews in small towns of southeastern Poland. He then wrote *Bilder fun a provints-rayze* (Scenes from a Journey Through the Provinces, 1891) where he describes the harsh conditions and the poverty. Peretz's text can be read in the context of other writing, of authors such as Peretz Smolenskin, Hayim Nahman Bialik and even Shmuel Yosef Agnon (in *Oreakh natah lalun, A Guest for the Night*), who explored cities and people after pogroms and wars, in order to provide poetic testimonies of the destruction.

2. All quotes are taken from the English translation of *In the Land of Israel*, unless stated otherwise.

3. The title of this chapter in Hebrew is "Rak Binah" and in English is "Just a Peace." In Hebrew Abu-Azmi uses the word "binah," which is an Arabic pronunciation of the Hebrew word pinah—a corner, meaning "just a corner," suggesting that his people only need just a little corner for themselves.

4. At that time, Oz could not have imagined that this split would lead to a horrific validation in the 1995 assassination of Prime Minister Yitzhak Rabin. As he admitted later, "when I reread what I had written there, I found the warning that Rabin or Shamir are about to be assassinated. There was something in the air, then, it wasn't only what I, the psychopath, was saying" (in Dror Eydar).

5. See Dani Sade.

6. https://www.youtube.com/watch?v=MBNWHTipwEA.

7. *Fighters' Discourse* [translated as *The Seventh Day* in its English edition], edited by Avraham Shapira, was based on a series of recorded conversations after the war with kibbutzim members, including Muki Tzur, Amos Oz, and Yariv Ben-A'haron, among others.

8. Hence I do not agree with Orly Lubin, who criticized Oz for failing to make any clear political statements in the book.

9. Berlowitz also perceives Oz's travels and the book as a response to a debate held in Tzavta in 1981 on Amos Kenan's book *El Artzech, El Moladetech* (*On Your Country, On Your Homeland*). The evening was entitled "How to return to Eretz Israel" and Oz was one of the speakers (Berlowitz 76).

Works Cited

Amir, Eli. "11 Shanim aharei: Amos Oz, po va-sham be-eretz Israel be-stav '82" ["11 Years Later: Amos Oz Here and There in the Land of Israel"]. *Yediot Aharonot weekend supplement*, 3 September 1993, p. 35. [Hebrew].

Baram, Nir. *Ha-aretz she-me'ever la-harim* [*A Land without Borders: My Journey Around East Jerusalem and the West Bank*]. Am oved, 2016. [Hebrew]. Translated by Jessica Cohen, Text Publishing, 2017.

Behar, Uzi. "Shome'a ve-eino roeh" ["Hears and Cannot See"]. *Ha-ir Tel Aviv*, 17 June 1983.

Ben-Dov, Nitza. "Haomnam menuha le'ahar ha-se'ara?" ["Is it Really Resting after the Flood?"]. *Ve-hi tehilatecha: iyunim biyzirot S. Y. Agnon, A. B. Yehushua ve-Amos Oz* [*And That is Your Glory: Studies in the Works of S. Y. Agnon, A. B. Yehoshua and Amos Oz*]. Shoken, 2006, pp. 275–84. [Hebrew]

Berlowitz, Yaffa. Po va-sham be-eretz Israel Be-stav 1982"—Masa u-poetika [*Here and There in the Land of Israel*: in Autumn 1982, *Journey and Poetics*]. *Sefer Amos Oz* [*Amoz Oz's Book*]. Edited by Aharon Komem and Isaac Ben-Mordecai. Ben Gurion UP, 2000, pp. 71–92.

Brinker, Menachem. "Noche'hut ha-sofer ba-hevra" ["The Author's Presence in Society"]. *Sovev Sifrut: Ma'amarim al gvul ha-philosophia ve-torat ha-sifrut* [*About Literature: Essays on the Borderline of Philosophy of Art and Literary Theory*]. Magnes, 2000, pp. 321–32. [Hebrew].

Eydar, Dror. "Omrim li she-ani elita. Ani lo mevin et mashmaut ha-mila ha-zot" ["They Tell Me I'm Part of the Elite. I Don't Understand the Meaning of this Word"]. *News1*, 14 May 2017, https://www.news1.co.il/Archive/003-D-119978-00.html.

Freedland, Jonathan. "The Radical Empathy of Amos Oz." *The New York Review*, 14 Jan. 2019, https://www.nybooks.com/daily/2019/01/14/the-radical-empathy-of-amos-oz/.

Gibson, Andrew. *Postmodernity, Ethics and the Novel*. Routledge, 1999.

Grossman, David. *Ha-zman ha-tsahov* [*The Yellow Wind*]. Ha-kibbutz ha-meuhad, 1987. [Hebrew].

Grossman, David. *Nokhehim nifkadim* [*Sleeping on a Wire*]. Ha-kibbutz ha-meuhad, 1992. [Hebrew].

Grossman, David. Epilogue.*Po va-sham be-eretz Israel: Be-stav 1982* [*Here and There in the Land of Israel: In Autumn 1982*], by Amos Oz. Keter, 2009, pp. 193–99. [Hebrew].

Hadar, Alon. "Esrim Shana le-'Po va-sham be-eretz Israel'—Bikur be-veit Shemesh" [20 Years to *In the Land of Israel*—A visit to Beit Shemesh]. *Kol ha-ir Jerusalem*, 18 October 2002.

Kenan, Amos. "Po va-sham be-eretz Israel" ["Here and There in the Land of Israel"]. *Kol Tel Aviv*, 17 June 1983. [Hebrew].

Kimmerling, Baruch. *Ketz shilton ha-ahusalim* [*The End of Ashkenazi Hegemony*]. Keter, 2001. [Hebrew].

Kimmerling, Baruch. *The Invention and Decline of Israeliness*. U of California P, 2001.

LaCapra, Dominick. *Writing History, Writing Trauma*. Johns Hopkins UP, 2001.

Lev-Ari, Shiri. "Anahnu adayin sipur patuah: Re'ayon im Amos Oz" ["We're Still an Open Story: An Interview with Amos Oz"]. *Ynet*, 24 July 2009, https://www.ynet.co.il/articles/0,7340,L-3751058,00.html.

Lubin, Orly. "Poetika shel hit'hamkut" ["A Poetics of Evasion"]. *Siman Kri'ah*, vol. 18, May 1986, pp. 156–62. [Hebrew].

Mendelson-Maoz, Adia. "The Fallacy of Analogy and the Risk of Moral Imperialism: Israeli Literature and the Palestinian Other." *Humanities*, vol. 8, no. 3, 2019, pp. 1–18.

Mayer, Tamar. *Gender Ironies of Nationalism: Sexing the Nation*. Routledge, 1999.

Miron, Dan. "Bein hitbonenut le-bina" ["Between Observing and Wisdom"]. *Yediot Aharonot*, 27 May 1983, pp. 1–2, 7. [Hebrew].

Misgav, Uri. "Hiluch hozer" ["Replay"]. *Yediot Aharonot weekend supplement*, 8 July 2009, pp. 1, 7–12.

Misgav, Uri. "Ziffer tsodek be-davar ehad: 'Po va-sham be-eretz Israel' hu achen sifro he-hashuv beyoter shel Amos Oz" ["Ziffer is Right About One Thing: 'In the Land of Israel' is Amos Oz's Most Important Book"]. *Haaretz*, 29 Dec. 2018, https://www.haaretz.co.il/gallery/.premium-1.6788751.

Oriental Jew (pen name). "Amos Oz gila et eretz Israel shel shnot ha-shmonim, heziz ve-nifga" ["Amos Oz Discovered Israel of the 80s, Took a Peek and Was Injured"]. *Ba-ma'aracha*, vol. 272, 1983, pp. 3, 24. [Hebrew].

Oz, Amos and Shira Hadad, *Mima asui ha-tapuah? Shesh sihot al ktiva ve-al ahava, al rigshei ashma ve-ta'anugot aherim* [*What's in an Apple? Six Conversations About Writing and About Love, About Guilt and Other Pleasures*]. Keter, 2018. [Hebrew].

Oz, Amos. *In the Land of Israel*. Harvest Books, 1993.

Oz, Amos. *A Tale of Love and Darkness*. Translated by Nicholas de Lange, Vintage Books, 2004.

Oz, Amos. *Dear Zealots: Letters from a Divided Land*. Translated by Jessica Cohen, Houghton Mifflin Harcourt, 2017.

Sade, Dani. "Sefer shel Amos Oz ne'esar be-kele kziot" ["A Book by Amoz Oz Was Banned in Kziot Prison"]. *Yediot Aharonot*, 8 Aug. 1989.

Schwarz, Yigal. *Pulhan ha-sofer ve-dat ha-medina [Cult of the Author and the State Religion]*. Kinneret Zmora-Bitan Dvir, 2011. [Hebrew].

Schwarz, Yigal. "Ha-migdalor" ["The Lighthouse"]. *Haaretz*, 31 Dec. 2018, https://www.haaretz.co.il/literature/prose/.premium-1.6792030.

Shainfeld, Ilan. "Zimtei imut ba-meziut ha-Israelit" ["Conflict Crossroads in Israeli Reality"]. *Migvan*, vol. 83–4, December 1983–January 1984, pp. 61–62.

Shapira, Anita. *Yehudim hadashim, yehudim yeshanim [New Jews, Old Jews]*. Am Oved, 1997. [Hebrew].

Shapira, Avraham (ed.). *Si'ah lohamim [Fighters' Discourse]*. Friends of the Kibbutzim Movement, 1968. [Hebrew]

Wisse, Ruth R. "Matters of Life & Death (Book Review)." *Commentary*, 1 Apr. 1986, p. 68, https://www.commentarymagazine.com/articles/ruth-wisse/in-the-land-of-israel-by-amos-oz/.

Yehoshua, A. B. "Amos Oz ben 70: Litbol et ha-et be-keset ha-ha'im" ["Amos Oz is 70: To Dip the Pen in the Inkwell of Life"]. *Haaretz*, 8 Apr. 2009. https://www.haaretz.co.il/gallery/1.3347180.

Ziffer, Benny. "Amos Oz, 1939–2018: The Leader of the White Tribe Has Died." *Haaretz*, 31 Dec. 2018, https://www.haaretz.com/opinion/.premium-amos-oz-1939-2018-the-president-of-the-white-tribe-has-died-1.6790788.

Chapter 14

Oz against Himself

Between Political Romanticism and Social Realism in Black Box

JOSHUA LEIFER

When asked about the relationship between his politics and his novels, Amos Oz would often deny that there was one. "Novels for me have never been a political vehicle," he told *The Irish Times* in 2014. So separate were politics and fiction, he claimed, that he wrote his essays and his novels with different colored pens. "One black and one blue. One I use to tell stories and the other to tell the government to go to hell," Oz said. "And I never mix them" (Marlowe, 2014). In his public appearances, Oz would also lament that his readers looked for politics, and in particular political allegory, in his novels. "You think you have written a piece of chamber music, a tale of one family," he said in his 1992 acceptance speech for the Frankfurt Book Fair Peace Prize. "But your readers and critics say, 'Aha! Surely the mother represents the old values; the father is the government; and the daughter must be the symbol of the shattered economy'" (Oz, 1992). Oz described the experience of being read this way as "the fate of novels from troubled parts of the world"—a fate that he hoped his works would escape.

Yet Oz was an unambiguously political author. His fiction contains no small measure of social criticism: in his early work, of the ideological

275

pieties and quotidian frustrations of kibbutz life; in his subsequent work, of Israel's culture of militarism and the settler movement's messianic territorial-maximalism. In Oz's novels, time is suffused with, and defined by, the political—the internal debates of the Israeli Jewish polity, as well as the geopolitics of Israel's wars against its Arab neighbors. The unhappy family scenes of *My Michael*, for instance, are set against, and merge with, the precariousness of 1950s Jewish Jerusalem and the war of 1956. In *Fima*, a very different novel from *My Michael*, the eponymous protagonist's delusions, disappointments, and general condition of maladjustment are articulated in the terms of, and analogized to, Israel's protracted conflict with the Palestinians. Even in his fictional work that resists an allegorical reading, Oz, does not miss other opportunities to make a political point.

And then there was Oz himself. Oz wrote consciously as a national writer, even as he expressed ambivalence, even disappointment, that he was read as such. (Oz sometimes seemed to want to transcend the Israeli particularity that he embodied to the higher realm of "universal" Western literature, like Tolstoy.) For all his talk of telling the government to go to hell, he enjoyed proximity to power, to prime ministers and presidents, for much of his career. He was the only writer to give a eulogy at Shimon Peres's funeral in 2016. He cultivated his standing as ambassador (a political position if there ever was one), first representing one Israel to the others, then Israel to the West and, in turn, to the rest of the world.[1]

He took up this role with a combination of agony and relish. It is a combination that is most perceptible in his non-fiction. For instance, in his collection of reported essays, *In the Land of Israel*, Oz tours Haredi neighborhoods in West Jerusalem, the offices of a Palestinian newspaper in East Jerusalem, working-class Mizrahi districts in Beit Shemesh, and right-wing religious settlements in the West Bank as much to argue as to listen: an emissary of a waning Labor Zionism trying to explain itself to the country it founded but no longer led. The simultaneous, contradictory embrace and evasion of representativeness also appears no less frequently, albeit in different guises, in his fiction, whether in Oz-like characters or others speaking Oz-style truths. Yet no work concretized his representativeness more than *A Tale of Love and Darkness*, perhaps his most internationally acclaimed book, which merged his own family's story with the foundation of the state. Oz made this merger explicit with the controversial gesture of sending a copy of the book to Marwan Barghouti, the imprisoned former leader of Fatah's paramilitary wing, with a dedication that read, "This is our story, and I hope you read it and understand us better." Despite his habit of proclaiming that he was merely a teller of tales, Oz did little to meaningfully shake off the perception that he was, as David Stern put in a 1974 review of *Elsewhere, Perhaps* for *Commentary,* "a leading spokesman for the generation of sabras who grew up along with the state of Israel."

How, then, to read a writer who, in a sense, asks not to be read? Scholars and critics have offered different strategies for reading Oz's fiction in light of his disavowals, and anticipation, of attempts to read his books politically. Historian Gabriel Piterberg, in his book *The Returns of Zionism,* zeroes in on this dynamic in Oz's work—Oz's equivocation between representativeness and individuality, between criticism of Israeli policies and affirmation of its foundational myths. Piterberg reads Oz's expressed ambivalence about political allegory as a kind of strategy of dissimulation, as a reflection of what Piterberg calls Oz's "remarkable propagandist prowess." Piterberg charges that Oz composed "all his texts so that they can be drawn on as speeches to diverse audience, from potential donors to Israeli universities, to the American chapter of Peace Now, or as conversations with guilt-ridden liberal German intellectuals" (226), and that this polyvocality served, in the end, to reaffirm the hegemonic Zionist narrative. There is some truth to this: not only to the view of Oz the people-pleaser, the star of the global book-fair circuit, but to the idea that Oz's resistance to political readings of his novels had the paradoxical effect of making his book's ideological content more palatable. Yet to dismiss Oz's novels as mere propaganda is too simple. It is also wrong. For what made Oz such a successful political novelist was precisely the subtle knowingness with which he wrote against the grain of what readers expected of him.

There are other interpretative options. In *Rhetorics of Belonging,* Anna Bernard suggests a more productive model for reading Oz's fiction. Bernard writes that "the assumption that because we know Oz's politics, we know the politics of his work, tells us little about how his narratives achieve their end." In other words, it is insufficient to observe Oz's standing within Israeli politics, or the role he played as a literary intellectual on the international stage, and expect his novels to correspond. Instead, Bernard highlights how Oz's novels often "put forward national allegories only to cancel them, strenuously recuperating nationally resonant losses and conflicts as personal bereavements and domestic disputes" (96). But rather than undermining the national myths within and against which Oz writes, his "reframing" of the political into the private has the effect of reaffirming the political. "The very move towards the psychological recuperates and rejuvenates the political," Bernard writes. The imperatives of a settler-colonial polity—however much Oz's characters ironize, mock, or chafe at them—are presented to the reader as merely "the modest hopes and dreams of their fragile, fallible, and above all human characters" (97). And if human, then universal, and therefore not up for debate.

In this essay, I intend to read Oz against himself in two ways: first against his own disavowals that there is any political argument contained in his fiction; second against Oz's own well-known views about Israel/Palestine, the conflict, and the occupation. My contention is that *Black Box* presents a political reality that Oz often refused to acknowledge in his essays and non-fiction: the connection, and more important, the inseparability of "Israel proper" (within the boundaries of 1948) from the occupied territories beyond the Green Line, and the equal responsibility of the Ashkenazi Labor Zionist elite for the settlement enterprise. This observation, I argue, troubles conventional assessments of the tension between realism and romanticism in Oz's work. For while it is no doubt true that many of Oz's novels feature idealized Israeli archetypes, national myths, and romantic depictions of Israeli landscapes, Oz retained a commitment not only to the psychological realism for which he is best known, but also to a social realism that could depict the political terrain of Israel/Palestine in a way that Oz, in his non-fiction, could not. Confronted with the increasing unviability of the two-state solution, Oz clung to it with greater fervor in his essays and public interventions. His tireless invocation of the imperative of an impossible resolution became less a serious policy proposal than "a fortunate occasion for an emotionally satisfying mood, an aesthetic opportunity" (Schmitt xxxi). Ironically, then, it is in Oz's non-fiction and essays, so often written in the jargon of realism and pragmatism, where his vision is most idealistic and romantic.

First published in Hebrew in 1986 (and in English translation in 1986), *Black Box* is a drama of messy family entanglements, inheritance, and stubborn attachments. It begins with a request. Ilana Brandstetter writes to her ex-husband Alex Gideon, a politician science professor living in Chicago, seven years after their acrimonious divorce, to ask for help. Their son Boaz has become a violent teenager, uncontrollable; Ilana fears his future is in jeopardy. In the years since they severed contact, Ilana has since remarried to a man named Michel Somo—born in Algeria, educated in France—who works as a French teacher when not agitating with the religious settler movement and trying to buy land in the newly occupied territories. But Ilana and Michel are short on cash, and Boaz has just been thrown out of a boarding school. Ilana requests help from Alex to get Boaz into another school. To Ilana's surprise, Alex not only obliges, but sends a generous check as well.

The initial contact between Alex and Ilana expands into a lengthy correspondence that includes Michel, Boaz, and Alex's lawyer, Manfred Zakheim. After Alex accedes to Ilana's first request, she returns with another, when Boaz is in trouble again. From afar, Alex becomes increasingly enmeshed in the affairs of Ilana and her new family. Even after Alex asks Ilana and Michel how much he would need to pay them to leave him alone, he continues to open Ilana's letters. He sends larger sums of money, much to the frustration of Zakheim, who attempts to keep his client's best interests at heart, though not without looking for ways to cash in. Alex's contributions gradually reshape Ilana and Michel's life, financing a renovation of their apartment, an update to Michel's wardrobe and, eventually, enabling Michel to quit his job as a French teacher to focus on organizing the settler movement. But if at first Alex's decisions appear vexing, even ill-advised, by the end it is clear that through his money, he has managed to reinsert himself into Ilana and Boaz's life, and, perhaps most significantly, arrange the desired conditions for his death.

Black Box takes place within a single year: 1976. Six months after the date of the book's final letter, written by Michel, Menachem Begin would be elected prime minister. Begin's victory, Israel's first transfer of power from one party to another, ended the Labor Party's dominance, and with it, the unchallenged rule of old elite that had run the country since before its founding: the secular, nominally socialist, statist Israelis of East European descent. It marked, to borrow the phrase of the late sociologist Baruch Kimmerling, the end of Ashkenazi hegemony. The Jews from the Middle East, and North Africa, "the throngs of Sephardim, Bukharians, Yemenites, Kurds, and Aleppo Jews" that Oz wrote of encountering at Revisionist movement rallies in Jerusalem, could no longer be ignored. Begin, a man whom Oz recalls mocking as child for his unidiomatic Hebrew, does not himself appear in *Black Box*. But his presence is often felt in Michel's denunciations of Labor Zionist hypocrisies, and in Zakheim's intimations of a change in government "bound to entail the opening up of exciting new horizons in the Sinai, and the West Bank, and the Gaza Strip for forward-looking men like ourselves" (109). Zakheim, who plays the role of the amoral capitalist, may profess to have "no special feeling about the Territories," but neither does he have qualms about profiting from their exploitation (107). In the real world, of course, Begin would prove such predictions wrong by signing the peace deal with Egypt in 1979 and withdrawing Israeli settlements from Sinai by 1982.

But while Begin's 1977 election, the event still referred to in Israel as *hamahapakh*, the upset, delivered Labor Zionism's coup de grace, it suffered its own grievous, and self-inflicted wound, a decade earlier, in 1967. Labor Zionism's leaders had led the state to its surprise victory in the Six Day War and initiated the settlement enterprise. Yet the conquest of the Palestinian territories unleashed spirits that the Labor Zionists could not control. Religious Zionism surged, its leading lights heralded the "footsteps of the messiah"—the dawn of Redemption—and true believers moved, many of them from the United States, to settle the newly "liberated" territories. This movement would gain institutional form in 1974, following the Yom Kippur War, with the establishment of Gush Emunim (the Bloc of the Faithful). The settler movement consciously claimed to be taking up the "pioneering" mantle from the Labor Zionist movement (Oz often noted their similarities). Even by the early 1970s, Labor Zionism seemed exhausted (this too was a concern of Oz's). It had completed its historical task.

Black Box gives an expressly libidinal interpretation to the historic shift in power, dramatizing the conflict between one Israel, represented by Alex, on the decline and the other, represented by Michel, on the rise. The portrait of Alex that Oz paints is, as literary critic Ariel Hirschfeld wrote, one of the "horrific decadence of Ashkenaziness" (Piterberg 230). Alex, though he has decamped to the United States, leaving behind the land of Israel, is the inheritor of both a vast fortune, overseen by Zakheim, a large estate in Zikhron Yaakov that has fallen into decrepitude, and several other neglected properties across the country; Alex's father, Volodya, described as garrulous Russian former bon vivant, is interned in a sanitorium in Haifa. They appear, in the words of Zakheim, as "the Frenchified Russian aristocracy from the region of North Binyamina" (202). And while Alex never expresses the vulgar racism that Zakheim does, it is clear that Alex views Michel as a kind of primitive subject, Michel's effusive religiosity as representing the return of a repressed "Oriental-ness" that has now overwhelmed secular, rationalistic, and above all European, Zionism.

Alex is among Oz's most uncannily Oz-like characters, especially from the vantage point of the twenty-first-century reader: not only because of shared interest in fanaticism (Alex's area of academic research), but also the scars left by Israel's wars, the affinity for order and orderliness, the specter of terminal illness. Yet one can also read the character of Alex as a critique of a segment of the deposed Ashkenazi elite, or rather its children: the many thousands of Israelis who, over the decades, have departed Israel, whether in pursuit of ambition, wealth, or both, putting their personal success above the fate of the nation. Alex's books are praised worldwide, but the move has not left Alex happy. "DON'T LEAVE ME I'M MISER-ABLE," he writes in a telegram to Zakheim, after Zakheim threatens to resign as Alex's lawyer over what he sees as Alex's unreasonable generosity toward Michel (26). Like Oz's other characters, Alex's objections to the country's political direction are merged with his personal estrangement from his family, which makes his eventual, end-of-life return to Ilana and Boaz, and to Israel, not just a personal reconciliation but a reconciliation with the national polity. Reframing the political as the personal, Oz calls Israeli *yordim* home.

Throughout the novel, Alex's illness worsens. His desire for life fades. Even his "hatred is dying" (97). In the home, in bed, in politics, he has been replaced by Michel, who is everything that Alex is not. Whereas Alex is aloof and rigid, Michel is passionate and cloying. Alex's office is austere and colorless, while Michel's house is cramped and cluttered. Alex is born a *sabra*, but lives as a cosmopolitan, sending his letters from academic conferences in expensive hotels in London, Geneva, and West Berlin. Michel's trajectory is the opposite. Born in Oran, raised in Paris, Michel is a Diaspora Jew who ended his own exile and returned to the land of Israel. Alex has fought for the country but has since abandoned it. Michel claims to be ready to fight at any moment, but perhaps because he knows he won't have to. So stark is the contrast between Alex and Michel, so simple the dichotomy between West and East, that is it hard not to believe that Oz has exaggerated these binaries intentionally in order to call them into question.

Black Box is Oz's only novel to deal so directly with the relationship between Ashkenazim and Mizrahim, and it is worth asking what the epistolary form does, and does not do, in giving shape to the conflict between Alex and Michel. In a way, a novel of letters accords most directly with Oz's own expressed impetus for novel writing. "If I find more than one argument in me, more than just one voice, it sometimes happens that the different voices develop into characters and then I know that I am pregnant with a story," Oz said. "I write stories precisely when I can step into several antagonistic claims, diverse moral stances, conflicting moral positions" (1992). The epistolary form allows for a proliferation of narrators, and therefore a multiplicity of perspectives. Yet this does not make it impossible to read the text as a political allegory, however much Oz would like to avoid it. For *Black Box* is staged as a conflict between Alex and Michel, and at the end there is a winner.

Nor does it shield Oz from criticism for how the character of Michel appears within the text. Of course, Zakheim's relentless condescension toward Michel is not a reflection of Oz's own views. Yet there is no character, not even Ilana, who refers to Michel without terms of revulsion or ridicule. And while this may be a point about the ubiquity of Ashkenazi chauvinism, Oz does not write Michel in any way as a rebuttal. The voice Oz gives to Michel is a stereotypical one. Though Michel is described at one point as having studied at the Sorbonne, there is little erudition in his letters. Instead, they are parodically stuffed with religious quotations— from the Torah, Psalms, various proverbs. Michel appears as a caricature: a swarthy, scripture-quoting zealot with gold-rimmed glasses, a gold-chain watch, and bad cologne. At no point does the debate between Alex and Michel seem to be between two equals. Here, it is hard to argue with Piterberg's critical assessment that "*Black Box* is the expression of Oz's literary participation in the project to create the hegemonic Israeli of the state period" (231).

Still, there is another way of reading *Black Box* beyond straightforward political allegory or as a production of hegemonic Israeliness. While Alex and Michel are separated by a vast gulf—of ideology, religion, culture—they are bound together financially. Alex continues to offer Michel money, nominally to help with Boaz, even though he knows what Michel plans to do with it. Indeed, throughout the novel Alex expresses a kind of resigned indifference toward the settler movement that Michel represents. "I don't care what good cause it's for," Alex writes of the money he offers to Michel. "It could be for the conversion of the Pope for all I care" (61). Alex also sends money to support Boaz while he's living in Kiryat Arba, the militarized Jewish enclave on the outskirts of Hebron. Read from what might be called a dogmatic, patriotic left-Zionist perspective, Alex's willingness to fund Michel's messianic ambitions is a kind of curdled post-Zionism, an abandonment of good, ethical, democratic Israel to the zealots of Greater Israel. But read with a focus on the financial relationship between Alex and Michel, it is also a damning observation of the Ashkenazi establishment's complicity and participation in the settlement enterprise. And it isn't only Alex who funds the settlements. Zakheim, a through-and-through bourgeois who hopes for the end of the Labor Zionists' "Bolshevik" reign, brings Michel into a business venture with his son-in-law, and prepares to profit from the real estate boom in the occupied territories.

Indeed, the financial relationship at the core of *Black Box* reveals a truth that Oz was reluctant to admit. In his nonfiction, he often wrote as if the religious Zionists were almost entirely to blame for the settlement enterprise, for the country's drift to the right, for its fall from favor in the world's eyes. During a visit to the West Bank settlement of Ofra, which Oz describes in *In the Land of Israel*, he famously upbraided his settler interlocuters for their "messianic intoxication" and "moral autism." He blames them for having "brought about a collapse of Zionism's legitimacy" (142). But the fiction of *Black Box* is much closer to reality. No firm line of separation can be drawn between the Labor Zionists who led the country through 1967 and the settler movement that assumed Zionism's vanguard. Just as Michel could not have quit his job or purchased more property in the occupied territories without the aid of Alex, so the settlements would not have been successful without the support, sometimes tacit, sometimes explicit, of successive Labor governments. The occupation would not have lasted as long as it has if Labor Zionist leaders, members of the very Ashkenazi elite that lament the intractability of the conflict, had not helped perpetuate it.

In the final letters of the book, Alex and Michel debate the difference between the violent settlement of 1948 and those of 1967. "The truth is that you may be a great champion of the Arabs and a hater of the Jews, but you have shed Arab blood like water during the wars and perhaps even between them," Michel writes. "Whereas I, the so-called chauvinist and extremist, have never shed blood in my whole life [. . .] You are considered the peace camp and I am considered the vicious circle of bloodshed." (216, 217). Michel's assertion contains a hard kernel of naivete, exemplifying the kind of "moral autism" Oz denounced: even if the majority of settler activists have not themselves committed acts of violence, they are the beneficiaries of a massively violent apparatus. But his question is a fundamental one, which destabilizes the dichotomy constructed throughout the book between Alex and Michel and what they respectively represent. After all, was it not the Ashkenazi pioneers, the Zionist settlers from the Pale of Settlement, who were responsible for the violence that drove hundreds of thousands of Palestinians from their homes? Who were the kibbutzniks, the founders of communal towns and moshavim, who built their ethnic-exclusivist communities over the ruins of Arab villages, to lecture about morality? What *did* make 1967 different from 1948?

Oz's answer to this question remained the greatest blind-spot in his political vision. Until his very last days, he was prone to facile, often marital metaphors for solutions to the Israeli-Palestinian conflict, as if the language of domesticity so present in his novels had gradually whittled down his political vocabulary. What Israelis and Palestinians needed was "a divorce." They had to recognize that coexistence "would not be a honeymoon," that the land was like a house that needed to be divided "into two smaller next-door apartments." In his public appearances, he would often frame this approach as a realistic, pragmatic one, as a conscious choice rejecting an impossible peace in the hopes that a flawed one might be realized. "I do not believe in the possibility of a perfect peace," he said during his Frankfurt Book Fair Peace Prize acceptance speech. "Rather, I work for a sad, sober, imperfect compromise between individuals and between communities." By which he meant, with his stress on the effect of realism, a two-state solution.

Yet such a solution was not the most realistic one for much of Oz's career. As early as 1982, Meron Benvenisti, the former deputy mayor of Jerusalem, was warning that "the Government of Israel proceeded toward de facto annexation of the West Bank—and that the process has gone very far." It was, in Benvenisti's words "five minutes to midnight" for the two-state solution, before what became the Oslo peace process had even started (Lewis, 1982). By the late 1990s, and certainly the 2000s, it had become clear that a neat separation of the kind Oz advocated had ceased to be a possibility. Perhaps having witnessed the dawn of the settlement project, Oz always believed in its reversibility. But this made him unwilling to reconsider his position once the facts changed. Indeed, the more Israel changed, the more Oz stayed the same. A self-described opponent of fanaticism, Oz never wavered in his devotion to the two-state solution, even when it began to appear like the kind of messianic vision that he had spent his whole life opposing. Oz, as Avraham Burg wrote, became "a fanatic" himself (2017).

Oz is typically celebrated as an exemplary Israeli voice of conscience, and it true that he showed more moral courage than most. But his relationship to the Palestinian narrative was more equivocal. He had no trouble recognizing the injustice of forcing the Palestinians in the West Bank to live under perpetual occupation. And though he did not call for an immediate withdrawal from the occupied territories, as others on the Israeli left did, he was among the first and few Jewish Israelis to warn that a protracted occupation would lead to disaster—moral and political. He tried, though mostly unsuccessfully, to convince his fellow Jewish Israelis of this, imploring them to recognize that occupation for what it was. "If they feel themselves to be under occupation, then this indeed occupation," Oz said of the Arabs before the settler audience in Ofra. "One can claim that it is a just occupation, necessary, vital, whatever you want, but you cannot tell an Arab, 'You don't really feel what you feel and I shall define your feelings for you.' This is another manifestation of moral autism" (147). Oz, a man not often described as humble, may have overestimated his powers of persuasion.

But while Oz could speak eloquently about the need to accept Palestinians' feelings about 1967, he took a much different position when it came to their feelings about 1948. For Oz, 1967 was the beginning of the corrupting, unjust, and unjustifiable occupation; it was the primary obstacle to peace, and its end would mark, if not the end of the conflict, then the beginning of the end. Yet 1948, the violent displacement of roughly 700,000 Palestinians from their homes, was for Oz nonnegotiable and entirely morally justifiable. The Jews in 1948, he claimed, were like a drowning man, the Land of Israel its plank. "And the drowning man clinging to his plank," Oz wrote, "is allowed, by all the rules of the natural, objective, universal justice, to make room for himself on the plank, even if in so doing he must push the others aside a little" (148). But the cumulative effects of rapid Jewish settlement and the war of 1948 did far more than push the Palestinians "aside a little." They ended Palestinian society as it had existed for generations and turned an entire people into refugees.

Oz knew this. He knew that for Palestinians, 1948 was the Nakba, *the catastrophe*, and 1967 the Naksa, *the setback*, and not the other way around. And yet like many of his fellow liberal Zionists, that made little difference. Oz's view was the same as that expressed by Ari Shavit, who happened to call the ethnic cleansing of Lydda "the black box" of Zionism. "The choice is stark," Shavit wrote. "Either reject Zionism because of Lydda or accept Zionism along with Lydda" (2013). Oz, like Shavit, did not accept the Palestinians' feelings on this matter and demanded the right to define the legitimate way to think and feel about what had happened in 1948. For a writer who wrote so much about the imperative of empathy and of listening, who captured so sensitively the suffering of refugees and the "darkness of exile," Oz could not accept that for Palestinians there could be no resolving the conflict without addressing the wounds of 1948. It is a shame, too, because if Oz had been willing to use his considerable powers of imagination to envision what real, egalitarian Arab-Jewish coexistence might have looked like—as opposed to the image of unhappy divorce he so often fell back on—he might have made a significant contribution to humanity (perhaps one worthy of the Nobel prize that eluded him).

When a plane crashes, those investigating its causes look for the black box amid the rubble. A flight recorder, the black box documents the plane's last moments, its pilot and co-pilot's final words. A black box is hard to destroy. In Oz's novel, Alex and Ilana compare their relationship to a crashed plane, and their correspondence the black box: the archive of their failed relationship. In a sense, that is what the novel itself is. As a political allegory, it also a document of the cockpit struggle over Zionism. It is Michel who has the last word: Alex, the secular, liberal, Ashkenazi *sabra* passes from the scene, the religious, Mizrahi settler takes his place. And though one can read in this Oz's lament at Israel's direction, it is not an idealization of the Israel of Alex nor a simple condemnation of the Israel of Michel. And, indeed, one can read the novel as a black box in Shavit's sense too: as containing a dark, often unacknowledged truth about Zionism and the occupation. It may not be a great novel of a political dissent, but nor is it, contra Piterberg, mere propaganda. *Black Box* is far from Oz's best novel. There are parts of it, particular turns of phrase, that have not stood the test of time. Like many of Oz's other works, it features an untrustworthy, unfaithful female character with an overactive libido, a taciturn ex-military man, and other set pieces. Yet along with Oz's other novels, *Black Box* will endure in a way that his non-fiction and essays will not precisely because it remains open to readings and interpretation to which his essays will always remain closed. Even in a novel that asks so explicitly to be read as political allegory, other avenues of reading remain open.

Oz's critics often point to his romanticizations—of *sabra* masculinity, of Israel's landscapes, of the kibbutz—in his fiction, in contrast to the realism of his political vision. But it may be more accurate to say the reverse. Oz's political interventions were phrased in the language of realism and pragmatism, announced themselves as sober thinking about hard compromises. Yet Oz's actual politics were deeply idealistic, his vision of a viable two-state a romantic dream that, but for the brief hopeful years of the late 1990s, never had the force of reality behind it. Philosopher Guy Oakes's description of "the political romantic" in the Schmittian sense, who, "in the flight from the substance of politics into the fantasies of his imagination . . . escapes political reality and remains passive in the face of forces that define the field of political conflict" could very well apply to Oz (xxxi). Indeed, it is not too much of a stretch to call Oz the novelist, the realist, and Oz the essayist, the romantic. And to read Oz's novels against Oz the public figure is to find truths in the former that the latter would never acknowledge.

Note

1. Some of the ideas explored and developed in this article first appeared in more germinal form in my piece on the occasion of Oz's death, published in *Dissent*, Spring 2019.

Works Cited

Bernard, Anna. *Rhetorics of Belonging: Nation, Narration, and Israel/Palestine.* Liverpool UP, 2013.

Burg, Avraham. "Amos Oz, a Fanatic of the Two-State Solution." *Haaretz*, 26 June 2017.

Lewis, Anthony. "5 Minutes to Midnight." *The New York Times*, 1 Nov. 1982.

Marlowe, Lara. "Amos Oz: 'One Pen I Use to Tell Stories, the Other to Tell the Government to Go to Hell.'" *The Irish Times*, 14 June 2014.

Oz, Amos. *A Tale of Love and Darkness*. Houghton Mifflin Harcourt, 2004.

———. *Black Box*. Houghton Mifflin Harcourt, 2012.

———. *Dear Zealots: Letters from a Divided Land*. Houghton Mifflin Harcourt, 2018.

———. *Fima*. Harcourt Brace & Company, 1993.

———. *In the Land of Israel*. Harcourt, 1983.

———. *My Michael*. Bantam, 1982.

———. "Peace, Love, and Compromise." Acceptance speech for Friedenspreis des Deutschen Buchhandels, 1992.

Piterberg, Gabriel. *The Returns of Zionism: Myths, Politics, and Scholarship in Israel*. Verso, 2008.

Schmitt, Carl. *Political Romanticism*. Translated by Guy Oakes. MIT Press, 1986.

Shavit, Ari. "Lydda, 1948." *The New Yorker*, 14 Oct. 2013.

Stern, David. "*Elsewhere, Perhaps*, by Amos Oz." *Commentary*, July 1974.

Chapter 15

"Like Belfast, Rhodesia, or South Africa":

Oz and the Ideologies of Oslo

Moriel Rothman-Zecher

On January 2, 2021, a man was shot in the neck.

His name was Haroun Abu Aram, he was 24 years old, and he lived in a village called al-Rakiz, in the South Hebron Hills region of the West Bank. IDF (Israel Defense Forces) soldiers had arrived on "a routine assignment . . . of confiscating and evacuating an illegal structure" (Abraham). In a shaky cellphone video of the scuffle, you can hear Abu Aram and a few others asking, "Why are you taking our generator?" and see them trying to pull the generator back from the soldiers, yelling at the soldiers, "May God curse you," pushing them away from the generator. The soldiers raise their voices, push the men back, grab the generator. The men push the soldiers, grab the generator back. A woman outside the frame calls, "ya Haroun, Haroun!". Then there are gunshots outside of the frame.

"Qataluh," a man yells. They've killed him.

"Haroun," another man yells. "Haroun."

There are screams that contain no words, which cannot really be described in words: The screams of seeing your friend, your brother, your son shot in the neck at point blank range while trying to keep hold of an old generator.

Abu Aram was taken to the Ahli Hospital in Hebron in critical condition, kept alive by emergency doctors there.

He is now paralyzed.

∿

In the year 2020, "stay at home" became a global stand-in for "try to survive; try to keep yourself and your family and your community alive and well." By the end of 2020, the pandemic continued to rage around the world. In Israel, however, the vaccine rollout had gone more smoothly than anywhere else, thanks to a robust and efficient healthcare system, a prime minister desperate to hold on to power, and other factors. Around the same time in which the Israeli government began ramping up its vaccination drive, in late December 2020, the Israeli military jeeps and bulldozers drove into the village of al-Rakiz and demolished a number of homes. These homes had been built without permits. It is virtually impossible for Palestinians in the South Hebron Hills area of the West Bank to receive building permits from the "Civil Administration," the antiseptic codename for the bureaucratic arm of the Israeli military dictatorship in the West Bank. According to a recent report from *Haaretz*, over ninety-eight percent of such permit requests are rejected (Shezaf).

To translate this reality: If you are Palestinian living in al-Rakiz, you are almost certain to be denied a building permit. If you build without a permit, you are likely to have your home demolished, as happened in the "routine assignment" of late December 2020. In the heart of the winter of 2020, as the pandemic raged, a number of Palestinian families were left homeless in al-Rakiz, punished for being Palestinian in the West Bank in 2020. These families, whose homes, whose fates, whose futures, are under complete control of the Israeli military dictatorship in the West Bank, were not offered vaccination against the coronavirus, even as their homes were turned to rubble. To translate: We wish you luck getting a vaccination; in the meantime, stay at home; and forgive us if we come to destroy the home in which we recommend you say. We are only upholding the law.

∿

Haroun Abu Aram's family home was among those demolished in December. In the wake of such a loss—can you imagine? Can I? Not really. Yet somehow we *must* try to imagine his feeling when a foreign government, a military dictatorship that claims that it is temporary, though facts on the ground speak louder than words to anyone really paying attention, came to destroy his family's home in the middle of the global pandemic. The French Jewish philosopher Emmanuel Levinas wrote that the beginning of ethics stems from looking into the eyes of another, seeing their vulnerability and fragility, understanding your capacity to murder them, and choosing, from this point, not to carry out this act of murder, choosing instead to love them, to cherish them, even, in their fragile humanity. Destroying someone's house is not equivalent to murder, though the realities of the pandemic may complicate this equation. It is a few steps down, and so if we must look in the eyes of the other in order not to murder them, then perhaps to orient our ethics around this sort of occurrence, perhaps we must look around the room in which we sit, each of us, now, and imagine our own home or place of refuge crushed by the teeth of a bulldozer, its walls of safety made flimsy, then gone, its carefully wrought corners and quirks of comfort disappeared into air. In the wake of his loss, Abu Aram chose to act, essentially, as a Good Samaritan, as a neighbor, as a friend; from within his personal palace of loss and pain, he chose to spend his time helping others: On January 2, Abu Aram went to help rebuild a neighbor's home.

They brought a generator to help them work (needless to say, and yet it needs to be said: al-Rakiz is not connected to the electrical grid). And so, when the soldiers came on their "routine assignment," Abu Aram yelled, and pushed, and tried to keep hold of the generator, and they shot in him in the neck and almost killed him, and now the home he lived in is destroyed and the body he continues to live in cannot move, cannot help his neighbors rebuild a wall, cannot embrace his mother, his fiancé, his friends. Can you imagine? Can I?

This story is obscene, but hardly an aberration.

This has become the norm of Israel's military dictatorship, nearly five and a half decades since the 1967 occupation began.

In August 1967, shortly after the end of the Six Day War, the twenty-eight-year-old Amos Oz, published an article in the Labor daily, *Davar*, in which he warned of the "complete moral destruction that prolonged occupation wreaks upon the occupier." His essay was a response to a speech given by Defense Minister Moshe Dayan, in which Dayan spoke

of the need for "merhav-mihya,"—Hebrew for "Lebensraum,"—and was
reportedly met with thunderous applause and was echoed by other ministers in the weeks that followed.

"'To promise Lebensraum for Israel,'" Oz wrote. "I do not know how
Moshe Dayan's voice did not shake when he chose such an expression.
With all the horrific memories associated with it. 'Lebensraum' means
one thing: to disenfranchise the foreigner, the inferior, the 'savage,' to
make space for the superior, for the 'civilized,'—for the strong." Oz did
not detail a specific peace plan in this essay, but his articulation of the
moral and political position that must be taken was unequivocal: "We
must say to the residents of the occupied territories," Oz wrote, "We do
not desire your land. We did not come to Judaize you. We will remain
here until there is a peace deal, a year, a decade, or a generation, and on
that day—the choice is yours."

"We were not born to be a nation of lords," Oz continued. "The
shorter the occupation, the better. Even an unavoidable occupation is a
corrupting occupation." Oz knew that he was writing against the current:
"I am afraid that these simple words are likely to be heard almost as words
of blasphemy or treachery." This was a time in which the majority of his
fellow Israelis were celebrating their seemingly miraculous victory in a
war many had feared would lead to a second Holocaust; a time in which
messianic language—Oz castigated comparisons to the "days of Joshua
Ben Nun"—was already being wantonly flung about. Oz was then a young
writer, whose debut novel had just been published, and whose career was
far from established, as well as a reserve solider who had fought in the
war himself. Today, one can only marvel at his ability to step back from
the mass euphoria engulfing his country, or "the drunkenness of victory,"
as Oz called it, in order to issue these words of warning. For this alone,
Oz is owed an historical debt of appreciation by all of us who dwell in
the disheveled city known as the Israeli left, and in its suburbs.

And indeed, Oz was writing about Haroun Abu Aram, and the
generator, though Abu Aram was not yet born, and the specific madness
of the nearly lethal tug-of-war around this generator might have been
difficult for a young Oz to imagine. A decade and a half later, still long
before Abu Aram was born, in *In the Land of Israel* (1983) Oz wrote of
his visit to the settlement of Ofra, that if his "genial articulate hosts," who
were on the front lines of enacting the vision of Lebensraum that Dayan
called for, succeed in their cause, they may "turn Israel into a monster, like
Belfast, Rhodesia, or South Africa." Oz was not alone in this prognosis,

but he was still on the outskirts of public opinion. In the early 1990s, a few years before Haroun Abu Aram was born, Oz held steadfast to his position forged in 1967, advocating for compromise and for a two-state solution and an end to the 1967 occupation as one of the early advocates for dialogue with the Palestinian Liberation Organization (PLO). He was critical of those Israeli leftists who had retracted their support for dialogue with the PLO in the wake of the Gulf War. In a 1991 interview with Australian journalist Phillip Adams's popular radio program *Late Night Live*, Oz concurred with an analysis that viewed him as the "hawk of the doves," clarifying that "I never placed much hopes in the PLO, and consequently my position [in support of dialogue] has not changed."

Then, somewhere in the 1990s, something of a plot twist occurred. Or perhaps it was the year 2000, or perhaps 2005, or maybe even 2012. Whatever the year was, hindsight allows—and indeed, compels us—to see clearly that the Oslo Accords between Israel and the PLO and its concomitant ideologies of bilateral dialogue to achieve an internationally brokered two-state solution based on the 1967 borders, failed, not temporarily or partially, but unequivocally and permanently. Neither Clinton, nor Bush, nor Obama brought peace to the Middle East. This form of two-state solution is never going to happen, as some Palestinian thinkers have been arguing for decades, and as the Israeli Right and its allies have insisted for years now. Yet the ultra-hawkish American Israel Public Affairs Committee (AIPAC) proclaims its support for a two-state solution. Donald Trump said he "liked" the idea. Netanyahu himself claims to be a supporter of the notion. Surely this must give every serious thinker pause: There is no political risk in giving lip-support to the two-state solution, because the two-state solution is no longer on the table, if ever it was.

Writing in 1999, Edward Said declared that "The alternatives are unpleasantly simple: either the war continues (along with the onerous cost of the current peace process) or a way out, based on peace and equality (as in South Africa after apartheid) is actively sought, despite the many obstacles." Ironically, it is only the Israeli liberal camp (which claims to be anti-messianic in its outlook), that continues to hold onto a belief that Oslo and its ideologies might be brought back from the dead. But as the liberal American Jewish journalist Peter Beinart belatedly came to recognize in a 2020 series of essays, the dream of a two-state solution must finally be put to rest: "Events have now extinguished that hope" ("I No Longer Believe"). Unfortunately, Beinart's sober reflection and change of heart remains the exception, rather than the norm. Most in the Israeli liberal and leftist camps still seem to cling to the idea that a future exists in which Israel can be both a Jewish State and a democracy. Perhaps this future did once exist; but it exists no longer. And so, progressive positions—such as support for dialogue with the PLO in order to achieve a two-state solution—that were brave and almost blasphemous in one era, have grown anodyne and even conservative in the era that followed. Consistency, in some cases, is to be admired; in others, it can lead to a tragic myopia. A particularly galling illustration of this can be found in Amos Oz's 2018 remarks in his interview with *Deutsche Welle* to the effect that Donald Trump was right to move the American embassy to Jerusalem, and that every country in the world should follow suit. "But simultaneously," Oz hastened to add, "there should be an embassy of all countries in the world in East Jerusalem as the capital of the state of Palestine." This sort of position might make sense, one supposes, if one genuinely believes that the two-state solution may still be on the horizon; but in the meantime, it amounted to Oz lending his beloved name and moral standing to Donald Trump and Benjamin Netanyahu and their obscene political theatrics.

The question must be asked: When does the future tense turn into the present?

Oz warned in 1967 that the occupation may corrupt Israel, and in 1983 that Israel might turn into Rhodesia: at the start of 2021, with Haroun Abu Aram lying paralyzed in the hospital, his family home turned into rubble, is it not time to speak clearly and simply, as Oz did in 1967, or in 1983? It is not that the occupation may wreak absolute moral corruption on Israel in some hypothetical future: that moral corruption has now been wrought. It is not that Israel may become Rhodesia at some hypothetical juncture down the road: Israel *has* become Rhodesia. The time has passed for warnings of what might occur in some ominous but nebulous future; it is time to look directly at the present, without sentimentality for what might have been, and even if so doing is seen as "blasphemy or treachery." Must not our ideas evolve alongside reality? Is not, in a certain sense, the proclamation of eternal hope in that which has become a political impossibility—namely, an Oslo-style two-state solution—a resignation to the status quo?

Unfortunately, the two-state solution will not march over the horizon to unravel our Rhodesia, our Belfast, our South Africa; Oslo will not rise from the dead to redeem us from our utter moral corruption.

A few weeks after Haroun Abu Aram was shot in the neck for trying to rebuild his neighbor's demolished home, the Israeli human rights monitoring organization B'Tselem ("In the Image of God") issued a paper in which they held that Israel practices apartheid, not only in the occupied territories, but from the river to the sea. "Over time," wrote B'Tselem, "the distinction between the two regimes [of Israel proper and Israel's rule in the occupied territories] has grown divorced from reality. . . . In the entire area between the Mediterranean Sea and the Jordan River, the Israeli regime implements laws, practices, and state violence designed to cement the supremacy of one group—Jews—over another—Palestinians." This regime, B'Tselem clarified, didn't come into being in a single day. Instead, "it is a process that has gradually grown more institutionalized and explicit, with mechanisms introduced over time in law and practice to promote Jewish supremacy."

B'Tselem, in essence, had taken on the task of updating Oz's clarion call from 1967 and 1983, saying, in so many words, that Israel of 2021 is Rhodesia, or Belfast, or South Africa; that a solution will necessarily require putting to rest antiquated, Oslo-era notions of separation or "divorce," as Oz so often put it; that the grim future predicted back then is now, and that now we must change our understanding of the past and present if we are to have a future that is less laden with wickedness and unnecessary violence, less punctuated with everyday occurrences of homes being destroyed, of young men being shot in the neck, of one population being tormented and repressed, and of the other losing what's left of its collective soul and conscience by the hour. Predictably, their position led to B'Tselem's being labeled as blasphemous and treacherous. Days after the report was issued, Israeli Education Minister Yoav Gallant banned groups "that call Israel false derogatory names" from entering schools around the country. A Haifa principal who chose to disobey this ban and invited B'Tselem to address students was immediately summoned by the government to face disciplinary action.

What might Amos Oz, z"l, have said about all these developments?

The answer, I believe, is different if we are speaking of the younger Oz or the older Oz, though the two held positions that were virtually identical to one another. I am quite confident that both the younger and older Oz would have readily and vociferously condemned what was done to Haroun Abu Aram.

I am less confident that Oz's continued allegiance to the principles he established during the first era of occupation, from its beginning in 1967 until the mid-1990s, say, would have allowed him to see the broader reality that has taken hold in the subsequent era, namely, that apartheid is not a thing of some hypothetical future. Oz was a longtime member of B'Tselem's public council. His statements of support for Netanyahu's and Trump's embassy charade notwithstanding, Oz was consistent in his recognition that what transpired in the occupied territories is a moral catastrophe. Yet I am less certain that the older Oz, who remained unbendingly faithful to an expired vision, would have joined B'Tselem in recognizing that we cannot eternally claim that we are "at risk" of becoming Rhodesia; that utter moral corruption is not merely on the horizon but has in fact arrived; that the grim future predicted by visionaries like the twenty-eight-year-old Amos Oz has become our tormented present.

Works Cited

"A Regime of Jewish Supremacy from the Jordan River to the Mediterranean Sea: This Is Apartheid." *B'Tselem Report*, 12 Jan. 2021, https://www.btselem.org/publications/fulltext/202101_this_is_apartheid.

Abraham, Yuval. "He Grabbed His Generator. They Shot Him in the Neck." *+972 Magazine*, 3 Jan. 2021, https://www.972mag.com/al-rakiz-shooting-israeli-army/.

Beinart, Peter. "I No Longer Believe in a Jewish State." *The New York Times*, 8 July 2020, https://www.nytimes.com/2020/07/08/opinion/israel-annexation-two-state-solution.html.

"Israeli Writer Amos Oz: Trump Did One Thing that every other Country Should Also Do." *Deutsche Welle*, 14 May 2018, https://www.dw.com/en/israeli-writer-amos-oz-trump-did-one-thing-that-every-other-country-should-also-do/a-43404637.

"Late Night Live Summer—Amos Oz." *Late Night Live with Phillip Adams*. 10 Sept. 1991, https://www.abc.net.au/radionational/programs/latenightlive/late-night-live-summer---amos-oz--20-years-of-phillip-adams/3678482.

Oz, Amos. *In the Land of Israel.* Mariner Books, 1993.

———. "Sar haBitahon / v'merhav haMihya" ("The Defense Minister / and Lebensraum"). *Davar*, 22 Aug. 1967.

Said, Edward. "The One-State Solution." *The New York Times*, 10 Jan. 1999, https://www.nytimes.com/1999/01/10/magazine/the-one-state-solution.html.

Shezaf, Hagar. "Israel Rejects Over 98 Percent of Palestinian Building Permit Requests in West Bank's Area C." *Haaretz*, 21 Jan. 2020, https://www.haaretz.com/israel-news/.premium-israel-rejects-98-of-palestinian-building-permit-requests-in-west-bank-s-area-c-1.8403807.

TOI Staff. "Education Minister Bans Major Human Rights Groups from Entering Schools." *The Times of Israel*, 17 Jan. 2021, https://www.timesofisrael.com/education-minister-bans-major-human-rights-groups-from-entering-schools/.

Chapter 16

And They Lived Separately Ever After

The Two-State Solution as Literary Ending

Vered Karti Shemtov

The name of the game for Israelis and for Palestinians, as I see it, is a fair and decent and painful divorce rather than a honeymoon bed together. I think Israelis and Palestinians should separate land and assets, divide the land between the two nations and live in peace like two ex-people rather than try to reconcile in the way of living together.

—Amos Oz, "Remembering Israeli Author and Peace Activist Amos Oz"

What does a failed love tell us? That the failure is inside ourselves? I think that this is what cultures can explore through failed love stories.

—William Gleason, Love between the Covers

Amos Oz is remembered, among other things, as a great orator. He was able to use the power of poetic language to explain and persuade his audience. I witnessed it personally, seeing the reaction of many students from different backgrounds to his lectures. The power of his rhetoric was, among other things, in his use of metaphors. In this chapter I will employ literary exemplars in order to better understand the metaphorical mapping of Oz's political discourse. My goal is not to promote, question, or evaluate in any other way Amos Oz's political vision but rather to pay close attention to the language he uses to describe the Conflict, and to point out the connections between the language of his essays and that of his literary fiction. My role as literary critic here, is to turn the metaphors from powerful tools of persuasion to the vehicles of investigation. To that end, I will read Oz's political metaphors of "separation" and "divorce" and compare them to descriptions of failed literary romances between Palestinians and Israelis in stories written by Oz and by others. I will argue that the poetic language of Oz's political essays can be fully understood only against the background of literary works that "open" these metaphors and turn them into imagined scenarios.

An Amicable Divorce

One of Oz's main arguments throughout his career was that the Israeli-Palestinian Conflict can be resolved by creating two states. Oz was one of the main public figures to suggest the two-state solution. He started speaking about it after the Six Day War as part of his involvement in the Peace Now movement and continued advocating it for over forty years. His persistence led Avraham Burg to call him "a Fanatic of the two-state solution," and Joshua Leifer to write that as "a self-described opponent of fanaticism, Oz never wavered in his devotion to the two-state solution, even when it began to appear like the kind of messianic vision he had spent his whole life opposing."[1] Knowing that his life was coming to an end, Oz in his last lecture addressed the urgent need to create two states, and presented it as his dying wish. In a prophetic tone, Oz warned his audience that "if we do not form two states, and fairly quickly, we will end up with one state. If we end up with one state, it will not be a bi-national state [. . .] It will be an Arab state."[2]

In lectures, essays, and interviews Oz focused on several metaphors and a few other rhetorical and poetic devices to describe his argument and to persuade his audience. Metaphors have long been seen not just as ornaments to political discourses, but as media of political contestation in their own right, capable of substantively shaping and affecting political speech.[3] Politics is a linguistic activity, and metaphor set the terms. One way in which Oz chose to speak about the two-state solution was by referring to the genre conventions of literary fiction—in particular, narrative endings. The Conflict, he wrote in his last book, is "not a Hollywood Western pitting good against bad, but a tragedy of justice against justice."[4] And in a 1993 interview he said, "I'm a great believer in a compromise. I think where there is a clash between right and right there can be either a Shakespearean type of solution, namely the stage in the end is covered with dead bodies and justice over us high above. Or else a Chekhov-like solution. In the end of a Chekhov tragedy everybody is embittered, grumpy, disillusioned but alive. And I have been working for a Chekhov solution not a Shakespeare solution for this particular conflict."[5] Oz repeatedly dismissed the utopian abstract notion of peace. It is impossible, he argued, "after a hundred years of conflict to put both sides in one bed."[6]

One of the most central metaphors in Oz's political thought was of the two-state solution as a divorce, or in his own words: "A two-state solution, a partition of the land. A divorce not a honeymoon."[7] The divorce, for Oz, was the perfect Chekhov-like ending to the story of the Conflict. In 2004 he published a book entitled *Help Us Divorce*, which comprised two essays, one of them bearing the same title.[8] As a metaphor for conceptualizing political agreements, divorce is not unique to the Israeli-Palestinian Conflict—we can see it, for example in the recent conversations about Brexit.[9] Jonathan Charteris-Blackin in his book *Politicians and Rhetoric: The Persuasive Power of Metaphor* explains the "metaphor scenario" of this political metaphor:

> A scenario provides details of the scenes and plot and therefore turns a series of political events, such as the negotiations between European states over EU membership, into a narrative about marriage and relationships that is accessible—because—like a televised soap opera—it involves love and sex. In the classic scenario, countries joining the EU are described as "getting engaged," "marrying," "flirting," and "getting into bed" with each other. However, our knowledge of the problematic nature of human relationships also has the potential to be used in political debates to construe other representations so they might also "fall out of love with" or "divorce" each other.[10]

To speak of divorce as a solution to a political conflict, according to Charteris-Blackin, is to participate in a more general metaphorical discourse that maps political arrangements onto romantic or sexual ones. But for

Oz, the metaphor of divorce doesn't gain meaning from the analogy of politics to love. Rather, it imagines the Conflict as a divorce specifically in divorce's juridical or legal ascription, as a process of separation. Oz does not seem to want his readers and audience to imagine a love story that failed. He wants a divorce without a marriage, a separation without a relationship. When speaking about the two-state-solution as a divorce, he often modifies the metaphor and explains that Arabs and Jews never were a family. In his 2015 lecture at the Institute of National Security Studies in Israel, Oz said: "The Palestinians and us cannot suddenly turn into one big happy family because 'us' and 'them' are not a family, or united or happy. We are two unhappy families. We need a fair divorce rather than a honeymoon." For Oz, the two peoples are already divided in every aspect besides the space. "The idea of a bi-national state," he argues, "is a sad joke [. . .] it is impossible to become a happy family. We need a fair divorce and a two-family home in this country."[11] For Oz, the divorce metaphor mobilizes a productive semantic field for discussing different aspects of the Conflict. By presenting the Conflict as a failed relationship, it evokes the idea of Israeli-Palestinian relations as an endeavor of compromise and mutual accommodation; as in a divorce, both sides must come to the table to discuss the division of assets, and they must imagine their independence after a final settlement is reached. With its suggestion of tolerable, if bitter, compromise, the language of divorce served Oz better than his descriptions of the two-state solution as a surgery, another image of splitting off or disjoining that he sometimes used.[12] Divorce allowed Oz to present the Conflict as having two sides that just don't get along, "justice" vs. "justice." The word "divorce" evokes pain, resentment, or other strong emotions between the two sides, but it shifts the focus from these emotions to the moment after "the marriage counseling," when the couple's narratives are placed aside, and the more pragmatic, colder, and more bureaucratic process of separation begins.

Logically, it does not make sense to speak of a divorce without a relationship. But Oz intervenes in the metaphor's logical operation to negate it, steering explicitly away from the suggestion of a once-intact marriage between the Conflict's two sides even as he invokes it through the language of divorce. For Oz, the divorce metaphor does not emphasize much more than a wish for partition, or a wish to disconnect, as Bernard Avishai explains:

> In recent years, Oz coined perhaps his most influential turn of phrase, which has been picked up by virtually all politicians

in the peace camp and implies the solidarity of that "slimmer" Israel. Namely, he said that Israelis and Palestinians must "divorce," that they must split "this small house into two little apartments." Superficially, the claim is inarguable: most on each side want to exercise political sovereignty in separate entities. And many Palestinians revere Oz's humanism; the President of the Palestinian Authority, Mahmoud Abbas, wrote a letter paying tribute to Oz. But divorce is not a neutral metaphor, and Oz made clear that he meant something quite radical by it: that the two peoples should get more or less entirely out of each other's lives. (He often quoted Robert Frost on the virtues of "good fences.") In effect, he was saying that the two-state solution should finally solve what the 1948 War did not.[13]

Political metaphors are cognitive mechanisms that enable the audience to "make sense of the political world by drawing from previous knowledge and experience in nonpolitical domains."[14] This "previous knowledge," as I see it, is not just the immediate personal experience, but includes also secondhand experiences gained by reading and watching fictional characters. Fiction contributes to the emotional associations that political metaphors can evoke and activate. In the case of Oz's political metaphors, Hebrew literature adds another layer of complexity. Many stories, novels, and films use the political metaphor to tell stories of romantic or sexual encounters between Israel and other nations. Amos Oz's "divorce" cannot be fully understood, then, without reading it first in the context of his own literary work, and then in the context of "separation" as a literary ending in Hebrew literature about the Conflict. In the next section I discuss literary partitions in Oz's fiction and argue that Oz activates the metaphor of the Israeli-Palestinian relationship as an erotic or romantic encounter, but he stops short from imagining an actual affair. In his literary works much like in his essays, Oz presents us with a "divorce" without a relationship. His reluctance to entertain the possibility of successful romantic interactions sets him apart from many other contemporary writers.

Literary Partitions in Oz's Work

A well-known example for "nations as couples" in Hebrew literature is a short story written by Samuel Yosef Agnon during the Holocaust. This tale, entitled "The Lady and the Peddler," describes the seductive and dangerous relations between Joseph, a Jewish merchant and Helena, a lady vampire. It is a gothic horror story, and it is often read as an allegory to the relationship between the Jews and the West. In the story, the peddler escapes being murdered by the vampire thanks to a last-minute decision to stick to his Jewish ritual and go outside to recite a prayer. Agnon's story addresses the dangers of being "hosted" in another nation's home. But, as many argue, his story is also a warning against assimilation, and against "flirting" and "getting into bed" with other nations.[15]

Amos Oz admired Agnon's writings and even devoted an entire book to reflecting on some of his stories.[16] His descriptions of psychological and symbolic encounters with Arabs as the Other share some similarities with Agnon's tale. In Oz's short story "Nomad and Viper" and in the novel *My Michael*, the "oriental Arab Other" is seen through the lenses of attraction and fear. The stories were written in the 1960s and are often included in studies that focus on the image of the Arab in Hebrew literature. In Oz's early work the encounter with the Other stays in the liminal space between fantasy and memory. The mistrust of the Other, and the fear of violence are never fully supported by the stories' details, and the question of whether they are justified or not remains open. The memories/fantasies of rape, like the bloodthirsty vampire in Agnon, can be seen as another kind of dangerous physical union with an Other, and with otherness in general.[17] Yochai Oppenheimer argues that "Oz contributed more than any other writer in the 1960s to the internalization of the 'siege mentality,' which tends to establish national contrasts. This concept defines a situation in which group members believe that other groups have negative intentions towards them, and in response they may develop a hostile attitude and distrust towards these groups."[18] Oz questions these intentions in the story, but does not dismiss them, and as a result the Arab remains a possible threat.[19] There is not much love or romance in the short encounters in "Nomad and Viper," nor in *My Michael*; these are not even "failed encounters" as in Agnon's tale but merely expressions of what Oz defined as "the trauma, the fantasies, the lunacies of Israeli Jews, natives and those from Central Europe."[20]

The mistrust and fear of the Other are based on the collective trauma of being a "guest" in a dangerous house. This is not to say that the fear is not justified, but only to point out that Oz's arguments for splitting the house are associated with being a persecuted minority in Europe. There is the fear of survival, the fear of assimilation, the fear of the Orient, the fear from one hundred years of conflict in the land of Israel, and more personally, all the fears and emotions of growing up in Jerusalem of the late 1940s. His negation of any possibility of a romance, and the insistence in the essays and literature to not even imagine a "honeymoon" is justified by the past: "I do not want to be a minority anywhere ever again," Oz says, "not after what my parents and grandparents told me."[21] This might partially explain why Oz did not change his language about the Conflict throughout his entire career despite the rapid and constant shifts in the political, social, and cultural environments. [22]

In his memoir, *A Tale of Love and Darkness*,[23] Oz returns to the traumas of his childhood. In this novel he combines his political, personal, and fictional worlds. When presenting the events that lead to the partition plan, the Nakba, and the creation of the state of Israel, Oz tells a story about a failed encounter with Aisha, a young Arab girl. Oz skillfully weaves together the personal experience and the symbolic one, as, for example, in the following sentence: "All excited and perhaps a little in love with her and yet trembling with the thrill of national representativity, eager to do anything she wanted, I instantly transformed myself from Jabotinsky into Tarzan."[24] The personal acts are justified by the ideas and myths of the time, and a story is presented as a metonym as well as an allegory to the political tensions of the late 1940s. The story serves, as I will demonstrate here, as an argument in favor of the partition, and as an explanation for the events before and after it.

For Oz, as he said, "The UN decision to divide the Land of Israel into two states was the right decision. Unintentionally they did the right thing. The borders of the division were unjust, because we received almost nothing but desert. But the very idea of dividing the country was already then a right decision."[25] The failed encounter between Aisha and the young Amos in this short tale from his childhood demonstrates the impossibility of a coexistence with the Arab neighbors. The story takes place during "mounting tensions between Arab and Jew, distrust and hostility, the rotten fruit of British intrigues and the incitement of Muslim fanatics who painted us in a frightening light to inflame the Arabs to hate us." The young Oz sees the visit as "a little diplomatic mission," a last opportunity to entertain the possibility of living together. But despite the innocence of youth, and the pastoral setting,[26] the young Amos can see Aisha and her family only through the lenses of the elder's prejudice and stereotypes.[27]

The setting for the story is the garden outside the Arab family's house. The building is surrounded by a thick stone wall that concealed an orchard shaded with vines and fruit trees. "My astonished eyes looked instinctively for the tree of life and the tree of knowledge." It is in this beautiful space of "birds in the orchard, and the trickle of the fountain" that the young Amos meets Aisha, an Arab girl. Oz activates the trope of innocent love in the Garden of Eden, and of a romantic encounter space of courtship and romance. Yet cultural stereotypes intrude. He learns from his Uncle Staszek that "in the eyes of our more respectable and enlightened Arab neighbors, who adopted a more Western European culture most of the time," and that "we modern Jews were mistakenly portrayed as a sort of rowdy rabble of rough paupers, lacking manners and not yet fit to stand on the lowest rung of cultural refinement." "Any inappropriate behavior," Oz's uncle explains, "particularly in Arab society, which was, he assured us, well known to be extremely sensitive, easily hurt, and inclined to take offense (and even, he was inclined to believe, vengeance), would not only be impolite and a breach of trust but might also impair future mutual understanding between the two neighboring peoples; thus—he warmed to his theme—exacerbating hostility during a period of anxiety about the danger of bloody warfare between the two nations." "In brief," Uncle Staszek said, "a great deal, maybe far more than an eight-year-old child can carry on his shoulders, depends on you too this morning, on your intelligence and good behavior" (317).

Oz allows his reader for a slight moment to imagine the possibility of an erotic and symbolic opening for a union, or at least, a romance. However, this hopeful prospect is raised only to be immediately negated and dismissed as naivete: "for an instant her knees appeared, the knees of a grown-up woman already, then her dress straightened again. She looked slightly to my left now, where the garden wall peered at us among the trees. I therefore adopted a representative position and expressed the view that there was enough room in this country for both peoples, if only they had the sense to live together in peace and mutual respect." The impossibility of this option becomes apparent when the encounter turns into a disaster that will haunt Oz for many years. The young Tarzan, unintentionally, causes an accident in which Aisha's little brother is badly hurt. With this the innocence is lost, the boy and his family are expelled from Eden, and the idea of living together in love and peace evaporates. The young Oz looks at Aisha as he leaves and describes "loathing, despair, horror, and flashing hatred came from her eyes, and beneath the loathing and the hatred there was also a sort of gloomy nod of the head, as though she were agreeing with herself, as if to say I could tell right away, even before you opened your mouth I should have noticed, I should have been on my guard, you could sniff it from a long way away. Like a bad smell." He then sees "a furious man [. . .] hitting Aisha, not punching her with his fists, not slapping her cheeks, but hitting her hard, repeatedly, with the flat of his hand, slowly, thoroughly, on her head, her back, her shoulder, across her face, not the way you punish a child but the way you vent your rage on a horse. Or an obstinate camel."

The feeling of guilt turns into reflections about the period. The "I" can be replaced with "we," as Oz shifts from speaking about the actions of the little kid that jumped like Tarzan on the tree to a compassionate critique of the muscular Judaism that raised the youth to be "lions among lions." "This awesome tree lion," Oz writes, "that I was exultantly acting the part of in front of Aisha and her brother was unaware of approaching doom. He was a blind, deaf, foolish lion." As foolish as these actions might seem, they were, perhaps, inevitable. "Instead of approaching her like the New Hebrew Youth approaching the Noble Arab People, or like a lion approaching lions," he writes, "perhaps I could simply have approached her like a boy approaching a girl. Or couldn't I?"

This is not an open-ended question. Oz leaves his reader with the sense that living together would not have worked. There is too much suspicion, too many stereotypes, too much bad history, and unbridgeable cultural differences. The alarming act of violence that ends the encounter, and the Arabs reluctance to connect with his family after the unfortunate incident, leave no hope for "living happily ever after." [28] If it was not clear to the reader at the beginning of this short tale, it is definitely clear at the end: the only way forward is partition.

I read the ending of this tale in the book through the narratological terms of Meir Sternberg that were later developed by Noël Carroll.[29] According to this approach, a sense of closure is achieved when the major gaps in the story are addressed. Oz's storytelling and the rhetorical question at the end brings closure to the post-Zionist doubts that the "we" could have acted differently. The question at the end functions as a way to doubt the doubt. Could things have turned out differently? Could the two families live happily together instead of being as separated as possible? Oz's storytelling leads the reader to believe that given how each group perceives the Other, and given the threat of violence, no other scenario besides separation could have worked.

In *Metaphor, Morality, and Politics*, George Lakoff discusses the "nation as family" as one of the most common political tropes.[30] According to Lakoff, the metaphor is often used for describing the government's role in terms of a conservative family structure. Oz believed that nations are families in the sense that they should be separate units, independent from any shared political sphere. Families have their own private space, their own home, and they are not expected to share their dwelling with another family. In this metaphorical world, of "nation as family," it makes sense that two families should divide their space to create a separate dwelling unit for each one of them. The two opposing metaphors, "the Palestinian and Jews as a couple in the process of divorce," and "each nation as a separate family" are combined in Oz's essays and speeches into a verbal net of shifting images in order to create an emotional and convincing argument for the necessity of the two-state solution. Through these metaphors Oz leads his audience to conclude that the only sensible thing to do when (1) a couple cannot get along and (2) two families that do not get along are sharing one household is to "divide up this little house into two even smaller apartments. Into a duplex."[31]

What do failed love stories tell us? If you accept my reading of this story as a prelude and an argument for partition, then according to Amos Oz, failed stories are a warning. The fictional world becomes here part of the experiences onto which we map the metaphor of the divorce between the nations, and part of the emotions that are evoked by the political metaphor. In *A Tale of Love and Darkness*, the childhood story is used as an argument, and as such, limits the literary imagination and allows the romance to exist only to the extent that it serves the rhetorical purpose.

Literary Endings and Political Solutions

Many Hebrew stories about Palestinian-Israeli romantic or sexual encounters end with a version of "and they lived separately ever after."[32] A separation is the anticipated ending in Hebrew literature about the Conflict. Readers come to expect that the romance will not lead to the creation of a new family. "There is an attraction," says Yochai Oppenheimer, "but this attraction actually emphasizes the stable boundaries that cannot be exceeded: none of the Jewish figures in Hebrew literature is converting to Islam, just as none of the Muslim or Christian figures convert to Judaism. Living together is not a goal, neither of the fictional characters nor of their creators."[33] The "separation" ending creates a closure, not necessarily for the individuals involved, but for the collective myths. When these stories are read through the metaphor of the nation as a family, then "they live separately ever after" can be seen like a return to the accepted social order. The love affair or the sexual encounter is a threat to the nation's wish to be in its own separate space, or in other words, a threat to the wish to be "a free people" in "our own land," as stated in the Israeli national hymn. This wish is the "happy ending," of the Zionist narrative, which—after reading Oz—can be seen as very similar to a "happy divorce."

Barbara Herrnstein Smith argued that the wedding is a closure in the sense that it provides a "stable conclusiveness, finality, or 'clinch,'" because "everything that could follow is predictable."[34] This is not quite the situation in Palestine/Israel. Literary endings of Israeli-Palestinian romance stay away from "they lived happily ever after." The narratives do not seem to be ready to see a union as a predictable and socially and politically stable solution. Yochai Oppenheimer argues that in the Arab-Jewish love stories the failed romance is a failure of the national literature: "We see the helplessness of literature. Instead of producing new options that reality has not yet dreamed of, it actually forms itself according to reality. This is one of the most obvious failures of Israeli literature. It recycles borders without undermining them." For David Zonshin, these stories mirror the current situation: "In general," he says, "Israeli literature reflects the reality of segregation in Israel."[35] These stories, according to Oppenheimer and Zonshin, fail to provide a new vision for the future.[36] I argue that this is not exactly the case. While it might be an accurate account of Oz's work, other major writers' disposition toward the trope of a "separation" ending is more ambivalent. Hebrew-language authors find different ways to question the status of the "separation" as a narrative horizon even when their works does conclude in an Ozian kind of "divorce."

A. B. Yehoshua's novel *The Lover* (1977) is a natural starting point for any conversation on this issue.[37] It is the first canonical Hebrew novel to include the voice of a Palestinian character. The plot originally focused on an affair between an expatriate Jew, Gabriel, and a married woman, Asya. In the process of writing, Yehoshua decided to add another plot line and include an affair between the novel's primary character Adam and Asya's daughter, Dafi, and an Arab teenager, Na'im, who works in her father's car shop.

The notion of a lover, in this book, represents the possibility of expanding the family beyond the nuclear unit, and including Others in the closed group. In the last scene of the book, Dafi's father (Adam) separates the young couple after he finds them together. He gets Na'im into the car and drives him to the border with Lebanon. The solution here, if understood symbolically, is not to divide a shared geographical space but to expel Na'im, because "he is an Arab, a stranger, a different world," and "talk will be useless here, the solution is simply to get rid of him" (432). But as Gilead Morahg argues:

> the distinctly nationalistic overtones that figure in Adam's deci-
> sion to forego the possibilities of dialogue and to ruthlessly rid
> himself of Na'im, regardless of the consequences to the boy,
> reflect the expanded symbolic context of this narrative and
> manifest the dehumanizing effects of denying confirmation
> on both the individual and national levels. Adam's insidious
> drive towards the Lebanese border is also a drive towards the
> border of his own humanity as well as of the humanity of the
> society of which he is a symbol.[38]

Adam ends up not depositing Na'im at the border but returning him to his village, a move that constitutes a separation, but it is not exactly Oz's "divorce." Adam and Na'im will still remain within the same borders, in the same country, and with the same strong emotions. Na'im explains that he is prepared to marry Dafi, and as Morahg argues, Na'im turns into the "loving stranger," the expansion of the family which "the quest for Gabriel (the ex-patriot Israeli) had failed to provide."

The separation is not completed also because Adam cannot drive back home after bringing Na'im to his village. His car is stuck: "I try to turn the car but the engine goes dead. The lights fade. The battery is absolutely dead. [. . .] A smell of fields around, the sky full of stars, a broken side road. Somewhere in Galilee. Old lives, new lives—He will go and I shall have to start from the beginning. My state of mind—Standing beside a dead old car from '47 and there's nobody to save me. I must look for Hamid—But still I don't move. Silence envelops me, deep stillness, it's as if I'm deaf."

Adam's monologue is followed by Na'im's words, which are the final words of the novel:

> What do I care if they don't let me see her I shall remember
> her a thousand years I shall not forget I miss her already—I've
> been burned with kindness—And he doesn't move from there.
> He's switched off the lights. From behind a fence of cactus I
> see him lift the hood and try to start up. Not moving . . . a big

tired shadow . . . stuck . . . Let him work a little, he's forgotten
how to work—"Go back to school" he said and I've forgotten
what school is. A good man, a good and tired man, and they
got on poor Adnan's nerves so—It's possible to love them and
to hurt them too—He's stuck there he can't do anything. But
if I go back to help him he'll attack me better to go and rouse
Hamid. The people will wonder what's happened to Na'im that
he's suddenly so full of hope.

Thus, the novel ends with a separation, but also with an understanding
that the two people can only move forward together, that a relationship,
a connection, already exists. This connection, the love and care that is
expressed at the end of the novel, the hope, the dependency, stays open,
unresolved. It cannot be socially accepted and at the same time it cannot
be ignored. The story does not provide closure or comfort, and the separation seems temporary. The story "freezes" rather than being resolved.[39] If
there is a vision of a future here it is not one that presents the separation
as a solution but rather an anticipation of "being stuck" indefinitely in a
status quo, and in a state of ambiguity.

Yehoshua sees the relationship as one threatening to the Palestinian-Israeli identity, and not to the Jewish Israelis. His position here is
very different from Oz's, which presents the separation as a preemptive
measure, as a way to avoid violence. In a recent conversation I had with
A. B. Yehoshua, he said that the fear of assimilation that he tried to convey
in the novel is that of the occupied, not the occupier. Na'im, a name that
means *pleasant*, "tried too much to please the Jews, to be like them, and
was losing his identity," and "Adam was saying to him: you have gone
too far in order to be Jewish, you cannot be Jewish. You can keep your
Palestinian identity and Israeli-Palestinian identity with the Bialik verses,
and with the Hebrew that you know, with your easy relationship to the
Jews that you have, but don't lose your own identity."[40]

The Lover was perhaps the most canonical Hebrew book to fully
entertain the idea of love between Palestinians and Jews. It was added to
school curriculums and was widely read. As such it contributed to establishing "the separation" of the couple as the anticipated ending. At the
same time, *The Lover* also created the possibility of reshaping the cultural
and national boundaries in literature. Imagining the next generation as
capable of connecting emotionally and physically expanded the possibilities
of the future, even if the story did not end with the traditional wedding.

Maybe nothing speaks to the openness of the ending more than A. B.
Yehoshua's future works, which continued to explore the possibilities of
crossing boundaries. In *The Liberated Bride*,[41] published around the same
time as Oz's *A Tale of Love and Darkness*, Yehoshua creates a fictional world
in which Jewish and Palestinian characters enter each other's bedrooms,
bathrooms, and other private spaces. The text itself is hybrid and includes
Hebrew and Arabic. Yehoshua, in his work and his political writings, continues to explore the interactions with other nations, and even if he does
not provide us with a different ending, he still creates a fictional world full
of encounters and exchanges. For Yehoshua, in his more recent political
writings and interviews, separation is no longer a possibility, as he said:
"I am very much concerned about the fact that we cannot have anymore
the two-states solution [. . .] there are four hundred thousand Jews in the
West Bank and we cannot take them out. We cannot evacuate them. And
so we have now to think about a real bi-national state. To give rights, civil
rights little by little to the Palestinian in the West Bank [. . .] I remember
my friend, Amos Oz, was very nervous when I shared this with him."[42]

Yehoshua's books are examples of the way Israeli literature creates
futurity (to use Amir Eshel's term) even within the conventional ending
of a separation. Israeli literature and film find ways to "widen the language and to expand the pool of idioms we employ in making sense of
what has occurred while imagining whom we may become."[43] The many
stories of romance or erotic encounters between Palestinians and Israelis
that were written in the last twenty years, often do end with separation,
but they go much further than Yehoshua in imaging love affairs and questioning the logic of the separation. Many of the stories describe in detail
romantic and erotic encounters—expanding the pool of images that the
readers and viewers can see with comfort. By doing so they normalize
the relationships—if not in reality, at least in the fictional world. As Shani
Litman argues, "Arab-Jewish love stories are no longer 'a big deal.'[44] In
some cases the romance is extremely intense and believable, and the 'they
lived separately ever after' ending seems bizarre rather than acceptable."
This is the case for example, in Dorit Rabinyan's *All the Rivers*.[45] In other
works we can find variations and deviations from the conventional ending; Michael Mayer's movie *Out in the Dark*, for example, ends with the
couple planning to leave for France where they will live happily together.
The Israeli man is arrested (sacrificing himself for his lover's freedom)
and the Palestinian sails away, unsure what the future will bring.[46] In
other movies such as *Strangers*, romance is possible outside the country

and the separation takes place only when one needs or chooses to return to Israel, "the wedding" ending is presented as possible, just not possible in Israel.[47] Some stories end with the death of the couple rather than separation. The movie *The Bubble*[48] follows a tragic model—Oz's "Shakespeare-like solution"—where the couple dies together. While this is not a happy ending, it does break away from the "divorce" solution. The two lovers die together in the middle of Tel Aviv, and they burst the bubble and the illusion that Israelis can live happily separated from the conflict. And separated from the Arabs. Michal Govrin's *Snapshot* does not end with a wedding but with a pregnancy. It leaves the future open to a new beginning.[49] In the film *Jaffa*, the Jewish woman also gets pregnant and gives birth.[50] The couple is separated because the man goes to jail but they are reunited in the last scene. Pregnancy can become a form of embodying the Other, rather than living with the Other. There are many more examples for questioning what became the conventional "separation" ending. In the next section I will examine closely two story lines before returning to discuss Amos Oz's notion of a political divorce.

Loose Ends

In her famous book by the same name, Barbara Herrnstein Smith defines *poetic closure* as an ending that leaves us, the readers, with the sense that "we have no further expectations" nor "loose ends to be accounted for."[51] Russell Reising, in *Loose Ends: Closure and Crisis in the American Social Text*, looks at works that bring a closure to the plot but remain open in terms of the social contexts and the larger stories. At the narrative's close, these loose ends "function largely as provocations for the reader to re-problematize the very assumptions brought to the aesthetic experience and to reimagine the entire world of the work of art." These works, he argues, "conclude either by eliciting via their final passages, counter readings to the narratives, or by eliding the very tensions that need to be addressed for the works satisfactorily to 'conclude.'"[52] In literature about the Conflict, the conventional "separation" ending might reflect political realities and the social expectations, but the growing numbers of narrative loose ends suggest this figure's inability to provide a sense of closure.[53] Two examples for loose ends stories are Dorit Rabinyan's novel *All the Rivers*, and Sameh Zoabi's movie *Tel Aviv on Fire*.[54] Both works draw a clear parallel between the end of a narrated romance and the possible solution to the Conflict.

All the Rivers (in literal translation "A Living Fence") is based on true events. It tells the story of Liat, a Persian Jewish Israeli woman who meets Hilmi, a young Palestinian artist, during her stay in New York. Much like in *Stranger*, the neutral location allows the couple to meet, connect, and fall in love away from the Conflict. Being from the same part of the world, the two can share the feeling of outsiders in the city, the longing for home, the experience of being perceived as a Middle Easterner (in the post-911 era), and much more. The beautiful romance becomes tense when the couple starts to argue about the future of the relationship. For Liat, it is clear that they will separate when her visa expires, and she will need to return to Israel. Hilmi is upset when she treats the relationships as an affair "with an expiration date," and does not see a reason not to keep things open-ended. These positions are juxtaposed in the novel with the "two-state" and "binational state" solutions to the Conflict: "We're already glued together," Hilmi says, "tightly interlacing the fingers of both hands. 'What can you do? We're inseparable from you.' Then he opened his eyes wide, raised his eyebrows into the three horizontal creases on his forehead, and asked if, deep down inside, I didn't acknowledge that a binational country was what would happen in the end."[55] Liat insists that a binational solution is a bad idea, and in the heat of a conversation she says: "Are you going to guarantee that instead of defeated Zionist nationalism we won't get triumphant, vengeful Arab nationalism, drunk on its own victory?" In a recent interview Rabinyan explained: "Hilmi and Liat, very much like Hassan and me, argue about the future for this conflict. Liat holds on to the notion that the two-state solution is the only solution, and Hilmi claims that this is anachronistic, it is old school, and it is not relevant anymore. For him, one [bi-national] state is the only option. I'm embarrassed to say that these debates took place in 2002 between Hassan and myself, and I still didn't change my mind. The happily ever after endings do not take into consideration our tribal instinct. Ignoring the tribal instinct is part of the current liberal ethos. But people need a sense of belonging and it cannot just vanish by being infatuated by the idea of universalism."[56]

In many different ways, the story does not provide a clear or decisive resolution in the argument between Liat and Hilmi. When the time comes, Liat does return to her home and Hilmi to his. But the novel leaves the reader with many loose ends. To begin with, Liat is not relieved but pained by the feeling that this relationship cannot last:

On the train home after the movie, he lunged at me with urgent thirst, uncharacteristically ignoring the other passengers as he hugged and kissed me. His breathless fervor gave me the hurtling sensation that this train ride, the rest of the way to Brooklyn, was all we had left—that these few minutes until we crossed the river were our last. At night when I thought about how few chances I still had to love him, I gripped him with the same desperate pain.[57]

In another place, Liat thinks about an image that will stay alive even after the separation: "the living, beautiful image of me and Hilmi would stay burned in that mirror, scratched and blurred, preserved like a ghostly reflection even after we each went our separate ways" (197). The logic of the separation is also questioned, by the fact that the couple's homes are not far from each other: "in summer, he'll be in Ramallah, and tomorrow I'll be in Tel Aviv. Only forty-some miles will separate us, an hour and a half's drive. Yet we've barely spoken about it, knowing that even when we are so close we will not be able to meet. We know there is no straight line running between those two dots of ours, only a long and tortuous road, dangerous for me, impassable for him." (216). But what unties the ending more than anything else, is that the story does not end with their separation. Hilmi makes his way to Tel Aviv, where he drowns in the sea. The last part of the novel combines the voices of Liat and Hilmi, he stays alive in her mind, and their two voices—the two options—which were interrupted by an accidental death—remain as two possible endings, if the story would have had a chance to continue.

Not long after the book was banned from the high school curriculum in Israel, Rabinyan expressed her surprise at the decision, especially given the fact that the couple separates in the book. The Israeli Ministry of Education realized that things have changed in Hebrew literature since Yehoshua's *The Lover*. "Their argument for having this book banned," Rabinyan says, "is based on the fear that it will inspire young Jewish people to assimilate and to get romantically involved with Arabs. This fear of assimilation was relevant perhaps in the two thousand years of Jewish life in the Diaspora, as a minority within other cultures, but it is no longer relevant in Israel where we are free and masters of our destiny and a sovereign society. Why carry on with this terminology of fear of assimilation when we are the majority?" Rabinyan's two-state solution is a call for interactions more than for separation, and her images and language emphasize the joined path and the shared space:

> Despite the attempts to persuade us that the Palestinians are nothing but "shrapnel in the ass"; despite the political deadlock and Prime Minister Netanyahu's steadfast refusal to engage with the other side—despite all this, *All the Rivers* is an aperture for dialogue. Far away in New York, Liat and Hilmi, an artist and a student, discover their affinities and their shared fate. Theirs is a complicated love story. But it is suffused with our responsibility to see the other, to be able to recognize ourselves in them. Above all, it rests on the hope that whether we want to or not, whether we shut our eyes or plug our ears, whether we drag our feet or stomp our legs, we will sooner or later admit that we—us and them—sail on the same boat.[58]

By way of interesting contrast, Sameh Zoabi's 2018 comedy *Tel Aviv on Fire* directly addresses the question of how to end the Arab-Israeli conflict. The film's main character, Salam, is a production assistant on a popular Palestinian soap opera titled, like the movie itself, "Tel Aviv on Fire." The soap opera tells the love story between an Israeli military officer and a Palestinian spy in 1967. Salam works in Ramallah and lives in East Jerusalem, meaning he must pass through an Israeli checkpoint on his way to work. During a stop, Asi, the Israeli officer in charge of the checkpoint, learns about Salam's job and advises him on how to create the character of the Israeli officer in the show. Salam brings Asi's advice to the soap opera's screenwriters, and the resulting scenes win him a promotion to be a screenwriter himself. Salam then strikes a deal with Asi: Asi will continue giving Salam writing advice if Salam will ensure the show will end with a wedding—"with an ending like this" he says, "an Arab and a Jew fall in love and get married—it will be explosive!" Asi sees it as "a real statement: no more checkpoints, no trouble."[59] At some point, Asi's request turns into a demand, and the officer even kidnaps Salam, taking his Israeli ID hostage to enforce the terms of their agreement and impose his desired wedding ending on the soap. Salam, which means "peace" in Arabic, is forced to broker a negotiation between the Israeli officer, who wants a wedding ending, and the show's producers and writers, who want to separate the couple: "Why not surprise the audience?" Salam suggests to the main screenwriter, "what if Rachel marries Yehuda? More drama that way." But the screenwriter dismisses the suggestion on political grounds: "it's another Oslo Peace accord," he says, "the big illusion that changes nothing." Eventually, in a move that makes explicit the relationship between the necessities of plot and the limits of the political imagination, the soap opera's head writer becomes convinced that separating the couple would "kill the story," and he looks for alternative endings that will allow him to keep the show's narrative line going without ultimately wedding the protagonist couple. The suggestions he makes track familiar endings in the canon of Conflict literature: one of them dies from reasons unrelated to the conflict, the Palestinian spy blows herself and everyone around her up in a suicide bombing, and so on.[60] When Salam insists on a wedding as a happy ending and as a way to have another season of the soap opera, the main writer says: "My dear Salam, once you become a writer you have responsibility toward your people. I did not create this show out of nothing. I was there during the 67 War, I thought for liberation. We had the spirit then, but we lost it after Oslo. I am creating this show for you and for your generation to make up for everything we lost. I'm talking about history" [my translation]. To this Salam retorts, "How did history help us? What did it accomplish? Is there nothing in between bombs and surrender? I understand my responsibility, but we need a different direction. Keep the show going."[61]

The lovers in the soap opera do not "live happily ever after." Right before the wedding ceremony, they are taken to jail in a scene ending with the words: "together to jail, that's where you belong." They are not separated; their futures are entangled in a common unhappy ending. When Salam and Asi sit to discuss the last scene, they do so as two people who listen to one another and try to come up with a solution, their relationship no longer shot through with the power dynamics that permeated earlier scenes. Salem explains to Asi why the wedding ending is not possible: "look around. This wedding is not realistic. It's an illusion. It does not make sense now, and not in '67 either. The reality has to change for that wedding to happen."

The audience is left in the same state of limbotopia that characterizes so much recent Conflict literature—no wedding and no funeral, Chekhov's gun still hanging, unused, on the wall. A. O. Scott, in his review of the movie wrote

> Messiness may be Zoabi's moral as well as his method. *Tel Aviv on Fire* (in both incarnations) has to fulfill narrative

conventions that call for a measure of resolution in a setting
where the chances of resolving anything seem to diminish by
the day. The idea of a happy ending—or, for that matter, a tragic
ending, or an ending of any kind—is downright laughable.
Which may be to say that when optimism is in short supply,
a sense of humor can't hurt.[62]

The story never reaches a neatly self-contained conclusion, rather it
leaves us with loose ends that can keep the story alive. The soap opera
for which Zoabi's film is named (or is it the other way around?) ends in
a suspenseful scene, with the implication that we, the viewers, will need
to wait for the "next season" to see what befalls the jailed couple. The
wished-for wedding scene might still be possible, just not yet. Both plots'
resolutions—the soap opera's and the film's itself—are projected beyond
diegetic time, the stories' loose ends won't be sewn up within the space of
this narrative. This refusal to commit the future to paper is an invitation
to first rewrite the present social reality; the plot demands it.[63]

A Relationship with the Future

This chapter has sought to discuss how metaphors from ordinary political
discourse become structuring and, sometimes, limiting devices in literary
fiction. Metaphors "both shape and constrain political understanding";
they can "contribute to mental representations of political issues, making
alternative ways of understanding these issues more difficult, and in so
doing 'occupy' the mind."[64] One need look no further than the marriage
plot to see that stories of individual romances have long stood for unions
between social groups. So too in Palestinian and Israeli literature about
the Conflict, where authors have turned to romances among characters of
both nationalities to play out the relationship between political possibilities
and narrative endings in explicit and often challenging ways. These works
make clear the ways in which metaphor can narrow the discursive field
of politics. If the Conflict's fate must unfold according to the terms of a
romance, few options remain open; a story might end in a fantasy of union,
whether through marriage or tragically, in death, or it might end in some
equally fantastical figure of disunion, separation, or expulsion. (The lover
is driven to the border and discarded, so that both people may occupy
their respective homes, separate and whole.) The political reality of the
Conflict cannot accommodate such endings—they stick out as gimmicks,

devices that are simply not up to the task that's been handed to them. And so, increasingly, Conflict literature refuses to end at all, deferring the resolution of romantic plots beyond the space where the story is told. I have argued that these "loose ends" demand some resolution outside the space of the narrative. They also enliven the language of political contestation and make new forms of thinking, writing, and speaking about the Conflict possible by expanding our imagination.

Amos Oz will most likely be remembered, and rightly so, as one of Israel's loudest and most eloquent voices for peace. He was an impressive man, a gifted writer, and a true activist. His vision might very well be correct. My aim here has been to place his political arguments in the context of contemporary Israeli fictional stories. Read against the ubiquity of romance as a vehicle for narratives about the Conflict, Oz's insistence on the necessity of a complete separation between Israelis and Palestinians is problematic—that he chose to conceive of this separation through the strained figure of a "divorce without a marriage" says as much.

Emmanuel Levinas famously said that the Other is the future and "the very relationship with the Other is the relationship with the future."[65] To interact with otherness is to open yourself to change, to the unknown, and the unpredictable. The relationship with the Other is a relationship with your future self. The wish to separate from the Other can be defined then as a relationship with the past and with how our histories define us. While I do not argue against Oz's political position, I am trying to shed light on the direction of his argument and the segregation (for right, or wrong reasons) that his metaphorical language implies. Oz's political vocabulary is focused on closure, on leaving no loose ends, no room for the possibilities that can come out of an open conversation with the Other. Reading Amos Oz's "divorce" metaphor in the context of Israeli fiction helps us understand not only the power of his metaphor but also the ways in which Oz's rhetoric "occupies our mind" and limits our political imagination. Juxtaposing the political metaphor to its use in literary discourses can help us turn it from a vehicle of persuasion to a vehicle of questioning, of creative thinking, and of knowledge.

Notes

1. Burg, Avraham. "Amos Oz, a Fanatic of the Two-State Solution" (A review of Amos Oz's book Dear Zealots: Letters from a Divided Land). *Haaretz*, 26 June 2017, https://www.haaretz.com/israel-news/.premium-amos-oz-a-

fanatic-of-the-two-state-solution-1.5488621, and Joshua Leifer, "What Amos Oz Could Not See." *Dissent*, Spring 2019, https://www.dissentmagazine.org/article/what-amos-oz-couldnt-see.

2. Oz, Amos. "All the Reckoning Is Not Over." You Tube, 2018, https://www.youtube.com/watch?v=Pqrd4c8ZT1E. Accessed 3 June 2018, 2021.

3. "Over the past two decades, scholars from different research perspectives have extensively studied the effects of metaphorical framing on political persuasion (e.g., Charteris-Black, 2006; Mio; 1997; Musolff, 2014). Metaphors are often used to frame political issues (Mio, 1997), and these metaphorical frames are argued to affect how people reason on these issues (Bougher, 2012; Mio, 1997). For example, when the metaphor *a natural disaster* is used to refer to immigration, elements from the source domain of "disaster" are mapped onto the target domain of "immigration," providing a negative image of immigration (Charteris-Black, 2006). Politicians use metaphors to characterize themselves, their opponents, and their political agendas, and use metaphorical language in policy debates to steer the public toward a certain viewpoint (Ottati, Renstrom, & Price, 2014). Amber Boeynaems, Christian Burgers, Elly A. Konijn, & Gerard J. Steen (2017) "The Effects of Metaphorical Framing on Political Persuasion: A Systematic Literature Review." *Metaphor and Symbol*, vol. 32, no. 2, pp. 118–134, DOI: 10.1080/10926488.2017.1297623.

4. Oz, Amos. *Dear Zealots: Letters from a Divided Land*. Houghton Mifflin Harcourt, 2018, p. 128.

5. Oz often repeats arguments almost word by word in interviews and these arguments were also unusually published in newspapers and books. I chose here to refer to sources that are relatively easy to the reader to find online. This specific quote is from Charlie Rose, "An Interview with Amos Oz." *The Power of Questions*, 1993, https://charlierose.com/videos/28704. Similar statements can be found in many of Oz's political writings and interviews, see for example: ". . . a clash between right claims can be revolved in one of two manners. There's the Shakespeare tradition of resolving a tragedy with the stage hewed with dead bodies and justice of sorts prevails. But there is also the Chekhov tradition. In the conclusion of the tragedy by Chekhov, everyone is disappointed, disillusioned, embittered, heartbroken, but alive. And my colleagues and I have been working, trying . . . not to find the sentimental happy ending, a brotherly love, a sudden honeymoon to the Israeli-Palestinian tragedy, but a Chekhovian ending, which means clenched teeth compromise." Farnsworth, Elizabeth. "Coping with Conflict: Israeli Author Amos Oz." *PBS News Hour*, 23 Jan. 2002, https://www.pbs.org/newshour/show/coping-with-conflict-israeli-author-amos-oz.

6. From *Ynetnews*, 17 Feb. 2015, https://www.ynet.co.il/articles/0,7340,L-4627668,00.html (my translation).

7. Rose, 1993

8. Oz, Amos. *Help Us to Divorce*. Vintage, 2004.

9. Rose, 1993

10. Charteris-Black, Jonathan. *Politicians and Rhetoric: The Persuasive Power of Metaphor.* Palgrave-MacMillan, 2005, p. 37. For more on Musolff and "metaphor scenario" see: Musolff, A. "Metaphor Scenarios in Public Discourse." *Metaphor and Symbol*, vol. 21, no. 2, 2006, pp. 23–38.

11. From *Ynetnews*, 17 Feb. 2015, https://www.ynet.co.il/articles/0,7340, L-4627668,00.html (my translation).

12. "If I may use a metaphor," Oz said, "I would say that the patient, Israeli and Palestinian, is unhappily ready for surgery, while the doctors are cowards." Here Oz is referring to the differences between the public view and the political actions. In Cohen, Roger. "Sitting Down with Amos Oz." *The New York Times*, 29 Jan. 2013, https://www.nytimes.com/2013/01/29/opinion/global/roger-cohen-sitting-down-with-amos-oz.html. For the surgery metaphor see also: Oz, Amos. "But These Are Two Different Wars." (essays), Keter, 2002, p. 45.

13. Avishai, Bernard. "The Israel of Amos Oz." *The New Yorker*, 5 January 2019, https://www.newyorker.com/culture/postscript/what-israel-meant-to-amos-oz. Oz was not the only one to use this metaphor for discussing the two-state solution, but from what I read so far it seems that he used it more frequently than many others. For another example of the use of the metaphor to discuss the solutions to the conflict see: Dajani, Omar M. "Divorce without Separation? Reimagining the Two-State Solution." *Ethnopolitics*, vol. 15, no. 4, Aug. 2016, pp. 366–79, https://www.tandfonline.com/doi/abs/10.1080/17449057.2016.1210347?journalCode=reno20.

14. Bougher, L. D. "The Case for Metaphor in Political Reasoning and Cognition." *Political Psychology*, vol. 33, no. 1, pp. 145–63.

15. For the story see: "The Lady and the Peddler." Translated by Robert Alter. *Commentary*, vol. 42, no. 6, Dec. 1966, pp. 37–42. For the description of the story as a gothic horror story see: Grumberg, Karen. *Hebrew Gothic: History and the Poetics of Persecution.* Indiana UP, 2019, and Miron, Susan. "Catastrophe Always Looms." *The New York Times*, 21 May 1995, https://www.nytimes.com/1995/05/21/books/catastrophe-always-looms.html. For a reading of the story as allegory, see for example: Laor, Dan. *Shai Agnon.* Merkaz Zalman Shazar, 2008, p. 137.

16. Oz, Amos, and Barbara Harshav. *The Silence of Heaven: Agnon's Fear of God.* Princeton UP, 2000.

17. The depiction of Arabs in Hebrew literature as a whole and especially in Oz's early work has received quite a lot of attention in the Hebrew literature scholarship. See: Oppenheimer, Yochai. *The Representation of the Arab in Hebrew Fiction.* Am Oved, 2008. See also Laor, Yitzhak. *Narratives with no Natives: Essays on Israeli literature.* Hakibbutz Hameuchad, 1995. Ṭahā, Ibrahim. *The Mile of the Optimistic Lover* [*Hiyukho Shel Me'ahev Opsimiṭ: keri'ah Hashva'atit Ba-roman Ha-'Ivri veha-Palesṭini Be-Yiśra'el.*]. ha-Ḳibuts ha-me'uḥad, 1999.

And, Ramras-Rauch, Gila. *The Arab in Israel Literature.* Indiana UP, 1989. "Nomad and Viper" was published in: Oz, Amos. *Where the Jackals Howl.* Massada,

1965. Oz, Amos. *My Michael.* Translated by Nicholas de Lange. Mariner, 2005 (1967).

18. Oppenheimer, Yochai. *The Representation of the Arab in Hebrew Fiction.* Am Oved, 2008.

19. On how the "us" and "them" categories connect to the construction of space in Amos Oz's work see: Cleary, J. *Literature, Partition and the Nation State: Culture and Conflict in Ireland, Israel and Palestine.* Cambridge UP, 2002, and Grumberg, K. *Place and Ideology in Contemporary Hebrew Literature.* Syracuse UP, 2011.

20. Lansky, Thomas. "Amos Oz, Conjurer of the Tribe." *The New York Times,* 19 May 1978, https://www.nytimes.com/1978/05/19/archives/publishing-amos-oz-conjurer-of-the-tribe.html?module=inline.

21. Oz, Reckoning, 2018

22. I agree here with Avishai (2019) that "Oz's version of the two-state solution may gesture toward moral reciprocity, then, but as a practical matter it chases the past." However, unlike Avishai, I do not claim that the two-state solution is no longer possible (I limit my discussion to understanding the metaphor without making any predictions or analysis of the possible solutions)

23. Oz, Amos. *A Tale of Love and Darkness.* Translated by Nicholas de Lange. Mariner Books, 2005.

24. Due to COVID I have access only to online books. Since the online addition does not keep the same page numbers as the printed book, I cannot refer to the exact locations of the quotes. All of the quotes from *A Tale of Love and Darkness* are from chapters 40–41 in the English translation, and 41–42 in the original Hebrew.

25. Eidar, David. "I'm Told I'm an Elite. I Do not Understand the Meaning of that Word." *Israel Today,* 11 May 2017, https://www.israelhayom.co.il/article/475531.

26. "The setting for the story is the garden outside the Arab family's house. The building is surrounded by a thick stone wall that concealed an orchard shaded with vines and fruit trees. My astonished eyes looked instinctively for the tree of life and the tree of knowledge." It is in this beautiful space of "birds in the orchard, and the trickle of the fountain" that the young Amos meets Aisha, an Arab girl. Oz activates the trope of innocent love in the Garden of Eden, and of a romantic encounter space of courtship and romance.

27. See: "In the eyes of our more respectable and enlightened Arab neighbors, who adopted a more Western European culture most of the time, Uncle Staszek explained, we modern Jews were mistakenly portrayed as a sort of rowdy rabble of rough paupers, lacking manners and not yet fit to stand on the lowest rung of cultural refinement." And: "Any inappropriate behavior," Oz's uncle explains, "particularly in Arab society, which was, he assured us, well known to be extremely sensitive, easily hurt, and inclined to take offense (and even, he was inclined to believe, vengeance), would not only be impolite and a breach of trust

but might also impair future mutual understanding between the two neighboring peoples; thus—he warmed to his theme—exacerbating hostility during a period of anxiety about the danger of bloody warfare between the two nations. In brief, Uncle Staszek said, a great deal, maybe far more than an eight-year-old child can carry on his shoulders, depends on you too this morning, on your intelligence and good behavior."

28. "We received no answer from the Silwani family, either directly or via Mr. Knox-Guildford, Staszek Rudnicki's boss." (Oz, Tale Chapter 41)

29. Carroll, Noël. "Narrative Closure." *Philosophical Studies*, vol. 135, no. 1, 2007, pp. 1–15.

30. ". . . a common metaphor, shared by conservatives and liberals alike—the Nation-as-Family metaphor, in which the nation is seen as a family, the government as a parent and the citizens as children. This metaphor turns family-based morality into political morality, providing the link between conservative family values and conservative political policies." Lakoff, George. *Metaphor, Morality, and Politics, Or Why Conservatives Have Left Liberals in the Dust.* Copyright George Lakoff, 1995, http://www.wwcd.org/issues/Lakoff.html#CONFAM.

31. Oz, Amos. *Dear Zealots: Letters from a Divided Land.* Houghton Mifflin Harcourt, p. 124, Kindle edition. See also, in Rose, 1993: "Now this is going to be a funny divorce as the two divorcing parties are going to remain in the same apartment, building some partitions. Having to arrange something about taking turns in the kitchen and the bathroom."

32. The literary context provided here reflects some of the cultural conventions but does not necessarily present accurately the most common attitudes in the public towards interfaith relationships. Arab-Jewish relationships in Israel are rare and often seen as a taboo. See for example Alona Ferber's interview of scholars about this issue in *Haaretz* newspaper (https://www.haaretz.com/jewish/.premium-palestinian-poet-in-love-with-a-jew-1.5250557) or Yolande Zauberman's interviews of young Israelis and Paelstinians in her movie *Would You Have Sex with an Arab?* (2012, France). It seems to me that the fact that many see it as a taboo leads to a symbolic interpretation of Arab-Israeli romantic tale rather than seeing it as a possible experience, a story from everyday life.

33. Ben Nun, Sagi. "How Did the Arab Turn to a Secular Object in Hebrew Literature?" *Walla*, 2016. https://e.walla.co.il/item/2959548. My translation.

34. Herrnstein Smith, Barbara. *Poetic Closure: A Study of How Poems End.* U of Chicago P, 1968, p. 2.

35. Both quotes are from Ben Nun, 2016. My translation.

36. In another paper, Elana Gomel and I examine the tendency of Israeli literature to be stuck in the present. We defined these kinds of ending "limbotopia" in "Limbotopia: The 'New Present' and the Literary Imagination." *Comparative Literature*, vol. 70, no. 1, Mar. 2018, pp. 60–71.

37. Yehoshua, Abraham B. *The Lover.* Doubleday, 1978 [1977].

38. Morahg, Gilead. "Reality and Symbol in the Fiction of A. B. Yehoshua." *Prooftexts*, vol. 2, no. 2, May 1982, https://www.jstor.org/stable/20689034.

For more about the ending of Yehoshua's book in the context of the literature of the time see Gertz, Nurith. *Motion Fiction: Israeli Fiction in Film*. The Open University Publishing House, 1993, p. 184.

39. Nili Sadan-Lovenshtain in her book also points out to the luck of comfort at the end of the novel: "Yehoshua's preoccupation with the question of Israeli-Arab existence develops in *The Lover* into an analysis of the weak spot of the hot topic of the time." Yehoshua presents a "relationship between the young generation of the two people, which is doomed to fail because of the external interference." The couple "in their naivete will try to avoid the verdict of the social conventions at a time of war. [. . .] Immediately after the Yom Kippur War, Yehoshua writes "the bitterness and grief of the last war can only be overcome by peace, only peace can provide us with comfort." But not a single one of Yehoshua's works end with comfort, neither for the individual nor for the general public. "In this sense *The Lover* is not different from other works of Yehoshua, or of the atmosphere of the time" (my translation) in: Sadan-Lovenshṭain, Nili. *A. B. Yehoshuʿa: Monography*. Sifriyat Poʿalim, 1981, p. 206.

40. A. B. Yehoshua in conversation with my class: Reflection on the Other: The Palestinian-Israeli Conflict in Literature and Film, February 2021.

41. Yehoshua, A. B. *The Liberated Bride*. Harcourt, 2003.

42. A. B. Yehoshua in conversation, February 2021. See also "We cannot divide this land into two states [. . .] For 50 years, I was a zealot about a two-state solution, I always spoke out about it when no one wanted to hear. Unfortunately, we have missed the opportunity. What Trump is bringing, no Palestinian will accept. I can't believe he will decide the Palestinian future. They don't want to talk to him. It's too late. There are too many settlements to evacuate people. We have to find a one-state solution of co-existence as the two million Israeli Arabs have done. You could count on the fingers of one hand the number of Israeli Arabs killed by Israelis and the number of Israelis killed by Israeli Arabs during 70 years of co-existence. That's a success to honor both sides." Sue Fox, Interview with A. B. Yehoshua (2020), https://www.thejc.com/culture/interviews/i-thought-it-s-fine-i-ll-die-but-someone-had-other-plans-for-me-1.497679.

43. Eshel, Amir. *Futurity: Contemporary Literature and the Quest for the Past*. U of Chicago P, 2013. pp. 4–5.

44. A blog on this matter was published in 2014 in *Haaretz*: Litaman, Shani. "A Romance between an Arab Man and a Jewish Woman? Not a Big Deal." *Haaretz*, 1 January 2014, https://www.haaretz.co.il/gallery/cinema/.premium-1.2204403.

45. Rabinyan, Dorit. *All the Rivers*. Random House Publishing Group, 2017, Kindle Edition.

46. *Out in the Dark*. Directed by Michael Mayer. Israel, M7200 Productions, 2012.

47. *Strangers*. Directed by Guy Nattive and Erez Tadmotr. Israel, IFCFilms, 2007.

48. *The Bubble*. Directed by Eytan Fox. Israel, United King Films, 2006.

49. Govrin, Michal, and Barbara Harshav. *Snapshots*. Riverhead Books, 2007. Eshel commented on the futurity in Snapshots and argues that "Although Zuriel's child remains unborn, it also signals," Govrin adds, "an auda-cious gesture of hope." "Snapshots reveals the ability of literature to voice the unsaid and create a space for reflection on contemporary ethical and political concerns. In crossing the lines separating past, present, and future, works such as Govrin's provoke readers to rethink previously held 'judgments' and—to again use Richard Rorty's words—to go back in time prospectively. If literature can help us grasp the contingencies of our lives and 'our own moral vocabulary,' as Rorty thinks, Snapshots allows its Israeli readers and readers elsewhere both to accept the multiplicity of memories surrounding their homeland and to imagine inhabiting space in a different manner than they do today. With its metaphors and visual images, the novel supplements diplomacy's efforts to imagine an Israeli-Palestinian future with less humiliation and less suffering on both sides of the divide." Eshel, 2013, p.166.

50. *Jaffa*. Directed Keren Yedaya. Israel, Bizibi, Transfax, Rohfilm, 2009.

51. Herrnstein Smith, Barbara. *Poetic Closure: A Study of How Poems End*. U of Chicago P, 1968, p. 35.

52. Reising, Russell. *Loose Ends: Closure and Crisis in the American Social Text*. Duke UP, 1996, pp. 8–10.

53. Kermode, Frank. *The Sense of an Ending: Studies in the Theory of Fiction: with a New Epilogue*. Oxford UP, 2000.

54. *Tel Aviv on Fire*. Directed by Sameh Zoabi and Daniel Kleinman. Israel/Palestine, Cohen Media Group, 2018.

55. Rabinyan, Dorit. *All the Rivers*. Random House Publishing Group, p. 148, Kindle Edition.

56. Dorit Rabinayn in an interview with Vered Shemtov, January 2021

57. Rabinyan, Dorit. *All the Rivers*. Random House Publishing Group, p. 168, Kindle Edition.

58. https://time.com/4754208/all-the-rivers-dorit-rabinyan-book-ban/

59. *Tel Aviv on Fire*. Directed by Sameh Zoabi, Israel, 2018.

60. See for example the ending of Dror Zehavi's movie *For My Father* (2016).

61. Amos Oz also used the metaphoric language of the negotiations as a union, and he talked about the agreement as a baby: "Let's start in Oslo. I was among the godparents. I do not know if Oslo was a good baby or a bad baby, but both his parents did not like him from the first moment and did not mean to have him seriously. Arafat, as you said, thought it was a tactical step and the sequel would come. Rabin and Peres, the day after Oslo, flooded the West Bank with a huge wave of settlements. No one liked this baby." Eidar, David. "I'm Told

I'm an Elite. I Do not Understand the Meaning of that Word." *Israel Today*, 11 May 2017, https://www.israelhayom.co.il/article/475531.

62. Scott, A. O. "'Tel Aviv on Fire' Review: Mideast Conflict as Soap Opera and Farce." *The New York Times*, 1 Aug. 2019, https://www.nytimes.com/2019/08/01/movies/tel-aviv-on-fire-review.html.

63. Zoabi's claim in the movie, that two sides are not ready for a wedding, is not very far from Oz's argument that any discussion of sharing the space (either as shared markets or a federation) should be done not from the position of extreme imbalance of power, not as "occupier" and "occupied," but as a conversation between two independent entities. Oz writes: "we and the Palestinians will not be able to become 'one happy family' tomorrow. We need a fair divorce. After a time, perhaps cooperation will come, a common market, a federation. But in the initial stage, the country must be a two-family home." Nevertheless, there is a big gap between imagining the possibility of a wedding in Zoabi's film and Oz's storytelling in which the romance fails before it even begins. For the quote from Oz see: "Amos Oz Has a Recipe for Saving Israel." *Haaretz*, 13 March 2015, https://www.haaretz.com/.premium-amos-oz-has-a-recipe-for-saving-israel-1.5335960.

64. Bougher, Lori D. "The Case for Metaphor in Political Reasoning and Cognition." *Political Psychology*, vol. 33, no. 1, 2012, pp.145–63. Quotation appears on p.159.

65. Levinas, E. *Otherwise than Being or Beyond Essence*. Translated by Alphonso Lingis. Kluwer Academic Publishers, 1978.

PART 5

DREAMERS, ICONOCLASTS, AND TRAITORS

Chapter 17

Of Howling Jackals and Village Scenes

A Lament

Yaron Peleg

The publication of Amos Oz's first collection of short stories, *Where the Jackals Howl*, in 1965, has ushered him almost immediately into the nation's literary hall of fame. It was not only the purple of his prose and its psychological darkness that attracted attention, so different from the more realistic idiom of some of his immediate predecessors like Shamir, Mossinshohn, and Kaniuk. It was also the profane way Oz walked into one of the most hallowed chambers of Labor Zionism, the kibbutz, and left muddy tracks all over it. Although Oz repeatedly explained that he did so out of love, *Jackals* was one of the first trees felled in the Zionist forest that actually made a sound. It was another reason people paid attention to Oz. Shortly after it, in the early 1970s, critic Gershon Shaked anointed him officially as prophet, and in doing so established his own role as kingmaker. From then on, until the end of his life, Oz continued to sit under the proverbial tree and prophesy over his people.

Toward the end of his life in 2009, Oz published another collection of short stories called, *Scenes from Village Life*. It was an obvious homage to *Jackals*, in which the narrator revisits the hallowed chamber he defiled in the past only to find it in ruins. Instead of young people, full of vigorous faults, fighting lustily with their imperfect Zionist elders as in

Jackals, Oz's later village is populated with dying labor party apparatchiks, old maids and weary teenagers, and choked by commerce that grows like a parasitic plant over the old, defunct farms. There are no trees to fell here anymore because the forest the narrator visits is petrified, haunted by Zionist ghosts of the past.

Separated by forty-four years, the two collections bookend Oz's literary career; the first בקול ענות גבורה, with a loud and mighty voice, the last בקול ענות חלושה, with a whisper, as the saying goes. Both epitomize the fortunes of the old Zionist guard in the previous century and the role of its literary prophets, for whom Amos Oz served as titular head. For unlike many other writers, Oz willingly accepted the prophetic call and worked in the service of Israeli culture throughout his life as both author and sage. And yet, as the differences between the two collections of stories make clear, while Oz dutifully showed up for work, toward the end of his life, the number of callers who visited him under his tree dwindled. To wit: if Oz's early critique was highly relevant and has paved the way for the later excoriations of post-Zionism, the works he wrote toward the end of his life seem almost irrelevant, mere epitaphs.

In some measure, this is not Oz's fault, if fault is the right word here. Oz was asked once if he thought authors are prophets: if they can see the future. He dismissed the notion but insisted that what they can do is detect delicate tremors that run through the cultures they inhabit and warn of earthquakes to come. Authors who are attuned to these tremors and turn them into literature can sometimes be taken for prophets. One is reminded here of Oz's celebrated collection of essays from the early 1980s, *In the Land of Israel*; essays that surveyed the Israeli land during the very changing of the political guard from Labor to Likud. It demonstrates precisely what Oz described: a prophecy in slow motion that speaks of two such tremors, the first was national religious fervor, the second was Mizrahi indignation. Both soon turned into full-scale quakes. Oz was not the first to spot them or write about them. He did detect the depth to which they ran and the force that both were packing.

Later, in *Black Box*, Oz combined the two and gave them vent as the conflict between the privileged Ashkenazi patriarch, Alexander Gideon, and the upstart Mizrahi, Michel Somo, two cocks who in typical Ozian fashion fight for power over the bodies of the woman in their lives. Such works, socially attuned and culturally political, together with his frequent pronouncements on the general state of the nation, kept Oz relevant for many years. It was the stuff that earned him the prophet's mantle in an

Israeli society that had cultivated such figures from its early days. Writers and intellectuals have served as such seers over the house of Israel since the early days of Haskalah. Oz, like other men (sic) before him, A. D. Gordon, Y. H. Brenner, S. Y. Agnon perhaps, became a secular rabbi in the new Jewish society that formed in the Yishuv and in the new state of Israel later. The habits of the old Jewish world did not seem to die in the brave world of the new Hebrews as much as transform when the traditional Jewish "church" was replaced with a newer Zionist ecclesia.

However, the role of seer depended on a number of conditions and on the existence of a distinct cultural and political community that shared the kind of values that created the role of prophet to begin with. That is, both the function and the resonance such watchmen had in the community depended on a social contract, a convention that stuck for many years. Eventually, however, the contract began to lose its force, and when it did, the role of prophet began to lose its relevance as well. Oz, as noted above, took an active part in this change. After all, he was one of the first to examine closely the Zionist foundations that were laid in the Yishuv and drew attention to some of the faults in the walls that were built upon those foundations after independence—ideological rigidity, militarism, the relations with Arabs, with Mizrahim. When others followed suit and leaned more heavily against them, the walls were eventually breached and exposed the distinct community they once encircled to outside influences that began to change it in unpredictable ways.

Oz sensed these changes and, in his magnum opus *A Tale of Love and Darkness*, provided a telling commentary on them; a commentary whose irony may have escaped him. For in that work, Oz seems to accept the fact that his moral domain has shrunk to the confines of just one of several tribes that are jostling for hegemony in *fin-de-millénaire* Israel, the white privileged tribe, to use an ungainly American import. The confessional power of the novel cannot be denied, nor can the personal pain Oz shares with readers about losing his mother, even if he profited by that pain, as some have suggested. The question of profit is, if fact, the crux of the change in Oz's writing and the shift in his public position. An autobiography is by definition confessional, or at least based on its writer's life. But it does not have to be nostalgic. Has Oz used confession and nostalgia here in order to stay relevant in a changing Israel that has progressively diminished the size and the pertinence of his province?

This is not to say, that Oz is a "provincial" writer. His popularity in Israel and abroad defies such assessments. Oz was a consummate raconteur, who knew how to tell a story, even though and perhaps because he embedded it in a concrete here-and-now, as the cliché about universalism goes. And yet, to some extent, Oz's works are also the stories of a very small community, encoded in Israeliana that require deciphering. His early writings derive much of their meaning from familiarity with the ideological fervor of the kibbutz movement in its heyday. His later works continued to rely on this code, even when they introduced other elements to the literary formula. For many years, this was the very reason for his great moral authority in Israel as Keeper of the Seal, the seal of an allegedly original Zionism that stood for secularism, liberalism, socialism, and appeasement.

Perhaps because *A Tale of Love and Darkness* is a summative work, which Oz wrote toward the end of his life, it is also his most nakedly ideological work, in which the author's life becomes the biography of the state itself. The fact that he grew up on the wrong side of the Zionist ideological tracks as the scion of a revisionist family serves him well in this regard, because it allowed Oz to cast his own story of awakening and rebellion as symbolic of a larger Zionist tale. Except that in 2002, when the book came out, much of the symbolic capital of that story had been spent or lost value, not just by years of profligate spending, but also because it was crowded out by other tales of Israelis who originated elsewhere.

Hence the confession and nostalgia. The personal confession allows Oz to participate in the discourse of identity, which in the late postmodern age has confined politics almost exclusively to the realm of culture. A confession is also a mark of authenticity and a painful confession even more so. Both are important elements in the politics of identity, which derive its meaning from the personal and its power from powerlessness. By casting himself in this role, the writer of *A Tale of Love and Darkness*, who once prophesied over an entire nation, is fighting for the viability of his reduced flock and for the primacy of its Zionist story.[1] Nostalgia is instrumental here as well because it serves up the past with enough sentiment to blunt its more painful parts without pushing them out of sight. And since that past is, after all, also the nation's past and the story of its origin, readers cannot but sigh with bittersweetness, irrespective of their own personal story or point of view. Postmodernists aside, grand narratives are very compelling, and the grand Zionist narrative is compelling indeed.

It is tempting to say that Oz is employed a cheap trick here, that his use of confession and nostalgia was calculating, designed to elicit quick sympathy from readers through stories of pain and glory. Only, there is nothing cheap about *A Tale of Love and Darkness*, which relates a remarkable history with impressive sweep and great depth and uses personal stories to tell a much bigger tale. But herein lies the tragedy of a book, written by a king who lost his kingdom, to use a political metaphor this time. The astounding story of the people who founded Israel and the great vision that united them, told with great flair by Oz, is inevitably undermined by the bitter fight over that legacy in the present. The fact that Oz does not devise an ironic narrator that could put some distance between him and the text, as Meir Shalev did, for example, in *The Blue Mountain*, implicates him personally in an ongoing culture war; a war Oz and his shrinking camp appear to be losing.

And this is also the reason why *Scenes from Village Life* seems irrelevant. By the time the narrator of those tales is paying his visit, the place he describes has become as meaningful as the world "village" is in modern Hebrew. That is, not meaningful at all, a European import that was never acculturated properly in Hebrew, except in naïve illustrations of kibbutz and moshav in early Zionist graphic art.[2] Looking at some of these images today, in children's books, on cardboard game boxes and on posters, one is struck by the blond and blue-eyed children, frolicking in verdant meadows, surrounded by green mountains and one blue lake. These images never reflected a concrete Palestinian reality as much as the visual references of their European-born illustrators and their Zionist fellows.

Scenes from Village Life engages in a similar exchange, except that at the dawn of the twenty-first century, one hundred years after the rise of Zionism, these reference points have become almost meaningless. Not as a matter of principle, as a matter of course. "They looked pretty stupid," says Pesach Kedem, an octogenarian and former Knesset member for Labor in one of the stories, "when Ben-Gurion upped and went to London to flirt with Jabotinsky behind their backs." The old man is dredging up ancient feuds with former members of a political party that has all but disappeared. But so have the readers Oz imagines and for whom he has written all his life. It may be that the critique in *Village Life* is just as biting as that in *Jackals*, about the death of a purer form of Zionism and the fall from grace, except that no one is listening because no one cares anymore. Zionism is no longer the garden, which Kedem's literary predecessor and fellow prig, Shimshon Scheinbaum, tends with showy fuss in Oz's early story, "The Way of the Wind." It is now a petrified forest where trees cannot even be cut down anymore.

There may be some consolation, certainly to the memory of Oz and to his legacy, that the Zionist sensibility he stood for throughout his life died with him. It is a kind of pyrrhic consolation, a poetic justice of sorts in which the House of Israel is losing its seer just as it is losing its own old self. To paraphrase the writer himself, "Amos Oz's last day, opened with an inglorious sunset."

Notes

1. The point has been developed at length by Eran Kaplan in, "Amos Oz and the Politics of Identity: A Reassessment." *Journal of Israeli History*, vol. 38, no. 2, 2020, pp. 259–74.

2. Arab "villages" is another absurd misnomer of Israeli Hebrew, where many Arab communities continue to be called villages long after they have grown to the size of cities.

Chapter 18

Exultation, Disillusionment, and Late Inspiration

Oz's Once and Future Kibbutz

RANEN OMER-SHERMAN

It could be that the kibbutz will have a sort of comeback sometime. They won't dance the *hora* in the dining hall and they won't make love on the threshing floor at night. That's finished. But there might be a more mature version of what those people tried to do . . . not out in the countryside, maybe not even in Israel. Perhaps in the future there will be more urban communes that will try to establish something similar to the extended family, with security in old age, with greater mutual responsibility in raising children. Actually, they already exist today: a few of my grandchildren are members of fascinating urban communes. I don't know about you, but what I see here . . . is a huge number of people working beyond their capacity in order to make more money than they actually need, to buy things they really don't need, to impress people they don't even like. Some are fed up with that. Not the majority. The majority will remain competitive, that's human nature. But there will be some who search for an alternative. And those people might draw from the original ideas of the kibbutz the good concept of some sort of extended family, without changing human nature, without perfect equality, without peering into other people's rooms to see who has an electric kettle and who doesn't.

—Amos Oz, "A Room of One's Own:
Amos Oz in Conversation with Shira Hadad"

335

It hardly seems an exaggeration to say that when Amos Oz fled his father's home to begin a radically new life at Kibbutz Hulda, he was in a state of great turmoil and that, not unreasonably, he may have pinned impossible expectations on the kibbutz as a haven of salvation and consolation, perhaps serving as a surrogate parent in place of the mother he had lost, and the father he had bitterly forsaken. Late in life he described those agonizing days to David Grossman:

> I hated my father in my youth, because I thought it was he who caused my mother to kill herself. And then I hated my mother, because how could she do something like that to me? How could she leave the house without saying where she was going? She was the one who demanded from each of us, whenever we left the house, to leave a note underneath the vase saying exactly where we were going . . . And mostly I hated myself because if my mother killed herself, I must not have been lovable enough for her. How could it be? Even the mothers of Nazis loved their sons, and my mother didn't? . . . only when I had my own children, did I begin to have compassion for my parents, and to love them. Only then was I able to understand them. And when I wrote *A Tale of Love and Darkness* I actually was a bit a "parent of my parents."[1]

For generations, the kibbutz invariably presented an alluring front to youthful outsiders like Oz with its promise of a life of social enlightenment and bucolic harmony. Even visitors who might otherwise doubt the existence of utopia were inclined to express admiration for the bold confidence of communities that seemed to promise their collective harmony had managed to overcome the meanness that prevails elsewhere in human societies. Given its famous egalitarianism, there could be no such thing as a lonely, marginalized, or persecuted residents on the kibbutz. Many who have been in thrall to the kibbutz dream at one point or another cherished this precious illusion with every fiber of their being. The visionary power of such a perfectly engineered society could effectively scour away any minor human limitations and frailties that might happen to linger like stowaways from their previous lives.

By the time he began writing, Oz already knew otherwise and from the very beginning his portrayals of kibbutz drew on both that heartbreak and his persistent humanism. In one of the more confessional interviews of his final years, Oz spoke to the writer Shira Hadad unflinchingly (perhaps guiltily) of the pain the kibbutz had inflicted not only on him in his formative years but subsequently on his children. It is surely telling that in the late mellowing that produced the more benevolent portrait of the 2012 collection *Bein Haverim* [*Between Friends*] there is at least one that touches directly on that raw reservoir of pain. In "Little Boy" even the kibbutz's native-born exhibit vulnerability and traumatic estrangement. The protagonist's mother submits to the urgings of kibbutz pedagogues dismissing her five-year-old child's bedwetting and tears: "The Committee for Preschoolers instructed Leah . . . to be firm . . . in order to wean him off this self-indulgent behavior" (85). Embracing the gospel of collectivist orthodoxy, she "didn't like unnecessary touching and talking. . . . She adhered to all the kibbutz tenets with a zealot's fervor" (86). Thus, during the child's wrenchingly brief visits, she "saw to it that . . . if he cried, she punished him for being a crybaby. She was against hugging . . . the children of our new society had to be strong and resilient" (85).[2] Speaking of what he felt he had accomplished in "Little Boy," Oz told Hadad it had captured the traumatic reality better than any other words he had ever expressed on the subject:

> The communal children's house was a Darwinistic place. The kibbutz founders, both men and women, thought, like Rousseau, that a person is born good and it's only circumstances that corrupt him. They believed, as did the Christian Church, that innocent children are actually small angels who have not yet tasted sin, and that the kibbutz children's house was a Garden of Eden filled with affection, friendship and kindness. What did they know, those founders of the kibbutz? They'd never seen children in their lives. They themselves were children. What did they know about what happens when you leave children unsupervised? It's enough to stand at the fence of a kindergarten to know once and for all that it should not be done. They developed entire theories: that if the children saw only each other, it would prevent them from imitating the negative aspects of their parents' behavior. But at night, after the adults said goodnight and left, the children's house sometimes turned into the desert island from *Lord of the Flies*. Heaven help the weak. Heaven help the sensitive. Heaven help the misfits. It was a cruel place.[3]

By the time Oz's youngest child Daniel had reached the age of two, the cooperative children's education system at Hulda had undergone reform, and the children moved in with their parents. Four years later, the family departed for Arad, due to Daniel's acute asthma. But on two separate occasions in his interview with Hadad, Oz expresses consternation for ignoring the damage done to his older daughters, Fania and Galia, in the children's houses:

> I regret and am ashamed that when my daughters were bullied, I didn't have the courage to intervene and go to war to protect them. . . . I knew very well what happened in the children's houses to children who were a little weaker or a little unusual. I knew from my own experience. I can't hide behind the excuse that I didn't know what was going on because I went through all of it. Maybe for me it was even worse than for my daughters. As a "boarding child," I was beaten every day. They beat me for being white when they were tanned, for not playing basketball, for writing poems, for speaking well, for not knowing how to dance, and also I was the victim of what they call in the Israel Defense Forces a "preemptive counter-attack," because they knew I would leave the kibbutz one day. My two roommates, who both left the kibbutz twenty-five years before me, supplied preemptive beatings because it was absolutely clear that I wouldn't stay on the kibbutz. ("A Room of One's Own")

Without ever quite being able to dismiss the profound allure kibbutz ideology once held for him (not to mention his conviction that for any writer kibbutz was probably "the best university to study human nature") as a parent Oz came to regret not having left during his daughters' difficult years in the children's communal education system ("A Room of One's Own").[4] However, the story of what precisely transpired during that time has become complicated by the story of abuse, physical as well as emotional, that Galia Oz says was directed toward her and on at least one occasion, toward her mother as recounted in her 2021 memoir *Something Disguised as Love* ([Hebrew] *Kinneret Zmora-Bitan Dvir*). Though vehemently disputed by her siblings, readers who want a fuller account of the Oz's family life should seek it out.

Following the 1965 publication of *Artzot Ha-Tan* [*Where the Jackals Howl*] undoubtedly his most provocative story collection (brimming with violent episodes and kibbutz characters who often fall well short of the virtuous myth of the Sabra), the reactions of many of Oz's fellow kibbutzniks was (perhaps not too surprisingly) one of hurt and dismay. Avner Holtzman recalls the "surprise and indignation" of some, quoting a leader of Ha-Shomer Ha-Tza'ir and Mapam, who charged that the book had failed to offer "a positive or [even] a balanced portrayal of kibbutz life" and had effectively "distorted" its essence.[5] Of course the fate of kibbutz artists has often been a lonely one and Oz was hardly the first kibbutz writer to cause umbrage. Consider the infamous case of David Maletz (1899–1981), a bestselling novelist in the Yishuv and a recalcitrant figure throughout his lifetime. A founding member of Kibbutz Ein Harod (1923) and an ardent follower of A. D. Gordon's sacred exaltation of labor and landscape, Maletz's 1945 novel (translated as *Young Hearts* though its Hebrew title *Ma'agalot*, denotes "cycles"), caused an unprecedented level of controversy. Immediately after publication, the book sold out entirely. Today it is not easy to comprehend the reasons for the intense furor that greeted the book's Hebrew publication, which overwhelmingly seems an ardently ideological, even naïve affirmation of the kibbutz project. Yet simply voicing the mildest notes of dissent in its pages caused dismay throughout the kibbutz movement.[6]

In Maletz's work, the protagonist broods over the collective's pervasive atmosphere of cold institutionalization, at one point anguishing whether "in striving after full equality and justice you lost all elementary human feeling?"[7] The novel is distinguished by its careful attention to matters such as the intergenerational war of secularism and religion waged in those early days. In one salient example, a character pleads forcefully with his entire community to validate the need for a spiritual life of some kind: "I know that if there is meaning to the life of Jews as Jews anywhere in the world, it is here. . . . I'm not denying the importance of bread and butter—aren't we giving our full time and effort to producing bread from the soil? Yet man does not live by bread alone and there's a pretty good likelihood that neither does he live by social and national ideals alone. He has to have a higher principle" (154). While in many ways exhibiting a faithful adherence to the norms and codes of the secular Zionist enterprise of the day, *Young Hearts* is also a novel that urgently and poignantly gestures toward the need for inner fulfillment as much as it underwrites the goals of Jewish nationalism and by daring to suggest that some human needs

and foibles are not resolved by socialism, its author aroused great anger.[8]
Little wonder that Oz found it a source of inspiration for confronting his
own difficult truths.

From an historical perspective, "Nomad and Viper" ("Navadim
va-tsefa") which appeared in Oz's 1965 debut short story collection, later
revised and republished in 1976, constitutes one of Hebrew literature's
most pertinent portrayals of the encounter between Zionist settlers and the
indigenous Arab. In language that manages to be both lyrical and almost
unbearably suspenseful, the story traces the growing tensions between
kibbutz farmers and migratory Bedouin driven north by severe drought.
Through its sly inversion of the tropes of Orientalism and Zionist certainties, Enlightenment and primitivism, the story (along with A. B. Yehoshua's
"Facing the Forests" published the same year) helped inaugurate a tradition
of boldly subversive portrayals of the clash between Jewish homecoming
and indigeneity in Israeli literature. Tensions are inflamed over suspicions
of petty nocturnal thefts by the Bedouin. Oz's story is narrated by an
unidentified kibbutz member who, lacking any individuation, speaks for
the "We" throughout, reinforcing the author's caustic perspective on the
triumph of moral agency in a hyper-conformist and self-righteous community. Exposing the kibbutzniks' tenuous hold on their putative values
(liberalism, egalitarianism, and rationalism) in the wake of that spurious
accusation, Oz's story is a masterful cultural deconstruction, strikingly
unsettling in its ancient and contemporary resonances.

In a *sulha* (ceremonial reconciliation) arranged to resolve the festering tensions and misunderstandings between the two groups, Oz portrays
the pettiness of the commune's Orientalist condescension toward the
indigenous Bedouin. In terms of the kibbutz's own defense of its values,
it is important to note that, whereas their secretary speaks benevolently
of "the brotherhood of nations," promising to initiate a series of courtesy
visits between the two communities, the younger men immediately begin
to plot "an excursion one night to teach the savages a lesson in a language
they would really understand" (*Where the Jackals Howl* 37). Thus, "Nomad
and Viper" challenged its early Hebrew readers' sacrosanct presumptions
regarding the "civilizing" potential of the young Jewish nation's utopian
energies (it is worth stressing that the Bedouin pose no existential threat
beyond their occasional theft of crops and small tools).

In the story's crucial subplot, a young woman from the kibbutz
struggles against her amorous attraction to a Bedouin youth with disastrous consequences for both, thus introducing the transgressive theme

of Jewish-Arab romance that remains almost a taboo in Hebrew fiction even in the present day.[9] After an ambiguous nighttime encounter in an orchard with a Bedouin youth in which she experiences erotic attraction that causes her subsequent shame, a young woman issues a false accusation of sexual assault. In the story's explosive conclusion, a mob from the kibbutz sets off on a vengeful raid. As Robert Alter once observed of Oz's early kibbutz stories, "the most crucial motif . . . is that of enclosure. The kibbutz enterprise is seen as a dream of overweening rationality, an attempt to impose a neat geometric order on the seething chaos of the natural world . . . a reflex of turning away from the unsettling darkness of reality to an illusory light."[10] That dimension of Oz's often tragic plots is a familiar touchstone of the early fiction. But what has been perhaps less recognized is the fact that it cemented Oz's long-term, active empathy for the Negev's Bedouin, expressed through public acts of solidarity well into the final years of his life. In 2010, Oz joined a group known as the Culture Guerrilla poets, to protest the repeated razing of the homes and orchards of Al-Arakib, an unrecognized Negev Bedouin village, due to pressure from the Jewish National Fund, which wanted to plant a forest in its place. In his public statement, Oz bemoaned the fact that "Tens of thousands of people live in inhumane conditions, without running water, without electricity, without jobs. The state doesn't provide the Bedouin people the most basic infrastructure it gives to its citizens. The village I visited this morning is the most radical example of a ticking time bomb."[11] Thus, the "overweening" grain that Oz wrote against in his early career, demonstrating that an artist can and must be both a fierce lover of his society while also challenging the corrosive repercussions of its insidious complacency and cultural chauvinism, never lost its tragic urgency.[12]

In his magisterial survey *Modern Hebrew Fiction*, Gershon Shaked evocatively renders the irresistible secular mystique that first drew Oz and others of his generation: "kibbutz society was supposed to be an instrument of Zionist settlement as well as a gem of social justice. . . . Since the collapse of the religious congregation, whose commandments, rituals, and ceremonies had in the past saved the individual from himself, loneliness had become the sin afflicting the modern Jew. Community was to serve as a new religion, its commandments the practical objectives of labor Zionism."[13] In 2012, nearly fifty years after publishing his first book of stories on kibbutz life (*Where the Jackals Howl* [1965]), Oz revisited these and other sacred promises of the kibbutz, not in its contemporary severely diminished form, but in its fresh vigor as he first encountered it in the 1950s. For Oz, his transformative years on kibbutz, following what he later described as his painful betrayal of his father, proved critical to his vocation and self-understanding as both a Zionist and a writer even years after moving away to his present dwelling in the desert town of Arad: "The truth is that I never completely left . . . Many of my dreams take place there, and reflect an unresolved relationship with the kibbutz . . . There were a few things I didn't like about kibbutz life. But I feel the absence of those things that I did like."[14] That enduring preoccupation inspired the slim and delicately interwoven stories of *Between Friends* (*Bein Haverim*, 2012).

This time out, "Yekhat" served as the curious name of his fictional kibbutz and when asked what drew him to it, Oz reflected on the word's singular duality:

> I chose it because of the distant association [in Hebrew] with something sharp and dulled. The first ideal of the kibbutz was sharp: to transform human nature instantaneously. Effectively, they [the founders] set out as a youthful camp, in the innocent belief that they would remain 18 and 20 forever. A camp of young people who were liberated from their parents, from all the prohibitions and inhibitions of the Jewish village and Jewish religion—a camp in which everything is permitted, suffused with perpetual ecstasy, and where life is always at a peak. You work, argue, love and dance until your strength runs out. It was childish, of course. In time, it became dulled. And then what came to the fore were the constants of human nature. The vulnerability, the selfishness, the ambition, the materialism and the greed. It was a forlorn dream, imagining that it would be possible to triumph over all those forces, be reborn and create a new human being without the shortcomings of the old one.[15]

This statement seems altogether characteristic of Oz's enduring proclivity for paying heed to life's ambivalences in politics, art, and life itself; at once an emphatic affirmation of the great promise of kibbutz life as well as an honest reckoning with its inability to fully overcome human weakness. In recent years, many recent kibbutz narratives have been written by those raised during its era of unquestioned prestige, now eager to grapple with the complexity of what they left behind. Accordingly, in Oz's case, there seems to have been a desire to honor the memory of the great "world reformers," without sentimentalizing their accomplishments: "At the funeral of Moshe Hess, one of the veterans of Hulda, with the grave surrounded by "old people" in their sixties and seventies, their faces flushed and all of them wearing caps, one of the young people burst out, "You have to know that you are the most wonderful Jews we have produced since the destruction of the Temple. No other Jews bore on their shoulders what you bore, and none ever will after you. In *Between Friends* I look at these people one more time. Not only at the burden they bore. Also at their zealotry, their dogmatism and their quasi-religious devotion."[16] Accordingly, if most of the comrades of *Between Friends* struggle to uphold a sacred legacy the results are decidedly mixed.

As was long evident in works such as "Nomad and Viper" and *A Perfect Peace*, Oz steadily refrains from portraying kibbutz society as somehow immune to mainstream Israel's racism and xenophobic strains nor its occasionally militarist fervor—a few tense exchanges in *Between Friends* allude to that darkness. Still others bear witness to the disappointing reality behind the myth of gender equality, as when a certain "man of principle who fought constantly to improve kibbutz life" and would never contemplate leaving, nevertheless knows "in his heart that kibbutz life was fundamentally unjust to women, forcing them almost without exception into service jobs like cooking, cleaning, taking care of children, doing laundry . . . The women here were supposed to enjoy total equality, but they were treated equally only if they acted and looked like men: they were forbidden to use makeup and had to avoid all signs of femininity" (115). There is an especially resonant and empathic portrait of a young Mizrahi boarder in "Father." The story bears witness to the fact that during the 1940s and early 1950s, thousands of young North African and Iraqi immigrants were boarded on kibbutzim, a topic generally muted in Israeli fiction with the significant exception of Eli Amir's 1983 novel *Scapegoat*. Oz's character, sixteen-year-old Moshe Yashar, is more isolated than the young rambunctious immigrant cast of Amir's book, who at least have one another in their struggle against Ashkenazi elitism.

Moshe must cope alone with the kibbutzniks' condescension and discouragement whenever he wishes to travel to see his family. For some time, his appearance and deportment are reliable subjects for debate ("There was always something of the outsider about him . . . when we lay on the grass at night and sang nostalgic songs under the stars, he

was the only one who didn't put his head on the lap of one of the girls"
[61]). However eventually he is rewarded with a degree of acceptance as
the kibbutzniks approvingly note his good manners. Yet in the end, the
kibbutz teacher David Dagan's patronizing attitude seems to speak for all:
"On the whole, I have a very optimistic view of the Sephardim. We'll have
to invest a great deal in them, but the investment will pay off. In another
generation or two, they'll be just like us" (63).[17] Moshe stoically ignores the
community's casual racism, staying true to his independent value system
against their insistence on the historical necessity of revolutions and the
Marxist version of reality.

Though quite demonstrably not a Mizrahi, Oz nevertheless clearly
inscribed a part of his own story when imagining Moshe's indifference to
doctrinaire certainties, lured instead by the rich ambivalences of writers like
Dostoevsky, Camus, and Kafka: "Moshe was well aware that part of him
still belonged to the old world because he didn't always accept progressive
ideas, but rather than argue, he simply listened. . . . He was drawn more
to unsolved questions than to glib solutions" (73). Repelled by bloodshed,
a lesson on the French Revolution and his teacher's insistence on the
necessity of historical violence only reinforces his "simple conclusion that
most people need more affection than they can find" (65). A voracious
reader who prefers the library to the kibbutz clubhouse or joining his
peers on their nocturnal raids on the food storeroom, his encounter with
Das Kapital leaves him similarly skeptical: "He didn't like Karl Marx: he
felt that there could have been an exclamation mark after almost every
sentence, and that put him off. Marx claimed . . . that economic, social,
and historical laws were as clear and immutable as the laws of nature. And
Moshe had his doubts even about the immutability of the laws of nature"
(64). Yet he is also the kind of endearing young person who worries about
the conceivable selfishness of his own misgivings, perhaps intuiting that
such disaffection toward violence might ultimately lead to questioning the
premises of the Zionist cause itself and a more unbearable loneliness than
he already suffers: "He was suddenly disgusted with himself . . . scorn-
fully calling himself a bleeding heart, a label that [his teacher] sometimes
applied to those who recoiled from the necessary cruelty of the revolution"
(69). After a painfully unsatisfying visit to his ailing father in the hospital,
a pious man who shudders at the heresies and scandals of kibbutz life
(it turns out that the haughty pedagogue David Dagan is a philanderer
screwing his way through the kibbutz) Moshe begins the difficult journey
back distracted by thoughts of his peers' casual romantic dalliances on

the kibbutz lawns as they sing the "nostalgic songs" of an intoxicatingly rich past he cannot claim: "He would give everything he had to be there now. Once and for all to be one of them. And yet he knew very well that it would never happen" (82). Oz leaves his character at that unpromising juncture, adrift between worlds. And sadly, that is consistent with the fact that the kibbutzim failed to absorb many Mizrahi newcomers in spite of their "universalist" ethos.

In portraying the kibbutzniks themselves, they perhaps share more in common with Moshe Yashar than they are comfortable admitting. As was the case in A Tale of Love and Darkness (Sipur Al Ahava Ve-Hosheh) and later in Jews and Words (coauthored with his daughter the historian Fania Oz-Salzberger), Oz insistently aligns his work with the ghosts of their European past and the imperative of memory. Fittingly these recurring characters hold disparate perspectives on the historical Jewish condition. Keenly capturing the founding generation of ideologues warring with the youth who dared to seek a measure of personal fulfillment, Oz mischievously intimates that from a certain perspective the kibbutz, supposedly the wellspring of the New Hebrew, was little more than a reconstituted shtetl. Accordingly, in "Deir Ajloun" a temperate soul prophesizes that in the next generation:

> [T]he kibbutz will be a much more relaxed place. Now all the springs are tightly coiled and the entire machine is still shaking from the strain. The old-timers are actually religious people who left their old religion for a new one that's just as full of sins and transgressions, prohibitions and strict rules. They haven't stopped being true believers, they've simply exchanged one belief system for another. Marx is their Talmud. The general meeting is their synagogue. . . . I can easily picture some of the men here with beards and sidelocks and some of the women in head coverings. (158)

In spite of their self-mythologizing, Oz's halutzim are patently incapable of shrugging off the identity and behavior patterns inherited from centuries of life in the Diaspora (intriguingly, in accepting the Heine Prize in 2008, he remarked that "Israel–even today–carries European chromosomes" and that "The cross-roads is the only place where I am at home, where I really belong"). Indeed, throughout this collection philosophical questions concerning Jewish historical fate and solidarity often intrude.

A young man anguished that the kibbutz's doctrinaire majority will likely refuse his request to study abroad is upbraided by an elder chiding that after the Holocaust every member of his generation: "must see himself as mobilized to a cause. These are the most critical years in the history of the Jewish people." Unwilling to accede to living out his life in thrall to that trauma, he confesses: "The thing is I can't take it anymore. I have no air" (146). Still other characters, even if otherwise immune to their own suppressed longings, are beguiled in the quiet nights by dreams in which they inexplicably find themselves wandering through diasporic landscapes of elsewhere: frothing rivers, valleys, mountains, and Polish towns. In their unconscious lives the comrades seem bound to one another through unspoken losses and griefs.

Few literary portrayals of the kibbutz have managed to ignore the robust regulatory social role of gossip. Hence, the members of Oz's Yekhat are both sanctimoniously outraged and titillated when a high school girl departs the collective dorm to move in with a man her father's age (the teacher David Dagan who ultimately helps nurture Moshe in "Father"). The title story ("Between Friends") views that scandal from Rashomon-like perspectives underscoring the strained relations in kibbutz society in the aftermath of scandal. We glimpse the girl's father, a widower (further bereaved after his son was killed in war) wounded by his daughter's conduct with his only friend, making his painful reentry into the kibbutz's most quintessential public space, the site of disapproving expressions and gazes, where the harsh judgments of gossip flow fast and furious: "Morning, noon and night he would appear in the dining hall to stand mutely in the queue at the serving counter, load his meal onto a tray and then sit down in a corner to eat, preferably in silence. He always sat in the same corner. People spoke to him gently, as if they were speaking to someone who was terminally ill, avoiding any mention or even hint of his problem, and he would answer briefly in his quiet, composed, slightly hoarse voice" (40). In such moments, the lives of Yekhat's halutzim are subject to unwritten but unyielding norms of conduct no less than the gentry peopling Jane Austen's novels. Throughout *Between Friends* we become intimately acquainted with other characters similarly fragmented between private and public selves and Oz masterfully takes us into the depths of their disquiet. Most significantly, these individuals reflect a late development in Oz's characterizations of kibbutzniks; multifaceted souls capable of reprehensible acts yet who still rise to the occasion to care for others.[18]

Throughout, the despairing nocturnal cries of jackals are a redolent refrain, a kind of eerie, ethereal soundtrack scoring the myriad forms of sadness, yearning, incompletion, and loneliness festering within (but unvoiced by) Oz's Sherwoodian characters. A lifelong trope of Oz's luminous prose, the cries of wild beasts once seemed to symbolize violent passions but here they may evoke his characters' restlessness, the inner tug of needs and existential quandaries for which their meticulously engineered community offers no ready solution. In "At Night" a character confronted by the monotony of nighttime guard duty discovers a hitherto dormant capacity for spiritual introspection. As he goes about his duties in the silence, a sudden epiphany of all that the demands of routine obligation threaten to stifle reminds him to live more mindfully:

> The night was cold and clear. The croaking of frogs punctu-ated the silence and a dog barked somewhere far off. When Yoav looked up, he saw a mass of low clouds gathering above his head and said to himself that all the things we think are important really aren't, and he had no time to think about the things that really are. His whole life was going by and he had never contemplated the big, simple truths: loneliness and longing, desire and death. The silence was deep and wide, broken occasionally by the cries of jackals, and Yoav was filled with gratitude both for that silence and for the cries of the jackals. He didn't believe in God, but in moments of solitude and silence such as this, Yoav felt that someone was waiting for him day and night, waiting patiently and silently, soundlessly and utterly still, and would wait for him always. (116)

Yet the gift of such transcendent awareness can be a curse for Oz's charac-ters, for in the aftermath it is hard to return to ever be fully satisfied again. Though many of the stories in *Between Friends* are imbued with similarly compelling interior drama, for this reader by far the most memorable here is "Esperanto," the book's delicate and bittersweet coda portraying the intermingled lives of a dying idealist, an abandoned woman, and a young newcomer. The title itself seems especially apt because for many socialists the kibbutz, like the language invented in 1887 ("Esperanto" translates as "one who hopes"), expressed a poignant dream of the universal more than it did a nationalist striving.

The center figure is Martin Vandenberg, a man is perceived by his
comrades as Yekhat's paragon of morality (such a legend that he is dubbed
"the Gandhi of Kibbutz Yekhat" by one wag) and someone observes that:
"Martin worked in the shoe-repair shop as if he had taken upon himself
symbolic responsibility for every step we took" (196). Stubbornly loyal to
his unwavering conviction that "property was original sin" he even left his
former kibbutz when it allowed Holocaust survivors to keep their German
reparation money in private accounts. Martin's deepest passion, to dissem-
inate Esperanto, which he taught in prewar Rotterdam, offers intriguing
echoes of one of Oz's own most oft-repeated declarations on the critical
nexus of ethics and language: "Martin said that imprecise words poison
relations between people everywhere, and that's why clear, accurate words
can heal those relationships, but only if they are the right words spoken
in a language that all people can understand" (192).[19] Yet these stories
succeed precisely because Oz's empathy extends to all of his flawed and
prickly characters; Oz the polemicist never overrules the imaginative artist.

In these stories (as throughout Oz's oeuvre), one voice is invariably
supplanted or opposed by another perspective, a plethora of pluralistic
discourse. And so it is here when Moshe the thoughtful Mizrahi high
school student of "Father" makes a memorable return, respectfully he
attends to the saintly founder's dying plea for a universal language yet
doggedly stumbles on toward his own vital truth: "Moshe Yashar said
nothing, but thought that the sorrow in the world was born long before
words." (192). And this too might directly reflect a component of Oz's
thought. A deeply appealing figure devoted to the kibbutz's most visionary
values, Martin dwells alone with a respiratory condition resulting from
years of smoking and is dependent on an oxygen tank. In Oz's portrayal
his comrades perceive him as the living essence of their ideology. Yet
ironically, in his universal yearnings, he seems to poignantly resemble
most of all the lonely immigrant iconoclasts and dreamers of the Jerusalem neighborhood he describes in *A Tale of Love and Darkness*. And
for that very reason, of all the memorable characters Oz has created, I
would argue that Martin most embodies Oz's unflinching insights into
both the transcendence inherent in the most far-reaching ideals of the
kibbutz—and the utter impossibility of their genuine realization. Idealistic
protagonists pitted against their imperfect societies. The indelible relation
between heartbreak and humanism that forms the unifying essence of all
of Oz's kibbutz narratives over the decades.

Martin's idiosyncratic vision of the kibbutz ultimately encompasses a far more ambitious aspiration than a nationalist enterprise: "It was his belief that states should be abolished and replaced by an international, pacifist brotherhood that would reign after the borders between peoples were erased" (173). Faulting Ben-Gurion for what he deems excessively hawkish policies (a trait he shares with both Shmuel Ash of *Judas* and Oz himself), Martin passionately insists that "all governments, without exception, are completely unnecessary because the Jews had already shown the world how a people can exist and even thrive spiritually and socially for thousands of years without any government at all" (181). But if Martin is perhaps overly sanguine about the world's willingness to learn from the Jews' survival as a Diaspora, he has no illusions when it comes to the prospects of the kibbutz in future generations on whom the values of labor and austerity would be lost: "The kibbutz was doomed to slide slowly into the petty bourgeoisie. . . . In another twenty or thirty years, kibbutzim would become nothing more than well-kept garden communities replete with material pleasures" (183). By way of stark contrast, he refuses to keep even a private kettle in his room, his austerity an anachronistic relic hearkening back to chalutz days. After a lifetime diligently serving as the kibbutz cobbler he refuses to rest from his labors until firmly coerced into retirement by the kibbutz secretary. Were this quixotic figure the whole focus of the narrative, "Esperanto" would be little more than a reverential elegiac portrait of one man's solitary grace. Instead, on the whole, "Esperanto" performs a larger purpose as the collection's coda, bringing back other character to take their final bow in order to affirm that in the end, Martin is not entirely alone. Not only does he continue to stir the moral growth of young Moshe, but Osnat, a cynical woman hurt by her husband's abandonment, is so overcome by Martin's incapacitated state that she emerges from her cocoon of self-pity to care for him (evocative of the transformation of Shmuel Ash in caring for the elderly invalid Gershom Wald in *Judas*).

The critical dialectic, which enlivens "Esperanto," speaks well for the clarity of Oz's final statement on the historical drama of the kibbutz, the grandeur of its struggle to transform human beings. In stark counterpoint to the dying man's idealistic certainties ("Man is by nature good and generous. It's only the injustices of society that push him into the arms of selfishness and cruelty" [177]), Osnat's bitter experience with betrayal convinces her that there is more cruelty than virtue in the world:

"kibbutz . . . makes small changes in the social order but man's difficult nature doesn't change. A committee vote will never be able to eradicate envy, pettiness or greed" (179). Yet ultimately, in spite of her own genuine suffering and hard-bitten view of humanity, Osnat transforms into a deeply affecting model of compassionate selflessness to the extent that when a representative of the Health Committee encourages Osnat to accept four hours of credited work hours to compensate for her care for Martin, she firmly insists "that she took care of him . . . out of friendship, and there was no need for compensation. The evening hours she spent with the sick man, their brief conversations, his gratitude, the world of ideals and thought he opened to her—she treasured them all and trembled at the idea that their relationship might end soon" (188). Hence, in bringing these disparate characters together, contrasting their divergent worldviews and emotional histories, Oz does much more than merely expose the conflicts and contradictions of kibbutz life by ultimately affirming the potential of human beings to rise to the occasion when confronted by the naked vulnerability of others. When considering the cumulative impression left by the quiet but luminous morality of such characters, it becomes strikingly clear that *Between Friends* more than fulfilled its author's desire to honor the memory of the great "world reformers" without sentimentalizing their accomplishments. In short, if the earlier work was contained the sharp thorns of skepticism and disillusionment, the late phase was imbued with a kind of love, one of sighs and a limited reverence, that can only be distilled over time.

It seems telling that Oz told his interlocutor and sometime editor Shira Hadad that "even though I used the same drawing of the kibbutz for the [Hebrew] cover of *Between Friends* that had appeared on the first cover of *Where the Jackals Howl*, the distance between the former kibbutz stories and the latter ones is great, very great. In *Between Friends* I tell the stories in almost a whisper, compared to *Where the Jackals Howl*."[20] When Oz was a young man, the kibbutz was in its heyday and so was its sacrosanct stature in Israeli society. Oz being Oz could he resist telling Israel difficult truths about its inherent flaws, the presence of casual sadists in the heart of utopia? When Oz reached old age and his beloved country had been permanently altered by the ravages of privatization, he had to bear witness to what had been lost along the way. Hence the journey from the almost gleefully scathing portraits of *Where the Jackals Howl* to the reverential homage to the old idealists of *Between Friends*.[21] What happens to those of us who drop out after many years living on a kibbutz? Do we simply pick up where we left off before our immersion in such a radically different community? Speaking for myself and many others I know, our kibbutz sojourns transformed us irreparably. Even if disillusionment has shaken the enchantment of pristine ideology, we are never again quite as selfish (and, shudder, we never embrace libertarianism) in how we see ourselves and society or the crucial obligations that individuals owe the collective and vice-versa. We tend to embrace progressive causes. Our faith may be shaken but we maintain an almost sickly nostalgia for its aura. And so it surely was with Oz who in spite of all remained unwavering in his conviction that the social system of the kibbutz is "the least bad, the least unkind."[22] Certainly, after reading the resolutely unsentimental but empathic stories of *Between Friends* most readers will likely share Karen Grumberg's impression that cumulatively they are sustained by a "quiet, moderate hope."[23] Others in this volume have written about grimmer aspects of Oz's "prophecies" but here we can at least heed Oz's reflections in the year of his death on the potential for a kibbutz "comeback" of sorts. To borrow Grumberg's phrase, it is surely worth extending that "quiet, moderate hope" to the ever-growing phenomenon of the urban kibbutz (*"irbutzim"*), both in Israel and North America.[24] As kibbutz scholar Yuval Dror concludes of such communities, they vigorously lay credence to the fact that, no matter how intensely individualist hedonism and materialism have transformed mainstream Israeli culture, a yearning for a meaningful life derived from a more collectivist ethos inherited from the past may yet endure in the youngest generation of Israelis. Moreover, the members of these communities may not succumb to the alienating pressures and stifling conformity that led many young people to abandon the traditional kibbutz in the 1970s.

Even wider manifestations of the kibbutz's enduring inspiration can be found in the fact that while Israel has not always been generous to the thousands of African migrants that have sought refuge there, there are African agricultural experts who have expressed profound admiration for the kibbutz system and are developing kibbutz-inspired communities, creating hundreds of new jobs in flourishing rural areas in South Sudan, Angola, Niger, and elsewhere. Dozens of young Africans in Israel have studied community development and strategies for economic and social independence as well as cooperative approaches that they intend to implement on the Israeli-style kibbutzim they established. For its part, Israel sent a delegation of IsraAID workers to Ethiopia and South Sudan to lend a helping hand.[25]

Finally, an important annual study conducted by Harvard suggests interesting trends in the progressive thinking of young Americans toward the economic systems governing their lives. For those who grew up during the Cold War, capitalism meant freedom from the Soviet Union and other totalitarian regimes. Yet for those born later, capitalism (especially under the duress of recent and perhaps future pandemics) starkly signifies a financial crisis from which the global economy still hasn't completely recovered and seems to them unsustainable.[26] Moreover, Harvard's questions accord with other recent research on how Americans think about capitalism and socialism.[27] Given our increasingly dire global climate emergency, the crisis of many post pandemic economies, and the widespread collapse of ecosystems, it seems clear that we may very well face the urgent prospect of designing a new human project, as economist Paul Mason forcefully argues, "based on reason, evidence and testable designs, that cuts with the grain of history and is sustainable by the planet."[28] Perhaps new variations on the old cooperative kibbutz model will yet emerge in forms as yet undreamt of but ultimately commensurate with Oz's humanistic vision.

Notes

1. As recalled by David Grossman, "Amos Oz Expressed the Painful Turbulence of Israeli Life." Translated by Danielle Harris. *The Guardian*, 5 Jan. 2020, https://www.theguardian.com/commentisfree/2020/jan/05/amos-oz-painful-turbulence-israeli-life-books.

2. Apropos of my comments in the Introduction to this volume, it may be tempting for some readers (as it has been for myself) to speculate whether the story's subtext constitutes a gender inversion of Galia and her father, a confession of sorts. Yet, if this characterization was Oz's conscious (or unconscious) attempt at a perhaps too subtle mea culpa, the fact is that Galia remained permanently estranged, her bitter unhappiness erupting into shocking accusations of abuse and an international scandal following the publication of her 2021 memoir *Something Disguised as Love.*

3. "A Room of One's Own: Amos Oz in Conversation with Shira Hadad." Translated by Sondra Silverston. *Granta*, vol. 145, 15 Nov. 2018, https://granta.com/a-room-of-ones-own/.

4. To be fair, that delay may owe in part to the fact that at the time Amos and his wife Nili had no money of their own, nor any reasonable expectation of being able to earn enough from Amos's writing: "We had nothing . . . and I had no profession: I was a high school teacher without a teaching license. . . . What could I have done? Perhaps Nili could have found a job as a librarian. . . . We were terrified. What could I do? I didn't know then that the day would come when I would earn money from writing books . . . I didn't even dream of it" ("A Room of One's Own").

5. Holtzman, Avner. "Strange Fire and Secret Thunder: Between Micha Josef Berdyczewski and Amos Oz." *Prooftexts*, vol. 15, 1995, pp. 145–62. Quotation appears on p. 149.

6. In Shula Keshet's comprehensive account of the resulting controversy she observes that "even urban workers displayed great interest in it, and worker's councils throughout the country invited the author to literary gatherings to discuss the book and its conclusions about life in the kibbutz. . . . Many kibbutzim convened meetings and discussions attended by [Maletz], which took the form of a kind of 'literary trial' of the work and its author alike" ("Kibbutz Fiction and Yishuv Society" 148). She cites a front-page article that appeared in the newspaper *Ha-Boker* under the banner headline ("Stormy Debates in Kibbutzim Over Maletz's Book"): "In the kibbutz settlements and the left-wing camp in general the book by Mr. D. Maletz . . . has generated a great storm. All the kibbutzim in the country have held, and are holding, literary trials of this book by one of the first members of the Third Aliyah [wave of immigration, 1919–23], who in his book has condemned the kibbutz. At Ein Harod a week-long literary trial was held at which the members of Faction B [Mapam] condemned the book and the author, whereas the members of Mapai defended it. At the same time many voiced complaints against Am Oved for publishing a book such as this that vilifies the kibbutz. The book, *Circles*, extensively discusses kibbutz life and its negative aspects. Its conclusion is that the individual in the kibbutz is repressed and dominated by those able to push their way forward. The Hashomer Hatza'ir kibbutzim have even banned its entry to them, and it has been declared one of the heretical books proscribed for reading in kibbutzim. Despite all the proscriptions, the book is in great demand and is being read extensively in the young kibbutzim." In "Kibbutz Fiction and Yishuv Society on the Eve of Statehood: The *Ma'agalot* (Circles) Affair of 1945." *Journal of Israeli History: Politics, Society, Culture*, vol. 31, no. 1, 2012, pp.147–65. Quotation appears on p. 149.

7. Maletz, David. *Ma'agalot*. Am Oved, 1945. *Young Hearts: A Novel of Modern Israel*. Translated by Solomon N. Richards. Schocken Books, 1950. Quotation appears on p. 182.

8. Intriguingly, in the Author's Note to his 1982 novel *Menuhah Nekhonah* (*A Perfect Peace*), perhaps in acknowledgement of Maletz's death the previous

year, Oz declares his indebtedness to the earlier writer's courageous example as both kibbutz lover and critic.

9. Pertinent examples of the few who have daringly imagined romantic relationships across the Jewish-Palestinian divide (they seem to appear once every decade or so though there are signs that this trend may be accelerating), include A. B. Yehoshua's classic *The Lover* (1977), Sami Michael's *A Trumpet In the Wadi* (1987), and recently Dorit Rabinyan's recent *All the Rivers* (2014), and if we include books by Israelis writing in English, Moriel Rothman-Zecher's *Sadness is a White Bird* (2018). In the country's current political and cultural climate, these are sometimes construed as too transgressive for the public good (would Yehoshua's famous novel featuring a pair of infatuated Arab and Jewish teens be required reading in Israeli schools as it once was?). Rabinyan's *All the Rivers*, a tender story exploring the relationship between a Palestinian male artist and an Israeli woman (its Hebrew title *Borderlife* seems more resonant), was banned from school curriculum by Israel's Education Ministry, a move that naturally led to soaring sales.

10. Alter, Robert. *Modern Hebrew Literature*. Behrman House, 1975. Quotation appears on p. 331.

11. Khoury, Jack and Maya Sela. "Amos Oz: Situation of Bedouin in Negev Is 'Ticking Time Bomb.'" *Haaretz*, 17 Aug. 2010, https://www.haaretz.com/1.5101538.

12. For more analysis of Oz's earliest kibbutz fiction see: Nehama Aschkenasy's discussion "The Biblical Intertext and the Dialogic Encounter: Between New and Old in Oz's Fiction" elsewhere in this volume; also: Omer-Sherman, Ranen. *Imagining the Kibbutz: Visions of Utopia in Literature and Film*. Penn State UP, 2015, pp. 67–103.

13. Shaked, Gershon. *Modern Hebrew Fiction*. Translated by Yael Lotan. Toby Press, 2000, pp. 124–25.

14. See Lanir, Niva. "Amos Oz Makes Room for His Loneliness." In this interview, Oz credits the kibbutz for teaching him "much of what I know about human nature" and that if he had spent those decades elsewhere "I would not have had the slightest chance of becoming so intimately acquainted with 300 souls."

15. See Lanir, Niva. "Amos Oz Makes Room for His Loneliness."

16. See Lanir, Niva. "Amos Oz Makes Room for His Loneliness."

17. It's worth noting a similar portrayal of paternalism in Yehoshua Kenaz's 1986 novel *Infiltration* where Alon, a haughty kibbutz soldier, disparages Mizrahi immigrants: "The army . . . is our only hope. Only the army can educate them, turn them into Israelis, until they're like us. They don't know the country outside their *maabarot*, they don't know its history, its beauty, its culture. When they bring them to their new settlements, they don't want to get off the trucks. They're not used to hard work and living in the country and farming. So how can we expect them to like our songs? The army has to educate them—at least the young ones because the old ones may as well be written off. The generation of the wilderness" (92). In *Infiltration*. Translated by Dalya Bilu. Zoland Books, 2003.

18. Here I take to heart one anonymous reader's illuminating remarks concerning the marked contrast "between the baroque style of the early stories [with their] blacks and whites and the late stories that display the weakness and strengths of individual characters. . . . David Dagan is a lecherous individual, but he is a good teacher and he is the one that helps Moshe Yashar integrate and not be marginalized. He may not understand him, but he wants what is best for him on his own terms."

19. Cf. Oz, in the 1990s, reflecting on the crucial nexus of ethics and language: "Each time and each place human beings are referred to as undesirable aliens, burdens or parasites, it's only a question of time before those humans will be actually persecuted. . . . It's always a certain distortion of language which heralds impending atrocities. Hence, the particular responsibility for the choice of words. . . . Precision is a value . . . The moment we are precise with our nouns, adjectives, verbs, and adverbs, we are closer to doing justice, in a small way. Not universal justice. Not international justice. But the way I describe a person, a mode of behavior or even an inanimate object, the closer I am to the essence, the more I evade either exaggeration or incitement. . . . Words are important because they are one of the main means by which humans do things to each other. Saying is doing." Meyer, Lisa. "Employing Language in the Service of Peace." *Los Angeles Times*, 28 January 1998, https://www.latimes.com/archives/la-xpm-1998-jan-28-ls-12760-story.html.

20. Oz, Amos and Shira Hadad. *What Makes an Apple? Six Conversations about Writing, Love, Guilt, and Other Pleasures*. Princeton UP, 2022, p. 105.

21. Oz himself later called *Where the Jackals Howl* (written in the wake of the infamous Lavon Affair), the work of a young man "filled with the joy that comes with slaughtering sacred cows: the kibbutz ethos, the myth of the 'Father of the Nation' and all that." But by 2018, he had acquired a more phlegmatic outlook: "Today, when I see a swarm of slaughterers eagerly attacking one old sacred cow, the kibbutz, I suddenly feel that I've moved slightly to the side of the cow. Not because I worship it; I remember very well how it kicked and how it stank. But at least it gave milk that wasn't half bad" ("A Room of One's Own").

22. Oz, Amos. "The Kibbutz at the Present Time." In *Under This Blazing Light*. Edited by N. de Lange. Cambridge UP, 1996, pp. 125–32. Quotation appears on p. 128.

23. Grumberg, Karen. "The Greatness of Smallness: Amos Oz, Sherwood Anderson, and the American Presence in Hebrew Literature." *Journal of Israeli History, Politics, Society and Culture*, vol. 39, 2020, https://www.tandfonline.com/doi/full/10.1080/13531042.2020.1834913. Quotation appears on p. 19.

24. In one of the best accounts of the latter phenomenon, Yuval Dror describes urban collectivities as representing "a completely different mode of kibbutz life" that successfully synthesize the most enduring ideals of the past with the norms of postmodern culture. In some respects, especially concerning education, they aspire to be more inclusive than the traditional kibbutz, striving

to overcome the elitism that once separated the kibbutz from the lesser affluent communities surrounding them: [T]hey are intimate manifestations . . . comprising a few dozen partners, not a large community of hundreds of people; they are communal (in a "modern" way that permits the use of external resources), but not privatized in a way that flaunts the original principles that harken to the kibbutz ethos; they are based on personal autonomy and choice with respect to ways of self-actualization and advancement less on collective needs and systemic and individual constraints; they are committed to community values as a whole, with communality and commitment complementing each other; they actually live in urban development areas, and do not turn into patronizing external sponsors for [limited] periods . . . and they are a society eager to learn together on a weekly basis, not only a community that enables individuals to study." In "The New Communal Groups in Israel: Urban Kibbutzim and Groups of Youth Movement Graduates." In Michal Palgi and Shulamit Reinharz, editors. *One Hundred Years of Kibbutz Life: A Century of Crises and Reinvention.* Transaction Publishers, 2011, pp. 315–24. Quotation appears on pp. 323–24.

25. Oz, Sheri. "Former Refugees Have a Dream: A Kibbutz in South Sudan." *Haaretz*, 28 Aug. 2013, https://www.haaretz.com/.premium-ex-refugees-with-a-kibbutz-dream-1.5326603. See also: Messika, Ilana. "Successful Israeli Firm Helps African Development by Exporting the Kibbutz Model." *YnetNews*, 2 May 2017, https://www.ynetnews.com/articles/0,7340,L-4956457,00.html.

26. Harvard Kennedy School Institute of Politics Fall 2018 National Youth Poll: https://iop.harvard.edu/fall-2018-national-youth-poll?utm_source=IOP+National+Press+List&utm_campaign=a0f35b66d9-EMAIL_CAMPAIGN_2018_10_24_07_31_COPY_04&utm_medium=email&utm_term=0_e352da6aa7-a0f35b66d9-87867141.

27. In recent years, the Pew Research Center has found that people ages eighteen to twenty-nine were frustrated with the free-market system. In their study, forty-six percent had positive views of capitalism, and forty-seven percent had negative views—and with regard to socialism, by contrast, forty-nine percent of the young people in Pew's poll had positive views, and just forty-three percent held negative views. Hartig, Hannah. "Stark Partisan Divisions in Americans' Views of 'Socialism,' 'Capitalism.'" *Pew Research Center*, 25 June 2019, https://www.pewresearch.org/fact-tank/2019/06/25/stark-partisan-divisions-in-americans-views-of-socialism-capitalism/.

28. Mason, Paul. "The End of Capitalism Has Begun." *The Guardian*, 17 July 2015, https://www.theguardian.com/books/2015/jul/17/postcapitalism-end-of-capitalism-begun.

Chapter 19

From Tragedy to Betrayal

Judas *and the Subversive Politics of Oz's Last Act*

Sam Sussman

I can't think for you, you'll have to decide / Whether Judas Iscariot had God on his side.

—Bob Dylan, "With God on Our Side"

Introduction

Amos Oz's trademark is tragedy. It permeates his novels and nonfiction, his personal life and political conviction.[1] Most importantly, it defined the story he told of the Israeli-Palestinian conflict—until his subversive final novel *Judas*. Oz's last novel is structured not by tragedy, but by its archetypical antithesis: betrayal. The novel tells the story of Shealtiel Abravanel, an Ottoman Jew whose family has lived in Jerusalem centuries before modern Zionism. After negotiating a life between the Palestinian elite and burgeoning Zionist community, Abravanel was banished from the Jewish leadership in 1948 for objecting to the establishment of a specifically Jewish state. Abravanel's story collapses the established categories of nearly all Oz's previous work: Jew and Palestinian, nation and state, the just war of 1948 and unnecessary occupation of 1967. Most provocatively, it voices a radical departure from the labor Zionist two-state paradigm for which Oz was considered the most eloquent advocate for fifty years. The conflict between *Judas* and the remainder of Oz's oeuvre has received little critical attention, even as it remains a central unresolved question in the legacy of Israel's most prominent novelist. Why did the foremost representative of Ashkenazi labor Zionism make the champion of his final novel a Palestinian Jew who questions the very premise of a Jewish state?

TRAGEDY

For the fifty years in which Amos Oz reigned as the most prominent spokesman of Labor Zionism and the two-state solution, beginning with the *Davar* essays in the aftermath of the 1967 War that established his as a national voice, he told a tragic story of the Israeli-Palestinian conflict that was as poetic as it was singular. Oz's tragic telling of the conflict made him a champion of the peace camp and Israel's humanistic spokesman to the world, while drawing ire from the right for his implicit apologetics and from the left for suggesting the lyricism of Palestinian suffering even as he justified its regrettable necessity.

Oz's tragic telling of the conflict is never more elegiac than in a childhood memory narrated in his memoir, *A Tale of Love and Darkness* (2002) in which eight-year-old Amos walks innocently through a garden of fruit trees and blue-tiled pools adorned with water lilies and golden fish. He is a guest in the villa of a Palestinian merchant in Sheikh Jarrah, invited by the improbable chance necessary to draw together an affluent Palestinian with the child of lower-middle class European Jewish immigrants. Amos's uncle, a minor postal bureaucrat, has resolved in the merchant's favor a troubling matter involving a missing envelope and an accused son. Amos's uncle treats the invitation to the al-Silwani villa "as if we were entrusted with a diplomatic mission." Young Amos is warned that "inappropriate behavior" might "exacerbate hostility during a period of anxiety about the danger of bloody warfare between two nations" (306). As he wanders the al-Silwani garden, Amos encounters a girl his age, Aisha, and her three-year-old brother, Awwad. Amos promptly bows "to dispel any prejudices and to advance the reconciliation between our two peoples." When he glimpses the girl's bare legs, Amos finds himself taken by a confounding union of erotic and national feeling. He wants desperately to explain "how pure our intentions were, how abhorrent was the plot to stir up conflict between our two peoples." The conversation proceeds awkwardly, mainly because it has not occurred to Amos that he does not speak Arabic. Aisha asks—in Amos's language—if there is any Hebrew poetry. He impulsively recites Tchernichovsky, Kipnes, Jabotinsky, "and one poem of my own." She asks if he can climb trees, and Amos obediently transforms himself "from Jabotinsky to Tarzan." Scampering high into a mulberry tree, his hands find a rusty chain linked to an iron ball, which Amos whirs impulsively about his head "uttering wild war-cries . . . the resplendent new Hebrew youth at the height of his powers." The rusty iron ball flies from its chain and strikes three-year-old Awwad unconscious (311–12).

The idyllic garden instantly metamorphosizes into a chaotic scene of violence, blame, and terror. Fifty years later Oz cannot remember how he came down from the tree, but he recalls a man striking Aisha "hard, repeatedly, with the flat of his hand, slowly, thoroughly, on her head, her back, her shoulder, across her face." Later Oz daydreams about a return visit to the villa in which he makes clear "to the al-Silwani family in particular and to the Arab people in general how sorry and ashamed and embarrassed we were" (317). But no apology ever comes. Soon after the incident, in autumn 1947, the United Nations recommends partition and "it was not sensible to go those areas anymore." No member of Oz's family ever mentions the incident again. Oz is left with a scar on his chin for the remainder of his life, and a "forbidden longing" for the garden from which he has been expelled.

Amos Oz's formative experience in the al-Silwani garden gifted him the metaphorical material to make sense of the Israeli-Palestinian conflict. In this telling, the young Hebrew gentleman enters the Palestinian garden with all intentions of being a proper guest. His Palestinian host intends him no harm, but nor does she understand his motives. With benevolent designs he seeks to highlight their shared passions (poetry, tree-climbing) even as he misunderstands her desires. Then inexplicable error results in catastrophic violence. The young Hebrew is left with a scratch on his chin—it requires stitches but is nonetheless a scratch—while a Palestinian son is struck unconscious, and his sister beaten for failing to protect him against the unforeseen. The pastoral garden is transformed by bloodshed and blame against the intentions of all involved.

Later in *A Tale of Love and Darkness* Oz furnishes his metaphor with historicity. Palestinians and Jews share a historical oppressor in Europe, he argues, who traumatized Palestinians by colonial exploitation and Jews by pogrom and Holocaust. The tragedy of the Israeli-Palestinian conflict is that

> when the Arabs look at us they see not a bunch of half-hys-
> terical survivors but a new offshoot of Europe . . . that has
> cleverly returned to the Middle East . . . to exploit, evict, and
> oppress. Whereas when we look at them we do not see fellow
> victims either, brothers in adversity, but somehow we see
> pogrom-making Cossacks, bloodthirsty antisemites, Nazis in
> disguise, as though our European persecutors have reappeared
> here in the Land of Israel, put keffiyehs on their heads and
> grown moustaches, but are still our old murderers interested
> only in slitting Jews' throats for fun (330).

The Israeli-Palestinian conflict is thus for Oz a tragedy of faultless mis-recognition, infused with Freudian repetition compulsion. Oz relied on this formulation from the 1967 essays in *Hadar* that transformed him into his generation's most celebrated advocate of the two-state solution through his final essays. The conflict, he insisted for fifty years, was a tragedy of "justice against justice" and "right against right" (*Dear Zealots* 128, *Blazing Light* 91).

For Amos Oz, tragedy represents not merely political analysis but personal affect. His parents came of age in Europe of the 1930s, and Oz's descriptions in *A Tale of Love and Darkness* of growing up in the shadow of their suffering is an extraordinary primary source on the transmission of intergenerational trauma. Each of his parents lost family in the Holocaust, and neither entirely assimilated in Jerusalem. His father Yehuda Aryeh dreamt of becoming a professor at the Hebrew University but toiled most of his life as a librarian in the Jewish National and University Library, writing passionate essays in comparative literature by night. Oz's charming, depressive mother Fania was an evening storyteller with a taste for the surreal and forbidden who yearned to become a writer before dying "of disappointment and longing." Oz's parents invested their emotional lives in the dream of a Jewish state, but even after the achievement of the State they remained literally and figuratively on the outskirts of Zion. For Yehuda and Fania, Zionism offered the Hobbesian minimum: bodily security, but not the creative lives to which they aspired. The distinction was too great for Fania to suffer; she took her own life when Amos was twelve. Fania could not outlive the Holocaust that murdered her friends and family and haunted her into the recesses of indelible depression. She was one of Hitler's six million no less than Yehuda's brother, David, who refused to believe that a multilingual professor of literature should leave a cosmopolitan European capital simply because of a few Nazi hooligans. He remained in Vilna to teach literature "and died of it."

A Tale of Love and Darkness thus situates young Amos's life within a tragically inverted dayenu. If it was not enough that the world of his parents' youth was extinguished by the Holocaust, still they had to suffer cultural displacement in a new homeland that never became home. If it was not enough that their hopes were stifled as the exiles frantically gathered in a Yishuv unable to absorb so many tongues and dreams, still after the achievement of the State their aspirations remained beyond reach. If it was not enough that the achievement of the Jewish state could neither redeem their past nor illuminate their future, still its creation came at the expense of another national people with whom the Jewish fate became violently intertwined. What made Oz his generation's foremost literary voice is the skill with which he set these familial misfortunes within his tragic narrative of the Israeli-Palestinian conflict.

Oz's tragic telling of the Israeli-Palestinian conflict is compelling literature. But what does this tragic formulation foreclose? The nature of tragedy in its Greek variation is that its subjects are deprived of agency. Oedipus's attempt to flee Corinth and evade his fate leads him to fulfill it. "No one has the power to run away from evils which the gods themselves present," Eteocles declares in Seven Against Thebes. As Walter R. Agard observed, there is not a single surviving Greek tragic text in which at least one character does not bemoan that life is shaped by divine rather than human will (1933). The cruelty of tragedy is that fate is presented through the deceptive prism of choice. Tragic subjects believe in their own agency because, as Prometheus brags in Prometheus Bound: "I stopped men thinking of their future deaths / Inside their hearts I put blind hope." Agamemnon can either sacrifice his daughter to secure safe passage to Troy, or subject his ships to divine wrath at sea. Either decision will undo him; like all subjects of Greek tragedy, he is free in no meaningful sense.

By way of contrast, in Oz's narrative of the Israeli-Palestinian tragedy it is historical trauma rather than divine will that deprives the conflict's subjects of agency. European Jews flee annihilation only to displace another people who have also suffered at European hands. Young Amos proceeds in innocence to the garden but leaves amidst violence he mistakenly caused. Just as Oedipus's attempt to flee Corinth and evade his fate leads him to fulfill it, Amos's desire to befriend Aisha leads to Palestinian injury. But was the Zionist leadership—which young Amos proudly imagines himself representing in the al-Silwani garden—truly bereft of agency in the events that led to the creation of the State? Was the Nakba the only conceivable historic possibility? Was it an eschatological necessity, a sanctification of God's name, as some Hasidim believe of the Holocaust? What historical alternatives and future possibilities did these events foreclose? If we understand the violence that birthed Israel through the lens of agency—of *betrayal*—rather than tragedy, what forbidden relations between Jews and Palestinians remain plausible in our own time? These are the questions Oz takes up in his provocative final novel.

BETRAYAL

Amos Oz's last novel, *Judas*, published in 2014 when he was seventy-five, is a radical attempt to account for the agency that tragedy forsakes. *Judas* centers on Shealtiel Abravanel, an Ottoman Jew whose family has lived in Jerusalem for centuries before modern Zionism, and whose life is upturned by his attempt to belong to both the Palestinian cultural elite and burgeoning Zionist community. Abravanel is both a Palestinian, fluent in Arabic and in conversation with Arab peers across the Middle East, and a Jewish nationalist, "a representative of the Jerusalem Sephardi aristocracy in the Zionist movement" (287). He is an articulate lawyer fluent in Hebrew, Arabic, Ladino, English, French, Turkish, and Greek, gifted in navigating the disparate worlds his multinational heritage opens to him. Throughout the tense 1930s and 1940s, Abravanel remains both well-respected throughout the Arab world, from Jerusalem to Damascus, and a valued leader of the Zionist Executive Committee and Council of the Jewish Agency.[2] But Abravanel dies "the most lonely and most hated man in Israel," "reviled by everyone . . . his Arab friends on the other side of the new borders" and not a single Jewish friend left (204, 187). The betrayal for which Abravanel suffers this fate is his opposition to David Ben-Gurion's declaration of a Jewish state in 1948.

Abravanel believes that the purpose of Zionism is to ensure that Jews—both Ottoman Jews like himself and European Jews fleeing persecution—can live in their historic homeland. Abravanel came of age in the multinational Ottoman Empire, and believes that Jewish and Palestinian nationalism can coexist so long as neither people make exclusive claims to a state that will rule over the other. Abravanel envisions "a conglomerate of two communities, with neither threatening the other's future." He imagines joint trade unions, neighborhoods, schools, and universities. He believes fiercely in "abandoning the pretentious idea of setting up a separate state for Jews with a Jewish army, Jewish rule, and attributes of sovereignty that would belong to the Jews, and to the Jews alone" (223). Crucially, this is not the one-statism of binationalist thinkers such as those associated with Brit Shalom.[3] Abravanel believes that Jews and Palestinians should retain communal self-determination within a shared political framework that ensures one community will not overpower the other. The fatal mistake of the Zionist leadership, he argues, is insensitivity to Palestinian fear of becoming subjects in a state designed for Jews. The Palestinian objection to Zionism, he believes, is not against Jewish presence in the land but rather to a state exclusively for Jews. If Zionism makes such a claim, Abravanel prophesizes, violent confrontation will ensure neither Jews nor Palestinians are ever at ease in their homeland. "Zionism," he believed, "could not be achieved by confrontation with the Arabs" (206).

For these convictions Abravanel is mocked by fellow Zionists as an "Arab lover" and "the Grand Mufti." When he objects to Ben-Gurion's declaration of the State, he is expelled from the Zionist leadership and publicly labeled a traitor. No newspaper will publish his resignation letter. Later the letter is vanished from the national archives; Abravanel's rivals ensure he will not belong to history. He retreats to his home on the outskirts of Jerusalem, where he claims to belong to "a small handful of true Zionists who were not intoxicated with nationalism." He observes with horror as the violence of 1947–49 leaves the land "covered with cemeteries and strewn with the ruins of hundreds of wretched villages" (185–86). He dies over a morning newspaper.

Judas takes place more than a decade after Abravanel's death, in the winter of 1959–60. His argument with Ben-Gurion now seems from another century. The war has solidified Jewish support for the State, and the multinational ideas for which Abravanel sacrificed his name are no longer recognizable even to Israeli leftists. The new generation is typified by Shmuel Ash, a scraggly member of the Socialist Renewal Group who is quick to the tongue with "what Kropotkin said about Nechayev," but is never sure what the landlord wants from him. Shmuel has come of age in an Israel in which there was little discussion of the expulsion of Palestinians that made way for a Jewish state, except for the conventional wisdom that violence was an unpleasant necessity. Shmuel encounters Abravanel's history only through a series of events as fortuitous as those that drew young Amos into the al-Silwani garden. Jilted by his girlfriend, cut off by his struggling parents, frustrated by his doctoral research on Jewish views of Jesus, Shmuel comes to the Abravanel home after seeing an oblique advertisement for room, board, and pay for a humanities student "with an interest in history." Shmuel spends the next months in the alternative temporality of the Abravanel home, clumsily falling in love with Abravanel's widowed daughter, Atalia, caring for her aging father-in-law, Gershom Wald, and slowly learning Abravanel's obscured history.

Oz's work is often marked by generational disjunction, in early short story and novella collections such as *Where the Jackals Howl* and *The Hill of Evil Counsel* no less than in mature classics like *A Tale of Love and Darkness*. His treatment of Shmuel Ash's disbelief that Abravanel could have objected to the Jewish state in which Shmuel came of age is among the most sharply written of these generational schisms. Shmuel was thirteen in 1948; his political consciousness has been shaped by the statehood Abravanel sought to prevent. At stake in their conflicting views is not a generational difference in relating to Hebrew, Europe, kibbutz labor, or the sound of the jackal, but rather to the very purpose of Zionism. "How," Shmuel asks, "could someone who did not believe in a Jewish state have possibly called himself a Zionist?" How could anyone think the War of Independence was not a necessity? Was Abravanel, Shmuel would like to know, simply "a dreamer?" (185).

Atalia is unforgiving as custodian of her father's view: "You wanted a state. Flags and uniforms and banknotes and drums and trumpets. You shed rivers of innocent blood. You sacrificed an entire generation. You drove hundreds of thousands of Arabs out of their homes. You sent ship-loads of Holocaust survivors straight from the quayside to the battlefield. All so that there would be a Jewish state" (183). To Atalia, Abravanel was a pragmatist, the only Jewish leader who cared to understand Palestinian and Arab interlocutors, to know their language and envision a future acceptable to each community. Ben-Gurion was the dreamer, Atalia insists, convinced Jews could live in their homeland despite a war that would leave Palestinians living "day by day with the disaster of their defeat," while the Jews "live night by night with the dread of their vengeance" (185–86). Once war broke out, Abravanel believed, each side would be too traumatized to remember that they had once lived as civic neighbors. The grieving Wald lurks as a morose reminder of this prophecy. He knows his son would not have fought and died in 1948 but for Wald's own talk of "a sacred war . . . I took him myself and led him up to Mount Moriah . . . I programmed him. Not just me. All of us" (176–78). Wald tries to believe his son died so Israel might live, but when others say these words to him "Shealtiel's ghost makes them stick in my throat" (179). Wald can neither accept that his son died heroically for Israel nor believe that his death was in vain. Muted by grief, he never speaks of Micha, just as Amos Oz's family never speaks of the al-Silwanis. It is too psychically expensive to consider that the war for a Jewish state might have been a mistake rather than a necessity.

Shmuel can make sense of none of this. For him, a Jewish state was always the ambition of Zionism and the Nakba was an unfortunate accessory to this historical inevitability. The generational chasm that separates Shmuel and Abravanel has not resulted from accident, but political design. In Nachman Ben-Yehuda's masterful study of betrayal, he argues that accusations of betrayal are essential to demarcating the norms of any new social order (102). This is because the morality of betrayal is always subject to our own values. Accusations of betrayal draw controversy precisely because the accused—Paris and Helen, or Edward Snowden—provoke debate about the worthiness of their cause (true love, libertarian freedom). Benedict Arnold is a hero to the British cause and a villain to the American cause; how we judge his betrayal is subject to our beliefs about the legitimacy of each. Unlike tragedy, which relies on the deprivation of agency, betrayal centers on the charge of intentionally acting against the best interest of those who have reason to trust otherwise.

In Ben-Yehuda's account, new social orders require accusations of betrayal to define emerging moral and political boundaries. The Zionist movement once welcomed Abravanel as a spokesman for the Jerusalem Sephardi aristocracy, but the declaration of a Jewish state demands that he relinquish his Arab identity. His refusal to do so leads the Zionist leadership not only to silence Abravanel, but to write him out of Zionist history so completely that a mere decade later his identity and ideology are illegible to a new generation. To recall the shared Arab-Jewish past is, in the new social order, to become a Judas.

Judas relentlessly draws attention to the ways in which Abravanel's Ottoman Jewish identity is at odds with the Ashkenazi Israel that has been built over his objection. The Abravanel family home itself is situated in a landscape unrecognizable to Shmuel. When he first sees the home, he is struck that it does not resemble the new commercial buildings of downtown Jerusalem but is rather "sunk almost to its windows in the heavy earth." Shmuel perceives the Abravanel home as far from "the inhabited regions" of Jerusalem, although it is near the depopulated Palestinian villages of Sheikh Badr' and Deir Yassin (13). In the Abravanel home the food of choice is always fruit, yogurt, or tea. When Shmuel ventures out for sausages and fried eggs, Oz repeatedly describes the restaurant in which he eats as "Hungarian." When Shmuel meets a Jewish Israeli, it is usually with a European addendum: a speaker with "a distinct Romanian accent" (197), "a Viennese accent" (213), or who "came originally from a small town near Frankfurt." Abravanel's neighbor is named Sarah de Toledo. On Atalia's thirteenth birthday, Abravanel gives her an anthology of Middle Eastern poetry "in the hope that this book will explain to you where we are living" (281). Objects, too, are conscious of their origin. An Israeli café patron reads "a newspaper attached to a wooden stick, as was the custom in cafes in prewar Europe" (212), while Abravanel's sofa is adorned with "embroidered Arab cushions" and his desk is in the style of an Arab secretaire.

The novel's emphasis on the differences between Abravanel's Ottoman identity and the European Jewish society emerging around him never functions to undermine Abravanel's Jewishness. "Abravanel" is one of the most historic Sephardi names, which can be traced to prominent Jewish figures on the Iberian peninsula in the Middle Ages, and, some argue, to the Davidic court.[4] The house sunken into the earth is on Rabbi Elbaz Lane.[5] On its rusted iron arch is a Star of David. The Abravanel family home evokes a relationship to the land defined not by the apparatus of a state but rather its place in a shared social landscape both Jewish and Palestinian. The home once regularly hosted Palestinian and Arab public figures, union leaders, teachers, and intellectuals from Jerusalem, Cairo, and Damascus (205). But Abravanel's identity as an Ottoman Jew is one European Zionists cannot understand. His political opponents circulate rumors that his grandfather was an Arab, seemingly unable to comprehend that Abravanel is both Arab and Jewish. His is an identity the emerging order cannot easily tolerate. A specifically Jewish state defined by conflict with the Arab "other" requires Ottoman Jews to relinquish their non-Jewish identities. By insisting that Abravanel is a traitor and casting him from the history of Zionism itself, the architects of the nascent Jewish state ensure that Shmuel Ash's generation is never burdened by considering whether there was an alternative to a Jewish state and the expulsions of Palestinians required to achieve it. That Shmuel can make no sense of Abravanel's identity or ideology suggests the success of these ideological revisions. Shmuel is occasionally sympathetic to Abravanel's views, espe-cially that the conflict cannot be ended by Jewish military might alone (106), but he cannot understand how Abravanel believed that history could have justly culminated in anything other than a Jewish state. What, he asks throughout the novel, can it possibly mean for a Zionist not to believe in a Jewish state?

This question lingers through *Judas* as much as it shadows contemporary debate about Israel-Palestine. Oz returns his answer through a theological metaphor that culminates in defense of a Zionism deeply different from the one he spent his career articulating. Shmuel Ash is a failed doctoral student in Jewish views of Christianity, and no Biblical figure interests him more than Judas. For Shmuel, the story of Judas does not cohere. If he was a wealthy landowner, why would he betray Jesus for thirty pieces of silver? If Jesus was well-known in Jerusalem, why would Judas need to identify him with his infamous kiss? Embattled, accused, relegated to harsh historical judgment, Judas deserves—as Shmuel sees it—revisionist treatment. Shmuel imagines a radical alternative to the conventional story. He believes Judas is sent to infiltrate Jesus's inner circle and determine whether he is a threat or lunatic. But once in his company, Judas is taken by Christ's word. He believes he must orchestrate a miracle that will demonstrate Jesus's divinity. Judas campaigns for Christ's crucifixion. The Romans believe Jesus is "simply a demented beggar, sick with God like all the Jews." It occurs to no one to crucify him. Judas urges otherwise, claiming Christ is organizing an uprising against Roman rule (268). For his plan to succeed, Judas must lure Jesus to Jerusalem. Christ has no interest. He would prefer to remain "a mere Galilean healer traveling from village to village." Relentlessly Judas insists: you are the Son of God and must reveal yourself. Jesus fears the Romans and doubts his divinity; Judas's faith that Christ will survive the crucifixion is greater than Christ's faith in himself. So when Judas gives Christ to the Romans, it is an act not of betrayal but of faith.

Both Judas and Abravanel are cast out as traitors, Judas to Christ and Abravanel to Zionism. But as Judas believed in Christ more than Christ himself, so too does Abravanel believe in Zionism more than its official statesmen. Unlike Ben-Gurion, Abravanel is not willing to risk a war that threatens to uproot the Jewish community that has lived in Ottoman Palestine for centuries. Declaring a Jewish state means such a war with Palestinians, and so for Zionism to succeed it has to surrender any notion of an exclusive Jewish state, just as for Christianity to succeed Christ had to surrender his life. As Christ gained his life by sacrificing it, so too would Zionism achieve its deeper purpose: a homeland for Jews in historic Israel. The stakes of this disagreement could not be greater, as the victor will decide whether the emerging political order is an exclusive nationalist state or a multinational community shared between Jews and Palestinians.

This is a radically different story of the Israeli-Palestinian conflict than the tragic formulation Oz articulated for fifty years. No claim is more axiomatic in the Ozian canon than the justice of a Jewish state. Until *Judas*, the Israel of Oz's literature was almost exclusively Ashkenazi, with the rare Mizrahi character typically marked by philistine messianism, such as Michel of *Black Box* (1987) or the clamoring chorus who scold Oz on a visit to Beit Shemesh in his reportage collection *In the Land of Israel* (1983). Abravanel's convictions—his faith in a multinational Zionism committed to both Jewish and Palestinian autonomy in a shared federal state—represent political possibilities never entertained in Oz's oeuvre. Abravanel's vision is frustrated not because of faultless tragedy, but rather because Ben-Gurion's nationalism betrays Abravanel's multinationalism, and the Ashkenazi Zionist movement betrays centuries of Ottoman Jewish life in its homeland. But the most significant betrayal of *Judas* was surely committed by Oz himself in composing a final novel so deeply at odds with the ideas that defined his intellectual legacy.

In considering *Judas*'s place in Oz's legacy, it is essential to ask: are the ideas that animate *Judas* merely the utopian musings of an aging idealist, or a genuine political alternative rooted in the history of Zionism, one that has been—like Abravanel himself—silenced by history?

HISTORICITY

It is seductive to assume that the categories of the present—Jew, Palestine, nation, state—also governed the past. In 1850, decades before modern Zionism, more than ten thousand Jews lived in the four holy cities then in the Ottoman Empire: Jerusalem, Safed, Tiberias, and Hebron.[6] As an urban community, Ottoman Jews were intimate with Muslim neighbors. Jacob Yehoshua's memoir *Jerusalem in Days of Old*, set before the First World War, describes Jews and Muslims living in the same buildings, sharing public baths, interwoven by commerce, medicine, and family friendships. Ottoman Jews spoke Arabic and shared with Muslim and Christian neighbors not only a city but a nation. The Ottoman regime was a multinational civic empire in which the aspirations of citizens with distinct religions, ethnicities, and mother tongues were moderated by a shared public sphere (Campos 2011). The empire's 200,000 Jewish citizens were hardly spared discrimination but were largely granted civil rights and communal autonomy within the millet system, which offered cultural self-determination for the empire's various national communities.[7] Civic identity was thus often composed of multiplicitous identities: Jew, Arab, Jerusalemite, Ottoman. In his day there would have been many Abravanels.[8] Such varied identities shaped not only Ottoman Jewish but also Ottoman Palestinian identity. As Rashid Khalidi argues in *Palestinian Identity*, Palestinians in the Ottoman era held many simultaneous identities, including national, local, religious, familial. The story of the modern Israeli-Palestinian conflict is the story of the transformation of these multiplicitous identities into binary ethnocentric categories (Jewish Israeli, Palestinian Arab).

By 1914, after the first two aliyot, the Jewish population in Ottoman Palestine had grown to between eighty and ninety thousand, one-seventh of the population (Jacobson 108). Ashkenazi immigrants embarked on ways of life distinct from Ottoman Jews. While Ottoman Jews lived near Palestinian neighbors in urban centers, many Ashkenazim settled in kibbutzim on the rural coastal plains. Ottoman Jews were citizens of the empire, while Ashkenazi immigrants usually retained European citizenships and were protected by foreign consuls under negotiated capitulations. For Ottoman Jews, the refusal of Ashkenazi immigrants to take Ottoman citizenship or learn Arabic threatened to draw charges of betrayal against the entire Jewish community. In her comprehensive study of Ottoman Jewish newspapers between 1912–14, historian Abigail Jacobson found that a major concern of the community's public discourse was that, in an echo of Abravanel, Ashkenazim did not understand that "Jewish life in Palestine was subject to co-operation with the Arab community" (126). Ottoman Jews advocated for Ashkenazi immigrants to learn Arabic, replace their European citizenship with Ottoman citizenship, and build meaningful relationships with their non-Jewish neighbors.

The Ottoman Jewish community's belief in "Ottomanization" did not detract from enthusiasm for Zionism. As a minority within a multinational empire, Ottoman Jews were eager to invigorate Jewish political consciousness. The most prominent Palestinian Sephardic newspaper, *ha-Herut*, transitioned from Ladino to Hebrew in the 1910s in the belief that a shared language could build Jewish political power within the Ottoman framework, uniting Jewish communities from Palestine to Salonica in shared advocacy for increased cultural and educational autonomy. But few Ashkenazim were interested in Ottomanization. Many had fled Russian pogroms and were more drawn to politics of self-defense than mutual national accommodation. Ashkenazi newspapers in the same period emphasized a separatist politics that advocated strengthening the immigrant Jewish community. As Jacobson summarizes, "Only after the establishment of the Jews in Palestine as a national community would the co-operation and settlement with the Arabs be possible" (125).

One of the few Ashkenazim who argued for Ottomanization was a charismatic journalist named David Ben-Gurion. In the Ottoman Empire, Ben-Gurion argued, the Jews "have enjoyed national rights" for hundreds of years (Shumsky 190). Ben-Gurion wanted Jewish immigrants to engage in this political system "as both state [Ottoman] citizens and as Jews" (182). This meant renouncing European citizenships and becoming Ottoman citizens so as to end "all of the abnormality of our foreignness" (186). When the Empire abolished the capitulations that had permitted Jews to live under the protection of European citizenship, Ben-Gurion celebrated in pointedly patriotic terms: the day "should be given a place in Ottoman history" beside the Young Turk Revolution, which restored constitutional parliamentary rule (184). Ben-Gurion believed that the Ottoman frame-work, which promised Jews both civil equality and national self-rule, offered a brighter future even than the United States, where "there is only one spirit, the spirit of Anglo-Saxon culture" (194). He understood the difference between liberal equality and national self-determination and believed that Jewish survival depended on the latter.

Judas does not specify when Ben-Gurion and Abravanel came to know one another, but through the twentieth century's early decades they would have had a great deal in common. Each was shaped by the age of liberalizing empires in which he came of age. When Ben-Gurion argued for Ottoman Zionism he was following the ethos of the day, in which national communities sought self-determination not through homogeneous states that linked nation, state, and territory, but rather through self-governance within the multinational Ottoman, Russian, and Austro-Hungarian empires. Polish nationalism, for example, argued for increased self-determination within the Russian and Austro-Hungarian empires, but did not suppose that this required securing a specific territory over which a Polish state would cultivate Polish nationhood while governing exclusively Polish people. As Hebrew University historian Dmitry Shumsky argues in his 2018 book *Beyond the Nation-State*, many of the most influential early Zionist leaders—Leon Pinsker, Theodor Herzl, Ahad Ha'am, Vladimir Jabotinsky, and David Ben-Gurion—followed nationalist leaders of this era in aspiring to autonomy within the Ottoman Empire rather than an independent Jewish state. In Herzl's 1902 novel *Altneuland* the Jewish state is a region of the Ottoman Empire. Jabotinsky imagined a federal state that coordinated between national communities, and consistently referred to the Austro-Hungarian empire as a model. Critiquing the Balfour Declaration, Ahad Ha'am argued that "the land's different nations can ask no more than national freedom in their internal affairs, while the leadership of matters pertaining to everyone in the land must be determined by all the 'heads of household' together" (94). He compared this future political system to Swiss federalism.

The two decades after the end of the First World War brought severe political pressure to those who imagined a future accommodating Jewish and Palestinian national aspirations. The dissolution of the Ottoman Empire, paired with the Balfour Declaration, exacerbated the nationalist tensions against which Ottoman Jews had warned. Ottoman Zionists like Abravanel increasingly lost their voice in public affairs. *Ha-Herut* went out of publication in 1917, when its editor, Hayyim Ben-Attar, followed his Ottoman patriotism into the imperial army. Ottoman Palestine was home to one of history's most diverse Jewish societies—Sephardic and Ashkenazi, Ottoman and European, fluent in Arabic, Hebrew, Ladino, and European tongues—but by 1929 violence in Hebron[9], Safed, and Jerusalem consolidated Jews in Mandate Palestine into one national community under the authority of the (largely Ashkenazi) Zionist leadership. Through the 1930s, Jews in Mandate Palestine continued to build the separatist political and economic institutions that just two decades ago Ottoman Jews had vigorously opposed.

Against the background of this escalating nationalist violence Ben-Gurion argued for a federative solution. In 1931, he published a political blueprint that became the official Mapai platform, in which a shared federal government oversaw Jewish and Palestinian cantons that ensured national autonomy in education, culture, and language. It is not difficult to imagine a historical Abravanel as an ally of Ben-Gurion in this period. But while Abravanel was thoroughly committed to multinational politics in the Ottoman tradition, Ben-Gurion saw federalism as the solution to a specific political dilemma. The Zionist movement wanted neither to live as a minority under democratic institutions dominated by an Arab majority, nor to be seen as opposing democratic rule. Federalism was one way to resolve this dilemma, at least until a Jewish majority could be established

(Lin 20). So while Abravanel and Ben-Gurion might have appeared as ideological allies until the mid-1930s, the tumultuous following decade would turn their respective political camps against one another.

Ben-Gurion argued publicly for a multinational confederation until 1937, when the Peel Commission endorsed partition to create a Jewish-majority state. As late as February 1937, at the Thirty-Fifth Zionist Labor Federation Council, Ben-Gurion declared: "Arab residents of the land deserve all the civil rights, all the political rights, not just as individuals but also as a national collective, just like the Jews of Palestine" (Shumsky 207). But after the Peel Commission recommended partition in July 1937, Ben-Gurion stopped speaking of federalism and Arab national rights. Instead, he advocated "communal equality" and "communal autonomy," terms suddenly and suspiciously bereft of national prowess (213). The Peel Commission legitimized what the Zionist left had thought politically unpalatable: partition and population transfer in service of a specifically Jewish state. This possibility presented itself as Britain considered new Jewish immigration restrictions, under pressure from prospective Arab allies whom it needed to court against Italy's increasingly aggressive maneuvers in the Mediterranean. These restrictions were doubly dangerous, as they both undermined the prospect of a Jewish majority in Palestine and abandoned Jews desperate to flee Europe's descent into violent antisemitism (Lin 166–201). In a fierce speech in May 1938, Ben-Gurion argued that if Zionism could not achieve a solution to the problem of Europe's embattled Jews, it would soon be seen as an irrelevant political movement.

It was both the moral urgency and political opportunity of the escalating crisis of European antisemitism that would definitively turn Ben-Gurion from federative to nationalist solutions. By 1940, it was apparent that millions of displaced European Jews would never return home. The Polish and Czech governments-in-exile made clear their intent to expel much of their prewar Jewish population. The postwar period would see, in Chaim Weizmann's words, "the greatest mass migrations in the history of mankind as a result of Jewish homelessness" (Rubin 174). Ben-Gurion believed this mass migration fundamentally altered the scope and ambition of Zionism. In 1941 he wrote in *Notes on Zionist Policy* that rather than "a spiritual center in Palestine, effected through moderate Jewish immigration," Zionism now required a Jewish state achieved through mass migration. This meant rethinking the delicate balance with Palestinian neighbors: "The immediate need of the Jews for a country of their own is not to be measured by the number of Arabs who happen to be in Palestine, but by the number of Jews—many times greater—who have been completely and hopelessly uprooted from many countries of the Diaspora." Neighboring Arab countries were "too sparsely populated" and therefore "will be rather helped than hindered if they were willing to absorb the whole or part of the Palestinian Arab population." In 1942, Ben-Gurion admitted that while "I was one of those who strongly advocated parity between Jews and Arabs under the British Mandate," it had been under the assumption that Jews would remain a minority (Rubin 173–77). With the possibility of a majority Jewish state, the rationale for federation lost its allure.

The crisis of European antisemitism also eroded Ben-Gurion's last moral justification for federalism. He believed in a reciprocal liberal multinationalism: if the Palestinian nation was respected in a federal state shared with Jews, this would ensure the members of the Jewish nation were respected abroad. Jabotinsky shared this view. Rather than welcome the Peel Commission recommendation for a Jewish-majority state, he worried that the mutual ethnic cleansing that might accompany partition would be an "instructive precedent" of how European nations would treat their Jews (Shumsky 167). But European nations did not need to wait on events in Mandate Palestine to dispose of their Jewish citizens. As Ben-Gurion learned of the Holocaust, his determination to build an exclusively Jewish state vanquished any lingering commitment to federalism. If Jews were being eliminated from other nation-states, they needed—he argued—their own. The Biltmore Program, which Ben-Gurion guided through the Zionist General Council in October 1942, made no reference to Palestinian national rights. The historic realignment between nation, state, and territory demanded nothing less. "We are on the cusp," Ben-Gurion wrote, "of a new era in human history: the state is spreading its wings over more and more of those living in its borders, that is the central fact of our time. . . . For hundreds of years, the Jews comprised a kind of state within a state: in their social life, in their professions, in their manners, in their religious rituals. In the modern state, this uniqueness—both economic and spiritual—is increasingly threatened, and there is a doubt as to whether the Jewish people would continue to exist as the Jewish people without its own state framework" (Shumsky 218). One can hear Abravanel's objections. Simply because Europe has gone mad with nationalism does not mean Jews should imitate the act.

It was precisely the brutal nationalism of the 1930s that turned Abravanel against the idea of a Jewish state, just as it was turning Ben-Gurion toward it. As Wald tells Shmuel, Abravanel's opposition to a Jewish state intensified as he witnessed growing nationalist violence: "the Arab revolt in 1936, Hitler, the underground movements, the retaliation operations of the Jewish underground, the hangings by the British" (*Judas* 185). Wald remembers an evening in those days when Abravanel returned home from a tense meeting with Ben-Gurion at the Jewish Agency office and declared his one-time friend "a false messiah" (226). For Abravanel, Zionism was a "secular, pragmatic, modern movement" necessary to protect persecuted European Jews without betraying the delicate social landscape in which Ottoman Jews and Palestinians had long lived together. Ben-Gurion's decision to steer Zionism away from liberal multinationalism and toward Jewish nationalism was "deliberate exploitation" that could only lead to escalating conflict. "One day," Abravanel warned, the "irrational energies" of nationalism "will sweep away everything Zionism sought to achieve" by causing war that denies both Jews and Palestinians the peaceful enjoyment of their homeland.

Abravanel's concern was not merely that Jewish nationalism would lead to inexorable conflict in Palestine but that the violent nationalism of the 1930s would lead to inexorable conflict across the world. "Abravanel was never impressed by nationalism," Atalia lectures Shmuel. "At all. Anywhere. He was totally unimpressed by a world divided into hundreds of nation-states, like rows and rows of separate cages in a zoo" (184). In our age of nation-states, Abravanel's words may sound like poetic idealism. But they are the earnest ideals of a liberal intellectual who lived through the age of empires and the age of nations, and by the late 1940s had every reason to prefer the first.

Following Nachman Ben-Yehuda's notion that accusations of betrayal mark new political orders, this historical context reveals how essential Abravanel's ostensible betrayal was to the creation of the Jewish state. By publicly accusing Abravanel of betraying Zionism, the founders of the State make clear the terms of the new political order. Theirs will be a Jewish state in which any other identities are subordinate to Jewish nationalism. Ottoman Jews must relinquish their Arab identity and assimilate to the European Jewish society that has been built around their own, a demand soon to be imposed on the eight hundred thousand Mizrahi immigrants who fled Arab nations for Israel (Shohat 1988). The Jewish state requires a Jewish majority and will tolerate sympathy neither for the Palestinians it expels nor the Jews who argue that there are other political possibilities. One of the essential beliefs in the new order is that there is no alternative path: the Jewish state Ben-Gurion births will not be able to suffer the multinational potentialities he spent three decades advocating. Abravanel's very existence as an Arab Zionist is an act of betrayal against the new Jewish state. Ben-Gurion's purging of Abravanel is thus also a purging of his own multinational past, and that of the Zionist movement. But the irony of Abravanel's ostensible betrayal is that he is the only Zionist leader whose mind has not changed. He remains committed to a liberal multi-national future, while Ben-Gurion and his disciples forge an ethnic state that betrays the Ottoman Jews and Palestinians who have lived together through the Ottoman centuries. It is a palace coup so complete that had it not happened it would have had to be invented.

But why was Amos Oz the novelist to invent it? Why did Oz—child and champion of the Jewish state, prophet of the two-state solution, spokes-man of the Ashkenazi labor Zionist elite—choose to revive Abravanel's lost multinational legacy in his last literary act?

Uchronia

For fifty years Amos Oz was renowned as the most articulate advocate of the Jewish state and the two-state solution, the leading literary voice of his generation's Ashkenazi elite. So why then does his last novel take as its hero a Palestinian Jew whose critique of Israel's very founding is so radical that, like Abravanel, it has been silenced by history?

Perhaps it is not so difficult to glimpse dimensions of Oz in Abravanel: a public intellectual with literary and political gifts, so often decried as traitorous in his time. "You were never afraid to be called a traitor," said Israel's president and Oz's childhood friend, Reuven Rivlin, in eulogizing Oz. But Oz shares far more with the less charismatic of *Judas*'s protagonists, the addled Shmuel Ash. Both Amos and Shmuel are born to lower-middle class Eastern European immigrants who live on the figurative margins of Jewish Palestine. Shmuel is born in Kiryat Motskin, near Haifa, in a shack built by his father (*Judas* 89). This birthplace bears almost verbatim resemblance to the one-room "tumbledown hut in a field of thistles behind Kiryat Motskin" built by Oz's grandfather after he arrived penniless in Mandate Palestine in 1933, the year after Shmuel's parents (*Tale* 157, 180). Both Shmuel's and Amos's families believe through the 1930s that a Jewish state will redeem them from exodus. But when it is achieved, the Jewish state resolves the disappointments of neither family. Both Amos and Shmuel grow up as solitary children painfully conscious of the trauma and blunted aspirations of immigrant parents. The emotions of each cramped household are inescapably intimate. Shmuel sleeps in a "low-ceilinged passageway" between the kitchen and toilet, bracketed by walls sooty from the paraffin heater and beneath a damp ceiling, "staring at the cobwebs above" (*Judas* 129, 91). Amos grew up "in a tiny, low-ceilinged ground-floor flat" in which his parents' bedroom doubled as study, library, dining room and living room, as in Shmuel's home (*Tale* 1). As children, both Amos and Shmuel find solace from a silent mother and sloganeering father in intellectual adventure. Each is as diminutive as he is cerebral, more at home in imagined adventures than everyday practicalities.

For both Shmuel and Amos, the emotional suffocation of the home is mirrored by the public anxiety of the turbulent 1930s. Nowhere was this tension greater than in the two cities in which Amos and Shmuel were raised, Jerusalem and Haifa. Shmuel's childhood is interrupted by street fighting and mob violence. Amos hears routine gossip about the coming destruction of the Jewish community in Mandate Palestine. Apart from his visit to the al-Silwani villa, and a single shopping trip gone wrong, Amos never ventures beyond the Jewish quarters of the city into "the other Jerusalem . . . the alien, silent, aloof, shrouded Jerusalem, the Abyssinian, Muslim, pilgrim, Ottoman city . . . a secretive, malign city pregnant with disaster," "a veiled city"—both "menacing yet fascinating." Neither the Jerusalem of Oz's childhood nor the Haifa of Shmuel's can remember Jacob Yehoshua's Jerusalem, in which Ottoman citizens both Muslim and Jewish share public baths and housing compounds. The multinational politics that shaped Abravanel are unimaginable to Amos and Shmuel's generation. Shmuel becomes a passionate leftist who composes letters in his head chastising Ben-Gurion for compromising the humanist socialism of his youth, an act that strikingly mirrors Oz's youthful polemics in *Davar*. But Shmuel takes for granted the specifically Jewish state in which he comes of age (119). Atalia recognizes these limitations because she has observed the Jewish left evolve into them. "You may be a revolutionary, a socialist, a rebel," she tells Shmuel, "but you're still one of them" (183).

Shmuel should be the ideal receptacle for Abravanel's beliefs, a student of Jewish views of Jesus with an aspiration for universal love. But the events that separate his generation from Abravanel's have left a chasm too wide to cross. "Feel free to listen to what I'm saying," Wald tells Shmuel in their first encounter, "but a young man like you no doubt inhabits a totally different planet" (19). Even Shmuel himself, wondering what happened to Abravanel, asks, "What good will it do you to know?" (45). Shmuel spends every evening in immersive conversation with Wald and Atalia, but *Judas* is largely an exercise in the futility of generational transmission. By the end of the novel he still cannot understand how Abravanel could have been a Zionist without believing in a Jewish state. Wald and Atalia often allude to other young men who came through the house and left no wiser, and Atalia speaks with alienation of a generation "full of young men with thick voices and thick arms who were all, without exception, war heroes in the Palmach or the trenches" (275). In the months Shmuel stays in the Abravanel home he often wanders Jerusalem, coming up against the harsh borders of the divided city: rusty barbed wire, concrete walls, depopulated no man's land (194). But he is rarely able to consider the intellectual borders of his time. As Shmuel leaves the Abravanel home in the first months of 1960, gifted the knowledge of Abravanel's buried history and the alternative political possibilities it implies, Atalia offers him a blue jug of Hebron glass that was once given to Abravanel from a Palestinian friend. "I expect you'll break it," she tells Shmuel. "Or lose it. Or forget who gave it to you" (292). When he leaves the Abravanel home, Shmuel takes a bus to a development town, the most blunt symbol of the new Israel that is rapidly replacing the one Abravanel knew.

Amos Oz argued for a two-state peace twenty-five years before official diplomacy between Israel and the Palestine Liberation Organization, in the early 1990s. But Oz was never able to publicly suggest that Jews and Palestinians could do better than an amicable divorce. Something had already been lost by the time Shmuel Ash left the Abravanel home in March 1960, "the fields and hillsides covered in a dark green carpet dappled in places with rain flowers," and walked past the emptied Palestinian village of Sheikh Badr' on his way to a development town in the Negev (290–91). Read as a bookend to Oz's career—set before its beginning, written at its end—*Judas* is as intellectually honest a farewell as Oz might compose, one that speaks not to mute convictions he never found a way to voice, but rather to an aging novelist's self-awareness of the political possibilities foreclosed to his generation. Oz never renounced the political beliefs that defined his intellectual career, and that he subjects to withering critique in *Judas*. He offered no Abravanelean resignation letter, only the doubts that linger so forcefully in his final novel.

By the time Oz wrote *Judas*, in the twenty-first year of the ostensibly five-year Oslo process, and in a sixth decade of occupation and settlement growth, it was clear the two-state solution would not be achieved in Oz's lifetime. Oz knew well that conventional wisdom demands that, with the end of the two-state solution, Jewish life in Israel-Palestine must either be defined by undemocratic rule over Palestinians (the status quo), or the end of a Jewish state (the one-state solution). *Judas* revives a third, richly historic tradition of thought: a federative model more imaginative than the rigidities of contemporary nation-states, in which Jews and Palestinians each exercise national self-determination in communal affairs while sharing a federative state that coordinates between each community. Federation is the least charismatic of all solutionism, rich with technical political design, bereft of the charming slogans of one-statism (equality for all) and two-statism (Jewish democracy, Palestinian statehood). But as Abravanel articulates it, federation is the only political design that moves beyond the perfunctory categories that cage debate about Israel-Palestine: the insistence on seeing the conflict as between "Israelis" and "Arabs," even as more than half of Jewish Israelis are Mizrahi, or of differentiating between "1948 Israel" and "1967 Israel" despite there being Israeli and Palestinian communities on each side of the Green Line. Abravanel's multinational federation acknowledges that Israeli and Palestinian identity is each constituted both by aspirations for national self-determination and living communities across all of Israel–Palestine that prevent the alignment of nation, state, and territory. *Judas* thus gifts contemporary debate a richly historic alternative to the one state/two state paradigm, one that promises to shape future debate about justice in Israel-Palestine.

The multinational federation envisioned in *Judas* is rooted in a rich intellectual tradition that shaped Abravanel and Ben-Gurion's generation, even as it became forbidden to Ash and Oz's in an age of unforgiving nationalism. Read in this light, *Judas* is a rare and moving uchronia, one that does not reconstruct alternative historical events so much as suggest alternative ways through which his nation might have chosen to move through history. In structuring *Judas* by betrayal rather than tragedy, Oz emphasizes human agency in the construction of the Israeli-Palestinian past—suggesting that whether Abravanel's lost multinationalism belongs only to the past or also to the future is an open question.

Notes

1. I am grateful for commentary on this essay from Derek Penslar; William Lee Frost, professor of Jewish history at Harvard University; Ranen Omer-Sherman, JHFE endowed chair in Judaic studies at the University of Louisville; Kalypso

Nicolaidis, professor of international relations at the University of Oxford and chair in international affairs at the European University Institute; and Oren Kroll-Zeldin, professor of theology and religious studies at the University of San Francisco. I am also grateful for many conversations with Benzion Sanders, and to the Extend alumni group who read and discussed *Judas* in summer 2020. And to Daunt Books, on the Haverstock Hill in Belsize Park, London, where I first glimpsed *Judas*.

2. There was neither a "Zionist Executive Committee" nor a "Council of the Jewish Agency." There was an Executive Committee of the Jewish Agency, chaired by David Ben-Gurion from 1935–1948. It is unclear whether Oz's composite institutions signify a genuine confusion of the early Zionist bureaucracy, or a fictionalization designed in concert with the invention of Abravanel himself. With gratitude to Professor Derek Penslar for this observation.

3. Brit Shalom was the most prominent binational association in Mandate Palestine. It was made famous by its intellectual star power—members included Martin Buber, Gershom Scholem, Judah Magnes, and Henrietta Szold—but the organization lasted less than a decade, from 1925 into the early 1930s. See Flapan and Ratzabi.

4. There is a Ladino saying that signifies the prestige of the family name: "Ya basta mi nombre ke es Abravanel." This translates: "It is sufficient that my name is Abravanel."

5. The Elbaz last name has long been associated with prominent Mizrahi rabbis, especially in Morocco. Perhaps the best-known Mizrahi rabbi of Oz's generation was Rabbi Reuven Elbaz.

6. Jewish presence in these cities is often narrated as anticipation and legitimization of Zionism: in Hebron today, visitors will notice signs linking the centuries-long Jewish presence to criticisms of the Oslo Accords. This is what Shumsky calls "simplistic formulae . . . that link together the past ('Zionism') and the present ('the State of Israel') to form one deterministic totality."

7. *Millet* derives from the Arabic *millah* (ملة), which means *nation*.

8. One particularly intriguing candidate for the historical Abravanel is Abraham Shalom Yahuda, who was born to an affluent and erudite Sephardic Arabic-speaking family in Jerusalem in 1877. After an early academic career in Jewish and Arabic studies in Europe, Yahuda was offered a position at the Hebrew University in 1921. But he remained in Jerusalem only several months after clashing with Ashkenazi Zionist leaders, including Chaim Weizmann, who rejected outright his commitment to a shared Palestinian and Zionist cultural and political program. Yahuda consistently critiqued the Zionist leadership for its disinterest in Palestinian national aspirations, and later distanced himself from Zionism. Oz likely would have been familiar with him through Yahuda's correspondence with Joseph Klausner, the Hebrew University professor and great uncle to Amos. See Evri (2016) and Ukeles (2017).

9. Many Palestinians protected Jewish neighbors from the 1929 violence. One particularly courageous example is that of Abu Shaker Amro, who inserted himself between armed Palestinians and the home of the rabbi of Hebron. His great-grandson, Issa Amro, is a widely recognized leader of today's Palestinian civil disobedience movement. From Cohen (2015), with thanks to Benzion Sanders.

Works Cited

Agard, Walter R. "Fate and Freedom in Greek Tragedy." *The Classical Journal*, vol. 29, no. 2, 1933, pp. 117–26.

Ben-Yehuda, Nachman. *Betrayals and Treason: Violations of Trust and Loyalty.* Northwestern UP, 2001.

Campos, Michelle. *Ottoman Brothers: Muslims, Christians, and Jews in Early Twentieth Century Palestine.* Stanford UP, 2011.

Cohen, Hillel. *Year Zero of the Arab-Israeli Conflict: 1929.* Brandeis UP, 2015.

Evri, Yuval. *Translating the Arab-Jewish Tradition: From Al-Andalus to Palestine/ Land of Israel. Essays of the Forum Transregionale Studien.* 2016, https://perspectivia.net/receive/pnet_mods_00000497?q=evri.

Flapan, Simha. *The Birth of Israel: Myths and Realities.* Pantheon, 1987.

Jacobson, Abigail. "Sephardim, Ashkenazim and the 'Arab Question' in pre-First World War Palestine: A Reading of Three Zionist Newspapers." *Middle Eastern Studies.* vol. 39, no. 2, 2003, pp. 105–130.

Khalidi, Rashid. *Palestinian Identity: The Construction of Modern National Consciousness.* Columbia UP, 1998.

Lin, Nimrod. *People Who Count: Zionism, Demography and Democracy in Mandate Palestine.* 2018. University of Toronto. PhD dissertation.

Oz, Amos. *A Tale of Love and Darkness.* Translated by Nicholas de Lange. Vintage, 2005.

———. *Black Box.* Translated by Nicholas de Lange. Houghton Mifflin, 2012.

———. *Dear Zealots.* Translated by Jessica Cohen. Harcourt, 2019.

———. *Judas.* Translated by Nicholas de Lange. Harcourt, 2017.

———. *In the Land of Israel.* Translated by Maurie Goldberg-Bartura. Harcourt, 1983.

———. *The Hill of Evil Counsel.* Translated by Nicholas de Lange. Harcourt, 1978.

———. *Under this Blazing Light.* Translated by Nicholas de Lange. U of Cambridge P, 1996.

———. *Where the Jackals Howl.* Translated by Nicholas de Lange and Philip Simpson. Harcourt, 2012.

Rubin, Gil S. *The Future of the Jews: Planning for the Postwar Jewish World, 1939–1946.* 2017. Columbia University. PhD dissertation.

Ratzabi, Shalom. *Between Zionism and Judaism: The Radical Circle in Brith Shalom, 1925–1933*. Brill, 2001.

Shohat, Ella. "Sephardim in Israel: Zionism from the Standpoint of Its Jewish Victims." *Social Text*, vol. 19/20, 1988, pp. 1–35.

Shumsky, Dmitry. *The Zionist Political Imagination from Pinsker to Ben-Gurion*. Yale UP, 2018.

Ukeles, Raquel. *Abraham Shalom Yahuda: The Scholar, the Collector, and the Collections*. Leiden, 2017.

Afterword

About My Father

FANIA OZ-SALZBERGER

Like both my parents, I have been blessed and cursed with a long and detailed verbal and pictorial memory. Proust-like, it shoots up scenes and sounds, tastes and smells from the gentle haze of our earliest childhood. My mother remembers my grandparents, the kibbutz pioneers, still living in a tent in the Hulda pine forest. My father begins his autobiographical novel with his mother Fania tying the laces of his tiny first shoes. And I remember the L-shaped single-room apartment in which my parents slept and lived. Also the shady yard of one of the kibbutz "children's houses," where I and three other toddlers slept by night and lived all day, except a couple hours every afternoon, the parents-time.[1]

During those hours my father spent time with me, and later with my siblings. He spoke to us a great deal, as he would to adults, and sometimes even sang when no one else was in earshot. His best tone, one that lasted all his life, was a distinct blend of love and irony. Then he would use very high language, a trifle comic, which I absorbed into my little mind, but an instinct told me not to repeat it to my kindergarten mates. At times I sensed his delicate sarcasm—small children are able to sense it—a fond, almost respectful sarcasm, aimed above my head at absent patriarchs or professors or ideologues, whose grand phrases he unpacked to make a plaything for his daughter. Such were the lullabies he sang to me at bedtime, replete with the pathos and pomposity of early Zionism and the grand revival of Modern Hebrew. I remember not only the words but also the particular inflections of his young voice, for my father was only twenty-one when I was born, and my mother was not yet twenty-one.

The kibbutz of my childhood was a unique brink of modern culture, still very socialist, its founders speaking in heavy East European accents, its second generation often marrying young and raising the third generation within the collective fold. They farmed, argued, read world literature, and listened to classical music, a little jazz, and the fresh canon of Hebrew songs. Most of my own generation, the founders' grandchildren, left for a somewhat more bourgeois life, delighted to discover that Zionism had given us not only the kibbutz but also Tel Aviv. But my father took the opposite path. He came to the kibbutz seeking social justice and personal redemption, a lonely boy from Jerusalem, orphaned and traumatized. In Hulda he found my mother, the daughter of pioneers and the love of his life, and they made themselves a home. No matter how tiny it was. No matter—so they thought—that they must put their children to bed every night in a different house, a few minutes' walk away. Our socialist paradise—I am not being sardonic here, because I can easily imagine his gratitude and joy—was precisely what gave him the freedom to write, first by night, in the toilet next to the single room where my mother was sleeping. Later, a kibbutz committee debated and decided to grant him one day per working week for writing, and still later he was allotted a small studio of his own. The complete absence of financial worries was a tremendous gift. These are the plain facts, unknown to my parents at the time, and a cause of guilt and consternation only many years later: my kibbutz childhood was not happy, and Amos Oz would not have become a writer without the kibbutz.

Today we are wise enough to acknowledge—perhaps too fiercely— that kibbutz life was not ideal for many family relationships. For me, my father Amos was the best part of my childhood. Our father-daughter relations were blessed with a rare combination of cerebral and emotional understanding. We followed the Freudian normality, although neither of us is an admirer of Freud: very close in my early childhood, more distant in my adolescence and twenties, and very close again later in life, basking in his happiness with his grandchildren, authoring one book together, planning a second book.

Yes, cerebral affinity; we were fortunate. To the end of his life, he would sometimes plant a shy, stolen kiss on the top of my head, occasionally hug my shoulders, but our chief instrument was language. The language was Hebrew, and Hebrew had only recently been reborn. In the middle of the last century this modernized speaking tongue was a merry mess of highs and lows, pomposity, poetry and profanity, its fresh everyday speech pulling at the skirts of its glittering biblical phrases. It was my father's playground and mine too. I suspect he may have been practicing his rhetoric on me, but I was feisty enough to understand and to remember. I owe him the discovery that language can be an enormous pleasure. Most of my academic colleagues are yet to find this out.

Two or three years after discovering language, I discovered death. I can't remember what I said to my father, obviously in great distress, but I remember his response: "Don't worry, Fania. By the time you grow up, I will invent something against death." In retrospect, the answer looks like bad parenting. In retrospect, furthermore, it includes my name, his dead mother's name. Also in retrospect, I think he did invent something against death. I cannot name it, but it is made from words.

He was the only kibbutz father unashamed to cry openly. His eyes filled with a tear when he told me how Spinoza prophesied Zionism in one tiny footnote. He cried watching an old newsreel of the British tank brigades beating Rommel in the dunes of North Africa ("thus saving the lives of little Amos in Jerusalem and little Nili in the kibbutz," he explained). He was deeply emotional when Neil Armstrong stepped on the moon. He was sentimental on behalf of humankind, the Jews, the Arabs, the war dead, the old poets and professors still walking the streets of Jerusalem. But he was never sentimental about himself.

I liked him better with the twinkle in his eye, the loving sarcasm, distancing himself from all his father figures, the grand pillars of his upbringing, without bringing them down. He was a rebel, not a patricide. This balance, far darker, gives force to his first short stories and first novel, *Elsewhere, Perhaps*. The same decision, taken in his twenties, made him a life-long Zionist—humanist Zionism was the phrase we both used—even when fiercely attacked from the Left. He never forgot the fact—a proven fact, for no other options remained to them—that Zionism saved his parents' and grandparents' lives (at least for a while, in the case of his mother).

My father was about twenty-two and I was about one year old when he became known to me as a distinct person, *abba (Daddy) Amos*. I remember him still wearing his soldier's uniform. I remember me, the toddler, sitting at his small desk and overturning the aquarium, water spilling on his university notes, and *abba* Amos talking gently to me as he first rescued the fish, then wiped the water, then shook each paper and spread them out to dry.

My mother says he was almost deliriously happy with his wife, their first and second daughter (Galia is about three years younger than me; Daniel came fourteen years later), their cat Kasabubu, the tiny warm one-room home, and his writing. During the same years his first short stories were published. He thought, perhaps, that his calamity was over. I can still hear him narrating my early life for me in a gentle happy voice and a treasure trove of words. Biblical quotes were personalized, made our very own: "my daughter's smell is like the smell of the field blessed by god." Not that he believed in God, but his young adulthood was a miracle for him. At the same time, he was a political activist and a literary rebel, challenging the patriarchs—Abraham, Moses, Ben Gurion, Agnon, his own father and grandfather and their utopian nationalism, the kibbutz elders and their utopian socialism. But under his domestic happiness and young brave public voice, the shadows lurked.

He was methodical, at times obsessive with order and neatness, almost never spontaneous. He was often very funny. He labored under his bad memories but never told us a thing. Only at sixteen did I discover by chance that his mother Fania, that vague nonexistent person for which I was named, took her own life rather than just "died before you were born, and that's it." She remained an enigma for all of us until he published *A Tale of Love and Darkness*. Even later, we rarely mentioned her. It was a black hole in Amos's otherwise crowded, verbal universe. Another black hole was the Yom Kippur War of 1973, and what happened to him after he was rushed to reserve duty in the Golan Heights on that fateful Saturday. He returned with some shrapnel in one arm, sat in his uniform on the floor, and stared for several hours. Till his death, not a word.

His intellectual world was very masculine. Such were the times, and for many years he did not know better. His best friends were men about a generation older than himself. There was General Yisrael Tal ("Talik"), his fellow philosophy student, the father of Israel's armored corps, and the only man in history who designed and built a fighter tank based on Immanuel Kant's categorical imperative. There was the wonderful writer Yizhar Smilansky (S. Yizhar), and a handful of others. After they died, the good doctor and wonderful friend Marek Glazerman stepped in; "he is my gynecologist," Amos used to joke. His friendship and political cama-raderie with two great authors of his own generation, A. B. Yehoshua and

David Grossman, earned them the Israeli nickname "the three tenors." Few people are aware of their rare poetic collegiality, reading and commenting on each other's manuscripts with delicately brutal honesty. Such, too, was my father's friendship with the exquisite Israeli novelist Yehoshua Kenaz, whom he lovingly addressed by the French version of his name, Josué.

As to the younger and aspiring novelists and poets, who sent him thousands of letters and hundreds of manuscripts, Amos Oz made a point of reading their works and providing each of them with a detailed and honest personal response. When he thought praise was due, he was delighted to give it. He enjoyed nurturing young writers, students, and fledgling political activists. I watched him during those years with a critical adolescent's eye: of course he was basking in his own talents and fame, but I also saw him constantly striving to use both fame and talent for the greater good. This was miniscule part of his greater, secret universe, where logic and sentiment were, like his own parents, tragically mismatched.

And so we get to the heart. In stark contrast to Amos's intellectual side, his emotional depths, from tragedy to redemption, had been wrought by women: his mother, his wife, his daughters, and perhaps one or two others who came and went during his long life. I kept a healthy distance from some sentimental particulars of my father's life, but I know that he owed his happiness to my mother Nili. They had fifty-nine years of love. I was born nine months after their first Friday night together (it was his turn to be the kibbutz night watchman, she made him a midnight meal, and the next morning they walked together to the Hulda Forest with a dog named Dolly). Nili was Natasha to his Raskolnikov or Solveig to his Peer Gynt, but she is blessed with a sunny personality, without a trace of Russian gloom or Lutheran self-deprivation. When they married, he promised to make her laugh at least once a day, and I think he mostly did.

But in his novels and stories there are neither brainy women nor sunny women. Already as a teenager I found his female characters either shallow or darkly mysterious. Even Hannah Gonen, the female narrator of *My Michael*, which brought him a global readership at the age of twenty-eight, is a woman led by her (wonderfully crafted and phrased) feelings alone. When I became an adult, an activist, and an academic, I voiced my resentment. We are women, I told him, not cryptograms. I began to educate him in the ways of feminist theory. I suppose others did, too. And Amos, a longtime listener and learner, gradually changed. In his bluntly honest conversations with his friend and editor Shira Hadad, included their book *What Makes an Apple* published shortly before his death, he touchingly confessed to his crude ignorance about women in his early years.

We argued about ideas, about history and politics, women and men, human nature and the great writers who understood something about it. I was alert to his shortcomings and unimpressed—a daughter's privilege—by either his good looks or his growing fame. As we co-authored *Jews and Words* we explored our differences and placed them on the greater Jewish continuum: parent and child, woman and man, two distinct generations, a digital ignoramus and an Internet denizen. We had lovely arguments about electronic books: he lamented the disappearance of bookshelves in living rooms and the loss of a book's form and texture, touch and smell. I showed him how digital books allow you to search and find Ivan Petrovich, the chap who appears in every great Russian novel at around page 643. Of course, the overloaded reader can never remember exactly who Ivan Petrovich is. So here's a trick, *abba*: press "search." My father would follow my deft fingers, frowning, and that was an argument I never won.

Today I find it difficult to address our rare true quarrels and deeper disagreements, because my sister has savaged him post-mortem so completely. Her book, published in 2021, not only contradicts the detailed memories, indeed the life-stories, of my mother, my brother and myself; it also deprives me of my own wrestling with him, a far gentler battle. Let me just say this: Amos Oz, my father, was a good man. He was unassuming and kind to family, friends, and strangers. Though raised as a nationalist and rebelling amidst socialists, he was attuned to individuals, to private anguish, and to the little details that undermine big theories. He was a true and ever-developing liberal, conquering his own cultural DNA of extremism, both the chauvinist and the Marxist strains. His fiery battles for political justice seldom allowed principles to run over individuals, and when it did, he heeded criticism (including mine) and stood corrected. He was the best listener I ever met. He actively chose, and kept choosing, life over death, love over darkness, and persons over grand schemes. In the last decade of his life, he and I talked and agreed that at the end, only one "ism" remains morally sufferable, and that is humanism. We also invented together what we called "The Eleventh Commandment," which is superior to all others: Thou Shalt Not Inflict Pain.

And, as my brother Daniel put it, our father had true love for human beings and for cats.

Banking on my own academic field, I want to say something about his intellectual sources. Surprisingly few scholars have addressed them (they include Professor David Ohana in a beautiful obituary article). His childhood education was as topsy-turvy as his sad early years: the polished, polyglot but poverty-ridden parents; father Arie Klausner and uncle Joseph Klausner holding forth on Jewish genius, nationhood, and great books; mother Fania, melancholic, conveying her Polish romanticism and Russian high literature; her earthy dark fairytales from the depths of Ukrainian forests. The stories were not Jewish, they came from a deep strain of peasant memory, but in one of those forests, Sosenki, every single one of her relatives, friends, and teachers who did not flee on time was shot and piled in large burial holes. This is part of his intellectual history too.

Then there was Amos's tiny first school. His second-grade teacher, the wise Zelda Schneersohn, an ultra-Orthodox woman with light in her face, who was later to shine as one of Israel's finest poets. Then came rough years in a fanatically religious school, followed by even rougher years as an orphan in the kibbutz, where his humble but excellent high school teachers focused his mind on social justice, but did not prevent his roommates from beating him up. Another early teacher was novelist Aharon Appelfeld, of whom my father always spoke with tenderness and admiration.

Then came the army service, our Israeli burden, the mandatory, post-high school training in every shade of the human spectrum. My father was fortunate to serve as an educator, and lived to see his grandchildren follow in his steps. (This non-combatant role, I must add, is unique to the Israeli army; don't imagine a commissar but a social-minded youth leader of under-privileged kids slightly younger than you). The kibbutz then allowed him to go straight to the Hebrew University of Jerusalem, where he studied literature and philosophy. So I may have toppled that aquarium over his class notes on Shmuel Yosef Agnon, or perhaps on Immanuel Kant.

By then, the kibbutz was his home and safe haven. His first books tackle its founding fathers and mothers: old socialists, practical and pragmatic enough to evade Hitler, reinvent their Jewishness, build a new village and a new country, but idealistic enough to think that their new village and country could truly become a utopia. He loved arguing with them, and I can't even begin to tell you how they loved arguments. Here lay the deep dividing line between their homelands' tyrannical Marxism and Israel's labor movement. Many years later, in our conversations, he and I often dwelled on that ancient Jewish vaccination against dictatorship, our inherited respect for verbal quarrel and intellectual disagreement. My father knew it in his very bones: if violence can be verbalized, conflicts can be solved. At least political conflicts. Not human tragedies, and never in good literature. As my father learned from his beloved Anton Chekhov, all the words and ideas in the world cannot prevent men and women from hurting others or gnawing at their own souls.

The 1960s were his first decade as an adult and a writer, and the first decade in my life. In my "Baby's Diary" Amos recorded how I cried when our transistor radio suddenly blurted out a loud speech by JF Kennedy. His transistor radio was always at hand for the hourly news. In Jerusalem, my future husband's mother was testifying in the Eichmann trial. Ben-Gurion retired. The Egyptians deployed tank brigades along the Sinai border and blocked the Straights of Tiran.

I was a thin, awkward little girl, too articulate for her own good, lonely in the midst of the collective. My father's mental universe, or perhaps the small universe he created for me, was both gentle and spellbinding. We collected stamps, imagining together the fragrant tropical lands, the long-dead kings, the evil dictators. Along came the stamp honoring the Soviet dog-hero Laika who flew into space aboard a gleaming spaceship. My father carefully attached her stamp to the student's binder that served as our album, all country names written by his hand. With equal caution he kept me ignorant of the fact that the Russian scientists never intended to bring Laika back. Like many parents of his generation and their predecessors, he sometimes told his children benevolent lies. But the thousands of little stories "from his head" that he told me, my siblings, and our classmates were never lies; they introduced us to the unique set of truths that are not available through science or history, only through storytelling.

I thus became a juvenile witness to some of his greatest springboards. A book lay open, spine up, on the coffee table: Sherwood Anderson's *Winesburg, Ohio*. Amos later said that this volume of interwoven stories from a small town in the American Midwest opened a magic door for him. After reading Anderson he understood that a great writer does not need Paris or Moscow or Rome as his backdrop. The human universe is in the writer's own village and its humble populace. The same signals must have reached him when he read Balzac, Ibsen, and Faulkner. I remember their covers from before I could read. I knew they were not toys. Every young child should be allowed to hold books, including those without pictures; in pre-literate infancy they can enter your memory as sensual things, charmed objects.

My father's favorite authors hunched over his desk like a small troop of kind uncles. Some of them changed over the years. As a young man Amos loved Tolstoy, in his middle age it was Dostoevsky, but Chekhov was with him until the end. I think that the final and insoluble problem, for Amos Oz, was not the riddle of his own mortality (which haunts Tolstoy's Ivan Illich), or the mystery of redemption (which Dostoevsky grants Raskolnikov), but that which he called the greatest enigma of them all: the family. This was why my father loved Chekhov in the wisdom and sadness of his old age. "In Shakespeare's tragedies," he used to say, "the stage is littered with dead bodies when the curtain falls. Whereas in the end of Chekhov's tragedies everyone is disappointed, frustrated, unhappy—but alive!"

Beyond his warm humor lurked the mother's ghost. You can call it the Amos Oz paradox: had my grandmother's tragedy been written by Chekhov, she would not have overdosed on sleeping pills without as much as a word to her husband and twelve-year-old son. She would have remained unhappy but alive, like Chekhov's Three Sisters or like Hannah in *My Michael*; but would Amos Oz have become Amos Oz? I doubt it, and I think he doubted it too. "In order to become a writer, you need three things: a grandmother, a rooftop, and a wound," he once wrote. His wound led an obscure life of its own, pulsating in the dark.

In 1969–1970, on a young writer's Fellowship in Oxford, my father came upon two great influences. Oxford inspired his novella "Unto Death," with ample materials in the Bodleian Library to allow him to enter the skin, the soul, and the bloodshot eyes of Crusaders striving for Jerusalem. This was, I think, his first deep encounter with Christianity, through its fanatic gateways, which he would follow right down to the end of his life with the last novel *Judas*. The protagonist of this last novel, Shmuel Asch, traces the origins what my father called "the Chernobyl of antisemitism," Jesus and Judas, in order to save both of them from everything that happened later. Perhaps rewinding history itself, Crusades and pogroms and Nazis and the forest next to my grandmother Fania's hometown of Rivne, strewn with the naked bodies of her relatives and classmates, and even the body of Fania herself in her sister's spare room in Tel Aviv that night in 1952—but I am digressing here. The first inspiration from Oxford on the young Amos Oz was the study of fanaticism in all its guises. The Christian, the Jewish, the nationalist, the ultra-radical, every fanatic that would kill you out of sheer love for you, thus curing your errors or purifying your soul: from "Unto Death" to *Dear Zealots*, the small book that Amos saw as his last will and testament. Here was one of the rare themes that crossed the tight line between Amos Oz's literature and his politics: the fanatic mind, and how it might, perhaps, be changed.

The second great inspiration was the philosopher, Isaiah Berlin. I was nine years old with no English when I entered Oxford's wonderland, but by the time we returned to Kibbutz Hulda my mind was full of marvels: Alice, the Hobbit, and the kindly Sir Isaiah, sitting in an armchair with his eyes gleaming like a wise Jewish elf. "He was deeply suspicious," my father reminisced many years later, "of anyone pretending to teach us once and for all what is the good, and insisting on opening our eyes if we fail to choose it. I learnt from him that the good is tricky to define, but anyone can sense evil. Truth is slippery, but even a child knows that a lie is a lie. Berlin also taught me that one could be national without being nationalist, and patriotic without loathing or condescension for the patriotism of others. You can be a Zionist without ignoring Palestinian justice. There is a line between human compassion and sweeping 'Christian' forgiveness. In politics, Thou Shalt Not Romanticize."

Isaiah Berlin showed Oz that philosophy can circumnavigate grand schemes, avoid nihilism, embrace the simple fact that humans will never fully agree with each other, and even enjoy it. Here was "The Crooked Timber of Humanity," Kant's phrase, in Berlin's melodious rendering and liberal reworking. People can never be, nor should be, lined up to fit an ideology. We belong to groups, but never wholly so. Years later, Amos rephrased it this: "No man is an island, but every person is a peninsula." All this was, of course, music to the young novelist's ears. He had known this truth before, but now he had the philosophy.

As to Amos the political thinker, Sir Isaiah well and truly un-dog-matized him. Gazing though his owlish spectacles he shot sharp questions, prodding the young Israeli away from the excesses of nationalism and ultra-socialism. Amos had already warned his government against nascent imperialism in the immediate aftermath of the Six Day War. He already felt the depths of the Palestinian calamity. Isaiah Berlin helped him shake off the crude Israeli rhetoric of victimhood and self-redemption. Like Berlin, Oz remained a zionist throughout his life, but his zionism (we both liked the small "z") was now wedded to liberalism, and both were subjected to humanism. A decade later, my father put it thus:

> I must tell you that the rendezvous between a Jew like me and
> Western humanism . . . has no similarity to all the previous

rendezvous between Judaism and Hellenism, or Judaism and Islamic culture. This rendezvous with Western humanism is a fateful one, formative, constitutional, irrevocable. And if you should ask, "why is this meeting different from all the other meetings?" I would tell you that when we, my forefathers and I, met up with European humanism during the last few centuries, particularly in its liberal and socialist forms, perhaps we recognized in it certain astounding genetic similarities. Because Western humanism has Jewish genes as well. (*In the Land of Israel*; also in *Jews and Words*)

There was something very Jewish hovering above the two of them, the old professor and the young writer, because they shared the same feisty sarcasm toward the traditions they loved. Within Jewish intellectual genealogy they both belong to the rationalist and cultural school of "Lithuanian Jews," not merely in the geographic sense. Their ancestors shared an aversion to spiritual sects and miracle-making rabbis and all manner of personality-cult and divinely ordained extremism. The Enlightenment at its best was their touchstone as modern men. And then there was the humor, without which you cannot decipher this particular strain of Jewishness. Theirs was an irreverent humor, a sophisticated, verbal, God-spanking humor, that crossed over from rabbinic forebears to atheistic progeny. Isaiah Berlin and my father were secular Jews of the most informed, thoughtful, and articulate kind. Not a religious bone in their bodies, no God to wrestle with after Auschwitz, no apologetic bow to the Orthodox, and yet they were utterly Jewish.

Years passed, and Israel's society and politics traveled a great distance from my father's world, his childhood Jerusalem ("I lost my Jerusalem in the Six Day War"), and the kibbutz of his youth with its flawed and daring utopia. At the height of his political fame, an orator's fame, influential with the peace movement, speaking with Palestinians, helping create and phrase the Oslo Agreement, Amos Oz became a hated man. The radical anti-Zionist Left could not bear his insistence on liberalism, his humanist zionism with a small "z," his male Ashkenazi demeanor, and his bewitching linguistic fluency. He was accused of symbolizing the "hegemony" by people who had never heard of his rebellion against Ben-Gurion or his dark and utterly correct prophecy about the Six Day War. Far more numerous were his detractors from the nationalist Right, who denounced him as an Arab-loving traitor and even a conspirator against Judaism. Traitors had fascinated my father throughout his adult life, and he humbly acknowledged the accusation as a private badge of honor.

Between 1995 and 1997, my sons and Galia's children were born. My parents received all their four grandchildren in the spell of just two years, and they were wonderful grandparents. It was then that my father finally wrote a novel based on his own life story, sad and hilarious and ambitious, woven into the woeful and exhilarating annals of the State of Israel, *A Tale of Love and Darkness*. "This is for the grandchildren, mine and everyone else's," he told me. "This will be their hard disk." I think he was ready for death after the *Tale*, and after *The Same Sea*, his own preferred and most beloved of his books. And yet he lived on to write his wise, beautiful twilight works, among them *Between Friends* and *Judas*.

I loved my father very deeply. Our first three or four years together were filled with promises. Some of them he fulfilled very grandly, others he failed to fulfill. During my infancy he must have spoken to himself through me, and I do not resent it. He was a Kantian, after all, and no person was merely a means for him, always an end-in-herself or himself as well. I must have been a particularly sweet end-in-herself to him, an emblem of his new happiness, a wholly new rendering of his dead mother's name.

Shortly before he died, during a family car ride, I said something rather trivial, which I can't recall, and Amos replied that his mother was of the same opinion. "Well," I said, "I'm glad I agree with the First Fania." My father turned his face to look at me from the from the front passenger seat. "You are the First Fania," he said simply. This was, in effect, our last conversation.

Note

1. This essay was originally published in French in the Éditions Gallimard Quarto edition of *Amos Oz, Oeuvres* (Paris, 2022).

Contributors

EDITOR

Ranen Omer-Sherman serves as The Jewish Heritage Fund for Excellence endowed chair in Jewish Studies at the University of Louisville and was recipient of its 2020 Distinguished Faculty Award in Outstanding Scholarship, Research, and Creative Activity. He obtained an MA (1997) and his PhD (2000) from the University of Notre Dame. Throughout his career, he has written many book chapters, essays, and reviews addressing Amos Oz's oeuvre, from his earliest kibbutz stories to Oz's final novel *Judas*. Omer-Sherman's essays on Israeli and global Jewish writers have appeared in journals such as *Prooftexts, Journal of Jewish Identities, Texas Studies in Literature and Language, MELUS, College Literature, Journal of Modern Jewish Studies, Religion & Literature, Shofar,* and *Modernism/Modernity*. He is the author or editor of five books, including *Diaspora and Zionism in Jewish American Literature: Lazarus, Syrkin, Reznikoff, Roth* (2002), *Israel in Exile: Jewish Writing and the Desert* (2006) *The Jewish Graphic Novel: Critical Approaches* (2008), *Narratives of Dissent: War in Contemporary Israeli Arts and Culture* (2013), and *Imagining Kibbutz: Visions of Utopia in Literature and Film* (2015).

CONTRIBUTORS

Nehama Aschkenasy is professor emeritus of comparative literary and cultural studies at the University of Connecticut, founding director of UConn's Stamford Center for Judaic and Middle Easter Studies, and earned her PhD in English and comparative literature from New York University and degrees in English and Judaic studies from the Hebrew University in Jerusalem. She published four books (among them the Choice selection and award-winning *Eve's Journey*, reprinted in 2016 by the University of Pennsylvania Press in honor of its 150th anniversary), and numerous articles and book chapters in the areas of Biblical patterns in Hebrew and English literatures, women in Judaic literary tradition, geopolitics and society in modern Israeli narratives, and comparative literary theory. She served on the editorial boards of the *Modern Language Studies* and the *Journal of Modern Jewish Studies*, as associate editor of the *AJS Review*, the *Journal for the Association of Jewish Studies* for two decades, and as guest editor of its dedicated volume on the "Bible's Role in Modern Israel's Culture and Literature," a collection of essays by Hebrew scholars to which she contributed an essay and a methodological introduction, later selected for the *Posen Library*.

Avraham Balaban is emeritus professor of Hebrew at the University of Florida. He is a recipient of the Prime Minister Creativity Award for scholarship and poetry. He has served as a scholar and visiting professor in Hebrew at Harvard University and at the University of Michigan, Ann Arbor, and later as full professor at the University of Florida. His primary publications address Hebrew fiction of the second half of the twentieth century (books on Amos Oz, A. B. Yehoshua, Amalia Kahana-Carmon, and a panoramic examination of "postmodernist" trends in Hebrew fiction of the late 1980s and the early 1990s). He is the author of the acclaimed study, *Between God and Beast: An Examination of Amos Oz's Prose*. His Hebrew literary memoir *Shivah* (*Mourning*) was published subsequently in 2004 in English as *Mourning a Father Lost: A Kibbutz Childhood Remembered*.

Nitza Ben-Dov served as an associate professor at the department of near Eastern studies at Princeton University. In 1989, she joined the faculty of the University of Haifa, where she serves as professor of Hebrew and comparative literature. A literary critic and a scholar, Ben-Dov has written numerous articles and is the author of several books, published in Hebrew and in English, including *Agnon's Art of Indirection* (in English); *Unhappy/Unapproved Loves*; *Ve-Hi Tehilatekha: Studies in the Works of S. Y. Agnon, A. B. Yehoshua and Amos Oz* (in Hebrew); and *Written Lives: On Israeli Literary Autobiographies*. Her latest book, titled *War Lives: On the Army, Revenge, Grief and the Consciousness of War in Israeli Fiction*, won the prestigious Itzhak Sadeh Prize for Military Literature in 2018. She has edited several books, among them *The Amos Oz Reader* in 2009. She is the author of about 250 articles and reviews and has served as editor-in-chief of Haifa University Press/Zmora-Bitan (1996–2000) and as chair of the Academic TV channel (2001–2005). She has recently established two graduate programs at the University of Haifa: women and gender studies and cultural studies.

Nissim Calderon is Prof. Emeritus of Ben Gurion University of the Negev where he taught for many years. He has published six books in Hebrew on subjects such as the political context of Israeli literature, the plurality of Israeli culture, and the connection between Israeli poets and singer-songwriters. His most recent book is titled *A Biography of Meir Ariel* ([Hebrew] 2016).

Jessica Cohen was born in England, raised in Israel, and lives in Denver. She translates contemporary Israeli prose, poetry, and other creative work. She shared the 2017 Man Booker International Prize with David Grossman, for her translation of *A Horse Walks into a Bar*. Other major Israeli writers she has translated include Amos Oz, Etgar Keret, Ronit Matalon, and Nir Baram. She is a past board member of the American Literary Translators Association and has served as a judge for the National Translation Award.

Sidra DeKoven Ezrahi is professor emerita of general and comparative literature at the Hebrew University of Jerusalem and has taught at numerous universities in the US and Canada. She has written on subjects ranging from representations of the Holocaust in postwar Israeli, to European and American culture, to the configurations of exile and homecoming in contemporary Jewish literature. Her books include *By Words Alone: The Holocaust in Literature* (1980) and *Booking Passage: Exile and Homecoming in the Modern Jewish Imagination* (University of California Press, 2000). She has also published two books in Hebrew (*Ipus ha-masa ha-yehudi*, 2017; and *Shlosha Paytanim*, 2020) and many scholarly essays. In 2007, she became a Guggenheim Fellow for her current project, *Figuring Jerusalem: Politics and Poetics in the Sacred Center* (2021). In November 2019, she was awarded an honorary doctorate from Hebrew Union College-Jewish Institute of Religion.

Nurith Gertz is professor emerita of Hebrew literature and film at the Open University of Israel. She has served as head of the cinema studies program at the department of film and television at Tel Aviv University and headed the department of culture creation and production at Sapir Academic College. She won the prestigious Brenner Prize for Literature in 2009 for her book *Unrepentant*, which was also on the short list for the Sapir Prize for Literature. Among her recent books, *Captive of a Dream: National Myths in Israeli Culture* (2000); *Holocaust Survivors, Aliens and Others in Israeli Cinema* (2004, in Hebrew); *Palestinian Cinema: Landscape, Trauma and Memory*, with George Khleifi (2008); and *An Ocean Between Us* (2016). Her latest book is *What Was Lost to Time: A Biography of Friendship* (2020).

David Grossman was born in Jerusalem, where he still lives. He is the best-selling author of many works of fiction, nonfiction, and children's literature, which have been translated into thirty-six languages. His work has also appeared in *The New Yorker*. He is the recipient of numerous awards, including the Man Booker International Prize, the French Chevalier de L'Ordre des Arts et des Lettres, the Buxtehuder Bulle in Germany, Rome's Premio per la Pace e L'Azione Umanitaria, the Premio Ischia International Award for Journalism, Israel's Emet Prize, and the 2010 Frankfurt Peace Prize. In 2021 he was awarded Sweden's first Berman Literature Prize.

Liam Hoare is a writer and journalist based in Vienna, Austria. He is the Europe editor for *Moment Magazine*, for whom he has written profiles of Tom Stoppard, Simon Schama, and Bernard-Henri Lévy and a recreation of the libel trial *David Irving v Penguin Books and Deborah Lipstadt*. He has reported on European Jewish life, politics, and culture for a number of British and American Jewish publications including *The Jewish Chronicle*, *The Forward*, *Tablet*, *eJewish Philanthropy*, and *The Times of Israel*, contributed pieces on European politics to *Slate*, *The Atlantic*, and *Politico*, and written essays on European Jewish literature for *The Jewish Review of Books*. His work in German can be found in the *Wiener Zeitung* and the *Presse*. He first encountered Amos Oz's stories among the paperbacks in the English-language section of the library on Kibbutz Ein HaShofet where he was a volunteer in the spring of 2012. Since then, he has interviewed Oz and written numerous essays on and reviews of his literary and political work for, among others, *The Forward*, *Fathom*, and Vienna's *Jüdisches Echo*.

Sheila Jelen, associate professor of Hebrew and Jewish Studies in the department of modern and classical languages, literatures and cultures in the College of Arts & Sciences at University of Kentucky, was recently awarded the Zantker Professorship in Jewish Literature, Culture, and History. Jelen has published a variety of monographs and edited volumes including, most recently, *Salvage Poetics: Post-Holocaust American Jewish Folk Ethnographies* (2020), *Reconstructing the Old Country: American Jewry in the Post-Holocaust Decades* (2017), *Intersections and Boundaries: Modern Jewish Literatures* (2011), and *Intimations of Difference: Dvora Baron in the Modern Hebrew Renaissance* (2007). Her work has appeared in such journals as *Prooftexts, The Jewish Quarterly Review, The AJS Review, Religion and Literature, Comparative Literature Studies,* and *Hebrew Studies.* She is currently working on a manuscript titled, "Testimonial Montage: Holocaust Testimonies by Women in Israel" as well as an anthology titled "Images and Imaginings: Menachem Kipnis's Photographs and Folk Stories." This work will feature both folktales collected, and photographs taken by Menachem Kipnis (1878–1942), a singer, critic, photographer, and ethnographer of Yiddish song who died in the Warsaw ghetto.

Joshua Leifer is an assistant editor at *Jewish Currents*. Previously, he was an editor at *Dissent* and before that, editor at *+972 Magazine*. His work has appeared in *The Guardian, The Nation, Haaretz, n+1, Jacobin,* and elsewhere. He has reported from Israel and the occupied Palestinian territories, Hungary, Germany, as well as the US. He received a BA in history from Princeton University, where he wrote his thesis on the Service Employees International Union's shifting strategy in the late twentieth century—during what historian Daniel T. Rodgers has called "the age of fracture." He is currently based in Brooklyn, NY.

Adia Mendelson-Maoz is an associate professor in Israeli literature and culture at the Open University of Israel. She investigates the multifaceted relationships between literature, ethics, politics, and culture, mainly in the context of Hebrew literature and Israeli culture. Mendelson-Maoz is the author of numerous articles in books and journals. She has published three books, *Literature as Moral Laboratory* (2009, in Hebrew), *Multiculturalism in Israel—Literary Perspective* (2014), and *Borders, Territories, and Ethics: Hebrew Literature in the Shadow of the Intifada* (2018). Her book, *Territories and Borders in the Shadow of the Intifada: Ethical Reading of Hebrew Literature 1987–2007,* is a Hebrew adaptation of *Borders, Territories, and Ethics* and is forthcoming by Magnes Press. Also forthcoming in Hebrew is her textbook by the Open University Press titled *Center or*

Periphery: Identity Discourse in Israeli Literature. Her current research project, funded by an ISF grant, aims to present a comprehensive picture of Yoram Kaniuk's literary endeavor, based on his personal archive. She discovered Kaniuk's unpublished manuscript *Sabon* (2018, in Hebrew) and served as a scientific editor for its publication.

Oded Nir teaches and writes about Israeli culture and Marxist theory at Queens College, City University of New York. His first book, *Signatures of Struggle* (2018), provides an account of the relationship between the development of Israeli literature to socio-economic transformations, from a Marxist perspective. He is the editor of several volumes and journal special issues, on topics such as Marxist approaches to Israel/Palestine, global peripheral literatures' periodization of capitalism, and materialist analyses of Israeli culture. His articles have been published in venues such as *Prooftexts, Criticism, Rethinking Marxism, Journal of Modern Jewish Studies*, and others. Oded is the editor of the peer-reviewed quarterly, *CLCWeb: Comparative Literature and Culture.*

Fania Oz-Salzberger is an Israeli historian and writer, professor emerita of history at the University of Haifa School of Law and the Haifa Center for German and European Studies (HCGES). Oz-Salzberger was born in 1960 in Kibbutz Hulda, the eldest daughter of writer Amos Oz and his wife Nily. She is the great-great-niece of historian and literary scholar Joseph Klausner. She served as an officer in the Israel Defense Forces. Her doctoral thesis, on the politics of the Scottish and German Enlightenments (Oxford University, 1991), was mentored by philosopher Isaiah Berlin and published as *Translating the Enlightenment* (1995). She was fellow of the German Institute for Advanced Studies in Berlin, visiting professor for Distinguished Teaching at Princeton University, chair of Israel Studies at Monash University, visiting professor at LMU in Munich, and director of Paideia, the European Institute for Jewish Studies in Sweden. She was awarded an honorary doctorate from Uppsala University. At the University of Haifa, Oz-Salzberger is the founding director of the Posen Research Forum for Jewish European and Israeli Political Thought. Alongside numerous academic articles in the history of ideas and political thought, she published several academic books, including *Israelis in Berlin*, published in 2001 in Hebrew and German, which became a prism of Israeli–German dialogue. In 2012, the book *Jews and Words*, co-authored by Oz-Salzberger and her father, was published, reflecting a vibrant ongoing dialogue between father and daughter, novelist and historian, and offering a fresh secular perspective on Jewish culture from the Bible to the present. Her opinion articles on politics, culture, and current affairs have appeared in venues such as *Newsweek, International Herald Tribune, The Wall Street Journal, Le Figaro, Frankfurter Allgemeine Zeitung,* and *Haaretz.*

Yaron Peleg serves as the Kennedy Leigh Reader in modern Hebrew studies at the University of Cambridge. He teaches courses in the history of modern Hebrew literature from the late eighteenth century to the present and the formation of Zionist culture in the first half of the twentieth century and its legacy beyond that time. He is co-editor of the *Journal of Modern Jewish Studies* and associate editor of *Prooftexts*. He has written numerous articles and book chapters and his books include *Directed by God: Jewishness in Contemporary Israeli Film and Television, Orientalism and the Hebrew Imagination, Israeli Culture between the Two Intifadas, Derech Gever, Homoeroticism in Modern Hebrew Literature (1880–2000),* and *Identities in Motion: Israeli Cinema Reader,* among others.

Moriel Rothman-Zecher Mor is a Jerusalem-born novelist and poet. He is a 2018 National Book Foundation "5 Under 35" honoree and received a 2020 MacDowell Colony Fellowship for Literature. He is the author of the acclaimed novel *Sadness Is a White Bird* and his writing has been published in *The New York Times, The Paris Review, Haaretz,* and elsewhere. Moriel's second novel is forthcoming 2022.

Adam Rovner is associate professor of English and Jewish literature and director of the center for Judaic studies at the University of Denver. He served as a Lady Davis Fellow at the Hebrew University of Jerusalem (2015–2016). He has published academic work in leading journals and in scholarly volumes, including recent articles on Hebrew writing in the US in *Dibur,* Jewish modernisms in the journal *Partial Answers,* and an essay on Zionist plans to colonize East Africa in the edited volume *What Ifs of Jewish History.* His general interest articles have appeared in numerous outlets, including *The Forward, History Today, Jewish Renaissance, American History, Paper Brigade,* and *World Literature Today.* His acclaimed book, *In the Shadow of Zion: Promised Lands Before Israel,* was published in 2015. His current project focuses on the African adventures of a nineteenth-century Anglo-Jewish merchant-explorer.

Vered Karti Shemtov teaches Hebrew and comparative literature at Stanford University. She is the head of the Hebrew Project at Stanford and the founder and editor-in-chief of *Dibur Literary Journal*. Some of Shemtov's publications include: *Changing Rhythms: Towards a Theory of Prosody in Cultural Context*, several co-edited issues including: "Spoken Word, Written Word: Rethinking the Representation of Speech in Literature" (2015), "1948: History and Responsibility" (2013), and "Jewish Conceptions and Practices of Space" (2005), and numerous articles in *Prooftexts* and other journals, including "Limbotopia: Poetry and Dwelling: From Martin Heidegger to the Songbook of the Tent Revolution in Israel," "Limbotopia: The New Present and the Literary Imagination," "On Poetry That Is Written not out of Pain: The Poetics of Roni Someck," "Poetry and Dwelling: From Martin Heidegger to the Songbook of the Tent Revolution in Israel" (*Prooftexts*), and "The Rebirth of the Lyrical Subject in Yehuda Amichai's Late Poetry."

Sam Sussman is an accomplished writer and journalist who has won the BAFTA New Writing Contest, has had a short film featured at Cannes, and published his literary criticism and political commentary in *The Forward*, *Haaretz, Dissent, Asia Times, Huffington Post*, the *Tel Aviv Review of Books*, and more. He is also the founder of Extend, an initiative that introduces Israeli and Palestinian human rights activists to American audiences. Sam holds a BA in politics, philosophy, and literature with highest honors from Swarthmore College, and an MPhil in international relations from Oxford, where he studied as a Clarendon Scholar and was a finalist for the All Souls Exam. He has also served as a fellow with the Aydelotte Foundation and the American Middle East Network for Dialogue at Stanford.

Eric Zakim is a faculty member of the Middle East Studies department of the School of Languages, Literatures, and Cultures, and of the Graduate Field Committee in Film Studies. He also serves as a core faculty member at the Meyerhof Center for Jewish Studies and the Gildenhorn Institute for Israel Studies. Professor Zakim's research and teaching focus primarily on modern Hebrew literature and Israeli culture. He is the author of *To Build and Be Built: Landscape, Literature, and the Construction of Zionist Identity* (2006), and the co-editor of a special volume of the journal *Prooftexts: David Fogel and the Rise of Hebrew Modernism* (1993). He has published numerous essays on Israeli popular culture, Hebrew poetry, and Marxist and post-structural theory in the study of modernist music.

Further Reading

Critical Resources in English

Books

Balaban, Avraham. *Between God and Beast: An Examination of Amos Oz's Prose.* Pennsylvania State UP, 1993.

Ben-Dov, Nitza, editor. *The Amos Oz Reader.* Harcourt, 2009.

Bernard, Anna. *Rhetorics of Belonging: Nation, Narration, and Israel/Palestine.* Liverpool UP, 2017.

Mazor, Yair. *Somber Lust: The Art of Amos Oz.* Translated by Marganit Weinberger-Rotman. State U of New York P, 2002.

Oz, Amos, and Shira Hadad. *What Makes an Apple: Six Conversations about Writing, Love, Guilt, and Other Pleasures.* Princeton UP, 2022.

Schwartz, Yigal. *The Zionist Paradox: Hebrew Literature and Israeli Identity.* Brandeis UP, 2014.

Shaked, Gershon. *The New Tradition: Essays on Modern Hebrew Literature.* Hebrew Union College Press, 2006.

Essays, Articles, and Interviews

Aschkenasy, Nehama. "Deconstructing the Metanarrative: Amos Oz's Evolving Discourse with the Bible." *Symposium.* 55.3. Fall 2001, pp. 123–34.

Ben-Dov, Nitza. "The Brown Notebook of Dreams: On Amos Oz's *The Third Condition.*" *Modern Hebrew Literature,* vol. 7, 1991, pp. 30–31.

———. "Why They Write: The Political Impulse of Israeli Writers." *Middle East Review,* vol. 20, 1987/88, pp. 15–25.

Fuchs, Esther. "The Beast within: Women in Amos Oz's Early Fiction." *Modern Judaism,* vol. 4, no. 3, 1984, pp. 311–21, http://www.jstor.org/stable/1396303.

Guppy, Shusha. "Amos Oz, The Art of Fiction No. 148." *The Paris Review,* 140, 1996.

Holtzman, Avner, and Chaim Seymour. "Strange Fire and Secret Thunder: Between Micha Josef Berdyczewski and Amos Oz." *Prooftexts,* vol. 15, no. 2, 1995, 145–62, http://www.jstor.org/stable/20689416.

Kaplan, Eran. "Amos Oz and the Politics of Identity: A Reassessment." *Journal of Israeli History*, vol. 38, no, 2020, pp. 259–74.

Oz, Amos, and Hana Wirth-Nesher. "After the Sound and the Fury: An Interview." *Prooftexts*, vol. 2, no. 3, 1982, pp. 303–12.

Remnick, David. "The Spirit Level: Amos Oz Writes the Story of Israel." *The New Yorker*, 31 October 2004, https://www.newyorker.com/magazine/2004/11/08/the-spirit-level.

Films

A Tale of Love and Darkness. Directed by Natalie Portman, Voltage Pictures, 2015.

Amos Oz: The Nature of Dreams. Directed by Masha Zur Glozman and Yonathan Zur. Cinephil, 2009.

Censored Voices. Directed by Mor Loushy, Hilla Medalia, 2015.

The Fourth Window. Directed by Yair Qedar, KAN: Israeli Public Broadcasting (IL), The New Foundation for Cinema & TV, 2021.

Index

Printed in the USA
CPSIA information can be obtained
at www.ICGtesting.com
LVHW051817041023
760147LV00005B/51